U. S. Grant

# GRANT

AS A

# SOLDIER AND STATESMAN:

BEING A

## SUCCINCT HISTORY

OF HIS

## MILITARY AND CIVIL CAREER.

---

BY EDWARD HOWLAND.

---

"—— Our chief of men, who through a cloud
Not of war only, but detractions rude,
Guided by faith and matchless fortitude,
To peace and truth thy glorious way hast plough'd.

—— Yet much remains
To conquer still; Peace hath her victories
No less renown'd than War."

HARTFORD:
J. B. BURR & COMPANY.
1868.

TO

M. H.

WHOSE DAILY LIFE AND

CONVERSATION

DEMONSTRATE THE TRUTHS OF THE

PHILOSOPHY OF FREEDOM,

I DEDICATE THIS

BOOK.

Fruges et agris rettulit uberes,
Et signa nostro restituit Jovi
  Derepta Parthorum superbis
    Postibus, et vacuum duellis
Janum Quirini clausit, et ordinem
Rectum evaganti fræna licentiæ
  Injecit, amovitque culpas,
    Et veteres revocavit artes
Per quas Latinum nomen et Italæ
Crevere vires.—*Horace Car.* iv: xv.

# PREFACE.

It is the duty of every American to consider well the part his country is called upon to take in the great question of the development of the human race.

The discovery of this continent at the end of the fifteenth century confirmed the new theories of the physical formation of the earth, and gave an impetus to the study of physical science, which since that day has characterized the tendency of the thought of the civilized world. Again, early in the seventeenth century, America by affording an asylum for those desiring religious freedom, set an example to the world, the influence of which is still at work. Yet again, in the eighteenth century, this country, by realizing after an eight years' struggle the theory of a democratic form of government, held up before the world an example of the benefits of political freedom, which has had such an influence, that now in Europe even the most despotically inclined ruler claims only a constitutional right to his position.

The divine right of kings has become as great an absurdity as the dogma that the earth is flat, or that religious persecution is the best means for spreading the reign of the Prince of Peace.

Thus three times in the three centuries which have elapsed since the modern world obtained a knowledge of America, she has influenced the thought of the world, and always in the direction of freedom. Nor is her task wholly completed. It remains for her now, in the nineteenth century, to continue leading the van of the army of progress towards the realization of freedom in every interest of life. The struggle of the civil war through which we have just passed, has, by the abolition of slavery, secured the basis for the freedom of labor. But the work is not yet wholly done. The contest has been transferred from the field of battle to the field of politics.

As after the struggle of 1776, it was found that the constancy and caution of Washington which led us successfully through the war, were equally needed in organizing the results of victory, so now it will be found that the persistent self-reliance, the singleness of purpose, the fertility of resources, the application of common sense to action, which characterized General Grant, are the qualities now needed to organize in every interest of life the principles of freedom which the war vindicated, and which form the basis of our nationality.

To show his fitness to direct the energies of this country towards the further spread of the democratic idea, is the purpose for which this book is written. However imperfect and incomplete it may be, its faults may be excused in consideration of its purpose. If it can in any way, aid in calling our attention to the noble destiny of this nation, and to General Grant as an able leader of our exertions to attain it, then it will not have been written in vain.

To those of my personal friends who aided me in its preparation, and to those whom I can not thus qualify, but who have also kindly assisted me, I would here take the opportunity of returning my warmest thanks.

E. H.

NEW YORK, 1868.

# CONTENTS.

---

# APPENDIX.

# LIST OF ILLUSTRATIONS.

# GRANT

## AS A SOLDIER AND A STATESMAN.

---

### CHAPTER I.

#### INTRODUCTORY.—THE SITUATION.

THE history of a nation's great men is a history of the nation itself, since great men are possible only as they are the expression of a nation's great thoughts. They are the mouthpieces of their age, and give utterance, either in word or deed, to the collective spirit of their times. The history, therefore, of the growth of humanity is found in the history of the succession of great men, who have in turn been the result of this growth, and have aided in its development. The calmness and moderation of Washington, while serving to guide and direct the enthusiasm of the youthful nation who accepted him as their head, was an indication and a result of these qualities in the people. It was a new thing in the history of the world, that a nation should rebel in order to maintain a philosophic principle. Up to this time revolutions had been caused by abuses which had assumed such monstrous proportions as to become unbearable; the people had risen in the desperation of despair; but the American colonies, accustomed through generations to their own self-government, rebelled against the assumption of a right upon the part of the mother country to impose upon them taxation without representation. It was not a question of pounds to be paid, but of principles to be maintained. It was not a question of money to be saved, but of the majesty of self-government.

It is so also with the great man whose life forms the theme of these pages. His comprehensiveness of conception, his versatility of resource, his promptness of execution, are the fitting expression of a nation, which in less than a century has developed the railroad, the steamboat, and the telegraph as they are to be found nowhere else in the world; whose cities, situated where, within the compass of a single life, the wild beast roamed the trackless forest unharmed, now count their inhabitants by the hundreds of thousands; whose commerce scatters its white sails over every navigable sea of the earth's surface; whose energies and conquests have always been devoted to the increase and spread of industry and peace, of the dignity and majesty of productive labor, instead of the hollow glory of some ruling monarch; of a nation whose mission is to vindicate the freedom of republicanism, and not the constraint of despotism; whose wealth lies not in its few royal residences, but in its millions of homes; whose glory lies not in the tinsel splendor of a court, but in the well-being of its citizens; whose rule of conduct is not based upon the whims and fancies of a few, but results from the free development of the many.

In honoring the man who in his life and deeds makes these qualities manifest, we are therefore honoring ourselves, and proclaiming to the world the best convictions of our national life.

It will be well, perhaps, before entering immediately upon the facts in General Grant's career, to take a hasty glance at the condition of affairs which led to the crisis that furnished the fit field for the display of his great qualities as a military leader and a statesman.

The founders of our government had intended to establish a Republic, and hoped that they had succeeded in doing so. Unfortunately, however, they had left slavery undisturbed; and in the course of time, the culture of cotton having made this system of labor appear profitable, it had grown with the growth of the country, and finally threatened to rule it entirely in its own interests. It was intrenched behind the conventions of habit, of prejudice, of the rights of property, of the constitution, of respect for law, and the theory of state rights. Never in our history did it show so bold, and apparently so strong, a front. The press of the country, almost without exception, advocated its right to exist where it was. The journals which denied this right were so few in number, and so powerless in influence, that they counted for nothing in moulding public opinion. The clergy of the country were, in the enormous majority, engaged in advocating its right to maintain its position, on Bible grounds, as well as those of expediency. So strong was public opinion in this direction, that even the Republican party designed only to stop its extension: they were content with this.

But a nation grows as surely as the individuals that compose it grow. Its sentiments, its feelings, its opinions are matured by events, as those of the youth become manly by his increase in years. As men, we must morally either advance or retrograde. To remain stationary is to stagnate, and stagnation implies putrefaction and decay. As the particles composing our physical being are in a constant state of change, the old and worn-out portions being rejected and replaced by new, so is it with our mental condition: the habits of thought which once were new, become, in their turn, effete and worn out, and must be replaced by new. A man might as well hope to be physically well and in robust health without an active circulation of the blood, as hope to be mentally robust without a correspondingly active circulation in his thoughts. The vivifying streams which the pulsations of the great heart of mankind keep constantly in circulation, must be allowed to flow freely, and perform their destined office of change and renewal, or sickness, decay, and death are the result. There is a moral aneurism of nations, as there is a physical aneurism for the individual.

Slavery was like a bandage tied tight about the body politic, preventing the free circulation of ideas, of thought, of labor. The doctors all stood by, saying that the patient must rest quiet; that it was impossible he could be in a better condition; and had almost persuaded him that they were right. The real history of the secession conspiracy cannot be yet written. The leaders have not yet confessed; and until they do, it will always remain a mystery how the South was precipitated into so foolish, so reckless, and so criminal a revolution. But they took the step, and with the cannon shots against Fort Sumter, the whole loyal population of the North and West rose like a giant roused from a drugged sleep. At first we seemed almost helpless. Treachery had been actively at work. Those whom we had trusted, to whom we had delegated our affairs, had proved meanly derelict. We found our army scattered and in the control of traitors. Our navy was dispersed all over the world. Our finances were disorganized. The public positions of trust had been used by their occupants for private peculation. The nation and the Executive knew not whom to trust. The time had come for the new birth of the nation; and the American people seemed as helpless as a new-born babe. The strength and endurance of republicanism was put to the extremest test, and most nobly and completely has the principle of self-government vindicated itself. No greater crisis could ever arise in any nation's history, and no nation could ever meet it more promptly and fully than we have done.

Of the disasters which at first attended our military operations it is needless to say more than a word. Bull Run was a providential defeat. If we had been victorious then, slavery would have been left undisturbed. It required disaster to awake us thoroughly from the apathy with which we had so long regarded this system of organized injustice. The attention of the North was for a long time concentrated principally upon the operations of the army of the Potomac. It was the nearest scene of operations, and we had been too long accustomed to take party and sectional views of our interests. The idea of the national unity, of the oneness of this nation, of the identity of its interests, had hardly yet been practically demonstrated with such force as to become a universally received truth. The conduct of the war and its results have made this truth more impressive and more generally accepted. Our first success began at the West, under the direction of the hero of these memoirs, who was finally, after organizing success with our armies from the Ohio to the Gulf, to complete the work with the army of the Potomac, and by leading them to the crowning victory, redeem the continued course of disaster which for years had appeared to be the inevitable lot of this noble, courageous, indomitable, persistent body of soldiers.

Let us examine the causes which influenced the development of this soldier and statesman, whose influence, in turn, upon the future of this country, time alone will enable us to fully comprehend.

THE HOUSE IN WHICH GRANT WAS BORN.

## CHAPTER II.

### GRANT'S EARLY LIFE.—WEST POINT.

IN a small, one-story cottage, still standing in Clermont County, Ohio, on the banks of the river, and commanding a view of the stream and the opposite shore of the State of Kentucky, on the 27th day of April, 1822, a child was born, who is now known to the world as ULYSSES SIMPSON GRANT. He was at first christened Hiram Ulysses; but on going to West Point, his cadet warrant was made out, by accident, in the name of Ulysses Sidney, which name he took, and retained during his education, changing it, on his graduation, to Ulysses Simpson, in honor of his mother, whose maiden name he thus assumed.

His father's name is Jesse R. Grant, a descendant of a Scottish family, two brothers of which emigrated to this country in the early part of the eighteenth century, while we were still colonies of Great Britain. One of these brothers settled in New Jersey, and the other in Canada.

Jesse R. Grant was a descendant of the settler in New Jersey, and was born in Westmoreland County, Pennsylvania, in 1794. When eleven years old, his father having died, he was apprenticed to a tanner. Subsequently, with his mother and the rest of the family, he removed from Pennsylvania to Kentucky, and then to Ohio. This portion of the country was then still partially in the possession of the Indians, and in an unsettled state, so that, after several changes, he finally settled at Point Pleasant, in Clermont County, where, in June, 1821, he married Hannah Simpson.

Hannah Simpson was the daughter of John Simpson, and was born in Montgomery County, Pennsylvania, but removed with her family, in 1818, to Clermont County, Ohio.

Grant's parents were married in June, 1821, and ten months after, he was born as their first child. His father was an upright, hard-working, energetic, and honest man, while his mother was a kind-hearted and devoted woman.

As a boy, Grant was robust, strong, and cool, as he has since shown himself; but though many stories are now told of his boyhood, which display his sturdiness, and quickness of resource under difficulties, they are hardly of enough importance to be repeated here. There is a constant tendency to discover in a great man's youth the germ of the qualities which in after life have made him distinguished; but almost all such discoveries are accessories after the fact. To be childish in childhood is the best prognostic that the boy will be manly when he reaches man's estate; but in Grant's case, the only distinctive quality he appears to have manifested as a boy, and which appears distinctive in his after career, is a want of ambition. Whatever he had to do, he did thoroughly and well, but without any apparent ulterior design. Fortunately for his country, this habit appears to have grown with his growth and strengthened with his strength.

His education, like that of most boys whose lot places them in such an unsettled condition of society, was quite limited. There was too much hard and practical work to do, in conquering the soil and wresting from it the means of living by labor, to give him leisure for the luxuries of learning. He had to help his father, and so could attend the village school only during the winter months. Of these limited advantages he made, however, the best and fullest use, learning thoroughly whatever he did learn, and acquiring — what is of the greatest advantage — a habit of application and a desire for further knowledge.

When a young man he desired to go to West Point. It was known that at this national school education was not only gratuitous, but that the student, during his course, was supported well, and also paid regularly more than enough for his dress, &c., and that, when he graduated and had served his term of enlistment, the field was open for him either to remain in the army, or else, with the prestige which the graduation gave him, to interest himself in the industrial and engineering pursuits, which made the demand for competent men inexhaustible. The whole country was to be surveyed and improved; its roads and bridges were to be built; while the schools, which could prepare men for superintending and directing these works, were rarer even than now.

Such an opportunity was too good to be lost without a trial; and so application was made successfully to the Hon. Thomas L. Hamer, who represented the congressional district in which Grant resided, and who gave him the appointment. The preliminary examination at West Point is quite simple: reading, writing, spelling, arithmetic through decimal fractions, are all that is required; and Grant, having passed safely through this ordeal, was admitted a cadet on the 1st of July, 1839, being then seventeen years old.

At West Point he was no more distinguished than during his boyhood. He went through the whole course respectably. From September to June the cadets live in barracks, studying, riding, and fencing in the riding-school, and drilling in the open air when the afternoons are fine. From June to September they live in camp, being regularly drilled, and studying pyrotechny and civil engineering.

In his studies Grant suffered in competition with the members of his class, from his want of early preparation. The class numbered over one hundred in 1839, when appointed, and of these only thirty-nine graduated in 1843. In this list Grant stood the twenty-first. Among his classmates were William B. Franklin, who stood at the head of the class; Roswell S. Ripley, who fired with increased rapidity upon Fort Sumter, while it was on fire and the garrison were attempting to extinguish the flames; Rufus Ingalls, subsequently the Quartermaster-General of the army of the Potomac; Franklin Gardner, the rebel general who surrendered Port Hudson to Banks, and others.

Henry Coppée, Esq., who was with Grant at West Point for two years, gives the following account of him while there:—

"I remember him as a plain, common-sense, straightforward youth; quiet, rather of the old-head-on-young-shoulders order; shunning notoriety; quite contented, while others were grumbling; taking to his military duties in a very business-like manner; not a prominent man in the corps, but respected by all, and very popular with his friends. His sobriquet of *Uncle Sam* was given to him there, where every good fellow has a nickname, from these very qualities; indeed, he was a very uncle-like sort of a youth. He was then and always an excellent horseman, and his picture rises before me as I write, in the old, torn coat, obsolescent leather gig-top, loose riding pantaloons, with spurs buckled over them, going with his clanking sabre to the drill hall. He exhibited but little enthusiasm in anything: his best standing was in the mathematical branches, and their application to tactics and military engineering.

"If we again dwell upon the fact that no one, even of his most intimate friends, dreamed of a great future for him, it is to add that, looking back now, we must confess that the possession of many excellent qualities, and the entire absence of all low and mean ones, establish a logical sequence from first to last, and illustrate, in a novel manner, the poet's fancy about

'The baby figures of the giant mass
Of things to come at large.'"

On leaving West Point, Grant entered the army as brevet Second Lieutenant in the Fourth Infantry, and commenced his army life, which we will describe in the next chapter, after noticing the fact that the education of West Point, though it was strictly a national one, did not, as we see, inculcate such ideas of loyalty as prevented those who were indebted to the nation for its benefits from turning traitorously upon it in its hour of need.

Nor can this charge be brought against West Point alone. It applies with equal force to all the institutions of learning in the country; and the reason is very evident. In none of them has proper attention been paid to the study of our own history, our own institutions, our own national spirit. The nationality of America has had a growth as definite, if not as extended, as that of any nation of antiquity or of modern times. Even its literature — for we have a literature, though most of our educated men are unaware of the fact — has had a regular growth.

The democratic idea, which was the culmination of the great eighteenth century, and which is destined to change all our social relations, as here in this country, of all the world, it has substituted a representative government for the monarchical system which Europe inherited from the barbarism of the feudal ages, — the democratic idea leads to the unity of mankind. In political economy its culmination is the harmony of interests; in industry it leads to the abolition of all monopolies, the freedom of labor, the cultivation of the productive arts, and their union with science. In government it leads to peace instead of war; and in modern Europe, despite the obstacles in its path, spread by the various dynastic interests, we see its effects in a united Italy, a united Germany, and in the growing impatience of public opinion with the narrowness of national prejudices; in social life it leads to the freedom of the individual guaranteed by the law, which is the expression of the public interest as best understood by the community, and as we see, in our own times, has changed the whole tone of criminal legislation, has emancipated class after class from their legal disabilities, and proved that the strength, the wealth, the happiness, and the intelligence of a nation are in direct proportion to the freedom enjoyed by its population.

Here, in our own country, which in its theory of government realizes more fully than any other country this democratic idea, we find that the attention of our educated youth is turned, during the period they pass under the guidance of our "institutions of learning," to the study of every other subject but this, which is the all-important one. No wonder, then, that when the crisis came, many of those who had been educated for the nation, at the public expense, turned against it. They could quote glibly examples from Greece and Rome in their justification, but were wholly unaware of the new spirit and tendency of thought which separates the new from the old world, by a gulf wider than the ocean, or the ages which roll between us and them.

Had the tone of thought been turned in this direction, which is truly national and American, by our thinkers and teachers, slavery would have faded from the South, despite the adventitious aid it derived from the culture of cotton, as it did from the North, by a process similar to that which has modified the barbarous brutality of our penal codes; and the war would have become impossible for want of a moving cause.

Let us hope, however, that the lesson it has taught us of the power of ideas may not be lost; and that our education may become national and American in fact as well as in word, that our youth who enjoy its training may become impressed with the majesty and solemnity of the position America has to assume in the world's history, and be able to lead rightly those who look naturally to them for guidance, instead of being themselves only fit food for demagogues.

## CHAPTER III.

THE MEXICAN WAR.—RESIGNS FROM THE ARMY.—CIVIL LIFE.

THE graduates from West Point are attached to regiments, in the order of their merit, as supernumerary officers, to wait in turn for vacancies. Grant, according to this custom, was made a brevet Second Lieutenant in the Fourth Infantry, and began his service on the 1st of July, 1843. His regiment was then at Jefferson Barracks, near St. Louis, Missouri. The next summer it was moved to Natchitoches, Louisiana, and the next year, 1845, was sent to Corpus Christi, to watch the Mexican army then gathering on the frontier. In September of this year he was made a full Second Lieutenant in the Seventh Regiment, but made an application to the War Department to remain with the Fourth, which was granted.

On the 6th and 7th of May, 1846, he was present at the battles of Palo Alto and Resaca, and also took part in the bloody battle of Monterey, September 23, 1846.

When General Scott commenced his march from Vera Cruz to the city of Mexico, a distance of almost three hundred miles through the enemy's country, Grant's regiment was withdrawn from General Taylor's command, to make part of the invading army. He was at the siege of Vera Cruz in March, and on the 1st of April, 1847, was made regimental Quartermaster, and held this position during the rest of the war. This position is one requiring system, business ability, and patience, and in his administration of its duties Grant displayed these qualities with the same success that he has since shown in his more extended sphere of action. Though it is customary for the Quartermaster, since he has charge of the regiment's trains of supplies, to remain with them during an engagement, it is recorded, to Grant's honor, that he always rejoined his regiment on such occasions, and shared their fighting.

At Molino del Rey, September 8, 1847, he distinguished himself, and was brevetted First Lieutenant, but declined, since he became, owing to the casualties of the battle, a full First Lieutenant. At Chapultepec, September 13, with a few of his men, he joined a detachment of the Second Artillery in an attack on the enemy's breastworks, and was mentioned in the official report as having "acquitted himself most nobly."

Captain Horace Brooks, of the Second Artillery, in his report of the battle of Chapultepec, says, "I succeeded in reaching the fort with a few men. Here Lieutenant U. S. Grant and a few more men of the Fourth Infantry found me, and by a joint movement, after an obstinate resistance, a strong field-work was carried, and the enemy's right was completely turned."

The report of Major Francis Lee, commanding the Fourth Infantry, of the battle of Chapultepec, says, "At the first barrier the enemy was in strong force, which rendered it necessary to advance with caution. This was done, and when the head of the battalion was within short musket range of the barrier, Lieutenant Grant, Fourth Infantry, and Captain Brooks, Second Artillery, with a few men of their respective regiments, by a handsome movement to the left, turned the right flank of the enemy, and the barrier was carried. . . . Second Lieutenant Grant behaved with distinguished gallantry on the 13th and 14th."

The report of Lieutenant Colonel John Garland, commanding the First Brigade, of the battle of Chapultepec, says, "The rear of the enemy had made a stand behind a breastwork, from which they were driven by detachments of the Second Artillery, under Captain Brooks, and the Fourth Infantry, under Lieutenant Grant, supported by other regiments of the division, after a short but sharp conflict. . . . I recognized the command as it came up, mounted a howitzer on the top of a convent, which, under the direction of Lieutenant Grant, Quartermaster of the Fourth Infantry, and Lieutenant Lendrum, Third Artillery, annoyed the enemy considerably. . . . I must not omit to call attention to Lieutenant Grant, Fourth Infantry, who acquitted himself most nobly upon several occasions, under my own observation."

In this particular mention of officers for gallantry and good conduct, besides the officers of his own staff, Lieutenant Colonel Garland names but one other officer, besides Lieutenant Grant, out of his whole brigade.

General Worth's report, September 16, also speaks highly of Lieutenant Grant.

For this he received the brevet of Captain, for "gallant and meritorious conduct," which was awarded in 1849, but not confirmed until 1850.

Upon the close of the Mexican war, in 1848, the Fourth Infantry was sent first to New York, then to the frontier, and Grant served in the command of his company first at Detroit, and then at Sackett's Harbor. This year he married Miss Dent, the sister of one of his classmates at West Point.

In the autumn of 1851, the discovery of gold in California having made the presence of more troops necessary on our western frontier, in order to protect the crowds of emigrants from the Indians, the Fourth Infantry was ordered to Oregon, and one battalion, in which brevet Captain Grant was serving, was ordered to Fort Dallas, where he saw some service against the Indians.

In 1853, after a two years' absence from his family, Grant, having been promoted to a full captaincy, but seeing only a slight chance for further promotion during the continuance of peace, resigned his commission, and in July, 1854, commenced life as a private citizen.

During the next few years, until the commencement of the rebellion, he tried his hand at many various kinds of business, but with very indifferent success. He was by turns a farmer near St. Louis, a dealer in wool, an agent for collecting money, an auctioneer, a house agent, and finally, in 1859, entered into partnership with his father in a new leather and saddlery business in Galena, Illinois.

Here his probity, industry, and economy achieved a certain success; but it is more than probable that he would never have distinguished himself in trade. His mind is of a kind to grasp the large combinations of military science, to put in practice the great economies of a nation's finances, to seize and direct a nation's sympathies and feelings, rather than to master all the chicaneries of trade, to be interested in the petty details of business, and to foresee and take advantage of the rise and fall of markets.

Business, as conducted in the present system of isolated competition, offers no scope for the exercise of a generous and comprehensive mind, and, as a general rule, such natures cannot succeed in it. When the rare exceptions occur, they have to seek relief in philanthropy from the contracting tendency of trade. But even this is insufficient, since it is justice, and not almsgiving, which should regulate our relations with our fellow-men.

The present era of competitive commerce is represented in government by diplomacy, which is the trickery of trade transported to a higher sphere of action. Both of them find their congenial home in Europe, where the interests of the people are made subservient to those of the rulers. But here, where the government is the people, where the democratic idea has become a reality in the government, diplomacy is useless, and, as far as its votaries are represented by our politicians, injurious; and what we want is statesmanship, that is, the practice of common sense applied to all our political relations.

The time must come when commerce shall represent the same idea; and until then it is no wonder if a nature like Grant's finds itself singularly out of place in the petty competitions of trade. It is, therefore, to his credit that he made no brilliant success in his attempts to dwarf himself; and though nothing can compensate for the waste of blood and treasure caused by the civil war, yet we should rejoice that we finally found in our midst a man capable of grasping and directing the military energies of the nation, and also, as we shall see, capable of treating with a statesman's comprehension the political issues which arose from the new situation.

## CHAPTER IV.

ENLISTS IN THE ARMY.—APPOINTED BRIGADIER GENERAL OF VOLUNTEERS.—TAKES THE INITIATIVE.—THE AFFAIR AT BELMONT.

PROMPT in his response to the first call of President Lincoln for seventy-five thousand men, Grant in April aided in raising a company in his own immediate neighborhood, and in May went to Springfield, Illinois, and tendered his services to Governor Yates, to whom he had been recommended by a member of Congress from his state. Use was soon made of his experience in organizing the state troops, and he was appointed a mustering officer, and by his energy succeeded in raising the three months men, and received a commission as Colonel of the Twenty-first Illinois Volunteers.

This regiment was at first enlisted for three months, but subsequently, from their confidence in him, enlisted, one thousand strong, for three years. His first care was to drill and discipline his command, which soon became known for its order. He took command of them at Springfield, Illinois, and soon after marched them to Quincy, on the Mississippi, which was supposed to be in danger. Thence he was moved to St. Joseph, to defend the line of the Hannibal and Hudson Railway. Here meeting with other regiments, though the youngest Colonel, he was appointed commander of the combined forces; and thus acting as Brigadier General, his headquarters, on the 31st of July, 1861, were at Mexico, Missouri.

In August he received his commission as Brigadier General of Volunteers, to date from May 17, being the seventeenth in the list of the thirty-four original appointments of that date. He was now ordered to Cairo, and with two brigades took command of "the District of South-east Missouri." This district included both banks of the Mississippi, from Cape Girardeau to New Madrid, and the whole of Western Kentucky on the Ohio River.

The importance of Cairo as a strategic point is evident at a glance. Lying at the confluence of the Mississippi and Ohio Rivers, it is the natural base for a military movement upon the south, and is of equal importance in the line of defence for the extensive and rich country lying between the Ohio and Mississippi Rivers. It is also of great importance for river expeditions, for the gathering and transportation of supplies, and for the equipment and organization of gunboat fleets. The Tennessee and Cumberland Rivers, flowing parallel northward into the Ohio, include also a most important part of Western Kentucky, which Grant saw immediately was to become the scene of active hostilities.

The State of Kentucky, as will be remembered, attempted, in the commencement of the war, to hold the ridiculously incomprehensible condition which was called "neutral." As, however, the line separating Tennessee, which had seceded, from Kentucky, which had not, was simply an imaginary one, the practical results of neutrality were, giving free access to the rebel forces, and throwing all possible obstacles in the way of the Union armies. Of these advantages the rebels were not slow to make a decided use. Seizing first Hickman, then Columbus and Bowling Green, fortifying the Tennessee at Fort Henry, and the Cumberland at Fort Donelson, they established a strong line from the Mississippi to the State of Virginia, running through the "neutral" State of Kentucky.

Seeing this, Grant urged frequently upon Fremont, his superior in command at St. Louis, the importance of taking actively offensive measures, but could never get the permission necessary.

On the 5th of September he informed Fremont by telegram that the rebels had invaded Kentucky, and that he was "nearly ready for Paducah, should not a telegram arrive preventing the movement." Receiving no word from Fremont, he left Cairo on the night of the 5th, and occupied Paducah on the morning of the 6th, without meeting any resistance.

Paducah is a village lying at the mouth of the Tennessee River, and forms a valuable military post. Within nineteen days he had also taken possession of Smithland, situated similarly at the mouth of the Cumberland, and by these movements had effectually blockaded both these rivers, running up into the rebel states, and thus prevented any supplies from being forwarded to them in this direction; and had also secured two fine bases for further operations, and cleared out the guerrillas, who appear upon all occasions to have risen spontaneously throughout the rebel country, and who were now attempting to blockade the Ohio River below these points.

Placing a garrison sufficiently strong in each of these places to hold them, he still retained his headquarters at Cairo.

At the moment when Grant took possession of Paducah, he found secession flags flying in various parts of the city, in expectation of the speedy arrival of the rebel forces, which were reported as being not many miles distant, in a force numbering some thousands. Taking immediate possession of the telegraph, the railroad, and the public buildings, Grant issued the following proclamation to the inhabitants:—

PADUCAH, KY., September 6, 1861.

TO THE CITIZENS OF PADUCAH.—I am come among you, not as an enemy, but as your fellow-citizen; not to maltreat you nor annoy you, but to respect and enforce the rights of all loyal citizens. An enemy, in rebellion against our common government, has taken possession of, and planted its guns on the soil of, Kentucky, and fired upon you. Columbus and Hickman are in his hands. He is moving upon your city. I am here to defend you against this enemy, to assist the authority and sovereignty of your government. *I have nothing to do with opinions*, and shall deal only with armed rebellion and its aiders and abettors. You can pursue your usual avocations without fear. The strong arm of the government is here to protect its friends and punish its enemies. Whenever it is manifest that you are able to defend yourselves, and maintain the authority of the government, and protect the rights of loyal citizens, I shall withdraw the forces under my command.

U. S. GRANT, *Brigadier General commanding.*

This proclamation is of importance as being the first of the series of public documents in which Grant has shown that in statesmanship he is as reliable as in war.

It is the first of the series in which, seizing the salient facts of the situation, he applies good common sense to them, and arrives at just conclusions.

On the 14th of October, Major General Polk, of the Confederate army, addressed a note, from Columbus, Kentucky, to General Grant, proposing an exchange of prisoners; to which Grant returned the following terse reply:—

DISTRICT OF SOUTH-EAST MISSOURI,
HEADQUARTERS, CAIRO, October 14, 1861.

GENERAL: Yours of this date is just received. In regard to an exchange of prisoners, as proposed, I can of my own accordance make none. I recognize no "Southern Confederacy" myself, but will communicate with higher authorities for their views. Should I not be sustained, I will find means of communicating with you.

Respectfully, your obedient servant,

U. S. GRANT, *Brigadier General commanding.*

To Major General POLK, *Columbus, Ky.*

The time was now approaching when General Grant should show his powers in active operations. Having found by an expedition, which had returned successful, that the Confederates were concentrating at Belmont, Missouri, while on the opposite Kentucky side they had fortified their position at Columbus, so as to protect the camp at Belmont, and also blockade the Mississippi River, General Grant, at the head of two brigades, commanded respectively by himself and General McClernand, left Cairo on the 6th of November, 1861, for this point.

On the morning of the 7th the brigades landed, formed in line of battle, and immediately attacked the rebel works, where the enemy was in force under the command of General Cheatham. Having driven them out, the camp was destroyed, and then our forces fell back before the superior number of the enemy, who had been reënforced from Columbus.

The following description of this action, from a private letter from General Grant to his father, written on the night of the 8th, will give the best idea of the object and result of the expedition: —

"Day before yesterday I left Cairo with about three thousand men in five steamers, convoyed by two gunboats, and proceeded down the river to within about twelve miles of Columbus. The next morning the boats were dropped down just out of range of the enemy's batteries, and the troops debarked. During this operation our gunboats exercised the rebels by throwing shells into their camps and batteries. When all ready, we proceeded about one mile towards Belmont, opposite Columbus, when I formed the troops into line, and ordered two companies from each regiment to deploy as skirmishers, and push on through the woods, and discover the position of the enemy. They had gone but a little way when they were fired upon, and the ball may be said to have fairly opened.

"The whole command, with the exception of a small reserve, was then deployed in like manner and ordered forward. The order was obeyed with great alacrity, the men all showing great courage. I can say, with great gratification, that every Colonel, without a single exception, set an example to their commands that inspired a confidence that will always insure victory when there is the slightest possibility of gaining one. I feel truly proud to command such men.

"From here we fought our way from tree to tree through the woods to Belmont, about two and a half miles, the enemy contesting every foot of ground. Here the enemy had strengthened their position by felling the trees for two or three hundred yards and sharpening their limbs, making a sort of abatis. Our men charged through, making the victory complete, giving us possession of their camp and garrison equipage, artillery, and everything else.

"We got a great many prisoners. The majority, however, succeeded in getting aboard their steamers and pushing across the river. We burned everything possible, and started back, having accomplished all that we went for, and even more. Belmont is entirely covered by the batteries from Columbus, and is worth nothing as a military position — cannot be held without Columbus.

"The object of the expedition was to prevent the enemy from sending a force into Missouri to cut off troops I had sent there for a special purpose, and to prevent reënforcing Price.

"Besides being well fortified at Columbus, their number far exceeded ours, and it would have been folly to have attacked them. We found the Confederates well armed and brave. On our return, stragglers, that had been left in our rear (now front), fired into us, and more recrossed the river and gave us battle for a full mile, and afterwards at the boats when we were embarking.

"There was no hasty retreating or running away. Taking into account the object of the expedition, the victory was complete. It has given us confidence in the officers and men of this command, that will enable us to lead them in any future engagement without fear of the result. General McClernand (who, by the way, acted with great coolness and courage throughout, and proved that he is a soldier as well as a statesman) and myself, each had our horses shot under us. Most of the field-officers met with the same loss, besides nearly one third of them being themselves killed or wounded. As near as I can ascertain, our loss was about two hundred and fifty killed, wounded, and missing."

In his official report, General Grant gives great credit, by name, to the officers who were with him on this occasion, and shows — as he has shown through his whole military career — that he has none of the small fear and jealousy of his fellow-officers which so often characterize military men, in common with their fellows in every other pursuit in life. Conscious of his own merit, he has no need to prop up his own reputation by the detraction or neglect of the services and merits of others. This quality will become more brilliantly apparent as his sphere of action enlarges.

Although, in comparison with the subsequent military operations in which Grant took the lead, this affair at Belmont is insignificant, yet it was, in its place, of considerable importance, and deserves especial notice from the following considerations: It was, first, the commencement of Grant's active career. While the Fabian policy of waiting was that pursued by most of our generals in the field, this was an offensive move. The enemy was outwitted, his camp burned, and a successful retreat was made, when reenforcements enabled the enemy to outnumber us, and the whole affair was conducted in a soldier-like manner.

It was also a trial for our new western troops, and their behavior was such that, while it established their own confidence in themselves, it gave an earnest to their commanders of what could be expected from them in the future, and thus established a sympathy between the officers and the men.

Again, the objects of the expedition were fully accomplished, and even more, as Grant himself says.

It also was the commencement of the train of causes which led to the subjugation of Forts Henry and Donelson, an account of which will form the subject of the next chapter.

## CHAPTER V.

### FORT HENRY AND FORT DONELSON.—THE COMMENCEMENT OF UNCONDITIONAL SURRENDER.

THE proportions the war was destined to assume now began to be more apparent, and the importance of the "District of Cairo" to be more evident. On the 12th of November, 1861, General Henry W. Halleck, of the regular army, was sent to take command of the "Department of Missouri." This department included the States of Missouri, Iowa, Minnesota, Wisconsin, Illinois, Arkansas, and that portion of Kentucky west of the Cumberland River. General Halleck at once divided this large territory into districts, and of these the "District of Cairo" was the most important. On the 20th of December, 1861, the bounds of this district were extended, so that it included all the southern part of Illinois, all that part of Kentucky west of the Cumberland, and the southern counties of Missouri south of Cape Girardeau; and General Grant was appointed to command it, and assumed the position on the 21st of December, 1861, in an order dated from Cairo as his headquarters, and ascribing the positions of the forces under his command.

Having organized his forces so as to have them well in hand, ready for mutual support, and at the same time so disposed as to deceive the enemy concerning his strength, on the 10th of January Grant sent General McClernand, with a force of five thousand Illinois Volunteers, to penetrate into the interior of Kentucky in the vicinity of Columbus, and towards Mayfield and Camp Beauregard. On the 14th two entire divisions, under Generals Payne and C. F. Smith, were sent to act in concert with him.

General Payne moved from Bird's Point, with a column from Cairo, and General Smith with a column from Smithland, at the mouth of the Cumberland Grant himself accompanied the column from Cairo. The three columns combined made a force of nineteen regiments of infantry, four regiments of volunteer cavalry, two companies of regular cavalry, and seven batteries of artillery.

McClernand penetrated to within a mile of the defences of Columbus, and on the 20th was recalled, the objects of the expedition having been accomplished in gaining an accurate knowledge of the roads, and the topography of the country, which could serve in operating directly against Columbus.

This city is situated on the Mississippi, in the west of Kentucky, about twenty miles below the mouth of the Ohio, on bluffs two hundred feet high, which were strongly fortified with heavy batteries, sweeping the Mississippi above and below. The land defences of the city were being daily strengthened, and the design was, evidently, as the southern press stated, to make this position the Gibraltar of America, which should command the Mississippi until all nations should acknowledge the independence of the Confederacy.

From this point east, covering Nashville, the Confederates had, in August, 1861, strongly fortified Bowling Green, a small place on the Big Barren River, but with natural advantages of defence, and of great strategical importance, since it was on the line of the Louisville and Nashville Railroad. The Big Barren River is at times navigable for small vessels from Louisville, by the Ohio and Green Rivers. The river winds sharply through steep hills in the vicinity of Bowling Green, and all these points were covered with fortifications.

In this line of defences the Tennessee and Cumberland Rivers, flowing north into the Ohio, and almost parallel, were very important. The Tennessee is navigable for steamboats, at high water, up to Florence, at the port of Muscle Shoals; and the Cumberland, on the right bank of which Nashville is situated, is navigable, at high water, up to this city, nearly two hundred miles from its mouth, for large steamboats, and nearly three hundred miles farther for small steamboats.

It was, of course, a prime necessity for the Confederacy to close these streams against the passage of the Union gunboats. If they were left open, the Union army would have easy access to almost the heart of the Confederacy. For this purpose, therefore, they had erected two strong works, which they boastfully proclaimed were quite sufficient to secure their ends. The one on the eastern bank of the Tennessee was called Fort Henry. It mounted seventeen guns, and had accommodations for fifteen thousand men. The other, on the west bank of the Cumberland, was called Fort Donelson, and mounted about forty guns. The distance between these two forts was twelve miles, and they were connected by a good road and a telegraph. These forts served also to guard the railroad from Memphis to Nashville and Bowling Green, and were thought to be one of the strongest points in the line of defence running from the Mississippi at Belmont and Columbus, through Southern Kentucky and Northern Tennessee, to Cumberland Gap, and thence, by East Tennessee and South-western Virginia, to the positions around and beyond Richmond. Of such importance did the Confederacy rightly consider these points in this line, that all the troops which could be spared had been forwarded for their defence.

The problem before the government was, how to break through this line, and take the measures necessary for meeting and overcoming greater difficulties, such as the clearing of the Mississippi, the advance from Chattanooga, and the final suppression of the rebellion by sweeping from the face of the country all armed resistance in its favor.

Whether there was any one man in the country, at this time, who could look clearly so far in the future, and who had formed his plans for meeting and overcoming all these difficulties, is more than questionable. It is too much to expect that any one could do this. It is only as difficulties arise that they can be met, and among those in the country who displayed a versatility of resource, a comprehensiveness of view, which led always to attempting the most important thing first, and a far-reaching foresight of what the result of action would be, General Grant, as we shall see from his action here, and during the rest of his career, must be esteemed as holding one of the foremost, if not the foremost place.

It is impossible to follow his history without being struck with this, and without being also impressed with the manner in which he himself was educated by the deeds in which he acted so important a part; with each success in overcoming the difficulties then before him, the circle of his vision seems to have enlarged, his comprehension of the difficulties in his way, and of his means for overcoming them, to become clearer, and he goes on from one action to another, making each an aid in successfully terminating the next, until the final and absolute overthrow of the rebellion is attained. War thus conducted displays genius, and the genius for foresight and combination which makes statesmen as well as warriors.

During the autumn and early winter a fleet of gunboats had been prepared at Cairo, St. Louis, and other river towns, under the superintendence of Commodore A. H. Foote; and many of these were now ready to coöperate with the army in its operations. In order to obtain sailors to man these gunboats, General Grant issued the following important order: —

HEADQUARTERS DISTRICT OF CAIRO,
CAIRO, January 20, 1862.

CIRCULA

Commanders of regiments will report to these headquarters, without delay, the number of river and seafaring men of their respective commands who are willing to be transferred from the military to the gunboat service. Seeing the importance of fitting out our gunboats as speedily as possible, it is hoped there will be no delay or objections raised by company or regimental commanders in responding to this call. Men thus volunteering will be discharged at the end of one year, or at the end of the war, should it terminate sooner.

By order.

U. S. GRANT, *Brigadier General commanding.*

This call was promptly responded to, and the success which attended the operations of this branch of the service rendered it, for a time, very popular.

In accordance with orders from General Grant, General Smith, who was in command of one of the reconnoitring columns whose operations we have detailed, had, on his return, struck the Tennessee River about twenty miles below Fort Henry, and there having met Commander Phelps, who was patrolling that river in a gunboat, resolved, after a conference with this energetic officer, to run up in the gunboat, and survey Fort Henry himself. Having steamed up sufficiently near to draw the enemy's fire, and form an accurate idea of the strength of the place, General Smith, on his return to headquarters, reported to General Grant that he was convinced Fort Henry might be easily taken by three or four of the iron-clads, acting in conjunction with a land attacking force, if the attempt was made within a short time.

This report having been forwarded to General Halleck about the 15th of January, and no response having been received, on the 28th General Grant and Commodore Foote sent despatches, asking permission to attack Fort Henry. The next day Grant wrote an urgent letter to Halleck, requesting him to grant permission for the attack, and setting forth the feasibility of the plan, and the importance of putting it promptly in execution. On the afternoon of the 30th, despatches came to hand from Halleck, directing Grant to prepare immediately for taking and holding Fort Henry, and promising full instructions by messenger. Whether this plan of action was designed originally by Halleck or not, it certainly was conceived by Grant independently, and suggested to his superior officer, in entire ignorance as to what were the plans he had formed.

The preparations having been all made, on Monday, February 2, the expedition sailed from Cairo, its route being up the Ohio to Paducah, and thence up the Tennessee. The armament of Fort Henry consisted of one sixty-two pounder, one ten-inch columbiad, twelve thirty-two pounders, two forty-two pounders, and one twelve pounder. Twelve of these guns bore upon the river. Above and below the fort were creeks, defended by rifle-pits and abatis of timber, and around it was a swamp, with a sheet of water in the rear. The land approach was difficult, while on the other side of the river was an unfinished work, which was intended to assist the fort in stopping the navigation of the river. The defence of Fort Henry had been intrusted to Lloyd Tilghman, a Brigadier General in the Confederate service, of a Maryland family, which had been distinguished in the Revolution of 1776. He was a graduate of West Point, had served in the Mexican war, and was finally killed at Baker's Creek, near Vicksburg. The force under his command was over three thousand men, and the importance of the position intrusted to him had been impressed upon him in the orders appointing him to the command.

The fleet under Commodore Foote consisted of the iron-clads Cincinnati, Essex, Carondelet, and St. Louis, and the wooden boats Lexington, Tyler, and Conestoga. The Cincinnati was the flag-ship. At daylight on Tuesday, February 3, the fleet were three or four miles below Fort Henry. It was necessary they should proceed slowly, since information received from persons on the banks led them to drag for submerged torpedoes, several of which were secured, but so imperfectly constructed as to be harmless. At half past twelve, the Cincinnati, as she passed the head of Panther Island, within a mile of the fort, fired the first gun.

In the mean time the coöperating land army had been delayed by the bad condition of the roads, and the combined attack had been arranged for the 6th, at which time the army would have been in a position to coöperate. The following disposition had been made by Grant of his forces. He had moved to the combined attack with the divisions of McClernand and C. F. Smith thus disposed: McClernand, with the First Division, landing at Marbury's, three miles below, was to move in rear of the fort, to occupy the road leading to Dover and Fort Donelson,—thus to cut off the retreat of the garrison and prevent reënforcements from coming in, and also to be "in readiness to charge and take Fort Henry by storm promptly on receipt of orders."

Two brigades of Smith's (Second) Division, landing on the west bank, were to reconnoitre and occupy the unfinished work, Fort Heiman, and the surrounding eminences, and bring their artillery to bear on Fort Henry. The Third Brigade of Smith was to march up the east bank in the track of McClernand, and either to support him or form a special column of attack on the fort, as circumstances might prompt.

Had the fort made anything like the resistance which had been anticipated, there would have been an opportunity for the army to coöperate with the fleet, and the victory would have dated from the 6th of February, instead of from the 3d. The gunboats came into action in the following order, from right to left, after passing Panther Island by the western channel, and extending their line diagonally across the river: First, the iron-clads Essex, Carondelet, Cincinnati, and St. Louis; then, in a second line, just above Panther Island, the wooden boats Lexington, Conestoga, and Tyler. The firing from the boats was at once responded to by the fort, and a terrific cannonade commenced. The practice on both sides was excellent. The rifled gun in the fort soon exploded, killing three men, and wounding many others; the flagstaff was shot away; seven of the guns are soon dismantled and rendered useless; the garrison becomes discouraged; the three thousand men encamped outside become panic-stricken, demoralized, and flee, hardly waiting Tilghman's orders to save themselves. Some of them, fearing the approach of McClernand's column, fled by the upper Dover road, while others, taking forcible possession of a small steamer lying at the mouth of the creek above the fort, steamed up the river to a place of safety. Tilghman, the commander, is thus left, with about eighty or ninety artillerists, to surrender the fort, which he saw was his only course, since, having now but four guns bearing on the river fit for service, and "only fifty privates, and twenty sick," having done a private's duty himself, "covered with smoke, and personally pointing the guns," a further resistance was evidently as impossible as useless. He therefore struck the flag, hung out a white ensign, and surrendered at five minutes before two, the action having lasted one hour and a quarter.

The flag-ship, Cincinnati, had received thirty-one shots; the Essex, sixteen; the St. Louis, seven; the Carondelet, six. The iron sides of those vessels in the front rank had shed most of the shots; but one had penetrated the boiler of the Essex, and caused the wounding and scalding of twenty-nine officers and men, among whom was the commander, W. D. Porter.

Within an hour after the surrender, the supporting army came upon the scene, delighted at the speedy success of the attack, but disappointed, since it had deprived them of sharing in it. Commodore Foote turned over to General Grant the captured fort, with its munitions and prisoners; and the next step was in order.

Grant's brief report to Halleck's staff-officer, written the same day from Fort Henry, is as follows:—

CAPTAIN: Enclosed I send you my order for the attack upon Fort Henry. Owing to despatches received from Major-General Halleck, and corroborating information here, to the effect that the enemy were rapidly reënforcing, I thought it imperatively necessary that the fort should be carried to-day. My forces were not up at ten o'clock last night, when my order was written; therefore I did not deem it practicable to set an earlier hour than eleven o'clock to-day to commence the investment. The gunboats started up at the same hour to commence the attack, and engaged the enemy at not over six hundred yards. In little over one hour all the batteries were silenced, and the fort surrendered at discretion to Flag-officer Foote, giving us all their guns, camp and garrison equipage, &c. The prisoners taken are General Tilghman and staff, Captain Taylor and company, and the sick. The garrison, I think, must have commenced their retreat last night, or at an early hour this morning.

Had I not felt it an imperative necessity to attack Fort Henry to-day, I should have made the investment complete, and delayed until to-morrow, so as to secure the garrison. I do not now believe, however, the result would have been any more satisfactory.

The gunboats have proven themselves well able to resist a severe cannonading. All the iron-clad boats received more or less shots, — the flag-ship some twenty-eight, — without any serious damage to any, except the Essex. This vessel received one shot in her boiler that disabled her, killing and wounding some thirty-two men, Captain Porter among the wounded.

I remain your obedient servant,

U. S. GRANT, *Brigadier General.*

This brilliant victory carried dismay to the heart of the Confederate government; and though they then, when it was too late, found that the site of the fort was badly chosen,—that it was low, easily surrounded, and commanded by the ground on the other side of the river, — the effect of the victory was none the less decisive; and such discoveries only increased the folly of attempting to make a stand in a naturally weak position, by the military incompetence shown in selecting an improper place for defence. All that they thus urged to lessen the mortification of the defeat, only enhanced the credit due to Grant and Foote for having been sagacious enough to discover the weakness of what the Confederates had boasted was so strong a position.

The first result of this victory at Fort Henry was seen in the promptness with which Buckner evacuated Bowling Green. As early as September, 1861, by command of Albert Sidney Johnson, Buckner, with ten thousand men, had occupied this position, and boasted of its impregnable strength. But with the fall of Fort Henry he saw himself in danger, and fell back upon Fort Donelson, the rear-guard leaving Bowling Green on the 15th of February, while this position, upon which the Confederates had wasted all their powers of defence, which they had strengthened by a system of the most complex fortifications, was entered by General Mitchell, of Buell's column, so soon after its evacuation that he captured great stores of supplies in it. Fort Donelson was now in danger, and the safety of Nashville was threatened.

Immediately after the capture of Fort Henry, Commodore Foote sent Lieutenant Phelps up the Tennessee with three of the gunboats. He destroyed the railway bridge, twenty-five miles above Fort Henry, and, proceeding up to Florence, at the head of navigation, captured a large quantity of stores, and destroyed several steamers and other river craft, besides developing and giving an opportunity for expression to the loyal sentiments of many of the people of Northern Alabama, who had always looked with distrust upon the secession conspiracy.

The next step in order was, evidently, the reduction of Fort Donelson, of the strength of which the Confederates were more certain than they had been of either Fort Henry or Bowling Green; and to the performance of this task General Grant immediately devoted himself.

## CHAPTER VI.

### THE CAPTURE OF FORT DONELSON.

FORT DONELSON was designed and constructed by the Confederates for the purpose of blockading the Cumberland, as Fort Henry was intended to serve the same purpose for the Tennessee. No sooner had the victory over Fort Henry been gained, than Grant commenced active preparations for an attack upon Fort Donelson. He was fully aware of the great importance of following up the first blow instantly, without giving the enemy time to recover from their dismay. He reorganized his forces, and sent for all available reënforcements to Cairo. For this new service his army was formed into two divisions. The first, under General McClernand, was composed of three brigades, under Colonels Oglesby, W. H. L. Wallace, and Morrison; the second, under Brigadier General Charles F. Smith, of three brigades, under Colonels Cook, Lauman, and McArthur. A third division also took part in the affair, under Brigadier General Lewis Wallace, composed of a part of Smith's division, and the reënforcements sent forward by General Halleck. When the advance was first made, General Lewis Wallace was left in command of Forts Henry and Heiman, with garrisons taken from Smith's division.

The order of advance was thus arranged in Grant's

general field-order for February 11, 1862. One brigade of McClernand's division was to move by the telegraph road from Fort Henry directly upon Fort Donelson, and to halt when within two miles of it; three other brigades were to march by the Dover road to within the same distance of the fort, and then to unite with the first in forming the right wing in the investment of the fort. Two brigades of Smith's division were to follow by the Dover road, and were to be followed by the reserves as soon as these could be sent forward. The details of the attack could not be arranged until the forces were on the ground; but Smith was directed to occupy Dover, if practicable, and cut off all retreat by the river.

In accordance with these directions, McClernand and Smith marched across the country on the morning of the 12th, to attack the works on the land side, while six regiments were sent in transports, accompanied by the gunboats, up the Cumberland to join in the attack on the water front, or to be used as might be thought best under the circumstances. The movement was made very hastily. Hardly time enough to repair the gunboats had been taken; but Grant was fully aware of the great importance of every moment just at this juncture, and pushed forward as rapidly as possible.

The fort itself was most favorably placed, and constructed according to the best rules of engineering art. It was situated upon a high hill, on the left bank of the river, where it makes an abrupt turn from north to west, flowing in this last direction about a quarter of a mile, and then turning again towards the north. This peculiarity of its location enabled a large number of guns to be trained directly down the stream. At the foot of the hill, on the river side, were two strong water batteries. The armament of the lower, or main battery consisted of eight thirty-two pounders, and one ten-inch columbiad; the other battery contained one heavy rifled gun, carrying a bolt weighing one hundred and twenty-eight pounds, and two thirty-two pounders. Both of these batteries were sunken, or excavated in the hill-side. The fort itself was of irregular form, following the inequalities of the surface, and enclosing about one hundred acres. It was covered on one side by a creek, which is generally not fordable; and just above it a small creek separates it from the town of Dover, which is a mile above it on the river bank.

On the land side the defences were equally strong. The Confederates had taken advantage of the natural inequalities of the ground, which consist of a series of hills, knolls, valleys, and ravines; had cleared away all the timber which might serve to protect and conceal the enemy's advance, and erected field-works, from the extreme western angle of the fort, running along the southern direction of a ridge, and thus forming an outer line of defence. In front, also, of this outer line, encircling the fort and the town of Dover, was a line of rifle trenches, made of logs, forming a kind of parapet, with an abatis of timber in front. The land side appeared as strong as the water front, and the garrison seemed proportionally strong.

This garrison consisted of thirteen regiments from Tennessee, two from Kentucky, six from Mississippi, one from Texas, two from Alabama, four from Virginia, two independent battalions of Tennessee infantry, and Forrest's brigade of cavalry; and besides the armament of the fort and water batteries, six batteries of light artillery and seventeen heavy guns. The whole number of the defensive force amounted to at least twenty-three thousand men. The command of the position was placed in the hands of General Floyd, who had gained a somewhat unenviable reputation as Secretary of War under Buchanan, and who here was to cap the climax of his achievements by adding to his talent for dishonesty the proof of a genius for cowardice. He had been appointed to the command of Fort Donelson, by General A. S. Johnston, on the 13th, the day Grant commenced his operations, and had assumed the post without delay. His ignorance of military matters, of the fort, its topography, its garrison, &c., was as great as his insolence in peculation and in treason. Floyd assigned the next position in command below his own rank to General Gideon J. Pillow, giving him control of the left wing of the Confederate army in and around Dover. General Pillow had also arrived at the fort only on the 10th, and was, perhaps, as ignorant and valueless as Floyd, though the accurate settlement of their respective claims in this direction is difficult. The other commanders of the Confederate army were Buckner, who had command of the fort and the ground in its immediate vicinity, and B. R. Johnson, both of whom were graduates of West Point, and capable men.

Buckner had been appointed first to the command of the fort, but had been superseded by Pillow, who in turn was superseded by Floyd, and each of them had remained to serve under his superior.

The attacking army under Grant consisted of about fifteen thousand men, while in his artillery he was proportionally still more inferior to the enemy. The boldness and audacity of the attack must count, however, for something: by this he deceived the enemy, as he intended doing. The march began from Fort Henry on the morning of the 12th, and the columns under McClernand and Smith advanced, preceded by cavalry to clear the way, to within sight of the fort, in the early afternoon, without having met the enemy, who remained huddled in the fort, waiting to be attacked, instead of coming boldly out and disputing the passage of the attacking force. The night of the 12th was passed by our forces in their assigned positions, and the next morning the fight began by the Confederate batteries opening upon our troops, whose positions had been discovered by the advance of our sharp-shooters upon the enemy's line of pickets.

Here Grant rapidly posted his divisions. General C. F. Smith was placed on the left, opposite the northwest face of the fort, McClernand on the right, while the light artillery, with proper supports, was placed upon the various roads, and the heavy guns were directed against the armament of the fort. Grant's headquarters were located at a farm-house on the Dover road. The struggle soon commenced with a furious cannonade upon both sides, in which the practice was equally excellent. The design was to assault the works with infantry, and our artillery was to prepare the way. General McClernand formed a storming column under the command of Colonel Hayne, of the Forty-eighth

Illinois, and the Seventeenth and Forty-ninth Illinois, with McAllister's battery to cover the assault, the object being to make a lodgment upon the intrenchment. The attack was not, however, successful, though reënforced by the Forty-fifth Illinois: the fire of the enemy was so fierce, and the abatis so formidable an obstacle, that the assailants were forced to retire. The action was opened, however, and Grant's persistence was not to be lessened by a single repulse.

Meanwhile the gunboats were anxiously expected; they were to bring reënforcements and supplies. The weather now changed, and, from its previous mildness, became bitterly cold. A rain-storm also set in, and changed first to hail and then to sleet. The thermometer fell rapidly to only ten above zero, and our troops were without any shelter whatsoever, were in want of rations, and the majority of them, with the recklessness characteristic of new troops, had left or thrown away their overcoats, beguiled by the previous spring-like mildness of the weather.

The sufferings our army endured that night can be realized only by those who have passed through similar experiences; many of the wounded froze to death, and it was with great difficulty that the well could keep themselves from the same fate. The next morning dawned upon these hungry, shivering men, and the gunboats had not yet arrived with the desired reënforcements and supplies. Grant, keenly alive to the hazard of his position, despatched a messenger to General Lewis Wallace, at Fort Henry, with orders to bring up the garrison which had been left at that post. The messenger had, however, hardly set out, when a scout brought the enlivening news that a gunboat was in sight; and a distant cloud of smoke announced that the balance of the fleet was not far behind. The Carondelet was the gunboat in sight, and as soon as she came within range she opened upon the water batteries, which responded fiercely, and the contest began anew.

The reënforcements and supplies were landed about three miles below the fort; a road was rapidly cut through the woods, and having made their connection with the forces previously on the ground, rations were quickly distributed, ammunition was served out, and arrangements made for the comfort of the wounded.

The reënforcements which had just come up, together with the garrison from Fort Henry, constituted the Third Division, composed of eleven regiments, which were placed under the command of Wallace, and posted in the centre, so that the line was completed.

The attack of the gunboats now commenced. As at Fort Henry, Commodore Foote steamed up with his vessels in two lines; the iron-clads, the Pittsburg, St. Louis, Louisville, and Carondelet in the first line, and the wooden ships, the Conestoga, Tyler, and Lexington in the second. His purpose was to silence the water batteries, and take up such a position in the bend of the river as would enable him to enfilade the faces of the fort with his broadsides. To do this, however, he was exposed to the concentrated fire of both the batteries and the fort, which was at once both raking and plunging, and was probably as severe a test as any fleet has ever experienced. Still the fleet pressed on, approaching nearer and nearer the desired end. The practice of the guns on the boats was most excellent; they were within perhaps less than four hundred yards of the batteries, and for two hours remained giving and receiving this terrible cannonade. The upper water battery had been silenced; and though the boats had not been thoroughly repaired, after the damage they had suffered at Fort Henry, and had suffered still more from the present contest, it seemed as though a short time longer would suffice for success, when suddenly they were forced to fall back. The cross and plunging fire had done its work. A shot had cut the rudder chains of the Louisville, and sent her drifting, helpless and unmanageable, down the stream. The flag-ship, the St. Louis, had her steering-wheel shot away, the ball at the same time killing her pilot, who was standing at Commodore Foote's side, while he himself was injured in the foot by a splinter. On examination, her additional steering apparatus was also found to be disabled, and she herself rendered helpless and unmanageable. Fifty-nine shots had struck the St. Louis during the conflict, some of them raking her from stem to stern. The Louisville had been struck thirty-five times, the Carondelet twenty-six times, and her rifled gun had burst during the action. The Pittsburg had been struck twenty-one times. The fire of at least twenty guns had been concentrated upon these boats, while they could bring only twelve to bear upon the batteries in reply.

Thus two of the iron-clads being rendered unmanageable, and the other two being greatly damaged, Commodore Foote found himself, on the verge of victory, obliged to withdraw, having lost fifty-four killed and wounded.

On consulting with Grant, it was decided that the best course to be pursued was to send the gunboats back to Cairo to repair, while the army should hold the fort in a state of siege, until they could return with sufficient reënforcements to make the army competent to reduce the fort. Though the fleet had not been entirely successful, yet their services had been of great importance. They had relieved General Grant from the danger of attack while unprepared, and had enabled him to post his reënforcements and mature his plans. To hold the place invested until both the army and navy, reënforced, should be strong enough to insure victory, now seemed the plan most proper for action. Had the Confederates remained intrenched in their works, repairing their damages, and strengthening their fortifications, this plan would have been pursued.

On Friday night, however, a council of war was held at Floyd's headquarters at Dover, and the plan of action there adopted led to a change in Grant's action, and hastened the surrender of the fort. This council was composed of the Confederate division and brigade commanders, and they agreed unanimously to the plan of action proposed by Floyd. This plan was, to make an overwhelming attack upon our forces. The principal portion of the attacking force, about one half the entire Confederate army, with all of Forrest's cavalry under Pillow and Johnson, was to attack our right wing under McClernand, and drive them from the heights they occupied commanding the Cumberland River, and whose batteries, it was evident, would soon close the river above the fort. This being accomplished, this force was then to fall back upon that portion of our line occupied by Wallace with his division, while Buckner, with the remainder of the army which could be spared after leaving the necessary garrison in the fort, should sally out against our centre, and attack Wallace in front. If these attacks should prove successful, the whole of our right wing and centre would be thrown back upon Smith's division, and would thus be routed and destroyed. In case the plan was only partially successful, Floyd hoped at least that a way would be opened for the evacuation of the fort, and his own successful escape, which seemed to him the most important and pressing piece of business now on hand. The decision was, that the plan should be put in operation on the next morning, Saturday the 15th.

Accordingly, at five in the morning of the 15th, the attacking column, numbering about ten thousand men, with thirty guns, under Pillow and Johnson, marched out from Dover, with the purpose of crushing our right wing under McClernand, and cutting a pathway through them. Our lines at this point followed the contour of the rebel intrenchments, and with each brigade was a field battery. The attack was a surprise. Reveille was just sounding; the troops were hardly under arms, when it became evident that the right wing was seriously threatened. Promptly, however, our line was formed, and guided by the flashes of the enemy's guns, a partial change of front was executed in order to meet their advance. There was no time to be lost, for Pillow had sent his cavalry round to try and attack our rear, while he was attacking our right flank.

Our line stood firm for a time, but, pressed too

strongly by the constantly arriving fresh troops, was forced to fall back; and but for the coolness of the officers and their inspiring courage, a panic might have ensued. But though thus partially successful, the enemy did not advance with impunity. Our light batteries poured a withering fire into their advancing columns, and forced them frequently to falter and recoil, until pushed onward by the advancing masses behind them.

Our new line was formed, and the enemy held in check, when Buckner's force came out to attack our left flank. As soon as they were discovered, the threatened flank was strengthened, and two guns being rapidly brought to bear upon them, they were easily repulsed, but not without having had the effect of somewhat disheartening our men. We seemed to be attacked on all sides. The ammunition had given out, and signs of a panic began to appear. Many officers were wounded, and the crisis of the battle had arrived. General Wallace, however, formed a new line; the regiments which had borne the brunt of the attack were formed again in our rear, and given fresh supplies of ammunition.

Pillow had now sent an aid to telegraph to Nashville that, "on the honor of a soldier," the day was theirs. Having delayed some little time in plundering McClernand's camp, the enemy came forward again, flushed with success. They expected to finish the contest with an easy victory. But our line stood firm, and by their deliberate fire, and the excellent handling of the artillery, the Confederates were repulsed.

During the seeming success of the unexpected attack upon our lines, Grant had been on the flag-ship consulting with Commodore Foote, who was wounded. He saw, on his return, from the desperate character of the attack, that when it culminated, the enemy would give way, if he showed a bold front, and pressed them vigorously in return. Examining the haversacks of some of the prisoners captured, they were found filled with three days' rations; and at the sight of this evidence Grant exclaimed, "They meant to cut their way out; they have no idea of staying here to fight us. Whichever party now attacks first will whip, and the rebels will have to be very quick if they beat me." The evident truth of this shrewd common-sense conclusion inspired our troops with new courage. Riding to the front, Grant then ordered Wallace, who had first checked the enemy, to advance and recover the ground lost in the morning, while Smith should storm the works on the enemy's right. The result showed the accuracy of his foresight and the correctness of his reasoning. Wallace advanced, and drove the enemy back before him, and at five in the afternoon, just at dark, our line halted within one hundred and fifty yards of the enemy's intrenchments. During the whole of the following intensely cold night, our troops remained in the position thus gained, ministering to the wants of the wounded, and wishing eagerly for the morning. At daylight reënforcements were brought up, and preparations made for storming the intrenchments, when the display of white flags from various parts of the fort showed that the battle was won.

Let us now look at the manner in which affairs were conducted in another part of the field. When, in the afternoon of the 15th, Wallace was ordered to advance, Smith's division was also set the arduous and dangerous task of storming the enemy's works upon the right. While he is organizing his column of attack, a feint was made by Cook's brigade posted on his left, and the batteries of heavy artillery open fire upon the intrenchments and the fort. The attacking column was composed of five regiments — the Second Iowa, the Fifty-second Indiana, the Twenty-fifth Indiana, the Seventh Iowa, and the Fourteenth Iowa. It was nearly sunset, when Smith, hearing Wallace's guns, far away to the right, awaking the echoes with their angry roar, put himself at the head of his column, and with a few such inspiriting words as the ardor of battle suggests, told them of the work before them to be done, and offered to lead them himself. Riding at their head, his gray hair floating in the wind as he waved his hat upon the point of his sword, he led them to the attack. The murderous fire from the enemy's guns decimates his ranks, but nothing can make them waver with such a leader, and, at the point of the bayonet, they rush through and over the intrenchments. Planting their standards upon the captured works, they pour volley after volley upon the defeated Confederates, who flee precipitately in dismay. Four hundred of the gallant body of men who make this decisive charge have fallen, but the victory is won. Grant's audacity of conception and Smith's fearless valor, backed by the irresistible enthusiasm of his troops, has plucked victory from seeming defeat.

Wallace, holding his advanced ground, is informed of Smith's success, and night settles upon the scene. Our soldiers remain upon the ground, ready for action with the approach of daylight. Grant had shown that he was a general; that he had a genius for comprehending the entire situation. He had foreseen that the impetuous surge of the enemy's attack promised, by its very might, that it would recede; and he had also shown that he possessed — the rarest quality in a military commander — the skill of intuition which recognizes and selects the fit moment for prompt action.

During the whole of the following night, despite the cold, though without fires, and though mostly wanting food, our men remained upon the ground they had gained, awaiting the morning with impatience. The enthusiasm of success both cheered and warmed them, while the contemplation of complete victory in the morning kept them in spirits, and their valor would have been irresistible the next day. But while the Union army was in this condition, the Confederates were in the most thoroughly disheartened state of mind. The officers were more so than the men, while the leaders were more so than the officers. Floyd and Pillow were the worst frightened of all. To the first it seemed as though the whole action was undertaken simply for the purpose of capturing him. The consciousness of his treason, of the shameful manner in which he had abused the trusts confided to him, made him fear the just vengeance of an indignant people, and the only question with him was how to escape. He declared he would sooner die than surrender, but he preferred escape to either. At the council of war, held that evening at his headquarters, he proposed cutting his way out with his own brigade of Virginia troops; but such an apt illustration of the principle of state rights was not relished by his companions.

Pillow, the second in command, seemed actuated only by a similar fear of capture, and an equally strong desire for escape. Both of these worthies absolutely refused to retain the command; so Floyd transferred it to Pillow, who immediately passed it over to Buckner, who was the only one of the three who appears to have had any of the dignity of honor which is traditionally supposed to be the first requisite of a soldierly character. Having thus shifted the immediate responsibilities of their position, these two "valiant Pistols" escaped that night upon two small steamers from Dover, and succeeded in reaching Nashville. Their official reports, together with that of General Grant, will be found in the Appendix.

The command having thus devolved upon Buckner, and no other course remaining open to him than surrender, his army being in such confusion that further resistance would have been impossible, he sent an officer, at early daylight, as the bearer of the following letter to General Grant: —

HEADQUARTERS FORT DONELSON,
February 16, 1862.

SIR: In consideration of all the circumstances governing the present situation of affairs at this station, I propose to the commanding officer of the Federal forces the appointment of commissioners to agree upon terms of capitulation of the forces and fort under my command, and in that view suggest an armistice until twelve o'clock to-day.

I am, sir, very respectfully,
Your obedient servant,
S. B. BUCKNER, *Brigadier General C. S. A.*

THE SURRENDER OF FORT DONELSON.

This communication reached Grant in due time, and he returned the following answer, which has become historical, and from which dates his soubriquet among the armies of "Unconditional Surrender Grant:"—

HEADQUARTERS ARMY IN THE FIELD,<br>CAMP NEAR DONELSON, February 16, 1862.

TO GENERAL S. B. BUCKNER, *Confederate Army.*

Yours of this date, proposing an armistice and appointment of commissioners to settle terms of capitulation, is just received. *No terms other than an unconditional and immediate surrender can be accepted. I propose to move immediately upon your works.*

I am, sir, very respectfully,<br>Your obedient servant,<br>U. S. GRANT,<br>*Brigadier General U. S. A., commanding.*

The reply was far from a pleasing one to the rebel commander; but, on looking around his position, he found he could not stand another assault, and his followers were anxious for a cessation of the strife. He therefore sent the following acceptance of General Grant's terms of surrender:—

HEADQUARTERS DOVER TENNESSEE,<br>February 16, 1862.

TO BRIGADIER GENERAL U. S. GRANT, *U. S. A.*

SIR: The distribution of the forces under my command, incident to an unexpected change of commanders, and the overwhelming force under your command, compel me, notwithstanding the brilliant success of the Confederate arms yesterday, to accept the ungenerous and unchivalrous terms which you propose.

I am, sir, your very obedient servant,<br>S. B. BUCKNER, *Brigadier General C. S. A.*

This reply is most amusing, and suggests the singular mixture of folly and enthusiasm which seemed at this time to be the principal ingredients of the secession spirit. What is ungenerous or unchivalrous in unconditional surrender, when a man has staked all on the wager of battle, and lost? While what has any preceding success, however brilliant, to do with the present question? But the southern leaders having been so long accustomed to domineer with a high hand, both at home and in Washington, it required time for them to learn that they were subject to defeat, and that a Union victory was not intended especially and only as a personal indignity towards themselves. The foolish halo of chivalry in which they moved was as far apart from the stern practical common sense of the present world as their system of slavery was behind the present condition of labor. Yet as, in spite of the world's progress, they defended and fought for this last as at once the highest, most moral, and most economic system, it is not so very surprising that they felt aggrieved when the illusions of the other were suddenly destroyed by the realities of war.

Grant's terms were, however, accepted, and the surrender was immediate and unconditional. With the fort were captured (according to the figures given by Pollard, the southern historian) thirteen thousand five hundred men as prisoners of war, three thousand horses, forty-eight field-pieces, seventeen heavy guns, twenty thousand stands of arms, and immense quantities of supplies. The day after the capitulation two regiments of Tennessee troops, numbering fourteen hundred and seventy-five men, came to reënforce the garrison, and marched in with their colors flying, wholly unconscious of the surrender which had taken place, and, to their surprise and chagrin, were all taken prisoners. The Confederate loss in killed and wounded was twelve hundred and thirty-eight; the Union loss was four hundred and forty-six killed, seventeen hundred and fifty-three wounded, and one hundred and fifty prisoners. The disparity of numbers arose from the fact that the Union forces had to fight in an open field, while the enemy was protected by the works.

The results of this compaign were most important: first, it broke the outer line of the defence of the Confederacy, which extended from Columbus to Bowling Green, both of which places had been strongly fortified, and forced the Confederates to abondon them both, so that a few days after the victory of Fort Donelson, the Union troops entered both these places without any resistance. It filled also the whole loyal population of the country with rejoicing. In the midst of the uncertainty, the anxiety, the approaching despair which had followed the course of our arms in the east, this victory was most welcome; it gave assurance to those who, drawing deductions too rapidly, and from too limited a field of observation, began to think that our leaders were incompetent, that we had at least one man who could execute as well as plan, to whom the science of war was not only strategy, but who also understood the value of action; and it proved that our soldiers might be relied upon for endurance as well as valor. Following the universal expression of the people's wish, the government made General Grant a Major General of Volunteers, his commission to date from the day of the surrender of Fort Donelson. The following order, issued by General Grant to the troops under his command, gives a succinct account of the events we have been trying to describe: —

*General Orders, No.* 2.

HEADQUARTERS, DISTRICT OF WEST TENNESSEE,
FORT DONELSON, February 17, 1862.

The General commanding takes great pleasure in congratulating the troops of this command for the triumph over rebellion, gained by their valor, on the 13th, 14th, and 15th instants.

For four successive nights, without shelter, during the most inclement weather known in this latitude, they faced an enemy in large force, in a position chosen by himself. Though strongly fortified by nature, all the additional safeguards suggested by science were added. Without a murmur this was borne, prepared at all times to receive an attack, and, with continuous skirmishing by day, resulting ultimately in forcing the enemy to surrender without conditions.

The victory achieved is not only great in the effect it will have in breaking down rebellion, but has secured the greatest number of prisoners of war ever taken in any battle on this continent.

Fort Donelson will hereafter be marked in capitals on the map of our united country, and the men who fought the battle will live in the memory of a grateful people.

By order.

U. S. GRANT, *Brigadier General commanding.*

## CHAPTER VII.

THE EFFECTS OF THESE VICTORIES.—PREPARING FOR THE NEXT MOVE.

THE grand plan for the suppression of the rebellion was now more apparent than ever. While the army of the Potomac was checked in its advance upon Richmond, in Virginia, it became evident that, to crush all armed resistance against the government, it was necessary that the Mississippi should be open for navigation from its mouth to its source, and that, the Confederate power being thus broken, access to the interior would be had from the south-west, and thus finally the Confederacy be split to pieces by the driving in of these two wedges. In carrying out the principal operations of this vast plan, Grant took a singularly prominent part. Having been the chief agent in breaking the first line of defence made by the Confederacy in protecting their territory to the east of the Mississippi and south of the Ohio, he was now called upon to continue the work thus nobly begun. His sphere of action after the victory at Fort Donelson was enlarged, and it will be seen that his grasp of the situation and its necessities kept pace with the extension of his field for action.

On the 14th of February, 1862, by an order from

General Halleck, he was assigned to the new district of West Tennessee, embracing the territory from Cairo, between the Mississippi and Cumberland Rivers, to the Mississippi border. His headquarters were in the field, and he kept them there.

The department of the Ohio was at this time in command of Brigadier General Don Carlos Buell. It comprised the States of Ohio, Michigan, Indiana, that portion of Kentucky east of the Cumberland, and the State of Tennessee. In the new move his army was to operate with Grant's, and we shall find them together at the battle of Pittsburg Landing, or Shiloh. Clarksville, on the east bank of the Cumberland, was evacuated by the Confederates, and taken possession of by us on the 20th of February. The gunboats then hastened on to Nashville. This city was abandoned by Johnston as soon as he heard of the fall of Fort Donelson, and was occupied on Sunday evening, February 23, by our forces. On the 3d of March Columbus was also evacuated, and the Confederates were forced to seek a new line. The capture of Nashville and Columbus, which was the result of Grant's victories, was quite as terrible a loss to the Confederacy as the taking of Forts Henry and Donelson. Pollard compares the first to the shock of an earthquake, and the second was hardly less staggering.

Soon after taking command of the district of West Tennessee, Grant proclaimed martial law in the following order: —

*General Orders, No.* 7.

HEADQUARTERS, DISTRICT OF WEST TENNESSEE,
FORT DONELSON, TENN., February 22, 1862.

[EXTRACT.]

Tennessee, by her rebellion, having ignored all laws of the United States, no courts will be allowed to act under state authority; but all cases coming within the reach of the military arm will be adjudicated by the authorities the government has established within the state.

Martial law is, therefore, declared to extend over West Tennessee. Whenever a sufficient number of citizens return to their allegiance to maintain law and order over the territory, the military restriction here indicated will be removed.

By order of Major General U. S. GRANT.

J. A. RAWLINS, *A. A. G.*

He also issued an order from General Halleck, exhorting his troops to "let no excesses on their part tarnish the glory of their army." All supplies which had to be impressed were to be paid for, and such magnanimous justice as a great nation, confident, perhaps too confident, in its honor and material strength, could afford and would prefer to exercise, were to characterize the conduct of our troops. The "relation of master and slave" was not to be interfered with. Such questions were to be settled by the "civil courts." We were then in the early part of 1862. But it is impossible to make an army of free citizens a mere unthinking machine. It may be possible in Europe, where the people are distinct from the government, opposed in interest, antagonistic in feeling, and where the army is the tool of the government. But here the people are the government, and the army is a part of themselves. It is not a band of mercenaries, hired to do a despot's bidding, but a collection of freemen, who have volunteered to do a public work, in which each man of them has a personal interest. We shall see further results arising from this fundamental difference in the constitution of our nationality and of our army as a part and parcel of this, and that of European governments and European armies, before we get through our record.

About this time there was a misunderstanding between Grant and the Department at Washington. He had gone to Nashville, February 26, to consult with Buell, and this fact being reported to Halleck and at Washington, it was made a cause of complaint against him. Fault was also found with him for being remiss in reporting the condition of his army promptly; though it is evident that the constant active duty they had been engaged in made this impossible. To his astonishment, on the 4th of March he was ordered to turn over his command to General C. F. Smith, and remain at Fort Henry. A correspondence took place between himself and General Halleck, in which he asked to be relieved entirely from duty. But the whole matter was explained, and he was restored to command, resuming the position on the 14th of March. The real cause of the difficulty was, probably, some petty jealousy of his success, which, as it did not result in depriving us of his services, we need not now trouble ourselves with investigating.

## CHAPTER VIII.

### THE BATTLE OF SHILOH, OR PITTSBURG LANDING.

THE next line of defence necessary for the Confederacy was one which should protect the line of the Memphis and Charleston Railway, one of their great arteries of interior communication. Memphis was strongly fortified, and Corinth, a little town at the junction of the Memphis and Charleston Railway with the Mobile and Ohio Railway, was evidently a most important point to be guarded by one party and to be taken by the other. The Tennessee River, now that it was opened, gave an opportunity for our forces to penetrate far into the interior of the Confederacy, and our troops were concentrated rapidly at Savannah and Pittsburg Landing, two points upon the banks of this river, quite near to Corinth, being only about twenty miles distant. The approach of the Union army upon Corinth, down the Mississippi, was guarded by the fortifications at Memphis and those at Island No. 10, and other points above that city, while the strength of New Orleans, Vicksburg, and other points, was supposed by the Confederates to make the approach from the mouth of the stream equally impossible.

When, on the 3d of March, 1862, General Polk, the Confederate bishop, — who may perhaps be taken as a fair sample of the church militant, — evacuated and dismantled the works at Columbus, falling back upon the strong defences which had been constructed at Island No. 10, and which were intended to guard the passage of the Mississippi, in place of those abandoned at Columbus, which had become worthless at the fall of Forts Henry and Donelson. This island is situated in the stream, about forty-five miles below Columbus, and is the tenth island in the river, counting from Cairo; hence its name. The river here makes a series of bends, in the form of an ꝏ. The island lies in the mid-channel, and is about a mile long, and a half mile wide in its widest part. The armament placed here consisted of four heavy batteries on the island, and seven on the Kentucky and Tennessee shores. At the upper and lower ends of the ꝏ are New Madrid and Point Pleasant. Beside the works, a floating dock was brought up from New Orleans, armored, anchored, and converted into a floating battery. Forts were also erected at New Madrid, and the place was considered exceedingly strong. A detailed account of the operations of the coöperating army under General John Pope, and the fleet under Commodore Foote, by which this strong position was taken, with one hundred and .twenty-four guns, and some three thousand prisoners, as they do not enter strictly in an account of Grant's campaigns, need not be given here. Suffice it to say, that Polk evacuated Columbus on the 3d of March; Mackall, who was appointed to Island No. 10, took command there on the 5th, and the place was formally surrendered to us on the 8th. This was the completion of the next step in the opening of the Mississippi River.

Pittsburg Landing, at which and in the vicinity our troops were concentrated, is on the west bank of the Tennessee. The landing is flanked on the left by a short but precipitous ravine, along which runs the road to Corinth. On the right and left of the position are Snake and Lick Creeks, which would compel an attack to be made in front. The distance between the mouths of these creeks is almost two and a half miles. The landing was protected by the gunboats Tyler and Lexington. The army of the Ohio, under Buell, was coming up to effect a junction with Grant. On the 17th of March Grant arrived at Savannah, where he was most conveniently placed for overseeing the whole force at his disposal, which consisted of about thirty-eight thousand men.

The credit of the rebel plan is given to Beauregard, who conceived the whole movement in his headquarters at Corinth, and who, though Johnston was his superior, was looked on as the leader during the day, while Johnston was on the field, and after his fall on the afternoon of the first day of the battle, became nominally commander. Beauregard had collected his troops from every available point. Bragg's corps had been brought up from Mobile and Pensacola; Polk had brought the greater part of his from the evacuation of Columbus; Johnston had brought his, which had retreated from Nashville to Murfreesboro'. These forces, amounting to about forty-five thousand men, had been disposed along the Mobile and Ohio Railway from Bethel to Corinth, and on the Memphis and Charleston Railway from Corinth to Iuka. Unquestionably Beauregard hoped to crush Grant entirely, though in his report, made of course in the light of subsequent events, he claims to have done all he desired, which was only to stun our army, take their stores, and then return to his base at Corinth.

On the 2d of April there was slight skirmishing at Cramp's Landing. On the 3d General A. S. Johnston issued a proclamation to his army, and their advance began; and on the 4th a grand reconnoissance of our position was made, from which, however, they rapidly retired. Johnston's proclamation was couched in the following terms: —

SOLDIERS OF THE ARMY OF THE MISSISSIPPI: I have put you in motion to offer battle to the invaders of your country, with the resolution, and discipine, and valor becoming men, fighting, as you are, for all worth living or dying for. You can but march to a decisive victory over agrarian mercenaries, sent to subjugate and despoil you of your liberties, property, and honor.

Remember the precious stake involved; remember the dependence of your mothers, your wives, your sisters, and your children, on the result. Remember the fair, broad, abounding lands, the happy homes, that will be desolated by your defeat. The eyes and hopes of eight millions of people rest upon you. You are expected to show yourselves worthy of your valor and courage, worthy of the women of the South, whose noble devotion in this war has never been exceeded in any time. With such incentives to brave deeds, and with trust that God is with us, your General will lead you confidently to the combat, assured of success.

By order of

General A. S. JOHNSTON *commanding.*

On the evening of Saturday, the 5th of April, the Confederates arrived in position in front of our lines, having been delayed by the bad condition of the roads. The portions of the Confederate army nearest to our lines were allowed no fires that night, nor were the noises usual in a camp permitted. Nothing was done which should make us aware of either their position or their strength. Orders were issued for the disposition of the forces the next day, and the Confederate leaders held an informal council that night at Beauregard's headquarters, who, though weak from a recent illness, was full of exaggerated confidence, and announced that his men should "water their horses the next day in the Tennessee or in hell." From his spies and the residents of the country he had an accurate knowledge of the position and composition of Grant's army; and hoping that Buell would not arrive in time, he expected to attack us unawares, and with his generals was in high spirits over their expected success of the morrow.

The morning of the 6th was bright and clear. By three in the morning the Confederates had breakfasted, and stripped for battle. It was Sunday. The contest raged all that day, and until the afternoon the Confederates were successful. Our forces were driven back at all points, and concentrated round the Landing in so compact a body, that the lines extended only about a mile in length, running in a curve round the Landing. Though such concentration was forced upon us, yet it had the effect of consolidating our resistance. The last attempt of the Confederates, just before nightfall, to cross the ravine, seize the road, and cut us off from the Landing, though made with desperate and determined valor, was unsuccessful. Our artillery fire, aided by the guns from the boats, was too severe for them to pass, and they were forced to fall back. Beauregard, professing himself satisfied with the day's work, resolved to leave the final and utter overthrow of Grant's army until the next day, and his army slept upon their arms.

General Grant had been upon the field all day, and about five in the evening had visited Sherman, and, being yet ignorant of Buell's arrival, had ordered Sherman, with the aid of Lewis Wallace, who had been expected upon the field at an early hour of the morning, but by some accident, taking the wrong road, did not arrive until the evening, to assume the offensive in the morning. Here, as at Fort Donelson, he had seen that when the fury of the Confederate attack had spent itself, the plan was to assume the offensive. During the night Buell's forces were posted, and the steamers kept plying between the Landing and Savannah, bringing up reënforcements, so that we should be ready the first thing in the morning for an overwhelming advance.

Next morning, early, both parties commenced the offensive. Beauregard persisted in attempting to capture the Landing. His assault was of the most determined and vigorous kind, but was met with more than equal valor and persistence. By four in the afternoon the Confederates saw the hopelessness of further fighting, and at half past five were in full retreat, having burned their camp, and, protected by a strong rear-guard, hastened back to Corinth, and commenced to intrench. Yet Beauregard's genius for vaunting did not desert him, despite the failure of his attack, and the next day he sent the following despatch to Richmond: —

GRANT AND SHERMAN AT THE BATTLE OF SHILOH.

CORINTH, Tuesday, April 8, 1862.

TO THE SECRETARY OF WAR, Richmond.

We have gained a great and glorious victory. Eight to ten thousand prisoners, and thirty-six pieces of cannon. Buell reënforced Grant, and *we retired to our intrenchments at Corinth*, which we can hold. Loss heavy on both sides.

BEAUREGARD.

His boast of holding his position at Corinth, we shall find, is as empty as his vaunted victory. The following correspondence will also serve to throw some additional lustre upon the magnificent disregard for facts which prompted Beauregard's telegraphic despatch: —

HEADQUARTERS DEPARTMENT OF MISSISSIPPI,
MONTEREY, April 8, 1862.

SIR: At the close of the conflict yesterday, my forces being exhausted by the extraordinary length of the time during which they were engaged with yours on that and the preceding day, and it being apparent that you had received, and were still receiving, reënforcements, I felt it my duty to withdraw my troops from the immediate scene of the conflict. Under these circumstances, in accordance with the usages of war, I shall transmit this under a flag of truce, to ask permission to send a mounted party to the battle-field of Shiloh, for the purpose of giving decent interment to my dead. Certain gentlemen wishing to avail themselves of this opportunity to remove the remains of their sons and friends, I must request for them the privilege of accompanying the burial party; and in this connection, I deem it proper to say, I am asking what I have extended to your own countrymen under similar circumstances.

Respectfully, General, your obedient servant,

P. G. T. BEAUREGARD, *General commanding.*

To Major General U. S. GRANT, *Major General commanding United States Forces, Pittsburg Landing.*

HEADQUARTERS ARMY IN FIELD,
PITTSBURG, April 9, 1862.

General P. G. T. BEAUREGARD, *commanding Confederate Army on Mississippi, Monterey, Tenn.*

Your despatch of yesterday is just received. Owing to the warmth of the weather, I deemed it advisable to have all the dead of both parties buried immediately. Heavy details were made for this purpose, and it is now accomplished. There cannot, therefore, be any necessity of admitting within our lines the parties you desired to send on the ground asked. I shall always be glad to extend any courtesy consistent with duty, and especially so when dictated by humanity.

I am, General, respectfully, your obedient servant,
U. S. GRANT, *Major General commanding.*

In the mean time, while Beauregard was withdrawing his discomfited army to Corinth, Grant's army being "too much fatigued from two days' hard fighting and exposure to the open air, in a drenching rain, during the intervening night, to pursue immediately," they remained on the field; but the next day, the 8th, Sherman, with two brigades and some cavalry, reconnoitred the route of the retreating army; and in his abandoned and disordered camp, in the wounded left under the protection of hospital flags, and in the supplies scattered along the road, he found every evidence of a hasty and disorderly retreat.

Our loss in this two days' fighting numbered, all told, some fifteen thousand men. That of the Confederates was still greater. Beauregard confesses to seventeen hundred and twenty-eight killed, eight thousand and twelve wounded, nine hundred and fifty-five missing — total, ten thousand six hundred and ninety-nine; and as his army went into action forty-five thousand strong, and he could not on Monday, by his own account, bring twenty thousand into action, there must have been from fifteen to eighteen thousand stragglers.

During the engagement General Grant frequently exposed himself to the thickest of the fire, and during the second day headed a charge himself, and was slightly wounded in the ankle, but not enough to prevent his remaining personally in the field. The Confederate General Johnston, in the afternoon of the first day, received a wound in the leg from a minié ball, which subsequently proved fatal. The following report forwarded to the Department by General Grant, gives a succinct *resumé* of the two days' operations, and accords the credit due to his officers with that magnanimous generosity which has endeared him to the hearts of all those who have ever served actively under him: —

HEADQUARTERS DISTRICT OF WESTERN TENNESSEE,
PITTSBURG, April 9, 1862.

Captain N. H. MCLEAN, *Assistant Adjutant General, Department of Mississippi, St. Louis.*

CAPTAIN: It becomes my duty again to report another battle, fought by two great armies, one contending for the maintenance of the best government ever devised, and the other for its destruction. It is pleasant to record the success of the army contending for the former principle.

On Sunday morning our pickets were attacked and driven in by the enemy. Immediately the five divisions stationed at this place were drawn up in line of battle to meet them.

The battle soon waxed warm on the left and centre, varying at times to all parts of the line. There was the most continuous firing of musketry and artillery ever heard on this continent kept up until nightfall.

The enemy having forced the entire line to fall back nearly half way from their camps to the landing, at a late hour in the afternoon a desperate effort was made by the enemy to turn our left and get possession of the landing, transports, &c.

This point was guarded by the gunboats Tyler and Lexington, Captains Gwin and Shirk commanding, with four twenty-four pounder Parrott guns and a battery of rifled guns.

As there is a deep and impassable ravine for artillery or cavalry, and very difficult for infantry, at this point, no troops were stationed here, except the necessary artillerists, and a small infantry force for their support. Just at this moment the advance of Major General Buell's column and a part of the division of General Nelson arrived. The two Generals named both being present, an advance was immediately made upon the point of attack, and the enemy was soon driven back.

In this repulse much is due to the presence of the gunboats Tyler and Lexington, and their able commanders, Captains Gwin and Shirk.

During the night the divisions under Generals Crittenden and McCook arrived.

General Lewis Wallace, at Camp Landing, six miles below, was ordered, at an early hour in the morning, to hold his division in readiness to move in any direction it might be ordered. At eleven o'clock the order was delivered to move it up to Pittsburg; but, owing to its being led by a circuitous route, it did not arrive in time to take part in Sunday's action.

During the night all was quiet; and, feeling that great moral advantage would be gained by becoming the attacking party, an advance was ordered as soon as day dawned. The result was the gradual repulse of the enemy at all points of the line, from nine until probably five o'clock in the afternoon, when it became evident the enemy was retreating.

Before the close of the action, the advance of General T. J. Wood's division arrived in time to take part in the action.

My force was too much fatigued from two days' hard fighting, and exposure in the open air to a drenching rain during the intervening night, to pursue immediately.

Night closed in cloudy, with a heavy rain, making the roads impracticable for artillery by the next morning.

General Sherman, however, followed the enemy, finding that the main part of their army had retreated in good order.

Hospitals, with the enemy's wounded, were found all along the road as far as pursuit was made. Dead bodies of the enemy, and many graves were also found. I enclose herewith a report of General Sherman, which will explain more fully the result of the pursuit and of the part taken by each separate command.

I cannot take special notice in this report, but will do so more fully when the reports of the division commanders are handed in.

General Buell, commanding in the field, with a distinct army long under his command, and which did such efficient service commanded by himself in person on the field, will be much better able to notice those officers' commands, who particularly distinguished themselves, than I possibly can.

I feel it a duty, however, to a gallant and able officer, Brigadier General W. T. Sherman, to make a special mention. He not only was with his command during the entire two days of the action, but displayed great judgment and skill in the management of his men. Although severely wounded in the hand on the first day, his place was never vacant. He was again wounded, and had three horses killed under him. In making this mention of a gallant officer, no disparagement is intended to other division commanders, or Major Generals John A. McClernand and Lewis Wallace, and Brigadier Generals S. A. Hurlbut, P. M. Prentiss, and W. H. L. Wallace, all of whom maintained their places with credit to themselves and the cause.

General Prentiss was taken prisoner on the first day's action, and General W. H. L. Wallace was severely and probably mortally wounded. His Assistant Adjutant General, Captain William McMichael, is missing, and was probably taken prisoner.

My personal staff are all deserving of particular mention, they having been engaged during the entire two days in carrying orders to every part of the field. It consists of Colonel J. D. Webster, Chief of Staff, Lieutenant Colonel J. B. McPherson, Chief of Engineers, assisted by Lieutenants W. L. B. Jenney and William Kossac; Captain J. A. Rawlins, Assistant Adjutant General W. S. Hilger, W. R. Rawley, and C. B. Lagow, Aids de Camp; Colonel G. Pride, Volunteer Aid, and Captain J. P. Hawkins, Chief Commissary, who accompanied me upon the field.

The Medical Department, under direction of Surgeon Hewitt, Medical Director, showed great energy in providing for the wounded, and in getting them from the field, regardless of danger.

Colonel Webster was placed in special charge of all the artillery, and was constantly upon the field. He displayed, as always heretofore, both skill and bravery. At least in one instance, he was the means of placing an entire regiment in position of doing most valuable service, and where it would not have been but for his exertions.

Lieutenant Colonel McPherson, attached to my staff as Chief of Engineers, deserves more than a passing notice for his activity and courage. All the grounds beyond our camps, for miles, have been reconnoitred by him, and the plans, carefully prepared under his supervision, give the most accurate information of the nature of the approaches to our lines. During the two days' battle he was constantly in the saddle, leading the troops, as they arrived, to points where their services were required. During the engagement he had one horse shot under him.

The country will have to mourn the loss of many brave men who fell at the battle of Pittsburg, or Shiloh, more properly.

The exact loss in killed and wounded will be known in a day or two. At present I can only give it, approximately, at fifteen hundred killed and thirty-five hundred wounded.

The loss of artillery was great, many pieces being disabled by the enemy's shots, and some losing all their horses and many men. There were probably not less than two hundred horses killed.

The loss of the enemy, in killed and left upon the field, was greater than ours. In the wounded an estimate cannot be made, as many of them must have been sent to Corinth and other points.

The enemy suffered terribly from demoralization and desertion.

A flag of truce was sent in to-day from General Beauregard. I enclose herewith a copy of the correspondence.

I am, respectfully, your obedient servant,

U. S. GRANT, *Major General commanding.*

The news of the victory flashed all over the country, and the loyal heart of the people throbbed with joy. General Halleck, in an order, thanked Generals Grant and Buell, "and the officers and men of their respective commands, for the bravery and endurance with which they sustained the general attack of the enemy on the 6th, and for the heroic manner in which, on the 7th, they defeated and routed the entire rebel army."

There was, however, a great deal of dissatisfaction and technical criticism applied to Grant's action and conduct of the battle. The people had hardly yet realized that war is necessary slaughter; there had been so much talk of the bloodless victories to be gained by strategy, and this system of warfare was in such brilliant development in the management of the army of the Potomac, that most specious use was made, by the envious detractors of General Grant, of the terrible mortality attending his victories. The charge of drunkenness while on duty was also brought against him, and although the charge was untrue, yet as it has been brought against every public man in the country since the time of Washington, and was frequently urged against him, it would seem too much to expect that Grant could be an exception to this universal penalty of greatness. It was objected to him also that he had not intrenched his position, though Halleck in general terms had ordered it to be fortified; that he was on the wrong side of the river, since in case of defeat he would have been overwhelmed; that he was surprised; that the victory had been gained by Buell's fortunate arrival, which Grant could not have counted on; and so on through the entire gamut of petty criticism. There are critics who exult in finding flaws in Milton's rhetoric, and Shakespeare's faults in grammar are all that many persons can find in his plays. Military genius must be liable to similar attacks.

To those who still think that he risked too much by placing his army on the west bank, and thus came very near total defeat, we can only quote the words of General Sherman's letter, which will be found entire in the Appendix. "If there were any error in putting that army on the west side of the Tennessee, exposed to the superior force of the enemy, also assembling at Corinth, the mistake was not General Grant's; but there was no mistake. It was necessary that a combat, fierce and bitter, to test the manhood of two armies, should come off; and that was as good a place as any. It was not, then, a question of military skill and strategy, but of courage and pluck; and I am convinced that every life lost that day to us was necessary; for otherwise, at Corinth, at Memphis, at Vicksburg, we would have found harder resistance had we not shown our enemies that, rude and untutored as we then were, we could fight as well as they."

The following extract from a speech by General Sherman, delivered at St. Louis, on the 19th of July, 1865, may also be quoted here in reference to this affair. Having reviewed the incidents of the commencement of the war, the General continued: "Then came the landing of forces at Pittsburg Landing. Whether it was a mistake in landing them on the west instead of the east bank, it is not necessary now to discuss. I think it was no mistake.

"There was gathered the first great army of the West. Commencing with only twelve thousand, then twenty, then thirty thousand, and we had about thirty-eight thousand in that battle; and all I claim for it is, that it was a contest for manhood; there was no strategy.

Grant was there, and others of us, all young at that time, and unknown men, but our enemy was old, and Sidney Johnston, whom all the officers remembered as a power among the old officers, high above Grant, myself, or anybody else, led the enemy on that battlefield, and I almost wonder how we conquered. But, as I remarked, it was a contest for manhood—man to man, soldier to soldier. We fought, and held our ground, and therefore counted ourselves victorious. From that time forward we had with us the prestige. That battle was worth millions and millions to us, by reason of the fact of the courage displayed by the brave soldiers on that occasion; and from that time to this, I never heard of the first want of courage on the part of our northern soldiers.

"It then became a game of grand war; armies were accounted equal, and skill and generalship came into play."

The present advocates of bloodless victories are probably incorrigible; while General Smith and all the division commanders, together with Grant, were opposed to intrenching the position, on the ground that it would tend to injure the *morale* of the army, who should be made to trust in themselves, and not in their intrenchments. Nor can the charge that we were surprised be maintained in the face of the present evidence upon this point. The enemy came up in force, and we were obliged to fall back. There is a military logic in audacity which rises above the conclusions of the schools. This is Grant's justification for selecting his position with the river in his rear. He did so as Cortes burned his ships when he landed with his handful of men in

Mexico. It is reported that Grant once answered the question, What he would have done had he been forced to cross the stream? "We would have used the gunboats." "But," continued his questioner, "the gunboats could have carried over only ten thousand men at most." "Well," said Grant, "there would not have been more than ten thousand men to carry over."

It was this persistence which led him to order Sherman, on the evening of the 6th, before he knew of Buell's arrival, to take the offensive the next morning. What possibilities an *if* may conceal, no one can know. But it was enough for the loyal men of the country to know that Grant gained victories, to feel confidence in him, and take him to their hearts. It is said that Lincoln, having been told that Grant drank too much, said he wished he knew the brand of the whiskey he used, for he would send a barrel of it to every one of his generals. Many of these charges having been more than insinuated in Congress, Mr. Washburne, one of the representatives from Illinois, refuted them in a speech, extracts of which will be found in our Appendix.

One of the great benefits of this action at Pittsburg Landing was, that it served to give Grant a greater confidence in himself; and as we are, all of us, during our whole lives, either educated by circumstances or made their sport, he could not escape the effects of this universal law. The difference between the ordinary and the extraordinary man, between the large majority and the exceptional geniuses, lies in the ability of the last to derive the materials for education and development from the circumstances which surround them. Some men never seem to acquire the power for this, but drift all their days, to all appearance, as helplessly down the stream of life as logs and brushwood down the current of a river; while others, on the contrary, appear to obtain such mastery over the circumstances in which they are placed, that, in comparison with the others, they can be likened only to the steamboats which advance in their desired course, despite the opposing influence of the current or the wind. In this respect the analogies between individuals and societies are identical.

Another great benefit derived from this campaign was, that it offered the opportunities for Grant to become acquainted with the great abilities of Sherman. He had been pleased before with the promptness Sherman had shown in forwarding his reënforcements from Paducah during the campaign against Fort Donelson; and here he had an opportunity of seeing his value in the field. From this campaign, then, we can date the commencement of the warm friendship and the mutual recognition which exist between these two men, and which have already been so fruitful in admirable results for the benefit of their countrymen.

## CHAPTER IX.

### THE SIEGE OF CORINTH.

AFTER the battle of Pittsburg Landing, General Halleck took command of the combined army in person, issuing at the time an order confirming Generals Grant and Buell in their respective positions; and preparations were made for an advance against Corinth, to protect which Beauregard had sought and lost the recent engagement. This village, as we have said, derived its importance from the fact that it was situated at the junction of the Memphis and Charleston and the Mobile and Ohio Railways, and was therefore of great strategical importance upon the second line of interior defence taken up by the Confederacy, to prevent the Union forces from penetrating to the heart of their territory. Corinth itself is situated upon a low and clayey plain, but has natural defences in the ridges lying about it. In the country beyond, up to the Tennessee River, the surface is broken by ridges, streams, and marshes. Farmington on the east, and College Hill on the north, are the highest points in the vicinity of Corinth, and were occupied as the signal-posts of the vast intrenchments surrounding the position.

On the 8th of April, as we have seen, Sherman had reconnoitred the road used by the enemy in his retreat from Pittsburg Landing, and had found the roads very bad, but strewed with evident signs of his precipitate retreat. On the evening of the same day he returned to Pittsburg Landing, and reported the results of his observations. On the next day, the 9th, Halleck left St. Louis for the scene of action. Before his arrival Grant had not been idle; an expedition sent forward by his orders, under the command of Sherman, had proceeded up the Tennessee, accompanied by gunboats, as far as Eastport, and destroyed the railroad bridge over Big Bear Creek, east of Iuka. By this, Corinth was cut off in its connections, by this route, with Richmond. On the 22d of April, General John Pope arrived with his army, consisting of twenty-five thousand men, from New Madrid. On the 30th, an expedition under General Wallace succeeded in destroying the railroad bridge on the Mobile and Ohio Railway, four miles beyond Purdy; thus cutting off from the Confederates at Corinth all supplies and reënforcements from Jackson, Tennessee.

On his arrival General Halleck took command of the combined armies concentrated at Pittsburg Landing, and naming them collectively "the grand army of the Tennessee," divided them as follows: the army of the Ohio, under General Buell, holding the centre; the army of the Mississippi, under General Pope, holding the left; the army of the Tennessee, under General Grant, holding the right. The entire force was divided into sixteen divisions, eight of which formed the army of the Tennessee, four the army of the Mississippi, and four the army of the Ohio. Grant's force was divided into the right wing under General Thomas, and the reserve under General McClernand. The combined Union forces numbered about ninety thousand men.

At Corinth, Beauregard, after his failure at Pittsburg Landing, had concentrated all the troops he could gather. His force contained the remains of the army he had led against Grant at Pittsburg Landing; the combined armies of Van Dorn and Price, from Arkansas and Missouri; the forces which Lovell had withdrawn from New Orleans, when it was taken by the Union army on the 28th of April; and others sent from Alabama, Mississippi, and Louisiana. These, combined, numbered about sixty-five thousand men, comprising some of the best troops in the Confederacy; and under Beauregard they were expected to accomplish great things.

New Orleans, we must remember, had been captured on the 28th of April, and the Mississippi had thus been opened at its mouth. Island No. 10 had also fallen, and the Confederacy thus kept its hold of the great river only in those portions between these two points. The beginning of the end commenced to appear.

On the 1st of May, the grand army of the Tennessee was ready to move, and on that day it occupied Monterey, a small town about half way between Pittsburg Landing and Corinth. On the 8th, Beauregard, who appears to have been as presumptuous and as unfortunate with his pen as with his sword, issued the following grandiloquent order to the forces under his command:—

HEADQUARTERS OF THE FORCES AT CORINTH, MISS., May 8, 1862.

SOLDIERS OF SHILOH AND ELKHORN: We are about to meet once more, in the shock of battle, the invaders of our soil, the despoilers of our homes, the disturbers of our family ties, face to face, hand to hand. We are to decide whether we are to be freemen, or vile slaves of those who are only free in name, and who but yesterday were vanquished, although in largely superior numbers, in their own encampments, on the ever-memorable field of Shiloh. Let the impending battle decide our fate, and add a more illustrious page to the history of our revolution — one to which our children will point with noble pride, saying, "Our fathers were at the battle of Corinth." I congratulate you on your timely junction. With our mingled banners, for the first time during the war, we shall meet our foe in strength that should give us victory. Soldiers, can the result be doubtful? Shall we not drive back in Tennessee the presumptuous mercenaries collected for our subjugation? One more manly effort, and trusting in God and the justness of our cause, we shall recover more than we lately lost. Let the sound of our victorious guns be reëchoed by those of the army of Virginia on the historic battle-field of Yorktown.

P. G. T. BEAUREGARD, *General commanding.*

It is one of the singular pieces of poetic justice, of which the history of the rebellion is so full, that this appeal to the "soldiers of Shiloh and Elkhorn," in both of which fields they had been unsuccessful, was intended to stimulate their valor by an allusion to Yorktown, which was evacuated on the 8th, the date of the order, by the Confederate forces in Virginia. The pen is mightier than the sword, and is a more dangerous double-edged implement when wielded by those whose insolent ignorance is their only claim to its use.

On the 3d of May our advance had reached a point eight miles from Corinth; and the same day a portion of the army occupied Farmington, the garrison of which, numbering four thousand five hundred men, under General Marmaduke, retired to Corinth, after a very slight resistance. At the same time an expedition proceeded on the Memphis and Charleston Railway as far as Glendale, destroying the track and the bridges.

In this advance of the grand army of the Tennessee, Grant was the second in command; and the difference in its operations is sufficiently explained by this fact. The order of the day was intrenchment, and no advance was made in which the spade did not play a very important part as a subsidiary implement of war. On the 11th a consultation was held at General Halleck's headquarters, and a general advance decided on. On the 17th General Sherman came into actual conflict with a portion of the Confederate army, posted at Russell's house, on the road to Corinth, and drove them from this position. It was now decided that Corinth should be reduced by regular approaches, and Beauregard, as an engineer, knew that the result could only be a postponement of his surrender. Besides, too, as his position depended upon the Confederacy holding the Mississippi, and as it was questionable whether Memphis and Vicksburg would remain in their hands, now that New Orleans and Island No. 10 had fallen, it was his evident plan of action to evacuate the position. His apparent defence .was, therefore, nothing but a blind, in order to gain time, and his bold front nothing but a trick, to enable him to retreat unmolested. This he did on the 28th and 29th of May, just onc month after the siege commenced. On the 30th of May our troops occupied the town, and the second line of the interior defence, selected by the Confederates themselves, was taken by the Union army, and they were forced to fall back upon their third, the strategic points of which were Vicksburg, Jackson, Meriden, and Selma.

The pursuit was immediately begun, and continued until the 10th, when Beauregard, having taken up a strong position at Tupelo, where the railway is crossed by Oldtown Creek, one of the feeders of the Tombigbee, Halleck, anxious concerning his communications, and being desirous of strengthening his base, stopped the pursuit, and the army returned to Corinth.

At Tupelo, on the 13th of June, Beauregard wrote his report, in which he says that he had "accomplished his purposes and ends;" that he had twice offered battle to the Union army, which they declined; and the impression he would give is, that the occupation of Corinth was simply a temporary expedient, to be abandoned when other and more important matters were prepared and made ready for action. The best commentary on this report is the following list of dates. On the 28th *of April New Orleans had become ours.* Yorktown was evacuated on the 3d and 4th of May. Fort Pillow, on the Mississippi, was evacuated on the 4th of June; and Memphis, on the 6th, was captured by the fleet, after a most brilliant action, in which three of the largest Confederate vessels were sunk, one burned, and three captured, while in the Union fleet only one vessel was temporarily injured; no one was killed, and Colonel Ellet, the daring commander of the Monarch, the only man wounded. The time for even the South to place any confidence in the boasting promises of their leaders was past. But the unscrupulous rulers had seized the reins of power, and showed no intention to surrender their hold of them. They established a military despotism as severe and uncompromising as has ever been seen. A sweeping conscription act was passed by the Congress, giving the President power to impress all white men between the ages of eighteen and forty-five, for three years or for the war. Soon after camps of instruction were established in every state, and the levies were distributed proportionally among the states. In this way every nerve was strained to recover their lost ground and repair their broken fortunes. The result was a partial success in the East, marked by the successes in the Peninsula, the victories of the second Bull Run, and the advance into Maryland.

In the West the same efforts were made, and the manner in which they were met by Grant will form the subject for some future chapters. On the 15th of June, having been for some time in bad health, Beauregard left the army at Tupelo, relieving himself from duty, on the certificate of two surgeons, in order to recuperate by rest. He retired to Bladen Springs, turning over the command to Bragg during his absence, with instructions looking to the preparation of the army for the field at once on his return, which he anticipated would be in three weeks. No sooner, however, did Jefferson Davis hear of this step, than he telegraphed to Bragg to assume permanent command; declaring, passionately, that Beauregard, thus laid upon the shelf, should not be reinstated by him, though the whole world should urge him to it. Thus Beauregard passed out of prominence upon the scene, and was not to be heard from again during the war, except in an unimportant command at Charleston and the last campaign before Richmond, where he gave evidence that his genius for braggadocio and his talent for failure still flourished in unimpaired vigor.

## CHAPTER X.

NEW DISPOSITION OF THE FORCES.—THE CIVIL DUTIES OF THE MILITARY POWER.

On the 11th of July, General Halleck, by general orders from the War Department, was called to Washington, and assigned the command, as General-in-chief, of the whole land forces of the United States. This caused a new arrangement in the disposition of the armies in the West. New departments were created out of the original department of the Mississippi. General Buell was given the department of the Ohio, embracing the country north and east of the Tennessee River. Missouri was also made a separate department; while all the country from the Mississippi River to the western shore of the Tennessee, Cairo, Forts Henry and Donelson, the western shore of the Mississippi River, and the northern part of the State of Mississippi, were grouped into the department of West Tennessee, and of this Grant was given the command, with his headquarters at Corinth.

Memphis was surrendered on the 6th of June, 1862, soon after the evacuation of Corinth, and was immediately occupied by the Union troops, and became a very important post in Grant's department, both as a base for operations and for supplies. In the mean time, as there was but little fighting in his department from June till September, 1862, his attention was chiefly occupied with the reorganization of his forces, and his preparations for a campaign against Vicksburg, which was evidently the next point to be taken. It will be well here to consider, for a moment, the qualities of a statesman which he developed in his management of the turbulent and unconquered Confederate material which he found in his department, and particularly in Memphis. A selection of some of his orders, bearing upon the aid given by sympathizers with the rebellion to its armies; upon the suppression of illicit and contraband trade; upon the unmixed evils resulting from the guerrilla system, which flourished with great vigor about Memphis; and upon other similar subjects,—will be found interesting and instructive. There was one idea running through the whole of them—that loyalty to the government must be unconditional; and we also find in them early indications of the spirit of economy which has always characterized Grant's financial administration.

*Special Orders, No. 4.*

HEADQUARTERS DISTRICT OF WEST TENNESSEE,
OFFICE PROVOST MARSHAL GENERAL,
MEMPHIS, June 28, 1862.

. . . . . .

Passes issued for persons to pass out of the city will be understood to mean the person alone, and will not include goods, letters, or packages.

Where letters are found on persons passing out, without being marked PASSED by the Provost Marshal, Post Commander, or General commanding, they will be seized and delivered to the Provost Marshal, and the offender arrested.

Powder, lead, percussion caps, and fire-arms of all descriptions, are positively prohibited from being carried out of the city by citizens. Citizens are also prohibited from carrying them within the city limits on pain of forfeiture of such weapons, and ten days' confinement for the first offence, and expulsion south of our lines, to be treated as spies if ever caught within them thereafter, for the second.

By command of Major General U. S. GRANT.

WM. S. HILLYER, *Provost Marshal General.*

Finding that the above appeared to have had no effect in stopping the illicit traffic, General Grant issued the following, which was of great service in restoring the city of Memphis to order and loyalty: —

*Special Orders, No.* 13.

DISTRICT OF WEST TENNESSEE,<br>
OFFICE OF THE PROVOST MARSHAL GENERAL,<br>
MEMPHIS, TENN., July 9, 1862.

. . . . . .

All passes heretofore issued to citizens, either by the commanding General, the Provost Marshal General, the Provost Marshal of Memphis, or any other officer, which may have been issued without the party being required to take the oath of allegiance, or give the prescribed parole of honor, are hereby revoked.

No pass will be granted in any case hereafter, except upon the taking of the oath or parole.

The parole will be substituted for the oath only in special cases (at the discretion of the officer authorized to grant passes), where the party lives beyond the protection of our army.

By command of Major General GRANT.

WM. S. HILLYER, *Provost Marshal General.*

*Special Orders, No.* 14.

DISTRICT OF WEST TENNESSEE,<br>
OFFICE PROVOST MARSHAL GENERAL,<br>
MEMPHIS, July 10, 1862.

The constant communication between the so-called Confederate army and their friends and sympathizers in the city of Memphis, despite the orders heretofore issued, and the efforts to enforce them, induced the issuing of the following order: —

The families now residing in the city of Memphis, of the following persons, are required to move south, beyond the lines, within five days from the date hereof.

*First.* All persons holding commissions in the so-called Confederate army, or who have voluntarily enlisted in said army, or who accompany and are connected with the same.

*Second.* All persons holding office under or in the employ of the so-called Confederate government.

*Third.* All persons holding state, county, or municipal offices, who claim allegiance to said so-called Confederate government, and who have abandoned their families and gone south.

Safe conduct will be given to the parties hereby required to leave, upon application to the Provost Marshal of Memphis.

By command of Major General GRANT.

*Special Orders, No.* 15.

DISTRICT OF WEST TENNESSEE,
OFFICE OF THE PROVOST MARSHAL GENERAL,
MEMPHIS, TENN., July 11, 1862.

. . . . . .

In order that innocent, peaceable, and well-disposed persons may not suffer for the bad conduct of the guilty parties coming within the purview of Special Order No. 14, dated July 10, 1862, they can be relieved from the operation of said Order No. 14 by signing the following parole, and producing to the Provost Marshal General, or the Provost Marshal of Memphis, satisfactory guarantees that they will keep the pledge therein made: —

PAROLE.

*First.* I have not, since the occupation of the city of Memphis by the Federal army, given any aid to the so-called Confederate army, nor given or sent any information of the movements, strength, or position of the Federal army to any one connected with said Confederate army.

*Second.* I will not, during the occupancy of Memphis by the Federal army and my residing therein, oppose or conspire against the civil or military authority of the United States, and I will not give aid, comfort, information, or encouragement to the so-called Confederate army, nor to any person coöperating therewith.

All of which I state and pledge upon my sacred honor.

By command of Major General GRANT.

WM. S. HILLYER, *Provost Marshal General.*

As a warning to the guerrillas who were operating about Memphis, destroying cotton and plundering from friend and foe, the following order was also issued:—

*General Order, No.* 60.

HEADQUARTERS DISTRICT OF WEST TENNESSEE,
MEMPHIS, TENN., July 3, 1862.

The system of guerrilla warfare now being prosecuted by some troops organized under authority of the so-called Southern Confederacy, and others without such authority, being so pernicious to the welfare of the community where it is carried on, and it being within the power of the community to suppress this system, it is ordered that, wherever loss is sustained by the government, collections shall be made, by seizure of a sufficient amount of personal property, from persons in the immediate neighborhood sympathizing with the rebellion, to remunerate the government for all loss and expense of the same.

Persons acting as guerrillas without organization, and without uniform to distinguish them from private citizens, are not entitled to the treatment of prisoners of war when caught, and will not receive such treatment.

By order of Major General U. S. GRANT.

JOHN A. RAWLINS, *A. A. G.*

Though it is always undesirable to interfere with the freedom of the press, yet this term does not include license; and war being itself a condition to be greatly deprecated, it is manifestly impossible for an army in possession of a disaffected country to allow the unrestricted publication of impassioned appeals to the people. The press is, no doubt, a most powerful agent in the diffusion of intelligence, and the development of civilization among the people; but when it prostitutes itself, as the southern press did, to becoming merely a bitter partisan organ, misleading the people, concealing the truth, and diffusing error, it must be dealt with strictly and firmly. The following order shows Grant's action in such a case:—

HEADQUARTERS DISTRICT OF WEST TENNESSEE,<br>
OFFICE PROVOST MARSHAL GENERAL,<br>
MEMPHIS, TENN., July 1, 1862.

MESSRS. WILLS, BINGHAM & CO.,<br>
*Proprietors of the Memphis Avalanche.*

You will suspend the further publication of your paper. The spirit with which it is conducted is regarded as both incendiary and treasonable, and its issue cannot longer be tolerated.

This order will be strictly observed from the time of its reception.

By command of Major General U. S. GRANT.

WM. S. HILLYER, *Provost Marshal General.*

MEMPHIS, July 1, 1862.

*The Avalanche* can continue by the withdrawal of the author of the obnoxious article under the caption of "Mischief Makers," and the editorial allusion to the same.

U. S. GRANT, *Major General.*

TO OUR PATRONS.—For reasons apparent from the foregoing order, I withdraw from the editorial management of *The Avalanche.* Self-respect and the spirit of true journalism forbid any longer attempt to edit a paper. I approved and indorsed the articles in question. Prudence forbids my saying more, and duty less, to the public.

JEPTHA FOWLKES.

The ruinous system of guerrilla warfare continuing, and it being found almost impossible to stop the contraband trade, which was being carried on through Memphis, in aid of the rebellion, General Grant appointed General Sherman to the command of that city, with the full knowledge that his decision would soon check both these nuisances. On the 21st of July, 1862, General Sherman assumed the command, and from the following order we may judge of the vigorous means taken for the suppression of these illegal operations: —

U. S. MILITARY TELEGRAPH, CORINTH, July 26, 1862.

To BRIGADIER GENERAL J. T. QUIMBY, *Columbus, Ky.*

GENERAL: Examine the baggage of all speculators coming South, and when they have specie turn them back; if medicine and other contraband articles, arrest them and confiscate the contraband articles. Jews should receive special attention.

(Signed) U. S. GRANT, *Major General.*

The most stringent measures were also adopted against all guerrillas and their agents, and the following despatch is an evidence of the manner in which the orders were carried out: —

TRENTON, TENN., July 29, 1862.

GENERAL: The man who guided the rebels to the bridge that was burned was hung to-day. He had taken the oath. The houses of four others who aided have been burned to the ground.

(Signed) G. M. DODGE, *Brigadier General.*

On July 28, General Grant ordered General Sherman to take possession of all unoccupied dwellings, manufactories, and stores, within the city of Memphis, to hire them out, and to collect the rents for the United States government, in all cases where the owners were absent, engaged in arms against the United States. This plan was adopted to prevent the property being destroyed or abused, as well as to bring in a revenue from rebel sources to help pay the expenses of the war.

The large number of negroes who had found refuge within the Union lines being a serious tax upon the resources of the army, it was decided that they should be put at some useful employment. General Grant, therefore, to remedy the evil in his own special department, issued the following order, which contains certain regulations in relation to both the negro refugees and the carrying out of the confiscation law, as passed by the Houses of Congress, and signed by the President: —

*General Orders, No.* 72.

HEADQUARTERS DEPARTMENT OF WEST TENNESSEE,
CORINTH, MISS., August 11, 1862.

The recent Act of Congress prohibits the army from returning fugitives from labor to their claimants, and authorizes the employment of such persons in the service of the government. The following orders are therefore published for the guidance of the army in this matter.

1. All fugitives thus employed must be registered; the names of the fugitives and claimant given, and must be borne upon the morning report of the command in which they are kept, showing how they are employed.

2. Fugitives may be employed as laborers in the quartermaster's, subsistence, and engineer's department; and whenever by such employment a soldier may be saved to its ranks, they may be employed as teamsters and as company cooks, not exceeding four to a company, or as hospital attendants and nurses. Officers may employ them as private servants, in which latter case the fugitives will not be paid or rationed by the government. Negroes thus employed must be secured as authorized persons, and will be excluded from the camps.

3. Officers and soldiers are positively prohibited from enticing slaves to leave their masters. When it becomes necessary to employ this kind of labor, the commanding officer of the post or

troops must send details, all under the charge of a suitable commissioned officer, to press into service the slaves of persons to the number required.

4. Citizens within reach of any military station, known to be disloyal and dangerous, may be ordered away or arrested, and their crops and stock taken for the benefit of the government or the use of the army.

5. All property taken from rebel owners must be duly reported and used for the benefit of the government, and be issued to the troops through the proper department; and, when practicable, the act of taking should be accompanied by the written certificate of the officer so taking to the owner or agent of such property.

It is enjoined on all commanders to see that this order is executed strictly under their own direction. The demoralization of troops consequent upon being left to execute laws in their own way without a proper head must be avoided.

By command of Major General GRANT.

JOHN A. RAWLINS, *A. A. G.*

Advantage had been taken of the advance of our armies, by many of the lawless population of the South, to come within our lines, and thus escape the effect of the strict conscription acts of the Confederate government. These men were generally of a disreputable character, and made their living by following the army, robbing the soldiers, or trading with the rebels. To meet their cases, the following order was issued by General Grant from his departmental headquarters: —

*General Orders, No.* 74.

HEADQUARTERS DEPARTMENT OF WEST TENNESSEE,
CORINTH, MISS., August 16, 1862.

1. All non-residents of this department, found within the same, who, if at home, would be subject to draft, will at once be enrolled under the supervision of the local commanders where they may be found, and, in case of a draft being made by their respective states, an equal proportion will be drawn from persons thus enrolled.

Persons so drawn will at once be assigned to troops from the states to which they owe military service, and the executive thereof notified of such draft.

2. All violation of trade by army followers may be punished by confiscation of stock in trade, and the assignment of offenders to do military duty as private soldiers.

By command of Major General U. S. GRANT.

JOHN A. RAWLINS, *A. A. G.*

It must be remembered that this was in 1862, and that neither the government nor the people had yet reached the point of using the negroes as soldiers. While Grant as a soldier has the invaluable qualities of fully accepting the responsibilities of his position, when they devolve upon him naturally, he has also the not less important quality of a soldier, of following orders without comment.

We thus find that sound judgment, clear, good common sense, and an eminently practical mode of action characterize Grant's behavior in all the political emergencies which the anomalous position of our armies in the field forced frequently upon our generals; and also that he handles the pen as decisively as he does his sword.

## CHAPTER XI.

### THE BATTLE OF IUKA. — THE COMBINATION OF STRATEGY AND ACTION.

During the summer montns of 1862, the active operations in the field, in Grant's department, were confined generally to skirmishes; but by his constant cavalry reconnoissances he kept himself well informed of the whereabouts of the enemy. Under General Bragg, the Confederates had collected a force at Chattanooga, Tennessee, which was designed to make a flank movement through East Tennessee and Kentucky to the Ohio. Meanwhile General Pope, who had commanded the army of the Mississippi in the advance upon Corinth, had been called to take command of the army of the Potomac, and his place was given to General Rosecrans, who had gained so excellent a reputation in West Virginia. During the whole summer, also, the Confederates had been straining every nerve to make Vicksburg strong enough to withstand any attack which might be brought against it. It was their last stand on the Mississippi River, and one of their plans for its defence appears to have been to operate against Grant, and prevent his giving his whole attention to its capture. At the same time it was important that Grant, before advancing against Vicksburg, should protect himself from any attacks in his rear, by destroying the armies which could thus operate to annoy him. The details of the operations to secure these ends will occupy our attention before entering immediately upon the operations before Vicksburg.

Early in September, General Sterling Price, who had gained an unenviable reputation early in the war, in Missouri, advanced from the south to cross the Charleston and Memphis Railway at some point between Corinth and Tuscumbia, probably at Iuka. On the 10th of September he reached Jacinto, the small Union garrison of which fell back upon Corinth. Tuscumbia was also vacated by the Union garrison which held it, they falling back upon Iuka; while the garrison at Iuka was also withdrawn to Corinth. Price therefore occupied this latter place, and Grant's object was to discover what the enemy's plan was. The reports concerning Price's intentions were numerous and conflicting. By patient and shrewd observation Grant became convinced that Price's design was to make a feint of crossing the Tennessee as though to attack Buell, who was then falling back upon Nashville, in order to induce Grant to march against him, and, by withdrawing his army from Corinth, make that strong point an easy prey to Van Dorn, who was advancing against it with all possible haste.

Having fathomed this design, the next thing was to counteract it, and render it injurious, instead of beneficial, to its formers. It did not take long to conclude what should be the proper course of action. By his scouts Grant knew that it would take Van Dorn four days to reach Corinth, and within this time he determined to attack Price, to defeat, and if possible destroy, his army, and then return to his position at Corinth, in time to receive Van Dorn on his arrival. There were only four days for this, so that not an hour was to be lost.

He therefore directed General Ord, with a force of three thousand men, to move upon the left of the railway, through Burnsville to Iuka, while General Ross was telegraphed to advance at full speed from Bolivar, on the same route, and join Ord with three thousand five hundred more men. This combined force was to attack Price on the north wherever an opportunity should offer for so doing. At the same time Rosecrans was ordered to advance with his men, by way of Jacinto, to strike the enemy's flank, while Hamilton, moving round by the Fulton road, should cut off his southward retreat, or turn it to a rout. The force commanded by Rosecrans was about nine thousand men. This combined movement began on the morning of September 18. That night, after marching through a drenching rain, Rosecrans and his army arrived at Jacinto.

The next morning, advancing early, they pushed on to Iuka, and finding the enemy upon an exterior ridge, engaged him; and the fighting continued until night. The ground was very much broken, so that it was difficult to bring the troops into action in large masses; yet the fighting was very severe, and the loss very large. The guns of the Eleventh Ohio were lost and retaken three or four times during the day, and at nightfall remained in the hands of the enemy. This battery was one belonging to Hamilton's division, and, despite this result, was so admirably handled by that officer, that he received the special encomiums of both Grant and Rosecrans.

On the morning of the 18th, Grant had started with Ord's column, and expected on reaching the ground to be in constant communication with Rosecrans, so that the two divisions should be able to act together and simultaneously.

On arriving upon the ground, however, the tangled nature of the country rendered it necessary, it was found, to send despatches so long a way round, that they constantly arrived too late, caused frequent misunderstandings, and prevented the timely coöperation of the forces. The next morning Rosecrans was ready to recommence the action, but found that the enemy had retreated. Price hastened to Bay Springs, a place about twenty-seven miles south of Iuka, on the Fulton road. He had lost upwards of a thousand prisoners, and left his dead and wounded on the field. On their retreat Price's men committed all kinds of outrages, as we learn from Confederate accounts, upon the people of the country through which they passed. The men were completely demoralized, and their officers could not restrain them if they wished. Sending the following report of the engagement by telegraph from Iuka, on the 20th, Grant on the 22d withdrew his forces to Corinth, to prepare for the reception of Van Dorn's approaching attack.

IUKA, MISS., September 20, 1862.

TO MAJOR GENERAL H. W. HALLECK, *General-in-Chief.*

General Rosecrans, with Stanley's and Hamilton's divisions and Misener's cavalry, attacked Price south of this village about two hours before dark yesterday, and had a sharp fight until night closed in. General Ord was to the north with an armed force of about five thousand men, and had some skirmishing with the rebel pickets. This morning the fight was renewed by General Rosecrans, who was nearest to the town; but it was found that the enemy had been evacuating during the night, going south. Generals Hamilton and Stanley, with cavalry, are in full pursuit.

This will, no doubt, break up the enemy, and possibly force them to abandon much of their artillery. The loss on either side, in killed and wounded, is from four to five hundred. The enemy's loss in arms, tents, &c., will be large. We have about two hundred and fifty prisoners.

I have reliable intelligence that it was Price's intention to move over east of the Tennessee. In this he has been thwarted. Among the enemy's loss are General Little, killed, and General Whitefield, wounded.

I cannot speak too highly of the energy and skill displayed by General Rosecrans in the attack, and of the endurance of the troops. General Ord's command showed untiring zeal; but the direction taken by the enemy prevented them from taking the active part they desired. Price's force was about eighteen thousand.

U. S. GRANT, *Major General.*

The examination of the field, after the first excitement of the battle was over, showed a still more favorable result for the Union forces, as may be judged by the following despatch: —

HEADQUARTERS CORINTH, September 22, 1862.

MAJOR GENERAL HALLECK, *General-in-Chief.*

In my despatch of the 20th our loss was over-estimated, and the rebel loss under-estimated. We found two hundred and sixty-one of them dead upon the field, while our loss in killed will be less than one hundred.

U. S. GRANT, *Major General.*

8

General Grant, on the same day that he sent the above despatch, issued the following order, complimenting his officers and men upon their bravery, not forgetting those who fell on that occasion: —

*General Field Orders, No.* 1.

HEADQUARTERS DEPARTMENT OF WEST TENNESSEE,
CORINTH, September 22, 1862.

The General commanding takes great pleasure in congratulating the two wings of the army, commanded respectively by Major General Ord and Major General Rosecrans, upon the energy, alacrity, and bravery displayed by them on the 19th and 20th inst., in their movement against the enemy at Iuka. Although the enemy was in numbers reputed far greater than their own, nothing was evinced by the troops but a burning desire to meet him, whatever his numbers, and however strong his position.

With such a disposition as was manifested by the troops on this occasion, their commanders need never fear defeat against anything but overwhelming numbers.

While it was the fortune of the command of General Rosecrans, on the evening of the 19th inst., to engage the enemy in a most spirited fight for more than two hours, driving him with great loss from his position, and winning for themselves fresh laurels, the command of General Ord is entitled to equal credit for their efforts in trying to reach the enemy, and in diverting his attention.

*And while congratulating the noble living, it is meet to offer our condolence to the friends of the heroic dead, who offered their lives a sacrifice in defence of constitutional liberty, and in their fall rendered memorable the field of Iuka.*

By command of Major General U. S. GRANT.

JOHN A. RAWLINS, *A. A. G.*

## CHAPTER XII.

### THE BATTLE OF CORINTH.

WHEN Corinth had been in the possession of the Confederates under Beauregard, the line of defences constructed for its protection were so extended, reaching about fifteen miles, and requiring such numbers to man them, that Halleck, on taking possession of the place had had an interior line built, which could be manned by a much smaller number. Grant was not, however, satisfied with these, and said to General Halleck, that they would be admirable if we had an army of one hundred thousand men to defend them. When General Halleck, therefore, went to Washington, Major F. E. Prime, under Grant's direction, made a plan for a still further interior and more compact line of defences, the work upon which was pushed forward with vigor, so that on the 25th of September they were about completed. Upon this day, General Rosecrans, under Grant's orders, took command at Corinth, while Ord was stationed at Bolivar, which might be the point of Van Dorn's attack, and where, in any event, he would be within easy distance, while Grant removed his headquarters to Jackson. General Hurlbut was stationed with his division at Pocahontas.

The Confederates combined their forces for this attack. Price, after leaving Iuka, joined Van Dorn, by a circuitous route, at Dumas, and their united force moved northward to Pocahontas, where they met the troops under Mansfield Lovell, and the entire army then advanced by the railroad to Corinth. Rosecrans, having called in his outposts, awaited the attack, which came with impetuous force on the 3d of October. The Confederates were in large force, and pressed vigorously upon the works. During the day of the 3d, they gained ground; our troops being drawn in to concentrate in the works immediately surrounding the position. Deceived by the apparent ease of his first day's success, Van Dorn sent a telegraph to Richmond, announcing a great victory.

The next day, the 4th of October, the assault was repeated with even increased determination. The impetuousness of the assault was equalled only by the stubbornness of the resistance. At one time the head of the column penetrated into the town, but they were driven back by our artillery, supported by infantry. The battle raged with inconceivable fury the whole morning. Time after time the advancing wave of living men is broken by the murderous fire of our guns, and falls away only to re-form and surge again tumultuously against our defences, only to meet again with a similar reception. But the Confederate valor was of no avail. At noon the battle was ended. Having waited a short time, after the last repulse, for the enemy's reappearance, our skirmishers advance to find that they have retired. Rosecrans gallops along the whole length of our line, to give the information, to cheer our exhausted men, to give them rest and rations, and to inspirit them for the pursuit early the next morning. The enemy's loss was one thousand four hundred and twenty-three killed, and upwards of five thousand wounded. Two thousand two hundred and forty-eight prisoners were taken, with fourteen colors and ten guns.

Our infantry followed the retreating enemy forty miles, and the cavalry sixty miles; while on the morning of the 5th, near Pocahontas, they were met by Hurlbut, who drove them back towards Corinth. During the day, Ord, coming up, assumed the command, but fell, severely wounded, and Hurlbut took his place. The fighting here was again severe, and the retreating army was driven to make a circuit, and cross the Hatchie six miles above where they had intended. The following despatches from General Grant tell the story with military brevity and conciseness:—

HEADQUARTERS JACKSON, TENN.,
October 5, 8 A. M.

TO MAJOR GENERAL H. W. HALLECK,
*General-in-Chief United States Army.*

Yesterday the rebels under Price, Van Dorn, and Lovell were repulsed from their attack on Corinth with great slaughter.

The enemy are in full retreat, leaving their dead and wounded on the field.

Rosecrans telegraphs that the loss is serious on our side, particularly in officers, but bears no comparison with that of the enemy.

General Hackleman fell while gallantly leading his brigade.

General Oglesby is dangerously wounded.

General McPherson, with his command, reached Corinth yesterday.

General Rosecrans pursued the retreating enemy this morning, and, should they attempt to move towards Bolivar, will follow to that place.

General Hurlbut is at the Hatchie River with five or six thousand men, and is, no doubt, with the pursuing column.

From seven hundred to a thousand prisoners, besides the wounded, are left in our hands.

U. S. GRANT, *Major General commanding.*

HEADQUARTERS, JACKSON, TENN.,
October 5, 1862.

To MAJOR GENERAL H. W. HALLECK,
*General-in-Chief United States Army.*

General Ord, who followed General Hurlbut, met the enemy to-day on the south side of the Hatchie, as I understand from a despatch, and drove them across the stream, and got possession of the heights with our troops.

General Ord took two batteries and about two hundred prisoners.

A large portion of General Rosecrans's forces were at Chevalla

At this distance everything looks most favorable, and I cannot see how the enemy are to escape without losing everything but their small arms.

*I have strained everything to take into the fight an adequate force, and to get them to the right place.*

U. S. GRANT, *Major General commanding.*

The General issued also the following congratulatory order to the army.

*General Orders, No.* 88.

HEADQUARTERS DEPARTMENT OF WEST TENNESSEE,
JACKSON, TENN., October 7, 1862.

It is with heartfelt gratitude the General commanding congratulates the armies of the West for another great victory won by them on the 3d, 4th, and 5th instant, over the combined armies of Van Dorn, Price, and Lovell.

The enemy chose his own time and place of attack, and knowing the troops of the West as he does, and with great facilities for knowing their numbers, never would have made the attempt, except with a superior force numerically. *But for the undaunted bravery of officers and soldiers who have yet to learn defeat*, the efforts of the enemy must have proved successful.

Whilst one division of the army, under Major General Rosecrans, was resisting and repelling the onslaught of the rebel hosts at Corinth, another, from Bolivar, under Major General Hurlbut, was marching upon the enemy's rear, driving in their pickets and cavalry, and attracting the attention of a large force of infantry and artillery. On the following day, under Major General Ord, these forces advanced with unsurpassed gallantry, driving the enemy back across the Hatchie, over ground where it is almost incredible that a superior force should be driven by an inferior, capturing two of the batteries (eight guns), many hundred small arms, and several hundred prisoners.

To those two divisions of the army all praise is due, and will be awarded by a grateful country.

Between them there should be, and I trust are, the warmest bonds of brotherhood. Each was risking life in the same cause, and, on this occasion, risking it also to save and assist the other. No troops could do more than these separate armies. Each did all possible for it to do in the places assigned it.

As in all great battles, so in this, it becomes our fate to mourn the loss of many brave and faithful officers and soldiers, who have given up their lives as a sacrifice for a great principle. The nation mourns for them.

By command of Major General U. S. GRANT.

JOHN A. RAWLINS, *A. A. G.*

President Lincoln, on receiving General Grant's despatch giving the news of the victory, returned the following characteristic reply: —

WASHINGTON, D. C., October 8, 1862.

MAJOR GENERAL GRANT.

I congratulate you and all concerned in your recent battles and victories. How does it all sum up? I especially regret the death of General Hackleman, and am very anxious to know the condition of General Oglesby, who is an intimate personal friend.

A. LINCOLN.

The answer to the President's shrewd inquiry will show the results of the whole movement. The brief campaign had displayed Grant's military judgment, and the admirable clearness of his perceptions. He had divined the intentions of the enemy, had shown himself able to plan and execute a combined movement, and that he was a master of military strategy in the best sense of this much misused word. He had enticed Price to Iuka, and had defeated him there, and had thus obtained information which made his surmise a certainty that Price and Van Dorn were acting in concert. He had made the way clear for his campaign against Vicksburg, and had prepared himself and his soldiers for that brilliant military drama; and, further, these active operations in the field afforded him the means of becoming acquainted with the qualities of his officers, and enabled him to make that rare selection of his immediate aids which organized the final overthrow of the rebellion. The sum, it will be found, is capable of proof.

## CHAPTER XIII.

### A BROADER FIELD OF ACTION.—PREPARING FOR VICKSBURG.

By general orders from the War Department, dated October 16, General Grant was assigned to the department of the Tennessee. Since the departure of General Halleck for Washington, he had virtually held this position, but now assumed it officially, in the following order:—

*General Orders, No. 1.*

HEADQUARTERS DEPARTMENT OF THE TENNESSEE,
JACKSON, TENN., October 25, 1862.

I. In compliance with General Orders, No. 159, A. G. O., War Department, of date October 16, 1862, the undersigned hereby assumes command of the department of the Tennessee, which includes Cairo, Fort Henry, and Fort Donelson, Northern Mississippi, and the portions of Kentucky and Tennessee west of the Tennessee River.

II. Headquarters of the department of the Tennessee will remain, until further orders, at Jackson, Tennessee.

III. All orders of the district of West Tennessee will continue in force in the department.

U. S. GRANT, *Major General commanding.*

*General Orders, No. 2.*

HEADQUARTERS DEPARTMENT OF THE TENNESSEE,
JACKSON, TENN., October 26, 1862.

I. The geographical divisions designated in General Orders, No. 83, from Headquarters District of West Tennessee, dated September 24, 1862, will hereafter be known as districts. The First Division will constitute the "District of Memphis," Major General W. T. Sherman commanding; the Second Division, the "District of Jackson," commanded by Major General S. A. Hurlbut; the Third Division, the "District of Corinth," Brigadier General C. S. Hamilton commanding; the Fourth Division, the "District of Columbus," commanded by Brigadier General T. A. Davies.

II. The army heretofore known as the "Army of the Mississippi," being now divided and in different departments, will be continued as a separate army.

III. Until army corps are formed, there will be no distinction known, except those of departments, districts, divisions, posts, brigades, regiments, and companies.

By command of Major General U. S. GRANT.

JOHN A. RAWLINS, *A. A. G.*

Buell having been defeated by Bragg, at Perryville, on the 8th of October, he was superseded in command by Rosecrans on the 30th.

Before entering upon the details of the active campaign against Vicksburg, it will be well to glance for a moment at what Grant was doing while preparing for this campaign, and also to get an accurate idea of the difficulties in his way, and what had been done by others to remove them.

One of his first cares was to republish and carry out Halleck's order, limiting the baggage of the army, and cutting down to the smallest possible quantity the amount carried by the officers and men. To insure the carrying out of his orders, he himself set the example, and adhered so rigorously to it, that, during the ensuing campaign, his personal baggage was said to consist only of a tooth-brush, and nothing more. To prevent the demoralization of his troops, by giving way to the tendency to plunder, which is almost always the necessary and inevitable concomitant of warfare, the following order was issued:—

*Special Field Orders, No. 2.*

HEADQUARTERS DEPARTMENT OF THE TENNESSEE,
LAGRANGE, TENN., November 9, 1862.

Hereinafter stoppage will be made on muster and pay rolls *against divisions* for the full amount of depredations committed by any member or members of the division, *unless the act can be traced* either to the individuals committing them, or to the company, regiment, or brigade to which the offenders belong.

In all cases the punishment will be assessed to the smallest organization containing the guilty parties.

*Confiscation acts were never intended to be executed by soldiers;* and if they were, the general government should have full benefit of all property of which individuals are deprived. A stoppage of pay against offenders will effect this end, and it is to be hoped will correct this growing evil.

*It is not only the duty of commissioned officers to correct this evil, but of all good men in the ranks* to report every violation; and it is determined now that they shall have a pecuniary interest in doing so.

Assessments will also be made against commissioned officers, in the proportion of their pay proper.

Where offences of the nature contemplated in this order are traced to individuals, they will be summarily punished to the full extent formerly given to garrison court martials, or be arrested and tried by a general court martial, according to the enormity of the offence, and the severest penalties provided imposed and executed.

This order will be read on parade, before each regiment and detachment, for three successive evenings.

By order of Major General U. S. GRANT.

This excellent idea, by which the soldiers were made pecuniarily responsible for acts of this kind, was so sternly carried out into practice, that it not only stopped all tendency towards this disorganizing habit, but had also the admirable effect of making his army one of the best disciplined in the country, and cultivating among the men a high sense of personal honor and dignity —qualities which come only from a feeling of personal responsibility.

All cotton which came into the hands of the quartermasters south of Jackson, Tennessee, was, in another order, directed to be sent to that point, while that captured north of this place was to be sent to Columbus, and directed to be kept until orders were received to sell the same at public auction. Record was also to be kept of the names of the parties from whom it was seized. In this way the money thus gained was to aid in meeting the expenses of the government.

To look after the interests of the negroes, who gathered in great numbers in our camps, who were not yet declared free, and who, it was supposed, in some cases acted the part of spies for their former masters, and who, at any rate, were quite a burden upon his army for their subsistence, the following order was issued, by which a special camp was organized for their accommodation and protection, and their labor, as far as possible, made available for their support: —

*Special Field Orders, No. 4.*

HEADQUARTERS THIRTEENTH ARMY CORPS,
DEPARTMENT OF THE TENNESSEE,
LAGRANGE, TENN., November 14.

1. Chaplain J. Eaton, Jr., of the twenty-seventh Regiment Ohio Infantry Volunteers, is hereby appointed to take charge of all fugitive slaves that are now, or may from time to time come, within the military lines of the advancing army in this vicinity, not employed and registered in accordance with General Orders, No. 72, from Headquarters District of West Tennessee, and will open a camp

for them at Grand Junction, where they will be suitably cared for and organized into companies, and set to work, picking, ginning, and baling all cotton now outstanding in fields.

2. Commanding officers of troops will send all fugitives that come within the lines, together with such teams, cooking utensils, and other baggage as they may bring with them, to Chaplain J. Eaton, Jr., at Grand Junction.

3. One regiment of infantry from Brigadier General McArthur's division will be temporarily detailed as guard in charge of such contrabands, and the surgeons of said regiment will be charged with the care of the sick.

4. Commissaries of subsistence will issue on the requisitions of Chaplain J. Eaton, Jr., omitting the coffee rations, and substituting rye. By order of Major General U. S. GRANT.

JOHN A. RAWLINS, *A. A. G.*

The subject of trade in the insurrectionary states, after they had been brought within the lines of the Union army, had become a matter of great importance. The Treasury Department had laid down rules for its management, but they were in many cases deficient; while it also required very stringent military supervision, in order to prevent such traffic being made a means of affording aid and comfort to the enemy. Grant's first desire was to suppress all trade, and he was especially severe upon the Jews, particularly the German Jews, who followed our camp, and having no nationality, felt themselves in no way bound by oaths or obligations of any kind, but pursued their own private interests regardless of every other consideration. For some time he rigidly excluded them entirely from his department; and it is a singular fact that they fell under the equal displeasure of the Confederates. Grant's opinion was, that a certain amount of trade might be made even useful to the Union cause, provided it was carried on by honest persons, who were above all suspicion; but being pressed to name such persons, he refused, on the intelligent grounds that should he do so, it would not be a week before it would be made to appear that he was the partner and in collusion with every one of the persons so appointed. This was the just conclusion of common sense, and the result has been, that no one has dared to even insinuate that he made money by the war, while such a charge has been repeatedly brought against other of our Generals. In order to define the trade which should be carried on within the lines of the department of the Tennessee, the following orders were issued: —

*General Orders, No.* 8.

HEADQUARTERS THIRTEENTH ARMY CORPS,
DEPARTMENT OF THE TENNESSEE,
LAGRANGE, TENN., November 19, 1862.

I. In addition to permits from the Treasury Department, all persons are required to have a permit from the local Provost Marshal at the post before purchasing cotton or other southern products in this department, and shipping the same north.

II. *It will be regarded as evidence of disloyalty for persons to go beyond the lines of the army to purchase cotton or other products; and all contracts made for such articles in advance of the army, or for cotton in the field, are null and void, and all persons so offending will be expelled from the department.*

III. Freight agents on military railroads will report daily to the post Provost Marshal all cotton or other private property shipped by them; and when shipments are made by persons who have not the proper permits, notice will be given, by telegraph, to the Provost Marshal at Columbus, Ky., who will seize the goods for the benefit of the government.

IV. The Federal army being now in the occupancy of West Tennessee to the Mississippi line, and it being no part of the policy of the government to oppress, *or cause unnecessary suffering to those who are not in active rebellion*, hereafter, until otherwise directed, licenses will be granted by district commanders to loyal persons, at all military stations within the department, to keep for sale, subject to the Treasury regulations, such articles as are of prime necessity for families, and sell the same to all citizens who have taken, or may voluntarily take, the oath of allegiance, and who have permits from the Provost Marshal, obtained under oath, that all goods to be purchased are for their own and for their families' use, and that no part thereof is for sale or for the use of any person other than those named in the permit. Permits so given will be good until countermanded; and all violations of trading permits will be punished by the forfeiture of the permit, fine, and imprisonment, at the discretion of a military commission.

V. Particular attention is called to existing orders prohibiting the employment or use of government teams for hauling private property. All cotton brought to stations or places for shipment in this department by government teams will be seized by the Quartermaster's department for the benefit of the government, and persons claiming such property expelled from the department. It is made the duty of all officers, and especially of local Provost Marshals, to see that this order is rigidly enforced.

By command of Major General U. S. GRANT.

JOHN A. RAWLINS, *A. A. G.*

The following order, expelling the Jews, was also issued, but afterwards so modified that they were allowed to trade under certain regulations:—

*General Orders, No.* 11.

HEADQUARTERS DEPARTMENT OF THE TENNESSEE,
OXFORD, MISS., December 17, 1862.

The Jews, as a class, violating every regulation of trade established by the Treasury Department, also department orders, are hereby expelled from the department within twenty-four hours from the receipt of this order by post commanders. They will see that all this class of people are furnished with passes and required to leave; and any one returning after such notification will be arrested and held in confinement until an opportunity occurs of sending them out as prisoners, unless furnished with permits from these headquarters. No passes will be given these people to visit headquarters for the purpose of making personal application for trade permits.

By order of Major General GRANT.

Let us now look at the condition of Vicksburg. As early as the 12th of January, 1861, the Governor of Mississippi had sent artillery to be used in fortifying this place, which was supposed to be the strongest defensive point upon the Mississippi River, since it commanded, from an elevated position, the channel for miles, both above and below. As soon as Island No. 10 was taken, the works at Vicksburg were pushed vigorously towards completion, under the direction of the most skilful engineers in the Confederacy, until at last they were considered to be as strong as it was possible to make them, and capable of resisting any attack either by land or water. The Confederates had boasted the possession of several "Gibraltars," but heretofore they had, in turn, been found wanting when weighed in the balance. Here, however, they felt convinced that they possessed the real Gibraltar of America, and the city had, in fact, become a series of forts.

The importance of this point is evident from the testimony of both parties. Sherman, in a speech at St. Louis, said that the possession of the Mississippi River was the possession of America; while Jefferson Davis, in a speech to the legislature of Mississippi, on the 26th of December, declared that the fall of Vicksburg would "cut off their communication with the trans-Mississippi department, and sever the western portion of the Confederacy from the eastern."

In consequence of this evident fact, the Confederates had, on the 25th of November, fortified Port Hudson, a naturally strong point on the left bank of the river, twenty-five miles above Baton Rouge, and the terminus of the Clinton Railway. This kept quite a stretch of the river free from our gunboats, and kept open their communications with Texas and the south-west, upon which they depended in great measure for their supplies.

On the 20th of June, Brigadier General Thomas Williams had left Baton Rouge, and on the 25th was off Vicksburg, and unmolested had commenced to cut a canal across a narrow point enclosed in a sharp turn of the river at this part, by which the channel should be turned, and Vicksburg made an inland town, situated about six miles from the stream. This canal was to run from De Soto to Richmond, Louisiana, and, if successful, would have transferred a piece of territory from this state to Mississippi. It was apparently a slight work, and was soon finished by the labor of about twelve hundred negroes, taken from the neighboring plantations; but on the 22d of July, when it was completed, it was found that the current would not run through it, from some cause which has not yet been thoroughly explained. The channel of the Mississippi had often before this been changed by simply drawing a furrow with a plough from one point to another, and thus making a commencement for the current to take a new path; but the low condition of the river at this time may have been one of the principal causes of the failure. It having become evident from this failure that the position at Vicksburg was not to be turned in this way, Williams went back to Baton Rouge, and the canal was immediately filled up by the Confederates.

On the 7th of June — the day after the capture of Memphis — Farragut had steamed up to Vicksburg, and on the 8th had silenced the Grand Gulf batteries. On the 28th of the same month he had sent seven vessels past, silencing the lower batteries, and had joined, on the 1st of July, a fleet of four gunboats and six mortar-boats, sent down from the upper fleet, while Porter, with the remainder of Farragut's fleet, had engaged again the water batteries below; but after an ineffectual bombardment, the rapidly falling condition of the water forced the fleet to return to New Orleans, for fear lest they should run aground.

About twelve miles north of Vicksburg the Yazoo River empties into the Mississippi. Here the Confederates had constructed a formidable ram, the Arkansas, which came down to Vicksburg on the 15th of July, and was sent down to Baton Rouge, to aid in Breckinridge's attack upon that place on the 5th of August, where she was sunk by the Union ram Essex, under the command of Colonel Ellet.

## CHAPTER XIV.

### THE MOVEMENT AGAINST VICKSBURG BEGUN.

On the 4th of November Grant was ready to move. He had concentrated his troops from Corinth, Jackson, and Bolivar. As early as June 16, the Confederate government had intrusted the command in and about Vicksburg to General John C. Pemberton, whose unpopularity more than counterbalanced his military superiority to Generals Van Dorn and Lovell, over whose heads he was appointed to this position. Pemberton's army lay upon the line of the Mississippi Central Railway, principally at Abbeville, behind the Tallahatchie River, and in the vicinity of Holly Springs, Miss. Its advance was near Grand Junction and La Grange. On the 4th of November Grant moved to La Grange, three miles east of Grand Junction, on the Memphis and Charleston Railway, pushing the advance of the Confederate army back towards Holly Springs. Meanwhile Grant's cavalry reconnoissances had shown that the Confederates intended to hold the line of the Tallahatchie River, and were chiefly in force at Holly Springs and Coldwater, Van Dorn having fortified the river line.

While the main army was moving down from Grand Junction upon Abbeville, on the Tallahatchie, where the Confederates were strongly posted, Sherman was moving down in the same direction from Memphis, and a third coöperating force, amounting to about seven thousand men, under Generals Hovey and Washburn, were moving from Helena, for the purpose of flanking the enemy, clearing the country for Grant's advance, and gaining for him possession of Northern Mississippi, with its rich resources.

This plan and its results were thus stated by Sherman in a speech at St. Louis: "Grant moved direct on Pemberton, while I moved from Memphis, and a smaller force, under General Washburne, struck directly for Grenada; and the first thing Pemberton knew, the depot of his supplies was almost in the grasp of a small cavalry force, and he fell back in confusion, and gave us the Tallahatchie without a battle." The credit of this plan, which was as brilliantly conceived as executed, belongs to Grant. The movement was rapid: on the 29th of November Grant's advance was at Holly Springs, on the 30th at Waterford, and on the 1st of December a junction was made with Sherman. Starting on the 27th of November from Helena, on the 28th General Hovey was at Delta. From here to Cold-water, capturing a rebel camp; then southward, rapidly, along the Cold-water and Tallahatchie Rivers, to Garner's Station, just north of Grenada, destroying the railroad and bridges; then by other points to Grand Junction. The success was perfect. The railroad from Memphis to Grenada was destroyed. While the Confederates were pressed in front by Grant, their rear was seriously threatened, and nothing was left for them but to fall back, which they did, to Grenada. Still advancing, Grant's headquarters on the 3d of December were at Oxford, and his cavalry were driving Van Dorn out of Water Valley and Coffeeville, while our gunboats were in the Yazoo, threatening the enemy's rear, and perhaps to cut off their retreat.

Grant, having been thus far successful, proposed to General Halleck to hold the enemy south of the Yalabusha, and move a force upon Vicksburg from Memphis and Helena; and receiving the required permission, Sherman was selected for the command of the expedition, and notified in the following order: —

HEADQUARTERS THIRTEENTH ARMY CORPS,
DEPARTMENT OF THE TENNESSEE,
OXFORD, MISS., December 8, 1862.

MAJOR GENERAL W. T. SHERMAN, *commanding Right Wing.*

GENERAL: You will proceed with as little delay as possible to Memphis, Tenn., taking with you one division of your present command. On your arrival at Memphis, you will assume command of all the troops there, and that portion of General Curtis's force at present east of the Mississippi River, and organize them into brigades and divisions in your own way. As soon as possible move with them down the river, to the vicinity of Vicksburg; and, with the coöperation of the gunboat fleet under command of Flag-officer Porter, proceed to the reduction of that place, in such manner as circumstances and your own judgment may dictate.

The amount of rations, forage, land transportation, &c., necessary to take, will be left entirely with yourself. The Quartermaster at St. Louis will be instructed to send you transportation for thirty thousand men. Should you still find yourself deficient, your Quartermaster will be authorized to make up the deficiency from such transports as may come into the port of Memphis.

On arriving at Memphis, put yourself in communication with Admiral Porter, and arrange with him for his coöperation.

Inform me at the earliest practicable day of the time when you will embark, and such plans as may then be matured. I will hold the forces here in readiness to coöperate with you in such manner as the movements of the enemy may make necessary.

Leave the district of Memphis in the command of an efficient officer, and with a garrison of four regiments of infantry, the siege-guns, and whatever cavalry may be there.

U. S. GRANT, *Major General.*

The following letter of General Sherman to Admiral Porter gives his views of the movement:—

HEADQUARTERS RIGHT WING ARMY OF THE TENNESSEE,
OXFORD, MISS., December 8, 1862.

REAR ADMIRAL D. D. PORTER,
*Commanding U. S. Naval Forces, Cairo, Ill.*

The movement thus far has been eminently successful. General Grant, moving down directly upon the enemy's strong lines behind the Tallahatchie, while the Helena force appeared unexpectedly on their flank, utterly confounded them; and they are now in full retreat, and we are at a loss where they will bring up. We hope they will halt and re-form behind the Yalabusha, with Grenada as their centre. If so, General Grant can press their front, whilst I am ordered to take all the spare troops from Memphis and Helena, and proceed with all despatch to Vicksburg.

Time now is the great object. We must not give time for new combinations. I know you will promptly coöperate. It will not be necessary to engage their Vicksburg batteries until I have broken all their inland communication; then Vicksburg must be attacked by land and water. In this I will defer much to you.

My purpose will be to cut the road to Munroe, La., to Jackson, Miss., and then appear up the Yazoo, threatening the Mississippi Central road where it crosses the Big Black.

These movements will disconcert the enemy, and throw them on to Meridian, especially as General Grant presses them in front. All this should be done before the winter rains make General Grant's road impassable. I will leave for Memphis to-morrow, Tuesday night, and will reach Memphis with one of my old divisions Friday night. We ought to leave Memphis before the 20th, and I do earnestly desire you should meet me there. At all events, even if the larger gunboats cannot proceed at once, send those of light draught down, with Captains Phelps, Gwinn, Shirk, or some officer to assist me in the preliminary work. Of course Vicksburg cannot be reduced till you arrive with the large gunboats.

General Grant's purpose is to take full advantage of the effects of this Tallahatchie success.

I am, with great respect,

W. T. SHERMAN, *Major General commanding.*

As we have seen, it was expected that Sherman would be able, with the coöperation of the navy, to surprise and capture Vicksburg. If, however, he could not do this, it was supposed to be certain that he could take and hold Haine's Bluff, and thus operating against the enemy's lines, open up the Yazoo as a line of supplies to Grant, while he should press Pemberton in front, and hold him in the Yalabusha until the result of Sherman's attack should be known.

On the 14th of December General Grant telegraphed to Sherman, in cipher, as follows: —

I have not had one word from Grierson since he left, and am getting uneasy about him. I hope General Gorman will give you no difficulty about returning the troops that were on this side of the river, and Steele to command them. The twenty-one thousand men you have, with twelve thousand from Helena, will make a good force. The enemy are as yet in the Yalabushâ. I am pushing down on them slowly, but so as to keep up the impression of a continuous move. I feel particularly anxious to have the Helena cavalry on this side of the river; if not now, at least after you start. If Gorman will send them, instruct them where to go, and how to communicate with me. My headquarters will probably be in Coffeeville one week hence. In the mean time I will be at Springdale. It would be well if you could have two or three small boats, suitable for navigating the Yazoo. It may become necessary for me to look to that base for supplies before we get through.

Still pushing the enemy, Grant kept sending cavalry expeditions, threatening both his flanks, and, as he advanced, leaving adequate garrisons at all the posts in his rear. Among the points thus protected were Columbus, Humboldt, Bolivar, Corinth, Holly Springs, Cold-water, and others. His headquarters were at Oxford, Mississippi.

Sherman set about immediately organizing his expedition. The forces were to embark at Memphis, and rendezvous at Friar's Point, eighteen miles below Helena. The fleet consisted of one hundred and twenty-seven steamboats, in addition to gunboats. The infantry force was composed of western troops entirely, men who were hardy, daring, and used to a rough and adventurous life. The following order, issued by him on the 18th, will show what care was used in organizing the expedition:—

*General Orders, No.* 8.

HEADQUARTERS RIGHT WING THIRTEENTH ARMY CORPS,
MEMPHIS, TENN., December 18, 1862.

1. The expedition now fitting out is purely of a military character, and the interests involved are of too important a nature to be mixed up with personal and private business. *No citizen, male or female, will be allowed to accompany it*, unless employed as part of a crew or as servants to the transports. Female chambermaids to the boats and nurses to the sick alone will be allowed, unless the wives of captains and pilots actually belonging to the boats. No laundress, officer's or soldier's wife, must pass below Helena.

2. No person whatever, citizen, officer, or sutler, will, on any consideration, buy or deal in cotton or other produce of the country. Should any cotton be brought on board of any trans-

port, going or returning, the brigade Quartermaster, of which the boat forms a part, will take possession of it, and invoice it to Captain A. R. Eddy, Chief Quartermaster at Memphis.

3. Should any cotton, or other produce, be brought back to Memphis by any chartered boat, Captain Eddy will take possession of the same, and sell it for the benefit of the United States. If accompanied by its actual producer, the planter or factor, the Quartermaster will furnish him with a receipt for the same, to be settled for, on proof of his loyalty, at the close of the war.

4. Boats ascending the river may take cotton from the shore for bulkheads to protect their engines or crew, but on arrival at Memphis it will be turned over to the Quartermaster, with a statement of the time, place, and name of its owner. The trade in cotton must await a more peaceful state of affairs.

5. Should any citizen accompany the expedition below Helena in violation of these orders, any Colonel of a regiment or Captain of a battery will conscript him into the service of the United States for the unexpired term of his command. If he show a refractory spirit unfitting him for a soldier, the commanding officer present will turn him over to the captain of the boat as a deck hand, and compel him to work in that capacity without wages until the boat returns to Memphis.

6. Any persons whatever, whether in the service of the United States or transports, found making reports for publication, which might reach the enemy, giving them information, aid, and comfort, will be arrested and treated as spies.

By order of Major General SHERMAN.

J. H. HAMMOND, *Major and A. A. G.*

The call was entirely successful, and Sherman, locating his headquarters in the Forest Queen, arrived with his staff at Friar's Point on the 21st of December. From thence the expedition proceeding, a small force, under General Morgan L. Smith, was landed at Milliken's Bend, who proceeded to Delhi and Dallas, on the Vicksburg and Texas Railway, destroying these stations and the track, so as to cut off the retreat of the Confederates from Vicksburg. The main body of the expedition, having safely disembarked, on the 27th of December, 1862, at Johnston's Landing, near the mouth of the Yazoo River, prepared for an assault upon the northern works defending Vicksburg.

## CHAPTER XV.

### THE FIRST ATTEMPT TO CAPTURE VICKSBURG, HOW AND WHY IT FAILED.

Let us now return to Grant, whom we left advancing against the enemy, and examine the causes which prevented his supporting Sherman's expedition.

The cause was very simple. As Grant advanced, we have told how he left the important posts in his rear garrisoned with what he considered an adequate force. As soon as Van Dorn was aware of the return of Hovey's expedition, he formed the idea of attacking some of the garrisons left in Grant's rear, and thus, by threatening his base, force him to postpone his advance. On the 12th a skirmish took place at Corinth, and other points were similarly threatened; but in them all the enemy were boldly repulsed. The weak point, however, was found. Holly Springs had been left in the command of Colonel R. C. Murphy, who on the 20th surrendered his post to an attack of cavalry, without attempting to make the slightest resistance. Grant was at this time at Oxford, thirty miles away. This base surrender, opening as it did his communications, forced him to fall back upon Holly Springs, and postpone advancing upon Vicksburg, and supporting Sherman's expedition. It also freed the troops in Grant's front, who had been kept in check by his advance, and enabled them to hasten back to Vicksburg to assist in repelling Sherman.

This failure of so well combined a plan, caused as it was by the imbecility of one man, in whom circumstances had necessitated the placing of confidence, was the more unfortunate just at this juncture, since the season had been one of disaster in the East. Pope had been defeated at Centreville on the 28th of August. The battle of Antietam was not a complete victory. Buell at Perryville had gained anything but a victory over Bragg, while, on the 19th of December, the terrible slaughters had taken place at Fredericksburg. But though every one else might despair, Grant remained firm. His tenacity of purpose was perhaps never more severely tried, and never came stronger from the trial. He lost no time in regrets, but made preparations for putting a new plan in execution. Having returned to Holly Springs, and made his headquarters there, he investigated the conditions of the surrender, and issued the following order on the 24th of December: —

*Special Field Orders, No.* 23.

HEADQUARTERS THIRTEENTH ARMY CORPS,
DEPARTMENT OF THE TENNESSEE,
HOLLY SPRINGS, MISS., December 24, 1862.

[EXTRACT.]

It is with pain and mortification that the General commanding reflects upon the disgraceful surrender of the place, with all the valuable stores it contained, on the 20th instant, and that without any resistance except by a few men, who form an honorable exception; and this, too, after warning had been given of the enemy northward the evening previous. With all the cotton, public stores, and substantial buildings about the depot, it would have been perfectly practicable to have made, in a few hours, a defence sufficient to resist, with a small garrison, all the cavalry force brought against them, until the reënforcements which the commanding officer was notified were marching to his relief could have reached him.

The conduct of officers and men in accepting paroles, under the circumstances, is highly reprehensible, and, to say the least, thoughtless. By the terms of the Dix Hill cartel each party is bound to take care of their prisoners, and to send them to Vicksburg, or a point on the James River, for exchange or parole, unless some other point is mutually agreed upon by the Generals commanding the opposing armies.

By a refusal to be paroled, the enemy, from his inability to take care of the prisoners, would have been compelled either to have refused them unconditionally, or to have abandoned further aggressive movements for the time being, which would have made their recapture, and the discomfiture of the enemy almost certain.

The prisoners paroled at this place will be collected in camp at once by the post commander, and held under close guard until their case can be reported to Washington for further instructions.

Commanders throughout the department are directed to arrest and hold, as above, all men of their commands and all stragglers who may have accepted their paroles upon like terms.

The General commanding is satisfied that the majority of the troops who accepted a parole did so thoughtlessly and from want of knowledge of the cartel referred to, and that in future they will not be caught in the same way.

By order of Major General U. S. GRANT.

JOHN A. RAWLINS, *A. A. G.*

The following order of the 8th of January, 1863, shows that, after a careful investigation of all the circumstances, the blame was made to rest where it belonged, and fit punishment meted out to the offender.

*General Orders, No.* 4.

HEADQUARTERS DEPARTMENT OF THE TENNESSEE,
HOLLY SPRINGS, MISS., January 8, 1863.

1. The Major General commanding the department takes just pride and satisfaction in congratulating *the small garrisons* of the

posts of Coldwater, Davis's Mills, and Middleburg, for the heroic defence of their positions on the 20th, 21st, and 24th ultimo, *and their successful repulse of an enemy many times their number.*

The Ninetieth Illinois, at Coldwater (its first engagement), the detachment of the veteran Twenty-fifth Indiana and two companies of the Fifth Ohio Cavalry at Davis's Mills, and the detachment of the gallant Twelfth Michigan at Middleburg, are deserving of the thanks of the army, which was in a measure dependent upon the road they so nobly defended for supplies, and they will receive the meed of praise ever awarded by a grateful public to those who bravely and successfully do their duty.

These regiments are entitled to inscribe upon their banners, respectively, Coldwater, Davis's Mills, and Middleburg, with the names of other battle-fields made victorious by their valor and discipline.

It is gratifying to know that at every point where our troops made a stand during the late raid of the enemy's cavalry, success followed, and the enemy was made to suffer a loss in killed and wounded greater than the entire garrisons of the places attacked. Especially was this the case of Davis's Mills and Middleburg. The only success gained by Van Dorn was at Holly Springs, where the whole garrison was left by their commander in ignorance of the approach of danger.

2. Colonel R. C. Murphy, of the Eighth Regiment Wisconsin Infantry Volunteers, having, while in command of the post of Holly Springs, Mississippi, neglected and failed to exercise the usual and ordinary precautions to guard and protect the same; having, after repeated and timely warning of the approach of the enemy, failed to make any preparations for resistance or defence, or shown any disposition to do so; and having, with a force amply sufficient to have repulsed the enemy and protect the public stores intrusted to his care, disgracefully permitted him to capture the post and destroy the stores, — and the movement of troops in face of an enemy rendering it impracticable to convene a court martial for his trial, — is, therefore, *dismissed the service of the United States — to take effect from the* 20*th day of December*, 1862, *the date of his cowardly and disgraceful conduct.*

By order of Major General U. S. GRANT.

JOHN A. RAWLINS, *A. A. G.*

Let us now follow the movements of Sherman's expedition, and the subsequent events, which for a time delayed all active operations against Vicksburg.

The approach to Vicksburg by land, from Johnston's Landing, the place where the embarkation was successfully accomplished by the troops, after the armed vessels had silenced a battery planted by the Confederates to resist the landing, is peculiarly difficult. The town is on a hill, with a line of hills surrounding it at a distance of several miles, extending from Haine's Bluff, on the Yazoo River, to Warrenton, ten miles below, on the Mississippi River. The low ground in the vicinity is swampy, and filled with sloughs, lagoons, and bayous. The approach over such a country would, even in times of peace, be very difficult for a large force, and in war, with an enemy in front, it was almost an impossibility.

On the morning of the 27th of December, the army was drawn up in line, prepared to make the assault. Sherman was of course unaware of the disaster at Holly Springs on the 20th. The general advance commenced, and the enemy was driven back about one fourth of a mile from his original position. The next day the men pressed forward with great bravery; but the want of coöperation of Grant's command disarranged the plan of action, left Sherman's force too weak, and enabled the Confederates to be largely reënforced by the men who were freed by Grant's falling back, and could be used for this purpose.

During the next day, also, the 29th, the fighting was continued; but the attempt was futile, and General Sherman gave orders for the troops to reëmbark.

By the arrival upon the ground of General McClernand, who ranked General Sherman by over a month in the date of his commission, the command was transferred, and by the orders of the new commander, the vessels were withdrawn from the Yazoo to the Mississippi. The title of the army was also changed, and these facts were announced by General Sherman to the troops in the following order:—

*General Orders, No. 5.*

HEADQUARTERS RIGHT WING ARMY OF TENNESSEE,
STEAMER FOREST QUEEN, MILLIKEN'S BEND, January 4, 1863.

Pursuant to the terms of General Orders, No. 1, made this day by General McClernand, the title of our army ceases to exist, and constitutes in the future the Army of the Mississippi, composed of two "army corps," one to be commanded by General G. W. Morgan, and the other by myself. In relinquishing the command of the army of the Tennessee, and restricting my authority to my own corps, I desire to express to all commanders, to soldiers and officers, recently operating before Vicksburg, my hearty thanks for the zeal, alacrity, and courage manifested by them on all occasions. We failed in accomplishing one purpose of our movement — the capture of Vicksburg; but we were part of a whole. Ours was but part of a combined movement, in which others were to assist. We were on time; unforeseen contingencies must have delayed the others. We have destroyed the Shreveport road; we have attacked the defences of Vicksburg, and pushed the attack as far as prudence would justify; and having found it too strong for our single column, we have drawn off in good order and good spirits, ready for any new move. A new commander is now here to lead you. He is chosen by the President of the United States, who is charged by the Constitution to maintain and defend it, and he has the undoubted right to select his own agents. I know that all good officers and soldiers will give him the same hearty support and cheerful obedience they have hitherto given me. There are honors enough in reserve for all, and work enough too. Let each do his appropriate part, and our nation must. in the end emerge from this dire conflict purified and ennobled by the fires which now test its strength and purity. All officers of the general staff now attached to my person will hereafter report in person and by letter to Major General McClernand, commanding the army of the Mississippi, on board the steamer Tigress, at our rendezvous at Gaines's Landing and at Montgomery Point.

By order of Major General W. T. SHERMAN.

J. H. HAMMOND, *A. A. G.*

Before McClernand had assumed the command, General Sherman had conceived the plan of attacking Arkansas Post, and had consulted with Admiral Porter concerning the advantage and feasibility of so doing. McClernand concurring in this design, the army went up White River from the Mississippi, and then by a canal to the Arkansas. Moving up to Fort Hindman, this place was attacked on the 11th, and after about four hours' fighting surrendered. The following report details the operations: —

HEADQUARTERS ARMY OF THE MISSISSIPPI,
POST OF ARKANSAS, January 11, 1863.

MAJOR GENERAL U. S. GRANT,
*Commanding Department of the Tennessee.*

I have the honor to report that the forces under my command attacked the Post of Arkansas to-day, at one o'clock, having stormed the enemy's work. We took a large number of prisoners, variously estimated at from seven thousand to ten thousand, together with all his stores, animals, and munitions of war.

Rear Admiral David D. Porter, commanding the Mississippi squadron, effectively and brilliantly coöperated, accomplishing this complete success.

JOHN A. MCCLERNAND, *Major General commanding.*

## CHAPTER XVI.

### REORGANIZATION OF THE ARMY.—GETTING INTO POSITION BEFORE VICKSBURG.

GRANT had been from the commencement of his career gaining the confidence of the government, and the great importance of his plans of operation on the Mississippi becoming more and more apparent, he was finally furnished new troops in such numbers as required a new organization. He therefore issued the following order, organizing his army into army corps — a system which is French in its origin, but the advantages of which are so manifest, particularly in handling large bodies of men, that experience soon led to its adoption. One of its chief advantages is, that it gives to competent corps commanders a sufficient field for the display of their abilities, and relieves the chief from a great deal of official drudgery; the reports, &c., being settled at the corps headquarters, and only digests being handed in to the chief. On the field also orders are issued to corps commanders, and they are held responsible for their execution. In fact each corps is an independent army, regularly organized, and ready to act independently as well as in coöperation.

*General Orders, No.* 14.

HEADQUARTERS DEPARTMENT OF THE TENNESSEE,
HOLLY SPRINGS, MISS., December 22, 1862.

By directions of the General-in-chief of the army, the troops in this department, including those of the department of the Missouri, operating on the Mississippi River, are hereby divided into four army corps, as follows: —

1. The troops composing the Ninth Division, Brigadier General G. W. Morgan commanding; the Tenth Division, Brigadier General A. J. Smith commanding; and all other troops operating on the Mississippi River below Memphis, not included in the Fifteenth Army Corps, will constitute the Thirteenth Army Corps, under the command of Major General John A. McClernand.

2. The Fifth Division, Brigadier General Morgan L. Smith commanding; the division from Helena, Arkansas, commanded by Brigadier General F. Steele; and the forces in the "District of Memphis," will constitute the Fifteenth Army Corps, and be commanded by Major General W. T. Sherman.

3. The Sixth Division, Brigadier General J. McArthur commanding; the Seventh Division, Brigadier General I. F. Quimby commanding; the Eighth Division, Brigadier General L. F. Ross commanding; the Second Brigade of cavalry, Colonel A. L. Lee commanding; and the troops in the "District of Columbus," commanded by Brigadier General Davies, and those in the "District of Jackson," commanded by Brigadier General Sullivan, will constitute the Sixteenth Army Corps, and be commanded by Major General S. A. Hurlbut.

4. The First Division, Brigadier General J. W. Denver commanding; the Third Division, Brigadier General John A. Logan commanding; the Fourth Division, Brigadier General J. G. Lauman commanding; the First Brigade of cavalry, Colonel B. H. Grierson commanding; and the forces in the "District of Corinth," commanded by Brigadier General G. M. Dodge, will constitute the Seventeenth Army Corps, and be commanded by Major General J. B. McPherson.

District commanders will send consolidated returns of their forces to these headquarters, as well as to army corps headquarters, and will, for the present, receive orders from department headquarters.

By order of Major General U. S. GRANT.

JOHN A. RAWLINS, *A. A. G.*

We have now come to the 1st of January, 1863, the day upon which the proclamation issued by President Lincoln on the 22d of September, 1862, was ratified by a formal proclamation, enumerating the states and portions of states in which slavery was declared dead, and the slaves to be free. The justice and the benefit of this policy will probably be disputed now by no one; but at the time many even of our generals in the field opposed it, though probably there could not be a better school than active military service in a slave state for learning the folly and absurdity of slavery, considered only in an economic point of view, and disregarding any other higher and nobler considerations. Here, however, as everywhere else, Grant showed himself fully up to the situation, as the following extract from an order issued early in January will show: —

*General Orders, No.* 25.

MILLIKEN'S BEND, LA.

1. Corps, division, and post commanders will afford all facilities for the completion of the negro regiments now organizing in this department. Commissaries will issue supplies, and quartermasters will furnish stores, on the same requisitions and returns as are required from other troops.

*It is expected that all commanders will especially exert themselves in carrying out the policy of the administration, not only in organizing colored regiments, and rendering them efficient, but also in removing prejudice against them. . . .*

By order of Major General U. S. GRANT.

JOHN A. RAWLINS, *A. A. G.*

On the 29th of January, 1863, Grant obtained full and personal control of the operations against Vicksburg and on this day sent a portion of his troops to Young's Point, Louisiana, and another to Milliken's Bend, and, following soon after, established his headquarters at the former place. On a thorough inspection of the works, he became convinced that it was impossible to take Vicksburg from the water front, and his plan was to take it from the land side. To do so, the first thing necessary was to obtain a base for his operations. The principal routes proposed for arriving at this end were the following: First, Williams Canal; second, the route from Milliken's Bend; third, Lake Providence; fourth, the Yazoo Pass; fifth, Steele's Bayou. All of these were attempted; and though to give a minute account of all the details connected with these operations would more than occupy all our space, yet we will glance briefly at them all. It is, however, the great results we desire to call special attention to, for it is in them that we find the material for estimating the amount of praise and gratitude due by the country to the man whose comprehensive mind first clearly estimated the difficulties in the successful prosecution of the war, whose genius formed the plans for overcoming them, and whose persistent energy carried us finally through to victory.

We have already spoken of the failure of the Williams Canal, and of the results which would have followed from its success. After his corps had captured Arkansas Post, or Fort Hindman, McClernand had been ordered to Young's Point; and this was made the destination of the whole of the army of the Tennessee, less the garrisons left for the protection of important points in the rear and Logan's division. At the same time a large naval force, under Admiral Porter, had rendezvoused there. On the 2d of February Grant came down to superintend in person the work on the canal, which was pushed forward with great vigor. The river was rising rapidly, and in fact so fast that it threatened to break down the embankment erected to keep the water out until the canal was finished and ready to be opened. On the 8th of March this occurred. While the men were actively at work, the immense pressure of the rising waters of the Mississippi broke through the temporary barrier raised against their approach, and, sweeping through, carried away the dikes and implements, flooding the camp, to the great discomfort and danger of the troops. Hastily seizing their tents and equipments, the men rushed to the levee, the Confederates laughed at our discomfiture, and the plan of a canal at this point had to be abandoned. All that part of the peninsula south of the railway was under water. Grant was not, however, disconcerted at this failure. It was only one of his plans, and he had others in reserve. The work was to be done, and he intended to do it. His army was large, in good spirits and good condition, and he felt the certainty of success which distinguishes genius from foolhardiness.

Another channel had been reported as practicable by his engineers. This was a route through the bayous which run from near Milliken's Bend on the north and New Carthage on the south, through Roundabout Bayou to the Tensas River. Dredge boats were sent through to clear this channel, and a small steamer, with a few barges, was passing through to test it practically, when the sudden falling of the water caused this scheme to be abandoned.

While work was being executed upon the Williams Canal, Grant's attention was directed to the route through Lake Providence, and he had placed a large force at work upon it. This lake is situated about seventy-five miles from Vicksburg, and just south of the state line of Arkansas, and is only one mile west of the Mississippi, so that a canal was cut connecting them. The lake is six miles long, and is connected by Bayou Baxter with Bayou Macon, a channel which opens into the Tensas, and by the Washita and Red Rivers into the Mississippi. This route was a long and difficult one, and was principally of use as opening a means of communication with Banks at Port Hudson. The project was soon abandoned, but served for a time to keep our soldiers occupied and engaged.

The most promising of all these plans was that of the Yazoo Pass, and the most vigor was applied to its development. Yazoo Pass lies eight miles below Helena, and is a narrow, tortuously winding passage, running eastward from the Mississippi into Moon Lake, whence it issues in a winding eastward course until it empties into the Coldwater River, which finally empties into the Tallahatchie. It was known that the Confederates were building gunboats on both the Coldwater and the Tallahatchie. At high water the Tallahatchie is navigable as far above the mouth of the Coldwater as Wyatt.

Grant's plan was to get into the Coldwater with boats of light draught, to destroy the vessels the Confederates were building; and he hoped also that his boats would be able to penetrate to the Yazoo, and thus coöperate with a land force, in a new assault upon Haine's Bluff. The want of a sufficient number of vessels prevented a large enough number of troops from being sent upon this expedition, so that only one division was despatched upon this duty. On the 24th of February, 1863, after tearing away that portion of the levee of the Mississippi which closed the entrance, the fleet entered the pass, and on the 28th, after very slow progress on account of the obstacles in the way, the winding course of the channel, the thickness of the forest, which overarches and at times almost bars the passage, they arrived at the Coldwater. The difficulties in the way may be imagined from the rate of advance made by the boats, which averaged about one mile in three and a half hours. When even the current ran strong, it was impossible to drift with it, since the overhanging trunks would sweep the decks clean.

The Confederates also, having gained information of the expedition, had closed the lower end of the Tallahatchie River, into which the Coldwater empties, by building a fort just above Greenwood, where the Tallahatchie and the Yalabusha combine to form the Yazoo. This fort was called Fort Pemberton, and was well posted for defence. An attempt to silence its guns by the gunboats was unsuccessful, and the whole expedition withdrew, arriving at Milliken's Bend on the 23d of March.

The attempt by Steele's Bayou was also unsuccessful. The difficulties in the way of this tortuous route were as great as those in the other. The boats were to proceed up the Yazoo, seven miles, to Cypress Bayou, a short opening into Steele's Bayou, which after thirty miles connects by a short canal with Deer Creek. After following this stream eighteen miles, there is a connection by the Rolling Fork with the Sunflower River, ten miles distant. This last stream, after a flow of over forty miles, empties into the Yazoo, not far from Haine's Bluff, and about sixty miles from its mouth. This route was recommended by Admiral Porter, after a reconnoissance. One of its advantages was, that it would flank Greenwood, threaten the rear of those who held our boats checked there, and turn the flank of the defences at Haine's Bluff. General Grant accompanied this expedition to Black Bayou, and was a witness of the difficulties in its way. He then returned to Young's Point in order to send up a pioneer troop which should clear the way for the expedition. Here he received a message from Admiral Porter, asking for the coöperation of a military force: in answer Grant forwarded a division of the Fifteenth Army Corps, with Sherman in command. The number of steam transports being too small for the accommodation of the entire force, the larger part of them were sent up the Mississippi to Eagle Bend, a point where the river runs within a mile of Steele's Bayou. The Confederates having, however, obtained a knowledge of this operation, made ready to receive us, and it was thought best to abandon the plan when we were within a few hundred yards of the point which, had we reached it, would have assured our success.

## CHAPTER XVII.

THE FINAL MOVE.—THE FIRST STEP IN THE RIGHT DIRECTION SUCCESSFUL.

ALL of these plans having been tried with unvarying fortune, Grant resolved to occupy New Carthage, the plan now being to move his forces below Vicksburg on the Louisiana shore, so as to attack the Confederate works in the rear. The movement began on the 29th of March, 1863, the Thirteenth Corps taking the lead, followed by the Seventeenth and Fifteenth, while the Sixteenth was left in charge of the communications and supplies.

Before giving an account of this new move, it will be well to glance for a moment at the sanitary condition of Grant's army at this time, since attention to this point is one of the most important qualities of a good general, and since about this time the unfounded public rumors to the contrary, having culminated into official inquiry, were officially answered.

During the time passed in the movements described above, public attention was very strongly directed to Grant's army, and every rumor relating to it excited public interest. As also during the time these various expeditions were preparing, it was of absolute necessity that the strictest secrecy concerning them should be preserved, all private correspondence of the army with friends left at home had been prohibited, for fear that such letters might fall into the hands of the enemy through the agency of the prowling bands of guerrillas which swarmed all round the outside of the lines. This absence of regular communication had the effect of redoubling the anxiety of those at home, who had friends in the army, and rendering them doubly sensitive to all rumors of every kind. Where, of course, such a desire for news exists, the supply to satisfy it will not be wanting, since the unscrupulous speculators in sensational news increase equally with, if they do not surpass, the growth of the legitimate diffusers of information — the public press. Inquiry into the facts of the sanitary condition of the army was made by the Surgeon General, and Grant, under date of March 6, responded informally as follows:—

No army ever went into the field better provided with medical stores and attendance than is furnished to the army before Vicksburg. There was a deficiency in volunteer surgeons, but that is now supplied. The hospital boats are supplied with their own surgeons, nurses, and everything for the comfort of the sick. The purveyor's department not only has everything furnished the sick, but more than it ever dreamed of was furnished to the army, and more than the great majority of men could have at home. Then, too, there is not that amount of sickness that persons would be led to believe from the statements in the public prints. I question whether the health of the St. Louis force is better than that of this command. On my arrival here, the men having to put up with straw for so long a time, and then with camping on low ground and in the most terrible weather ever experienced, there was for a time, of necessity, a great number of sick.

U. S. GRANT, *Major General.*

The foregoing letter was informal; but on the 12th

General Grant sent, in answer to the official inquiry, the following document for registry in the departmental offices at Washington: —

HEADQUARTERS DEPARTMENT OF THE TENNESSEE,
BEFORE VICKSBURG, March 12, 1863.

BRIGADIER GENERAL W. A. HAMMOND,
*Surgeon General United States Army.*

SIR: Surgeon J. R. Smith's letter of the 20th of February is just received, inquiring into the sanitary condition of this command, and asking for suggestions for its improvement. *I know a great deal has been said to impress the public generally, and officials particularly, with the idea that this army was in a suffering condition, and mostly from neglect. This is most erroneous.* The health of this command will, I venture to say, compare favorably with that of any army in the field, and every preparation is made for the sick that could be desired.

I will refer Surgeon Smith's letter to my medical director for a fuller report of the condition of the medical department here.

I am, sir, very respectfully, your obedient servant,

U. S. GRANT, *Major General.*

On the 27th of the same month the following order was issued for the purpose of giving every facility to the Sanitary Commission in their self-imposed task: —

*Special Orders, No.* 86.

HEADQUARTERS DEPARTMENT OF THE TENNESSEE,
YOUNG'S POINT, LA., March 27, 1863.

1. The Quartermaster's department will provide and furnish a suitable steamboat, to be called the "United States Sanitary Store Boat," and put the same in charge of the U. S. Sanitary Commission, to be used by it exclusively for the conveyance of goods calculated to prevent disease — and supplement the government supply of stores for the relief of the sick and wounded.

2. No person will be permitted to travel on said boat, except sick officers of the army and navy (and they only on permits from

their proper commanding officers), discharged soldiers, and employees of said Sanitary Commission; and no goods whatever for trading or commercial purposes will be carried on said boat, and no goods will be taken for individuals, or with any conditions which will prevent their being delivered to those most needing them in the army or navy.

3. The contents of all packages to be shipped on said U. S. Sanitary Store Boat will be inspected before shipment, by an agent of said Sanitary Commission, at the point of shipment, unless an invoice of their contents has been received, the correctness of which is assured by the signature of some person of known loyalty and integrity. A statement, showing what goods have been placed on board at each trip, will be sent to the Medical Director of the department at these headquarters.

4. A weekly statement will also be made by said Sanitary Commission to the department Medical Director, showing what sanitary supplies have been issued by said Commission, and to whom issued.

5. All orders authorizing the *free* transportation of sanitary stores from Cairo south, on boats other than the one herein provided for, are hereby rescinded.

By order of Major General U. S. GRANT.

JOHN A. RAWLINS, *A. A. G.*

Shortly before the movement of the forces below the works of Vicksburg, Admiral Farragut had run by the batteries at Port Hudson, with his flag-ship, the Hartford, and her tender the Albatross, and on March 17 was lying off Natchez. On March 21 the Hartford arrived off Vicksburg, and anchoring below the batteries, her commander communicated with General Grant and Admiral Porter. On the 25th of March, two rams, which had been made by altering river steamboats, the Lancaster and the Switzerland, attempted to run by the batteries of Vicksburg, but were found not strong enough to stand their heavy fire; the Lancaster was sunk, and the Switzerland temporarily disabled. Admiral Farragut descended the stream with his two vessels, engaging the batteries at Warrenton and Grand Gulf, and on the 2d of April arrived at the mouth of the Red River.

In the mean time the army kept on the move, and on the 30th of March reached Richmond, a village in Madison County, Louisiana, a few miles inland from the Mississippi River, and in a line with Vicksburg. Here a portion of the Thirteenth Corps, after two hours' sharp fighting, drove out the Confederate cavalry, and took possession of the place. From here to New Carthage the roads were in a frightfully bad condition, so much so that in places it was necessary to drag the wagons by hand; but the corps kept on, and, when within two miles of New Carthage, it was found that, by a breakage in the levee, the current had flowed in and made New Carthage an island. It would seem as though Fortune was heaping up all kinds of unforeseen difficulties in Grant's way; but his indomitable perseverance never wavered. Boats and barges were collected from the neighborhood, and built; but, this operation taking too much time, the troops were marched round by a detour, which made the distance from Milliken's Bend thirty-five miles. The roads were horrible, but Grant exemplified the old proverb, that "where there's a will there's a way."

The army was now upon the west side of the Mississippi, below Vicksburg; and to operate against that place it was necessary that they should cross the stream, and to do this the transports and barges, together with the gunboats to protect the landing, had to be run past the batteries. The successful performance of this difficult and dangerous task was one of the most brilliant operations of the war. On the 16th of April Admiral Porter was ready to make the first attempt. In this three transports were used, the Forest Queen, Henry Clay, and Silver Wave, which were loaded with supplies, and their machinery protected by bales of cotton and hay. Together with these, eight gunboats, all iron-clad except one, and all further protected with cotton and hay bales, formed the little fleet, to make the first trial, which took place at night. The plan of action was as follows: —

The gunboats were to proceed in single file, engaging the enemy's batteries if discovered and fired upon, while the transports were to try and slip down the stream under the cover of the smoke, between the gunboats and the opposite bank. It was between ten and eleven at night when they came round the bend of the river, and for a short time they supposed they were going to slip by unnoticed; but all of a sudden two sharp and brilliant lines of fire gave the signal, and in an instant the whole length of the bluff was ablaze with the lurid flames of cannon. The gunboats returned the fire bravely, and in an hour and a quarter the batteries were passed. The damage done was as follows: The Forest Queen had received a shot through her steam drum, but was towed safely past, and soon repaired. The Henry Clay was the worst sufferer. Her protection of cotton bales was set on fire, and she was abandoned, a blazing wreck, to float at the mercy of the stream. The fire of the gunboats so intimidated the batteries at Warrenton, that they scarcely responded.

Inspired by this success, six more transports were got ready, towing twelve barges loaded with forage; and these were run by on the night of the 22d of April. One of these transports was sunk, and five damaged, but only so that they were easily repaired, while one half of the forage was safely landed.

The dangerous task of manning the transports on these expeditions was done by volunteers, who responded enthusiastically to the call; and Grant remarks in his report, that as far as his observation goes, there is nothing which the volunteer army of the United States is called upon to do, "mechanical or professional, that accomplished adepts cannot be found for the duty required, in almost every regiment." No higher compliment could be paid to the character of our army, or to the character of the loyal population of the country, of whom the army was a fit representative. Its occupation and its interests are thus shown to be in productive labor, and a nation so employed cannot but be manly, honest, and fittest to lead in the civilization of the nineteenth century.

The number of the transports for the army being still inadequate, Grant determined to move his force, by a circuitous route, to Hard Times, on the Louisiana shore, just above Grand Gulf, making thus the distance traversed by the army, since leaving Milliken's Bend, about seventy miles. The next step was crossing the river, and then after the navy had silenced the batteries at Grand Gulf, the position was to be stormed by the Thirteenth Corps, under McClernand, which was the only portion of the army that had reached this point.

On the morning of the 29th of April, at eight o'clock, the fleet moved to the attack, while a portion of the corps was held in readiness to land. Grand Gulf was an exceedingly strong post, on a high bluff, just south of the Big Black River. Its batteries were arranged in tiers, and the range of hills was lined with rifle-pits. On a tug in the stream, General Grant watched the action of the navy, and was greatly struck with the bravery they displayed. Bringing their vessels within pistol shot of the batteries, for five hours and a half they delivered and received a perfect hail of shot and shell. The lower batteries were silenced, but the upper tiers were so high as to be out of range of the guns on the boats, and it being shown that they were too strong to be taken by assault, this plan was abandoned.

Before leaving the north side of Vicksburg, and taking command in person, General Grant, being desirous of cutting the enemy's communications with that city, and to secure his own forces from attacks in the rear, should he find it necessary to invest the place, determined to send a cavalry expedition which should pass round their lines, destroying the railroads. The command of this expedition was intrusted to Colonel H. B. Grierson, of the First Cavalry Brigade.

On the 17th of April, 1863, this force left La Grange, Tennessee, about two in the morning, and after a series of most brilliantly daring adventures, the details of which would require almost a volume to do them justice, entered Baton Rouge about noon on Friday, the 1st of May. The value of this expedition can hardly be appreciated, but the following data may give some idea of it. In fifteen days this force had marched over six hundred miles, through the very heart of the enemy's country, had destroyed over four million dollars' worth of property, broken all the railroad communications, captured over five hundred prisoners and twelve hundred horses, and menaced the enemy at points where they thought themselves most secure — while its total loss from all causes was only twenty-four.

The announcement of the successful issue of the expedition was given to the country by General Grant in the following despatch: —

GRAND GULF, MISS., May 6.

MAJOR GENERAL HALLECK, *General-in-Chief.*

I learn that Colonel Grierson, with his cavalry, has been heard of, first about ten days ago, in Northern Mississippi.

He moved thence and struck the railroad thirty miles east of Jackson, at a point called Newton's Station.

He then moved southward towards Enterprise, demanded the surrender of the place, and gave one hour's grace, during which General Lormniey arrived.

He left at once, and moved towards Hazelhurst, on the New Orleans and Jackson Railroad. At this point he tore up the track. Thence he pushed to Bahala, ten miles farther south, on the same road, and thence eastward, on the Natchez road, where he had a fight with Wirt Adams's cavalry.

From this point he moved back to the New Orleans and Jackson Railroad, to Brookhaven, ten miles south of Bahala; and when last heard from, he was three miles from Summit, ten miles south of Brookhaven, and was supposed to be making his way to Baton Rouge.

He had spread excitement throughout the state, destroying railroads, trestle-works, and bridges, burning locomotives and railway stock, taking prisoners, and destroying stores of all kinds.

U. S. GRANT, *Major General.*

## CHAPTER XVIII.

ANOTHER ATTEMPT. — A FOOTING GAINED. — SHERMAN'S FEINT.

FINDING that Grand Gulf could not be taken by assault, the troops were again landed at Hard Times, and then marched across the upper end of Coffee's Point and De Shroon's plantation, to the Louisiana shore of the Mississippi, below Grand Gulf, and opposite Bruinsburg, while the navy and transports ran the batteries and joined them. A reconnoitring party having been sent to examine the best point for crossing the river, General McClernand reported on the 17th of June, that Bruinsburg was such a point; so that on the 30th of June, his corps was carried across the stream, and started, with three days' rations, to reach, as soon as possible, the high land, and succeeded in forming a line without meeting any resistance.

The advance was now upon the Vicksburg side of the river, and everything depended upon promptness, since success could be guaranteed only in this way. This plan of action was so daring, that its feasibility was doubted by the authorities at Washington, and it did not meet the views of many of Grant's own officers. Sherman went even so far as to present a written protest against it, though expressed in the friendliest terms. This fact appears from Sherman's own magnanimous declaration, after the capture of Vicksburg, and when the credit of this successful plan was attributed to himself. It is certain, however, that the conception of this plan belongs entirely to Grant, and his persistence and self-confidence, based upon a consciousness of gènius, the highest quality of a military commander, and the touchstone of which is success, is shown in his determination to carry it out, even against the opinion of all those about him. This determination is equalled only by Grant's modesty and want of ambition, since, but for Sherman's declaration, the credit of the plan could not have been with certainty given to him; for, if on no other grounds, his kind consideration for Sherman, his dearest friend, would have prevented him from ever claiming his own. The tender and exalted friendship, the mutual respect, recognition, and admiration, which exist between these two great men, are as fine an evidence of the nobility human nature is capable of, as can be culled from the pages of Plutarch, or any other record of the world's history. But if this plan of action was against the judgment of Grant's subordinates, most nobly and heartily did they aid him in its execution: there was no small jealousy among this body of men; their hearts and souls were in the work, and each did all he could to help the common cause. Herein also Grant has shown that he possesses the rare quality of judiciously selecting those upon whose aid he must rely, and then, by the generous magnanimity with which he treats them, infusing his own spirit into them. As the tyrant always produces a brood of sycophants and hypocrites, as slavery fosters only all the petty vices in the slave, so only freedom produces the manly virtues of freemen, and a nobly great man, whose life is justice, fosters only the best qualities in those he has about him.

The Seventeenth Corps followed as soon as possible, and Grant himself arrived also the same day. The enemy were first met eight miles from Bruinsburg, on the night of the 30th, and were driven back a considerable distance. The next morning they were met in force, about four miles from Port Gibson, and thirteen from Bruinsburg, strongly posted, under Major General Bowen, where two roads met, both leading, by detours to the right and left, to Port Gibson. The position was one where a small force could resist the advance of a large one. The roads were upon ridges, and the country upon each side was broken with ravines. The battle was immediately joined, and lasted about all day, but at evening our forces were successful. The Confederates fled, thoroughly defeated, across Bayou Pierre, towards Grand Gulf, destroying, in their flight, the bridges over this stream. On the next day, however, a new floating bridge was built by McPherson, and the army passed over in pursuit, to the banks of the Big Black River. The Confederates, in crossing this stream, attempted to destroy the pontoon bridge over which they had passed, but were prevented from so doing by our sharp-shooters.

This part of the army was now seven miles beyond Grand Gulf, and within eighteen miles of Vicksburg. From an examination of some prisoners captured, it was learned that Grand Gulf had been evacuated, and the magazine blown up. Proceeding with a few men to Grand Gulf, Grant found this to be the case, and made the necessary arrangements for changing his base of supplies from Bruinsburg to this place. The following modest report of the results thus gained was sent by General Grant to the department at Washington: —

GRAND GULF, MISS., May 3, 1863.

MAJOR GENERAL HALLECK, *General-in-Chief.*

We landed at Bruinsburg April 30, moved immediately on Port Gibson, met the enemy, eleven thousand strong, four miles south of Port Gibson, at two o'clock, A. M., on the 1st instant, and engaged him all day, entirely routing him, with the loss of many killed, and about five hundred prisoners, besides the wounded. Our loss is about one hundred killed and five hundred wounded.

The enemy retreated towards Vicksburg, destroying the bridges over the two forks of the Bayou Pierre. These were rebuilt, and the pursuit has continued until the present time.

Besides the heavy artillery at the place, four field-pieces were captured, and some stores, and the enemy were driven to destroy many more.

The country is the most broken and difficult to operate in I ever saw.

Our victory has been most complete, and the enemy is thoroughly demoralized.

Very respectfully,

U. S. GRANT, *Major General commanding.*

On the 4th of May Governor Yates, of Illinois, who was with the army, and who, it will be remembered, was the first to perceive and employ Grant's military ability, wrote from Grand Gulf as follows: "Our arms are gloriously triumphant. We have succeeded in winning a victory which, in its results, must be the most important of the war. On my way to Grand Gulf I saw guns scattered all along the road, which the enemy had left in their retreat. I consider Vicksburg as ours in a short time, and the Mississippi River as destined to be open from its source to its mouth."

The same night that Grand Gulf was occupied, several barges were sent past the batteries of Vicksburg; but the fire upon them was so heavy that they were set on fire by shells bursting in the midst of the cotton and hay, and those on board were compelled to surrender.

In order to divert the enemy's attention, and occupy a portion of his force elsewhere, General Grant ordered Sherman to make a feint upon Haine's Bluff, at the same time that he made his landing at Bruinsburg. Sherman's orders were received on the 28th of April, and proceeding up the Yazoo, he was at the mouth of the Chickasaw on the evening of the 29th; and the next day, the fleet, proceeding to within an easy range of the works, kept up an active fire for four hours. That evening Sherman disembarked his troops, in full view of the enemy, and made preparations as though to assault the works. Keeping up this show, the object of which was successfully gained, as was evident from the activity the Confederates displayed in moving their guns, bringing up their forces, and in various ways preparing for a desperate resistance, the troops were reëmbarked that night, and the next day was spent in making similar movements on both sides of the Yazoo. Then, quietly dropping back to Young's Point, the whole corps, with the exception of a garrison left at this place, marched to Hard Times, on the Louisiana shore, four miles above Grand Gulf, arriving there on the morning of the 6th of May, having marched sixty-three miles. During that night and the next day they were carried across the stream, and on the 8th commenced their march into the interior.

Both Sherman and Grant were aware that the army could discriminate between a feint and a genuine attack, and that their spirit would not be depressed by a seeming repulse; and the result showed that they had exactly understood the character of the men under their command.

In his report Grant shows that he felt the importance of prompt action, by the following allusion to a proposition he received from General Banks, who proposed to join him with twelve thousand men. Time was, however, of more importance than any prospective reënforcement. The iron was to be struck when hot.

"About this time (May 4) I received a letter from General Banks, giving his position west of the Mississippi River, and stating that he could return to Baton Rouge by the 10th of May; that by the reduction of Port Hudson he could join me with twelve thousand men.

"I learned, about the same time, that troops were expected at Jackson from the southern cities, with General Beauregard in command. To delay until the 10th of May, and for the reduction of Port Hudson after that, the accession of twelve thousand men would not leave me relatively so strong as to move promptly with what I had. Information, received from day to day, of the movements of the enemy, also impelled me to the course I pursued."

## CHAPTER XIX.

THE DEFENCES OF VICKSBURG.—A REPETITION OF STRATEGY IN ACTION.—MISSISSIPPI ELOQUENCE, AND ITS RESULTS.

HAVING now succeeded in establishing a foothold, before we attempt to follow Grant in his movements, it will be well to glance at the obstacles in the way of his approach. The town of Vicksburg is situated on a sharp bend, or bow, in the river, on a high line of bluffs, extending from Haine's Bluff, touching the Yazoo, on the north, to a point below Warrenton on the south, a distance of about fifteen miles. The river front was impregnable, and was, as we have seen, considered so by General Grant. Perhaps immediately after the fall of New Orleans it might have been carried, but the Confederates had been too busily engaged since then in strengthening its defences.

On the land side, at the time of Grant's approach, it was hardly less formidable. Pierre Bayou, with its steep banks, formed an outer line of defence; then came the Big Black River, with its tributaries, the Big Sandy, Five-mile, Fourteen-mile, and Baker's Creeks: besides this, the city itself was surrounded with defensive works, constructed with great skill, and taking every advantage of the natural strength of the position. It seemed, and was afterwards proved, that nothing but an attack by overwhelming numbers, secure from any interference by a succoring army, and able by a regular investment and siege to starve the defending army into surrender, could hope to obtain possession of the place. Yet this was the work Grant had proposed to himself and his army.

The defence of Vicksburg was intrusted to Lieutenant General John C. Pemberton, with about sixty thousand men. Having secured his position, General Grant went personally to Grand Gulf, to superintend the landing of supplies, and found that the Confederates had retreated in such haste as to leave behind them thirteen heavy guns. A careful study of the operations of the war which were carried on in Grant's department, affords more and more conclusive proof of how much the efficiency of the armies under his command depended upon his unwearied activity and his minute supervision. He was indefatigable, and inspired this quality in all of his subordinates. Computing the amount of work he did, the despatches he wrote, the orders he gave, the hours he must have spent in making himself personally almost ubiquitous, it seems nearly impossible that he could have found time to do so much in the short twenty-four hours of the day.

On the 8th of May, Sherman having reached him, the main army was at once marched forward to the Big Sandy. An army was gathering, under Johnston, to aid Pemberton, by operating upon Grant's rear, and he conceived the plan of cutting away from his base, and by deceiving Pemberton, hold him in check, then quickly advance upon Jackson, the capital of the state, at which place Johnston was posted, and be back in time to meet Pemberton outside of Vicksburg. It was a repetition of the bold tactics at Côrinth. The plan, however, when proposed, met with nothing but opposition from his subordinates. Grant, however, had learned from his experience at Holly Springs, that it was possible to support his army, without a base of supplies, from the enemy's country.

Meanwhile the Confederates were making every effort to raise all the troops possible, since they had become thoroughly alarmed at the situation. The governor of Mississippi, John J. Pettus, issued from Jackson, the capital of the state, a proclamation containing the following extracts: —

"Recent events, familiar to you all, impel me, as your chief magistrate, to appeal to your patriotism *for united effort in expelling our enemies from the soil of Mississippi. It can and must be done.* Let no man capable of bearing arms withhold from his state his services in repelling the invasion. Duty, interest, our common safety, demand every sacrifice necessary for the protection of our homes, our honor, liberty itself.

"The exalted position won in her name upon every battle-field where Mississippi's sons have unfurled her proud banner, and hurled defiance in the face of overwhelming numbers, forbids that her honor, the chivalry of her people, the glory of her daring deeds on foreign fields, should be tarnished, and her streaming battle-flag dragged to the dust, by barbarian hordes on her own soil.

"Awake, then; arouse, Mississippians, young and old,

from your fertile plains, your beautiful towns and cities, your once quiet and happy, but now desecrated homes; come and join your brothers in arms, your sons and neighbors, who are now baring their bosoms to the storm of battle at your very doors, and in defence of all you hold dear.

"Meet in every county with your arms; organize companies of not less than twenty (under the late act of Congress), forward your muster-rolls to this office, and you will be received into the service with all the protection and rights belonging to other soldiers in the field. Fathers, brothers, Mississippians! while your sons and kindred are bravely fighting your battles on other fields, and shedding new lustre on your name, the burning disgrace of successful invasion of their homes, of insult and injury to their wives, mothers, and sisters, of rapine and ruin, with God's help, and by your assistance, shall never be written while a Mississippian lives to feel in his proud heart the scorching degradation. Let no man forego the proud distinction of being one of his country's defenders, or hereafter wear the disgraceful badge of the dastardly traitor who refused to defend his home and his country."

Before Grant's army started on their expedition, the following congratulatory order was read at the head of every regiment, which the curiously accurate reader may compare with the one from which we have just given extracts, and by the comparison obtain some assistance in arriving at the spirit and motives which actuated the two armies:—

HEADQUARTERS ARMY OF THE TENNESSEE.
IN THE FIELD, HANKINSON'S FERRY, May 7.

SOLDIERS OF THE ARMY OF TENNESSEE: Once more I thank you for adding another victory to the long list of those previously won by your valor and endurance. *The triumph gained over the enemy near Port Gibson, on the* 1*st*, *was one of the most important of the war.* The capture of five cannon and more than one thousand prisoners, the possession of Grand Gulf, and a firm foothold on the highlands between the Big Black and Bayou Pierre, from whence we threaten the whole line of the enemy, are among the fruits of this brilliant achievement.

*The march from Milliken's Bend to the point opposite Grand Gulf was made in stormy weather, over the worst of roads. Bridges and ferries had to be constructed. Moving by night as well as by day, with labor incessant, and extraordinary privations endured by men and officers, such as have been rarely paralleled in any campaign, not a murmur of complaint has been uttered.* A few days' continuance of the same zeal and constancy will secure to this army crowning victories over the rebellion.

More difficulties and privations are before us; let us endure them manfully. Other battles are to be fought; let us fight them bravely. *A grateful country will rejoice at our success, and history will record it with immortal honor.*

U. S. GRANT, *Major General commanding.*

On his arrival at Rocky Springs, after leaving Hankinson's Ferry, Grant learned that the Confederates were concentrating at Edwards's Station, about twenty-five miles distant on the Vicksburg and Jackson Railway, and therefore resolved to keep as close to the Black River as possible, with McClernand's and Sherman's corps, and strike the railway somewhere between Edwards's Station and Bolton. McPherson, meanwhile, was to move by way of Utica to Raymond, thence to Jackson, destroying the railway, telegraph, &c., and then to join the main force by pushing west. By this means he would avoid fighting with Pemberton on the ground of his own selection, would keep his troops within distance for mutual protection, and at the same time divide the enemy by striking between Pemberton and the force at Jackson.

To deceive the enemy as to his intentions, was one of Grant's great objects, and, as we shall see, he succeeded thoroughly. On the 10th of May Grant heard again from Banks, earnestly asking reënforcements for his operations on the Red River, and replied, "It was my intention, on gaining a foothold at Grand Gulf, to have sent a sufficient force to Port Hudson to have assured the fall of that place, with your coöperation, or rather to have coöperated with you to that end. Meeting the enemy as I did below Port Gibson, however, I followed him to the Big Black, and could not afford to retrace my steps. Many days cannot elapse before the battle will begin which is to decide the fate of Vicksburg, but it is impossible to predict how long it may last. I would urgently request, therefore, that you join me, or send all the force you can spare, to coöperate in the great struggle for opening the Mississippi."

On the 11th of May Grant wrote to Halleck from Cayuga, "My forces will be this evening as far advanced towards Jackson as Fourteen-mile Creek, the left near Black River, and extending as nearly east and west as they can get without bringing on a battle. As I shall communicate with Grand Gulf no more, except it becomes necessary to send a train with heavy escort, you may not hear from me again for several days." Curiously enough, this was the date of a despatch from Halleck to Grant, to return and coöperate with Banks.

Fortunately the despatch did not come in time to prevent the move.

On the same day McPherson, who was now beyond Utica, was ordered, "Move your command to-night to the next cross roads, if there is water, and to-morrow with all activity into Raymond. We must fight the enemy before our rations fail, and we are equally bound to make our rations last as long as possible. Upon one occasion you made two days' rations last seven. We may have to do the same thing again."

On the 12th, at about 11 A. M., McPherson came upon the enemy, about five thousand strong, within two miles of Raymond. The lines were formed, and at two in the afternoon the advance was ordered; and before the reserves under Crocker, who was ordered up when the enemy were first discovered, reached the field, the Confederates were defeated and flying in disorder, and at five the army entered Raymond. Pemberton had been completely deceived. Supposing that Grant was advancing upon Edwards's Station, he waited there to receive him, and on the 12th telegraphed to Jefferson Davis, "That will be the battle-place." Instead, however, of assaulting the main Confederate army concentrating to meet him on his left, Grant pushed out his right, destroyed the opposition at Raymond, avoided a battle where he was expected, fought the enemy where they did not expect him, and opened the road for Jackson. The Confederates retreated direct to Jackson, where Johnston next day took command, having just arrived upon the ground. This flight confirmed Grant in his opinion, that a strong force of the enemy was at Jackson, on his right, and he immediately resolved to deflect his entire force in that direction. This place was also a railroad centre, and its destruction as such would be of great value in preventing any future concentration to interfere with his future plans.

On the night of the 13th Johnston arrived at Jackson, and found his available force about eleven thousand men. In addition to these, twelve or thirteen thousand more were on their way to join him from the east, for he had urged the Confederate government to make every exertion to aid him in preserving Vicksburg and the Mississippi. He also ordered Pemberton to come up from Edwards's Station, and attack Grant in the rear. "If practicable," he writes on the 13th, "come up in his rear at once. To beat such a detachment would be of immense value. All the troops you can quickly assemble should be brought. Time is all-important."

Sherman arrived at Raymond before McPherson left it, and was ordered to take immediately the southern road to Jackson. During this day McClernand also withdrew from his position near Edwards's Station, where his pickets had been within two miles of Pemberton's army. A portion of his force was drawn up in line of battle, and behind them the remainder retired, so that the movement was not discovered until too late to interfere. This force was then marched near to Raymond, where they were in position to coöperate with the others. That night Grant remained at Raymond, and on the morning of the 14th sent by a courier to Grand Gulf the first report he had made to Halleck since leaving that post, in which he ends by saying, "I will attack the state capital to-day."

GRANT AND HIS STAFF ENTERING JACKSON.

At nine in the morning the pickets of McPherson's corps engaged the enemy about five miles out of Jackson. While dispositions were making for the attack, a heavy rain storm set in, which came down in such torrents that the battle was deferred an hour and a half, for fear of spoiling the ammunition if the cartridge-boxes were opened. During this time, however, the positions for the forces were selected. About eleven, the rain having ceased, McPherson's line advanced, and the Confederates broke and fled, followed by our men, to within the range of the artillery in the defences of the city. Sherman meanwhile had advanced until checked by a line of intrenchments. Grant, who had been with Sherman all the morning, ordered a detachment sent to the right of this line to reconnoitre it; but as they did not return speedily, he rode to the right himself, accompanied only by his staff, and found the road open into the city. The enemy had abandoned the place, and Grant, with his officers, rode into the works. His son, a boy of thirteen, who was with his father through this campaign, spurred on his horse as the party reached the limits of the town, and was the first to enter the capital of the State of Mississippi, from which, a few days before, the grandiloquent proclamation for its defence had been dated by its now fleeing governor. The "scorching degradation" and "burning disgrace" of successful invasion were "written," while many of the Mississippians still lived.

By three the army was in possession of Jackson, and that night Grant slept in the house occupied by Johnston the night before. That afternoon Grant gave his further orders to his commanders from the State House.

Sherman was ordered to destroy the railroads, which he did most effectually, north, south, east, and west, for a distance of twenty miles. All the bridges, manufactories, arsenals, and everything which could be of use to the Confederates, were destroyed, and the importance of Jackson as a railroad centre for the concentration of troops and supplies was annihilated. There was slight pillaging by our soldiers, who had found some bad liquor; a hotel was burned, called the Confederate Hotel; but there was good excuse for this, since it was done by a party who had been led as prisoners through Jackson, but were soon after exchanged, and now returned as victors. On their previous visit they had been halted before this hotel, and on asking for water, had been refused with abuse and jeers. Here some of our soldiers, taking peaceful possession of the deserted State House, enacted a farcical burlesque of the Mississippi legislature, showing in so doing an adaptability for wit and humor which equalled their valor and endurance.

After leaving Jackson, Johnston retreated about six miles on the Canton road, and then encamped. From here he sent despatches to the approaching reënforcements to assemble at a point forty or fifty miles from Jackson, and also to Pemberton, giving information of the capture of Jackson, and saying, "As soon as the reënforcements are all up, they must be united to the rest of the army. I am anxious to see a force assembled that may be able to inflict a heavy blow upon the enemy." In the same despatch he asks whether Grant "could supply himself from the Mississippi. Can you not cut him off from it, and above all, should he be compelled to fall back for want of supplies, beat him?"

Grant had, however, cut himself off from the Mississippi, and for a week had obtained his supplies from the country, since with the exception of a train of two hundred wagons, which had set out from Grand Gulf on the 12th, and guarded by a division of Sherman's corps, under Blair, had arrived just before the battle, and the rations he had started with, he had nothing else to depend on.

## CHAPTER XX.

### THE BATTLE OF CHAMPION'S HILL. — PEMBERTON DRIVEN INTO VICKSBURG.

ON the 16th Grant had his divisions on the march to concentrate at Edwards's Depot, whence Pemberton, having disregarded Johnston's order to attack Grant, had finally set out for Dillon's, to cut Grant's communications, but on the 16th, having received positive orders from Johnston to unite with him by marching directly to Clinton, was now returning in order to obey. The persons from whom Grant received the intelligence that Pemberton's army was here, had passed through it the night before, and estimated the force at twenty-five thousand men. Up to this time it had been intended to leave one division of Sherman's corps still another day at Jackson, in order to complete the destruction of the railways and stores; but he was now ordered to move promptly to the support of the main army. "It is important," Grant writes, "that the greatest celerity should be shown in carrying out this movement, as I have evidence that the entire force of the enemy was at Edwards's Depot at seven P. M. last night, and still advancing. The fight may therefore be brought on at any moment. We should have every man in the field." In an hour from the reception of this order Sherman had his division in motion.

There are three roads leading from Raymond to Edwards's Station, known as the Southern, Middle, and Northern roads. McClernand was ordered to move the troops under Blair and A. J. Smith by the Southern road, to place Carr and Osterhaus on the Middle road, and Hovey on the Northern, which is the direct road from Bolton to Edwards's Station. This done, he was to feel the enemy with a line of skirmishers, but not to bring on a general engagement unless he felt certain of success. A messenger was sent to McClernand, to explain the situation to him, and urge him to come up promptly. At about seven, Smith's division was met by the rebel skirmishers on the Southern road, about a mile and a half from Edwards's Station. Hearing the guns, Osterhaus pressed forward on the Middle road, drove in a line of skirmishers, and uncovered the enemy in force. At about half past six, McPherson, having heard from Hovey that he had met the enemy in force, sent to Grant a despatch: "I think it advisable for you to come forward to the front as soon as you can." Seeing that a battle was imminent, and that McClernand was the ranking officer in front, McPherson preferred, as he afterwards explained, that Grant should be there in person.

The enemy was strongly posted, with his left upon Champion's Hill, over which the road to Edwards's Station runs. This hill is a ridge, rising sixty or seventy feet above the surrounding country, and its top, which was bare, made a commanding point for their artillery; the thick woods and deep ravines, however, covered the rest of the ridge, and made it a difficult matter to manœuvre troops. The Confederate line was about four miles long, running southward upon this ridge, its centre covering the Middle road, while its right was on the Southern road. Champion's Hill, on their left, was evidently the key of their position. The Confederate force, by Pemberton's report, was seventeen thousand five hundred men; but Grant estimated it at at least twenty-five; and this is evidently nearer the truth, as was seen afterwards by the numbers which were surrendered at Vicksburg. By eleven the firing between the skirmishers grew into a battle, and Hovey with his division gained the crest of the hill. The enemy, however, receiving reënforcements rapidly, recaptured the position; but fresh troops being sent to Hovey, he again carried the crest. This operation was again repeated, and with the aid of Logan's division, who turned the enemy's left, and threatened to cut off his line of retreat, between three and four in the afternoon the rout was complete.

While the battle was fighting, McClernand, despite Grant's repeated despatches to move promptly, was delaying through excess of caution, and consequently did not arrive on the ground until the battle was over. It is said that even during the pursuit, "when the beaten enemy came headlong across his front, McClernand, supposing this an assault, developed his troops, and prepared to receive a flank attack from the pell-mell fugitives."

In Hovey's and McPherson's commands, who did the whole of the fighting, Grant had about fifteen thousand men, all of whom took part in the battle, and were under fire. Our loss was severe — about twenty-five hundred killed, wounded, and missing. The enemy's was, however, greater; besides which, one of the divisions of the Confederate force, under Loring, which held the right of their line, and, being in McClernand's front, had not been seriously engaged, became separated from the rest of the army by the rapidity of Grant's advance after the battle, and, abandoning all their artillery, set out in the night to join Johnston, and, making a wide detour, succeeded in doing so after several days, having lost largely by desertion during the march. This entire division was thus taken from Pemberton's command. It appears that Pemberton had found, during the engagement, the same trouble with Loring that Grant found with McClernand — though he repeatedly sent him orders to come to the assistance of the left, he could not get him to stir, and the result was as we have stated above.

The rout of the Confederates was complete: two batteries of six guns each were left in their flight, and the ground was strewed with evidences of the precipitancy of their retreat. The Seventeenth Corps continued the pursuit until dark, while Hovey remained on the field. "The heroes slept on the field they had so dearly won. Men, horses, cannon, and all the wrecks of the battle were scattered around in wild confusion; rebels and Union men heaped upon each other, dead and dying; their struggles ended, their hot rage all chilled. The soldiers called the spot the 'Hill of Death.'"

Grant and his staff pushed on at the head of the column in pursuit until long after dark, and halted for the night at a house, when soon finding their position was unsafe, they returned, and passed the night in the vicinity of the column which was just going into bivouac on the road, under the porch of a house used as a Confederate field hospital. This night Grant received the despatch from Halleck, ordering him to return and cooperate with Banks. But the campaign was won.

At the time of the battle, Pemberton was on his way to join Johnston, and in a despatch to this last describing the route he was taking, he says, "I am thus particular, that you may be able to make a junction with this army;" adding in a postscript, "Heavy skirmishing now going on in my front." His next despatch to Johnston announced that he had been "compelled to fall back with heavy loss." The celerity of Grant's movements had enabled him to defeat both armies before they could combine.

Sherman left Jackson on the 16th, and was in Bolton the same day. That night he was informed of the victory at Champion's Hill, and ordered to march to Bridgeport without delay. Blair's corps was ordered to move to the same point by way of Edwards's Station, carrying the pontoon train with it; and by this arrangement Sherman's force was brought together at the best point for crossing the Big Black, and turning the enemy's flank, or striking Haine's Bluff, which was now a point of great importance, since the establishment of a base of supplies was a matter of urgent necessity. Though forage and beef had been found in great abundance in the country, other supplies were getting short. The main column pushed on the direct route for Vicksburg, and would thus be able to attack the flank of any force attempting to confront Sherman, or to defend Haine's Bluff, while, if the Confederates should oppose Grant in front, Sherman could cut off their retreat to Vicksburg, by interposing in their rear.

To Sherman Grant wrote, "I will endeavor to hold the enemy where he is, to give you time to cross the river, if it can be effected. The moment the enemy gives way, I will endeavor to follow him so closely that he will not be able to destroy the bridge."

At half past three on the morning of the 17th, the pursuit was resumed, and the enemy was found in force, strongly posted at the bridge over the Big Black. The stream at this point flows in a horse-shoe bend, the opening towards the east, while on the western shore high bluffs rise from the water's edge. The opening of the curve on the eastern side is about a mile wide, making a low, level bottom, surrounded by a stagnant bayou nearly twenty feet wide and two or three deep. Inside of this bayou, making a natural ditch, the Confederates had made a line of intrenchments, defended by twenty guns and a garrison of four thousand men — as many as could be used to advantage in the space. The intrenchments were commanded by the bluffs on the opposite side of the river, though the open space between them and the stream had no cover. The main body of the Confederate army had crossed. The pursuit having come up, the position was invested, and the flank being turned, the line of defence was carried by storm. Our men vied with each other in valor, being inspired by success, and friendlily emulous of each other's glory. The supports charged as soon as they saw the assaulting column start, and the Confederates, disheartened by the defeat of the day before, were completely demoralized, and broke and fled in confusion. Pemberton himself says, "Our troops on their front did not wait to receive them, but broke and fled precipitately. One portion of the line being broken, it very soon became a question of *sauve qui peut*." The troops on the other side of the river shared the panic, and set fire to their end of the bridge before those on the eastern side had crossed. A wild struggle to save themselves commenced, in which all distinctions of rank were lost, and only the blind instinct of life ruled. One entire brigade remained in the trenches, and surrendered. Seventeen hundred and fifty-one prisoners, eighteen cannon, and five stands of colors fell into our hands here.

Pemberton began to fear for Vicksburg. The rapidity of Grant's movements completely bewildered him. His report said, "The enemy, by a flank movement on my left at Bridgeport, and on my right by Baldwin's or other ferries, might reach Vicksburg almost simultaneously with myself, or perhaps interpose a heavy force between me and that city. I myself proceeded at once to Vicksburg to prepare for its defence."

The destruction of the bridge gave the Confederates twelve hours' start, for the Big Black is here wide and deep. During the day Grant sent the following to Sherman: "Secure a commanding position on the west bank of Black River, as soon as you can. If the information you gain after crossing warrants you in believing you can go immediately into the city, do so. If there is any doubt in this matter, throw out troops to the left, after advancing on a line with the railroad bridge, to open your communications with the troops here. We will then move in three columns, if roads can be found to move on, and either have Vicksburg or Haine's Bluff to-morrow night. The enemy have been so terribly beaten yesterday and to-day, that I cannot believe that a stand will be made, unless the troops are relying on Johnston's arriving with large reënforcements; nor that Johnston would attempt to reënforce with anything at his command, if he was at all aware of the present condition of things."

The labor on the bridges was continued all night, and on the morning of the 18th, at eight, the Thirteenth and Seventeenth Corps were again on the march for Vicksburg. On the 17th, at noon, Sherman reached Bridgeport, and found Blair with the pontoon train there. There was a body of Confederates intrenched on the other side of the stream; but on the appearance of the national forces, they displayed a white flag and retired. The pontoon bridge was laid, the troops passed over, and at daylight next morning, the 18th, Sherman pushed rapidly forward, and at half past nine the head of his column struck the Benton road, three and a half miles from Vicksburg, thus interposing a superior force between that place and the forts on the Yazoo.

When this column struck the hills, Grant was riding with Sherman, and together they mounted the farthest height, from which they looked down upon the Yazoo, and from which Sherman had been repulsed six months before. The two friends gazed in silence upon the goal they had so long desired, the high, dry ground to the north of Vicksburg, and the base for their supplies, when suddenly Sherman, turning to Grant, said, "Until this moment I never thought your expedition a success. I never could see the end clearly until now. But this is a campaign; this is a success, if we never take the town." To this the other made no response save his usual one of smoking his cigar in quiet. During the campaign, Sherman, with his corps, had not been much engaged in the active fighting, though they had had more than their share of the marching; and therefore he had not been stirred with the enthusiasm of success which victory gives. Now, however, he saw the results, and recognized the brilliancy and accuracy of conception on the part of his chief, with an enthusiasm as great as the imperturbable self-confidence of the leader.

## CHAPTER XXI.

VICKSBURG INVESTED.—THE UNSUCCESSFUL ASSAULTS.—THE REGULAR SIEGE BEGUN.

GRANT now directed Sherman to push on and occupy the right, while McPherson held the centre and McClernand the left. Sherman pushed forward his column, and by dark had reached the bluffs of the Mississippi. Possession was taken early next morning of the enemy's outer works, and many prisoners were made of those left behind in the hasty evacuation of his camps. At eight in the morning of the 19th of May, the north side of Vicksburg was encompassed, our right resting on the banks of the Mississippi, in full view of the fleet at the mouth of the Yazoo, and only about four hundred yards separating our lines from the line of Confederate intrenchments. The other portions of the troops were as successfully disposed, and on the 19th the siege of Vicksburg began.

Haine's Bluff was also immediately occupied, for the enemy had of course abandoned this stronghold as soon as Grant had pushed himself between it and Vicksburg. Chickasaw Landing was made a base of supplies, and roads built for bringing them up.

It was just twenty days since the campaign had begun. In that time Grant had marched more than two hundred miles, beaten two armies in five several battles, captured twenty-seven heavy cannon, sixty-one pieces of field artillery, taken six thousand five hundred prisoners, and put at least six thousand more Confederates *hors de combat.* He had forced the evacuation of Grand Gulf, captured Jackson, the capital of Mississippi, destroyed the railways for more than thirty miles, and invested the chief stronghold of the Confederacy on the Mississippi. Starting without teams, and with only ten days' rations, he had found his wagons and supplies in the country. Only five days' rations had been issued in the whole twenty days, yet there was no want or complaining in his army; and his entire loss had been four thousand three hundred and thirty-five. In this campaign Grant first displayed his original system of warfare in a conspicuous way. War in the western country was as different an affair from war in Europe, as the condition of the country and the character and life of the people differ from those in Europe. The country there is all known, and the Generals can study the movements of their own and the opposing armies as easily as they can study out a problem in chess. Here, however, much of the country is a wilderness, and the first surveys of it were made by the armies in the field; here, too, the country is not covered with a network of roads. The railroad runs through forests in order to connect villages, and is frequently the only means of communication for large tracts of country. Grant in this campaign showed his full appreciation of the strategical importance of the railroad. Here, too, he first put into practice the idea of living upon the country, and made the suggestion of Sherman's final campaign possible. In his ability also to plan a military combination, to appreciate the value of promptness and celerity in his movements, he showed himself a master mind. In fathoming also his adversaries' plans, judging what their course of action would be, in certain circumstances, from the character of the men themselves, he again showed himself a master; while in his power of infusing his spirit into his subordinates, gaining the enthusiastic confidence of his men, and influencing inversely his opponents, he showed himself unquestionably the most capable General the war had as yet produced.

The siege of Vicksburg was now commenced. The line of the rebel defences of the city was seven or eight miles long, exclusive of those on the water front. It consisted of a series of detached works, on prominent points, connected by a continuous line of trenches or rifle-pits. This line was, from the nature of the ground, irregular, and the works were placed at distances of from seventy-five to five hundred yards from each other. In fact, Vicksburg was rather an intrenched camp than a regularly fortified town, while the broken nature of the ground, making all attempts at rapidity and unity of movement impossible, made it a place of unusual strength. This evident strength of its defences, both natural and artificial, was well calculated to inspire new courage in an army, even though it had retired to the place after a series of defeats in the open field. This was found to be the case with Pemberton's men. Here they met some eight thousand troops, who had been left as the garrison, who had not therefore been demoralized by the recent defeats; and so no wonder that Pemberton felt, with his thirty thousand men, his two hundred cannon, well able to stand a siege, at least until Johnston should have time enough to collect another army and come to his relief.

On the 18th of May, however, while Grant was still advancing on the Jackson road, Pemberton received a despatch from Johnston, who had learned that he had been driven back into Vicksburg, as follows: "If Haine's Bluff be untenable, Vicksburg is of no value, and cannot be held. If, therefore, you are invested at Vicksburg, you must ultimately surrender. Under such circumstances, instead of losing both troops and place, you must, if possible, save the troops. If it is not too late, evacuate Vicksburg and its dependencies, and march to the north east."

Pemberton, on the receipt of this order, called a council of war, composed of all his general officers, to deliberate on the propriety of obeying. The unanimous opinion of this council was that "to withdraw from Vicksburg with such *morale* and *matériel* as to be of further use to the Confederacy, would be impossible." Pemberton therefore decided to remain, and did so.

Grant had at this time about thirty thousand men. His troops were flushed with success, and eager to carry the place by assault. He therefore, on the 19th, the first day of the investment, ordered his corps commanders to "push forward carefully, and gain positions as close as possible to the enemy's works, until two o'clock, P. M.; at that hour they will fire three volleys of artillery from all the pieces in position. This will be the signal for a general charge along the whole line." This assault was unsuccessful; the troops penetrated as far as possible, but were unable to make a permanent lodgment, and were forced to fall back. The result, however, of the attempt was of great value. It served to show the nature of the ground, and the obstacles to be overcome, and it showed that to take the place by assault was impossible.

The 20th and 21st of May were devoted to looking after the comfort of the army — bringing up supplies, a change of clothes, and bread, of which the army had felt the want: communications were opened, new roads laid, and all the needed arrangements for a besieging camp made. McClernand was ordered to open his communications with Warrenton, and for a time drew his supplies from there. On the 20th the mortar fleet was brought into position, and on that and the next day bombarded the city, but met with little response from the artillery in the defences; for Pemberton was desirous of saving his ammunition, and had forbidden both picket firing and artillery duels. The fire from the boats was so heavy that the citizens commenced digging caves in the sides of the hills for shelter. They had been desired to leave the town by the military commander, but refused to abandon their homes. The horses and mules were also driven out of the lines, since it was found too great a tax upon the resources of the garrison to feed them.

On the 21st Grant resolved upon another assault. He was led to this course by the following considerations. The distance to be passed over by the assaulting columns in no case exceeded four hundred yards, and in most cases partial shelter could be obtained to within one hundred yards of the enemy's line: he also felt that a resolute assault from the advanced position he had gained would succeed, if made with vigor and co-operation: then besides he knew that Johnston was gathering an army at Canton; that it was in daily receipt of accessions; and that if, instead of waiting to be attacked in his rear, he could take Vicksburg, and, sallying out from there, attack and defeat Johnston, he could destroy all the railroads, make the state secure, and save the government from the necessity of sending him re-enforcements, which were so much needed elsewhere at this juncture. The troops also were desirous of obtaining possession of the place; the weather was getting hot, and water among the hills was becoming scarce, and would probably fail during the summer; the army also would not work with as hearty a will in the difficult and laborious duties of the trenches, until they were convinced that all other means had been tried and failed. Grant has the ability of a great leader — to feel the spirit of his men, and to be influenced by it, as in turn he influences it. This spirit demanded an assault. On the 21st, therefore, orders were given for a general assault along the line the next day, at ten in the morning. The artillery was to prepare the way by a vigorous fire. The columns were to move at quick time, with fixed bayonets, carrying only canteens, ammunition, and one day's rations, and not to fire a gun until the outer works were stormed. "If prosecuted with vigor, it was confidently believed that this course would carry Vicksburg in a short space of time, and with very much less loss of life than would result from a protracted siege." Admiral Porter was informed of the intended assault, and requested to send up the gunboats and shell the city until half past ten, and also to mount and use the mortars from the opposite shore, the night before. This was done, and Porter kept six mortars playing rapidly all night upon the city and works, while at three next morning the cannonade from the land side began. Vicksburg was encircled with fire, and the thundering roar of the artillery continued until eleven. The bombardment was the most terrible one of the siege, and the sharp-shooters kept up so accurate a fire that the enemy was able to make only a partial response, and the attacking columns could form without molestation.

Grant held a position near McPherson's front, in the centre. All the corps commanders had set their time by his, and promptly at the appointed hour the three corps moved to the assault. No men could be seen above the works, except occasionally a sharp-shooter, who would quickly rise, fire, and disappear. A line of sharp-shooters was placed to keep them down. The assault was, however, like the first, a failure, and at two o'clock, it being evident the works could not be thus carried, the troops were all withdrawn. Prodigies of valor were performed, in every corps the colors were planted on the works, and some of them remained there all day, the sharp-shooters preventing any approach to them from either side; but it was impossible. Each corps had advanced, and had been driven back by the withering fire of the enemy. The position was too strong to be taken. At every point of the assault, the enemy had all the force necessary to repel it, while the nature of the ground outside rendered an attack by a column impossible. In many cases the riflemen, who had got too near to retreat with safety, stood still, exposed from head to foot, with their pieces ready to fire at any head that showed itself, and the fire from the works was always kept down where the Union troops had nerve enough for this desperate course.

The brunt of the first assault was over in an hour, and the result was seen to be ineffectual; but about twelve o'clock, Grant received a despatch from McClernand, saying he was hard pressed. Telling him to call on his reserves, Grant went round to Sherman's position, and there received another despatch from McClernand, saying he had carried two forts, and advising a bold push along the line, and soon a third, repeating this assertion, and asking for reënforcements. Although doubting the truth of these despatches, — four of which were sent, the last at half past three, — another trial was ordered; but it was as unsuccessful as the first. By these despatches the battle was prolonged, many lives lost, and no advantage gained. McClernand's corps had been as brave as the others, but they had gained no success which justified the despatches he had sent. About three thousand men were killed or wounded in this day's fight, but the spirit of the army was in no way shaken.

During the night the troops were withdrawn from the most advanced positions they had reached during the assault. Most of the wounded were carried off the field, but there was not time enough to bring back the dead, who lay for two days exposed between the two armies, since the enemy's guns commanded the ground where they lay. Pemberton then, being afraid that a pestilence would be caused in his garrison, proposed an armistice of two and a half hours, to enable Grant to remove them. The offer was promptly accepted, and the enemy took advantage of it to remove the dead horses and mules which lay before their works, and which had become very offensive by decomposition. During the armistice a good deal of intercourse took place between the soldiers on both sides; but there was no evidence of animosity between them, and an utter absence of insulting language. They had tested each other's manliness too well not to respect each other.

On the 22d Grant reported to Halleck the progress of the campaign since his arrival before Vicksburg. In speaking of the second assault, he said, "General McClernand's despatches misled me as to the facts, and caused much of this loss. He is entirely unfit for the position of corps commander, both on the march and on the battle-field. Looking after his corps gives me more labor and infinitely more uneasiness than all the remainder of my department."

The assaults having failed, preparations were immediately made for the siege. The troops retained the positions they had assumed when the place was invested, Sherman holding the right, McPherson the centre, and McClernand the left. Grant had now about forty thousand troops in line. Reënforcements had been received since his investment of Vicksburg, but he still felt the need of more men, in order to prosecute the siege vigorously, and at the same time protect himself against the efforts of Johnston to relieve Pemberton, to do which effectually, he should guard the line of the Big Black, and the Yazoo to Haine's Bluff.

Halleck clearly saw this need, and without waiting for an application from Grant, telegraphed that he would do all he could to help him. The army was, however, in want of almost all the appliances of a siege, and contained only four regular engineer officers; but with the materials at hand, the best was done that could be done.

The enemy was evidently short of ammunition, and his fire was consequently not very heavy, while our sharp-shooters were so effective that at the end of the first fortnight nearly all the artillery of the enemy was either dismounted or withdrawn. The first ground in the regular approaches was broken on the 23d of May. The history of this siege is another proof, if further proof were necessary, of the adaptability to circumstances, and fertility of resources, shown by our volunteers during the war. They could, after a few trials, perform all the various duties required of them; they were able to learn, which is more than half of the task of learning. The scarcity of engineer officers obliged Grant to give a great deal more personal superintendence to the works than he would otherwise have done. His military education fitted him for this, and every day he rode through the lines, directing, advising, overseeing the works, and infusing his spirit into his men. The aggregate length of the trenches was twelve miles; eighty-nine batteries were constructed during the siege. On the 30th of June there were in position two hundred and twenty guns, mostly light field-pieces; one battery of heavy guns, on the right, was manned and officered by the navy. The enemy slackened their fire, as the batteries were built, until towards the end they hardly responded at all: they also made sorties occasionally, and sometimes resorted to mines, to delay the approaches; but their general policy appears to have been to wait for another assault, and their indifference to the approach of the works was, at some points, amusing. The night working parties were protected by a line of pickets, and at one point the pickets of the two sides made an agreement not to fire upon each other at night. On one occasion our pickets, in order to allow the opening of another parallel, encroached upon the position of the enemy's line, so that the pickets became mixed, and after some discussion their relative position was arranged by a compromise, and they were stationed in places not more than ten yards apart, and in full view of each other.

While the investment of Vicksburg was thus proceeding, Grant's attention was directed to Johnston's menacing attitude in his rear, and on the 25th of May he wrote to Banks, "I feel that my force is abundantly strong to hold the enemy where he is, or to whip him should he come out. The place is so strongly fortified, however, that it cannot be taken without either a great sacrifice of life or by a regular siege. I have determined to adopt the latter course, and save my men. . . . The great danger now to be apprehended is, that the enemy may collect a force outside, and attempt to rescue the garrison. I deem it advisable that as large a force be collected here as possible. Having all my available force that can be spared from West Tennessee and Helena here, to get any more I must look outside of my own department. You being engaged in the same enterprise, I am compelled to ask you to give me such assistance as may be in your power. I would be pleased, General, to have you come, with such force as you may be able to spare."

On the 26th a force of twelve thousand men, under Blair, was sent against a body of the enemy, supposed to be gathering between the Big Black and Yazoo Rivers. Blair was absent nearly a week, and accomplished the objects of the expedition most thoroughly.

On the 31st of May Grant received a letter from Banks, asking for ten thousand men; to which Grant replied, "Vicksburg is the vital point. Our situation is, for the first time during the entire western campaign, what it should be. We have, after great labor and extraordinary risk, secured a position which should not be jeopardized by any detachments whatever. On the contrary, I am now, and shall continue to exert myself to the utmost to concentrate. I have ample means to defend my present position, and effect the reduction of Vicksburg within twenty days, if the relation of affairs which now obtains remains unchanged. But detach ten thousand men from my command, and I cannot answer for the result. I need not describe the severity of the labor to which my command must necessarily be subjected, in an operation of such magnitude as that in which I am now engaged. Weakened by the detachment of ten thousand men, or even half that number, with the circumstances entirely changed, I should be crippled beyond redemption. My arrangements for supplies are ample, and can be expanded to meet any exigency. All I want now is men."

On the 7th of June a body of the enemy attacked Milliken's Bend, but were driven back by the garrison of white and black troops occupying that place, under the command of Brigadier General Dennis. Grant also sent him reënforcements, with orders to drive the enemy beyond the Tensas. "Every vestige of an enemy's camp ought to be shoved back of that point."

On the 8th of June, a division of troops having arrived from Memphis, they were ordered to Haine's Bluff, which till then had been temporarily held by a garrison of the Marine Brigade, furnished by Admiral Porter. Haine's Bluff was now placed under the command of Washburne, with orders to so fortify it that it could be held by ten thousand men against a sudden movement, and could be capable of protecting at least forty thousand.

Reënforcements continued to arrive, until, on the 14th of June, Grant's force amounted to seventy-five thousand men, about half of whom remained in the trenches till the place surrendered, while the other half formed an army of observation, and watched closely all the movements of the forces gathering to relieve the town. On the 22d of June positive information was received that Johnston was crossing the Big Black, and Grant immediately gave the command in the rear to Sherman, with the orders, "Use all the forces indicated as you deem most advantageous, and should more be required, call on me, and they will be furnished to the last man here and at Young's Point."

To McPherson Grant wrote, "Sherman goes out to meet Johnston. If he comes, the greatest vigilance will be required on the line, as the Vicksburg garrison may take the same occasion for an attack also. Batteries should have a good supply of grape and canister." A line of works, quite as strong as those defending Vicksburg, were now constructed from the Yazoo River to the Big Black, so that if Johnston should attempt to attack the rear of the besieging army, he would find it as difficult as they found the attack upon Vicksburg.

On the 17th of June Grant received from Sherman and McPherson a formal protest against a congratulatory order, issued on the 30th of May, by McClernand to his troops, and which, besides being in direct violation of the army regulations and the orders of the department, which required all such papers to be forwarded to the superior officer, since it had not been seen by Grant, was also full of insinuations against the other officers and corps of the army, while it magnified the glory of its author. Enclosing the copy of the order, Grant wrote to McClernand, asking, if it was a true copy; and on receiving an answer in the affirmative, he immediately relieved McClernand of his command, appointing General Ord in his place, subject to the approval of the President. This was the end of the military career of a political general, whose incompetence and self-sufficiency had troubled Grant greatly during his entire connection with the army. Grant had frequently complained of him to the department at Washington, and finally, on the 14th of May, had received "authority to relieve any person who, from ignorance in action, or from any cause, interfered with or delayed his operations." He was also told that the government expected him to exert his authority, and would hold him responsible. This congratulatory order offered the opportunity so long desired, and immediate advantage was taken of it.

On the 14th of June Johnston had written to Pemberton, "By fighting the enemy simultaneously at the same points of his line, you may be extricated; our joint forces cannot raise the siege of Vicksburg."

The garrison began now to suffer both for rations and supplies. There was particularly a great dearth of percussion caps. On the 15th Pemberton sends to Johnston, "We are living on greatly reduced rations, but I think sufficient for twenty days yet. Our men, having no relief, are becoming much fatigued, but are still in pretty good spirits." On the 19th, "My men have been thirty-four days and nights in the trenches without relief, and the enemy within conversation distance. We are living on very reduced rations, and, as you know, are entirely isolated. What aid am I to expect from you?" The prices of food in the town had risen enormously. Flour was a thousand dollars a barrel, rebel money; beef, — very often the oxen killed by the shot from the Union army, and picked up by the butchers, — two dollars and a half a pound. The rich had eaten all the food they had, while the poor were nearly starved. There was scarce a building which had not been hit; women and children had been killed by the shells, and all who did not retire to the caves were in danger. Meanwhile the pickets met every night, and were always good-natured to each other. The conversation often turned on the merits of the war, and the question would be discussed vehemently, until, arguments being exhausted, they would separate, as one of them said, "for fear of getting into a fight upon the subject."

On the 25th of June Grant fired a mine which had

been prepared on the Jackson road. It extended thirty-five feet from the starting-point; fifteen hundred pounds of powder were placed in three branches, and seven hundred in the central lead: fuses were arranged to fire them all at once, and at half past three the explosion took place, and the earth was shaken as though with an earthquake, and huge masses were thrown into the air. The crater made was large enough to hold two regiments, and the parapet was partially destroyed. As soon as the result was discovered, a column of infantry, which had been held in readiness, rushed in and gained the crater, while the enemy retired to the interior line, only a few feet back, and no practical result was gained. Another mine was sprung on the 1st of July, but the effect was not more decisive.

Thus matters went on, and, as accurately summed up by Mr. Badeau, this was the condition: "A continuous siege, and a mighty battle imminent. A citadel surrounded by land and water. The bombardment almost incessant. The beleaguered garrison reduced to quarter rations; living on mule meat, and thinking it good fare. The population of the town hiding in caves to escape the storm of mortar shells exploding in their streets. A squadron thundering at the gates by night as well as by day. Mines trembling beneath their feet. What rare news came from Johnston, far from cheering; all hope, indeed, of succor quite cut off. Ammunition almost expended. The lines of the besieger contracting daily; his approaches getting closer, his sharp-shooters more accurate; his sap rollers steadily rising over the hills that Vicksburg had proudly declared impassable.

Every day some new battery opening from an unexpected quarter; every day the position detected from which to-morrow still another battery would surely begin its fire. To crown all, after a few more contractions of the coil, another mighty assault would bring the enemy beneath the walls, when, covered by their works, and more numerous than the besieged, the assailants, in every human probability, would storm the town, and all the unutterable horrors to which fallen cities are exposed might come upon the devoted fortress."

## CHAPTER XXII.

VICKSBURG SURRENDERED. — A FURTHER DISPLAY OF THE UNCONDITIONAL SURRENDER POLICY.

On the 27th of May, a courier, who had been intrusted by Pemberton with a despatch for Johnston, came into Grant's lines, and gave the document to him. This despatch read as follows: "I have fifteen thousand men in Vicksburg, and rations for thirty days—one meal a day. Come to my aid with an army of thirty thousand men. If you cannot do this within ten days, you had better retreat. Ammunition is almost exhausted, especially percussion caps." On the 28th of June the Union lines were thirteen hundred yards nearer the city than the original works, and the advance continued, and it was said among the troops that on the 4th of July an assault was to be made. On the morning, however, of the 3d of July, 1863, a flag of truce was displayed, at eight A. M., upon the works in front of that portion of the forces under General A. J. Smith; and soon after General Bowen and Colonel Montgomery left the fortifications, and being met at the Union lines, announced that they bore a sealed communication from Pemberton to Grant. The bearers being taken to the nearest headquarters, a messenger was despatched with all possible haste to acquaint Grant with the fact. The communication was as follows: —

HEADQUARTERS VICKSBURG, July 3, 1863.

MAJOR GENERAL GRANT,
*Commanding United States Forces.*

GENERAL: I have the honor to propose to you an armistice for — hours, with a view to arranging terms for the capitulation of Vicksburg. To this end, if agreeable to you, I will appoint three commissioners, to meet a like number to be named by yourself, at such place and hour as you may find convenient. I make this proposition to save the further effusion of blood, which must otherwise be shed to a frightful extent, feeling myself fully able to maintain my position for a yet indefinite period. This communication will be handed you, under a flag of truce, by Major General James Bowen.

Very respectfully, your obedient servant,
J. C. PEMBERTON.

To this General Grant replied as follows: —

HEADQUARTERS DEPARTMENT OF TENNESSEE,
IN THE FIELD, NEAR VICKSBURG, July 3, 1863.

LIEUTENANT GENERAL J. C. PEMBERTON,
*Commanding Confederate Forces, &c.*

GENERAL: Your note of this date, just received, proposes an armistice of several hours, for the purpose of arranging terms of capitulation through commissioners to be appointed, &c. The effusion of blood you propose stopping by this course can be ended at any time you may choose, by an unconditional surrender of the city and garrison. Men who have shown so much endurance and courage as those now in Vicksburg will always challenge the respect of an adversary, and, I can assure you, will be treated with all the respect due them as prisoners of war. I do not favor the proposition of appointing commissioners to arrange terms of capitulation, because I have no other terms than those indicated above.

I am, General, very respectfully, your obedient servant,
U. S. GRANT, *Major General.*

General Bowen expressed a wish to converse with

the General further on this important matter; but the latter at once declined. General Bowen then requested that General Grant would meet General Pemberton on neutral ground, as more could be arranged in one personal interview than could be by the interchange of numerous despatches. General Grant expressed his willingness to do this, and offered to meet Pemberton that afternoon at three, and then the interview closed. After the return of the messengers, hostilities continued until noon, when a cessation was ordered.

At three in the afternoon a signal gun from the Union side was answered by one from the works, and announced the approach of the Confederate commander. Pemberton was accompanied by the bearers of his despatch in the morning. Grant was supported by Generals A. J. Smith and McPherson. The interview took place in front of McPherson's line, on a spot which had not yet been trodden by either army, and under the branches of a gigantic oak. After shaking hands and introducing the officers to each other, Pemberton opened the conference by saying, —

"General Grant, I meet you in order to arrange terms for the capitulation. What terms do you demand?"

"Unconditional surrender," replied Grant.

"Unconditional surrender?" said Pemberton. "Never, so long as I have a man left me. I will fight rather."

"Very well," said Grant, coolly.

The appearance and manner of the two men showed their difference of character. Pemberton was greatly agitated, and his hot and impulsive nature could hardly be restrained by the dignity of his position. Grant, on

NDER OF VICKSBURG.

the other hand, was as collected and imperturbable as ever, and smoked his cigar with his accustomed coolness. Though the desired object of all his hopes and labors for months was now in his grasp, he did not appear elated in any way.

After this short conversation, as though by mutual but tacit consent, the two chiefs wandered off a short distance by themselves, and, seating themselves upon the grass in a clump of bushes, remained for a considerable time in conversation. The four companions of the Generals followed their example, while in a larger group their respective staffs remained in the rear. The interview ended with the understanding that Pemberton would submit the matter to a council of war, and would send his answer in the morning.

The oak tree under which this memorable scene took place has long since disappeared, its trunk being manufactured into relics of the occasion, and on the spot where it stood now stands a monument commemorating the surrender.

The monument is a pyramid twenty feet high, surmounted with a globe fifteen inches in diameter. On the principal side is a large American eagle, with widespread wings, which cover implements of defence; in one claw he holds the laurel, in the other an American shield, and in its beak a pennant, inscribed, "*E Pluribus Unum.*" The eagle sustains on its wings the Goddess of Liberty. On one side of the monument is inscribed, "To the Memory of the Surrender of Vicksburg by Lieutenant General J. C. Pemberton to Major General U. S. Grant, U. S. A., on the 3d of July, 1863."

After the conference, Grant, on his return to his headquarters, conferred with his corps and division commanders, and sent that same evening the following letter to Pemberton: —

HEADQUARTERS DEPARTMENT OF TENNESSEE,
NEAR VICKSBURG, July 3, 1863.

LIEUTENANT GENERAL J. C. PEMBERTON,
*Commanding Confederate Forces, Vicksburg, Miss.*

GENERAL: In conformity with the agreement of this afternoon, I will submit the following proposition for the surrender of the city of Vicksburg, public stores, &c. On your accepting the terms proposed, I will march in one division, as a guard, and take possession at eight o'clock to-morrow morning. As soon as paroles can be made out and signed by the officers and men, you will be allowed to march out of our lines, the officers taking with them their regimental clothing, and staff, field, and cavalry officers one horse each. The rank and file will be allowed all their clothing, but no other property.

If these conditions are accepted, any amount of rations you may deem necessary can be taken from the stores you now have, and also the necessary cooking utensils for preparing them; thirty wagons also, counting two two-horse or mule teams as one. You will be allowed to transport such articles as cannot be carried along. The same conditions will be allowed to all sick and wounded officers and privates, as fast as they become able to travel. The paroles for these latter must be signed, however, whilst officers are present, authorized to sign the roll of prisoners.

I am, General, very respectfully,
Your obedient servant,
U. S. GRANT, *Major General.*

The officers who received this letter stated that it would be impossible to return an answer before night; but very early next morning the following letter was sent to the Union lines: —

HEADQUARTERS VICKSBURG, July 3, 1863.

MAJOR GENERAL GRANT,
*Commanding United States Forces.*

GENERAL: I have the honor to acknowledge the receipt of your communication of this date proposing terms for the surrender of this garrison and post. In the main your terms are accepted; but in justice both to the honor and spirit of my troops, manifested in the defence of Vicksburg, I have the honor to submit the following amendments, which, if acceded to by you, will perfect the agreement between us. At ten o'clock to-morrow I propose to evacuate the works in and around Vicksburg, and to surrender the city and garrison under my command by marching out with my colors and arms and stacking them in front of my present limits, after which you will take possession; officers to retain their side arms and personal property, and the rights and property of citizens to be respected.

I am, General, yours, very respectfully,
J. C. PEMBERTON, *Lieutenant General.*

In his reply Grant showed his magnanimity: the proposition amounted to surrendering with the honors of war; and if so doing was any gratification to the wounded vanity of the vanquished, he had no objection to their enjoying it, particularly since it in no way affected the results of the victory he had gained. His reply to Pemberton's last letter was therefore as follows: —

HEADQUARTERS DEPARTMENT OF TENNESSEE,
BEFORE VICKSBURG, July 4, 1863.

LIEUTENANT GENERAL PEMBERTON,
*Commanding Forces in Vicksburg.*

GENERAL: I have the honor to acknowledge your communication of the 3d of July. The amendments proposed by you cannot be acceded to in full. It will be necessary to furnish every officer and man with a parole signed by himself, which, with the completion of the rolls of prisoners, will necessarily take some time. Again, I can make no stipulation with regard to the treatment of citizens and their private property. While I do not propose to cause any of them any undue annoyance or loss, I cannot consent to leave myself under restraint by stipulations. The property which officers can be allowed to take with them will be as stated in the proposition of last evening — that is, that officers will be allowed their private baggage and side arms, and mounted officers one horse each. If you mean by your proposition for each brigade to march to the front of the lines now occupied by it, and stack their arms at ten o'clock A. M., and then return to the inside and remain as prisoners until properly paroled, I will make no objection to it. Should no modifications be made of your acceptance of my terms by nine o'clock A. M., I shall regard them as having been rejected, and act accordingly. Should these terms be accepted, white flags will be displayed along your lines to prevent such of my troops as may not have been notified from firing on your men.

I am, General, very respectfully, your obedient servant,

U. S. GRANT, *Major General U. S. A.*

After a very short consultation with his general officers, the commandant of Vicksburg sent the following reply: —

HEADQUARTERS VICKSBURG, July 4, 1863.

MAJOR GENERAL U. S. GRANT,
*Commanding United States Forces, &c.*

GENERAL: I have the honor to acknowledge the receipt of your communication of this date, and, in reply, to say that the terms proposed by you are accepted.

Very respectfully, your obedient servant,

J. C. PEMBERTON, *Lieutenant General.*

This final reply was received by Grant on Sunday morning, July 4, 1863, and he immediately sent instructions to McPherson's headquarters, ordering the Seventeenth Corps under arms as soon as possible, to be ready to move into the city instantly upon receipt of orders. Shortly after ten the rebel works displayed a number of white flags along the entire lines, extending from right to left. This was the signal for surrender. The enemy soon after marched out by regiments, on McPherson's front, stacked their arms, and returned to the works, where they were paroled in a body prior to being paroled individually. This ceremony of stacking their arms took three hours. No one had been delegated by General Grant to superintend this process; with the high courtesy of a natural gentleman, he trusted the matter to themselves; we shall see how this nobility of breeding was returned by the Confederate officers. The probability is, that they could not understand it. It shot clear above their comprehension.

Pemberton, in his report, says, "If it should be asked why the 4th of July was selected as the day for surrender, the answer is obvious. I believed that upon that day I should obtain better terms. Well aware of the *vanity* of our foes, I knew that they would attach vast importance to the entrance on the 4th of July into the stronghold of the great river, and that, to gratify their national *vanity*, they would yield then what could not be extorted from them at any other time."

On the afternoon of the 4th of July, General Grant rode into Vicksburg, and proceeded to the rebel headquarters. Pemberton and his Generals were seated upon the porch. Grant dismounted, and saluted them. None of them rose, and Grant remained standing, until, for very shame, one of the officers rose and offered him a seat. The day was hot, and his ride had been dusty, and Grant asked for a drink of water.

He was referred to the house, and, rising, went in, where finally he found a negro who gave him what he wanted. On his return to the porch his seat had been taken, and during the rest of the interview he remained standing. This is the man whose vanity Pemberton flattered himself he could play upon. Modest, unassuming, patient, like all great natures, Grant disregards, because most probably he does not see, the petty conventions which bound the circle of most men's lives. Persistent, too, like all the great forces of nature, he slowly and silently prepares his plans, until, when the results follow, men stand amazed at the mighty power which is so suddenly developed. The thunderbolt that rushes from the bosom of an angry cloud and rends the stalwart oak which has for centuries defied the storm, excites the wonder and amazement of the vulgar, who stand awe-struck at this sudden display of irresistible force; while to the philosopher the even processes of nature, which slowly by evaporation keep the oceans and rivers of the globe in a constant circle of diminution and replenishment, are much greater causes for admiration and wonder. He knows that in these silent causes lies the storehouse of countless thunderbolts.

Of the crowds of tourists who year by year gaze with a fearful awe at the immense sheet of Niagara, as it plunges from the cliff down to the seething depths below, how many realize that quiet summer days have raised every drop of the water, which rushes now with such an angry roar over the falls, to many times that height, and that their mild influence exerts insensibly the force of countless Niagaras?

It was well that a negro should give the desired cup

of water to the captor of Vicksburg, while the proud enslavers of his race should sit in sullen silence by. Their haughty dominion was overthrown, and this tribute came the more fitly to him who had overthrown it, from the hands of one representing those made free men by his genius, than it could have come from the proudest of the conquered but unconverted who had opposed their futile resistance to the man representing in action the spread of the democratic idea in this country. This giving of a "cup of cold water" is one of the deeds which has not, and shall not lose its reward.

It was during this interview that Pemberton asked Grant to supply the garrison with rations, to which Grant immediately assented, and asked how many would be needed. "I have thirty-two thousand men," was the answer. This was the first intimation Grant had of the extent of his victory; he had supposed the garrison comprised not more, at the outside, than twenty thousand. But nothing showed his gratified surprise; he remained as coolly imperturbable as ever.

In less than four hours after the national flag had been flung to the breeze from the dome of the Court House, as an evidence of the surrender, the levee was crowded with steamers; up to that time at least seventy-five had arrived, and others were coming in constantly. All the boats from above and below the city came to swell the number, and give to the city the appearance of a busy inland commercial metropolis, which had so long deserted it for the sad desolation of war. The levees were almost instantly covered with busy, moving crowds, pushing here, there, and everywhere, while already, some of the steamers having commenced to discharge their cargoes, men and teams made an unwonted activity in the streets, while transporting the cargoes to their various destinations. It was a transformation almost like magic. The material results of the campaign were thus summed up by General Grant in his official report:—

"The defeat of the enemy in five battles outside of Vicksburg, the occupation of Jackson, the capital of the State of Mississippi, and the capture of Vicksburg and its garrison and munitions of war; a loss to the enemy of thirty-seven thousand prisoners, among whom were fifteen general officers; at least ten thousand killed and wounded; and among the killed, Generals Tracy, Tilghman, and Green; and hundreds, and perhaps thousands of stragglers, who can never be collected and organized. Arms and munitions of war for an army of sixty thousand have fallen into our hands, besides a large amount of other public property, consisting of railroad, locomotives, cars, steamboats, cotton, &c.; and much was destroyed to prevent our capturing it."

The following extract from General Halleck's report will also be read with interest in this connection:—

"When we consider the character of the country in which this army operated, the formidable obstacles to be overcome, the number of forces and the strength of the enemy's works, we cannot fail to admire the courage and endurance of the troops, and the skill and daring of their commander. *No more brilliant exploit can be found in military history.* It has been alleged — and the allegation has been widely circulated by the press — that General Grant, in the conduct of his campaign, positively disobeyed the instructions of his superiors. It is hardly necessary to remark that *General Grant never disobeyed an order or instruction, but always carried out to the best of his ability every wish or suggestion made to him by the government.* Moreover he has never complained that the government did not furnish him all the means and assistance in its power to facilitate the execution of any plan he saw fit to adopt."

When the news of the surrender reached President Lincoln officially, he wrote the following autograph letter to Grant:—

EXECUTIVE MANSION, WASHINGTON, July 13, 1863.

TO MAJOR GENERAL GRANT.

MY DEAR GENERAL: I do not remember that you and I ever met personally. I write this now as a grateful acknowledgment for *the almost inestimable service you have done the country.* I wish to say a word further. When you first reached the vicinity of Vicksburg, I thought you should do what you finally did — march the troops across the neck, run the batteries with the transports, and thus go below; and I never had any faith, except a general hope that you knew better than I, that the Yazoo Pass expedition, and the like, could succeed. When you got below and took Port Gibson, Grand Gulf, and vicinity, I thought you should go down the river and join General Banks; and when you turned northward east of the Big Black, I feared it was a mistake. I now wish to make a personal acknowledgment that you were right and I was wrong.

Yours very truly,

A. LINCOLN.

## CHAPTER XXIII.

THE RESULTS OF THE SURRENDER OF VICKSBURG. — PREPARING FOR FURTHER SERVICE. — THE FINAL CAPTURE OF JACKSON.

IT was not until the 6th that Grant took up his headquarters in Vicksburg. On the evening of the 4th he announced the surrender to the government as follows: "The enemy surrendered this morning. The only terms allowed is their parole as prisoners of war. This I regard as a great advantage to us at this moment. It saves probably several days in the capture, and leaves troops and transports ready for immediate service. Sherman, with a large force, moves immediately on Johnston, to drive him from the state. I will send troops to the relief of Banks, and return the Ninth Army Corps to Burnside."

Seven hundred of the garrison refused to be paroled, preferring to be sent north as prisoners. Pemberton protested against this, and wished Grant to force these men to be paroled; he also desired that Grant should allow him arms for some of his troops, to guard the others on their march home; but this also Grant refused, since it was desirable to have as many of them desert as chose. On the 11th the paroles were completed, and the garrison marched out between a guard of national troops, extending on both sides of the road, for some distance beyond the intrenchments. As they reached the fortifications, each man's name was called, and checked off on the rolls. Grant's orders were, "Instruct the commands to be orderly and quiet as these prisoners pass, to make no offensive remarks, and not to harbor any who fall out of ranks after they have passed." These orders were obeyed. In fact, immediately after the surrender the two armies affiliated. The rebels were treated with kindness, and appreciated it, and the late combatants were frequently seen walking arm in arm while they remained together.

One of the most immediate effects of the surrender of Vicksburg was the surrender of Port Hudson. On the 7th of July, the commander of that post, Frank Gardner, sent a despatch to Banks, asking if it was true that Vicksburg had surrendered; and on receiving an assurance that such was the fact, he proposed to do the same, and did so the next day, so that on the 8th of July the Mississippi flowed "unvexed to the sea." On the 16th of July the steamboat Imperial arrived at New Orleans from St. Louis, the first boat which had passed over the route for two years. On the 28th of the same month she returned to her wharf at St. Louis, amid the welcoming cheers of thousands who gathered on the banks to see her arrive.

After the capture of Vicksburg General Grant reported that several weeks' repose was necessary for his troops, who were worn out with the fatigue of their long and forced marches, the labors of the siege, and the excitement incident to the active operations of the past campaign. But as it was evident that Johnston was collecting a force, as soon as Vicksburg surrendered

Grant determined to attack and scatter it. It had been Grant's intention to order another assault on the works of Vicksburg on the 6th of July; but the surrender on the 4th having prevented this, he determined to send the expedition against Johnston as soon as possible. In answer to his inquiry when he could be ready to move, Sherman reported that he would move at once, and doing so, reached Jackson on the 10th, where Johnston had taken up his position. In his report, written subsequently to the events we are about to narrate, Johnston says that it was his intention to hold this place only until he could draw off his army and remove his stores; but from the amount of labor he had expended in fortifying the position, it would seem that he had formed his previous plans from the facts brought under his observation by the subsequent events. Though such a course of action is perhaps difficult, and certainly is somewhat unusual, yet we are almost tempted to believe that anything is possible to a commander who could publish such an order as we give below, even though it was for the purpose of "firing the southern heart." But, of course, a set of men who, in the nineteenth century, in a representative government like ours, in a time when the whole world is rising to the recognition of the dignity of productive labor, the right of the laborer to the result of his industry, and the necessity of guaranteeing this right in the amplest way, in order to preserve anything like stability in the social body, since this sacred right of labor is the corner-stone of all possible social life, — a set of men who, at such a time, had commenced a revolution to maintain and extend slavery, are not to be held to the ordinary rules. Their politicians in office, when the crisis came, showed their contempt for the restraints of honesty. Such restrictions may be well enough for a hireling crew, but not for the genuine chivalry. Their military men felt their obligations to the government sit as lightly upon them; and how, therefore, is it to be supposed that the shackles of rhetoric or the rules of logic should be expected to confine the expression of their ardent souls, any more than the rules of honesty or honor should have confined the aspirations of their pockets. Johnston's report, therefore, is the fit accompaniment of the following proclamation:—

HEADQUARTERS ON THE FIELD, July 9, 1863.

FELLOW-SOLDIERS: An insolent foe, flushed with hope by his recent success at Vicksburg, confronts you, threatening the people, whose homes and liberty you are here to protect, with plunder and conquest. Their guns may even now be heard as they advance.

The enemy it is at once the duty and the mission of you, brave men, to chastise and expel from the soil of Mississippi. The commanding General confidently relies on you to sustain his pledge, which he makes in advance, and he will be with you in the good work, even unto the end.

The vice of "straggling" he begs you to shun and to frown on. If needs be, it will be checked by even the most summary remedies.

The telegraph has already announced a glorious victory over the foe, won by your noble comrades of the Virginia army on Federal soil: may he not, with redoubled hopes, count on you, while defending your firesides and household gods, to emulate the proud example of your brothers in the east?

The country expects in this, the great crisis of its destiny, that every man will do his duty.

JOSEPH E. JOHNSTON, *General commanding.*

The orders given to Sherman on the 4th were as follows: "The orders will be made as you suggest, the moment Vicksburg is ours. Ord and Steele have both been notified to move the moment Vicksburg falls. I will let you know the moment Pemberton's answer arrives. I have no suggestions or orders to give. I want you to drive Johnston out in your own way, and inflict on the enemy all the punishment you can. I will support you to the last man that can be spared."

On the 5th Sherman's forces reached the Big Black, constructed bridges, crossed the next day, and on the 7th and 8th marched to Clinton. Johnston fell back on Jackson, and on the 9th Sherman arrived at that place. The Confederate works now protected Jackson by a line commencing and ending on the Pearl River, and encircling the city. Sherman resolved to hold the Confederate army there, and with infantry and cavalry destroy the railroads, at the same time threatening to cross the river, and destroy the enemy's only line of communications with his rear. Johnston hoped that Sherman would attempt an assault, but, finding that he would not, telegraphed to Davis, "If the enemy will not attack, we must, or at the last moment withdraw. We cannot attack seriously without risking the army."

On the 13th Sherman's army extended so that both flanks rested on the river, and he sent back for ammunition to commence the siege. Meanwhile his expeditions extended in all directions, some of them as far as sixty miles, destroying the railroads, and devastating the country. On the 16th his ammunition arrived, and Johnston, having received information of its arrival, resolved to evacuate the place; and the next day it was found that he had done so, the Confederates having crossed the river, burning the bridges after them.

Knowing that a pursuit under the hot July sun would be more injurious to his command than to the enemy, Sherman resolved to return, and after spending a few days more in completing his work of destruction, returned to Vicksburg, where he arrived on the 25th.

On the 8th of July Halleck replied to Grant's despatch, announcing the surrender, —

> "I fear your paroling the prisoners at Vicksburg, without actual delivery to a proper agent, as required by the seventh article of the cartel, may be construed into an absolute release, and that these men will immediately be placed in the ranks of the enemy. Such has been the case elsewhere. If these prisoners have not been allowed to depart, you will retain them until further orders."

This order came, however, too late, and unquestionably most fortunately. The parole had bound those who took it not to take up arms against the government until exchanged by the proper authorities, and its advantages to us were, that it did not necessitate the support of so many men, nor the guarding or transporting them, and thus left our men and vessels free for other uses. Besides this, the prisoners having been well treated, Grant supposed that they would by their presence tend to demoralize the South, and tend to disaffect them with the war; and it is hardly a question but that he was right.

Though this order may appear to find fault with his action, yet Grant was, however, appointed a Major General in the regular army for this capture, his commission dating from the occupation of Vicksburg, July 4, 1863.

The country at this period was greatly depressed; for a long time it had seemed as though disaster attended our arms. On the 4th of July, 1863, the entire loyal population was in an agony of suspense and doubt, since on that day Lee was at Gettysburg, and the battle was to be fought which should decide whether as a victor he should remain, or be driven out baffled and defeated. To receive therefore upon one day the news of two such victories as Gettysburg and Vicksburg, raised the country from doubt and despair to confidence and security. Perhaps at no period of the war did the loyal heart of the people throb faster at the receipt of joyful news than on this day, unless it may be when it was announced that Lee had surrendered.

At this time Grant recommended both Sherman and McPherson for promotion to the rank of Brigadier General in the regular army. "The first reason for this," he said, "is their great fitness for any command that it may ever become necessary to intrust to them. Second, their great purity of character, and disinterestedness in anything except the faithful performance of their duty and the success of every one engaged in the great battle for the preservation of the Union. Third, they have honorably won this distinction upon many well-fought battle-fields. The promotion of such men as Sherman and McPherson always adds strength to our army."

These promotions were made, and also many others of the same kind, which Grant also suggested.

The army under Grant's command having finished its immediate work, and being desirous of some rest, he issued the following order:—

*General Orders, No.* 45.

HEADQUARTERS DEPARTMENT OF THE TENNESSEE,
VICKSBURG, MISS., July 20, 1863.

In pursuance of section 32 of an act entitled "An act for enrolling and calling out the national forces, and for other purposes," approved March 3, 1863, furloughs may be granted for a period not exceeding thirty days at one time, to five per centum of the non-commissioned officers and privates of each regiment, battery, independent company, and detachment, present with their respective commands in this department, for good conduct in their line of duty, by their immediate commanding officers, approved by intermediate and army corps commanders. Furloughs thus granted are intended for the benefit of well men, and the sick who have become so from fatigue or exposure in the line of duty.

Under no circumstances will furloughs be given to men who have shirked duty, or straggled on the march, or from camps. Such men must be made to perform extra fatigue duty by their immediate commanding officers; and in cases where this is not regarded as sufficient punishment, they will be fined in an amount not beyond that which a regimental court martial is authorized to impose. The amount of such fine will be entered on the proper muster and pay rolls, opposite their respective names, and the cause for which it is imposed stated.

By order of Major General U. S. GRANT.

T. S. BOWERS, *A. A. G.*

Finding that many of his soldiers, who took advantage of their furloughs to return home, were charged exorbitant fares by the captains of the steamboats which commenced immediately to ply on the Mississippi, he issued a special order, fixing the price of passage from Vicksburg to Cairo at five dollars for enlisted men, and seven dollars for officers; and the necessity of obeying it was impressed upon the captains by making one of them, who had overstepped the limits, refund the overcharge, or submit to imprisonment, and to having his boat confiscated.

On the 4th of July the Secretary of the Treasury, Mr. Chase, wrote to Grant, "I find that a rigorous line within districts occupied by our military forces, from beyond which no cotton or other produce can be brought, and within which no trade can be carried on, gives rise to serious and to some apparently well-founded complaints." The Secretary, therefore, urged the propriety of "substituting bonds, to be given by all persons receiving permits, for the rigorous line now established; or, at least, of substituting them partially." To this letter Grant responded, on the 11th, as follows: —

HEADQUARTERS DEPARTMENT OF THE TENNESSEE,<br>VICKSBURG, MISS., July 21, 1863.

SIR: Your letter of the 4th instant to me, enclosing a copy of a letter of same date to Mr. Mellen, special agent of the treasury, is just received. My Assistant Adjutant General, by whom I shall send this letter, is about starting for Washington; hence I shall be very short in my reply.

My experience in West Tennessee has convinced me that any trade whatever with the rebellious states is weakening to us of at least thirty-three per cent. of our force. No matter what the restrictions thrown around trade, if any whatever is allowed, it will be made the means of supplying the enemy with what they want. Restrictions, if lived up to, make trade unprofitable, and hence none but dishonest men go into it. I will venture to say that no honest man has made money in West Tennessee in the last year, while many fortunes have been made there during that time.

The people in the Mississippi Valley are now nearly subjugated. Keep trade out for a few months, and I doubt not but that the work of subjugation will be so complete, that trade can be opened freely with the states of Arkansas, Louisiana, and Mississippi; that the people of these states will be more anxious for the enforcement and protection of our laws than the people of the loyal states. They have experienced the misfortune of being without them, and are now in a most happy condition to appreciate their blessings.

No theory of my own will ever stand in the way of my executing, in good faith, any order I may receive from those in authority over me; but my position has given me an opportunity of seeing what would not be known by persons away from the scene of war; and I venture, therefore, to suggest great caution in opening trade with rebels.

I am, sir, very respectfully,

Your obedient servant,

U. S. GRANT, *Major General.*

HON. S. P. CHASE, *Secretary of the Treasury.*

Grant's conviction was, that military success alone could finish the war, and that until this should be done, all political, commercial, or other considerations should be held subservient to military success. On the 26th of July he said, "I am very much opposed to any trade whatever until the rebellion in this part of the country is entirely crushed out." On the 13th of August, "My opinion is, that all trade with any enemy with whom we are at war is calculated to weaken us indirectly. I am opposed to selling to or buying from them whilst war exists, except those within our lines." On the 26th of August he wrote to the Secretary of War, "If trade is opened under any general rule, all sorts of dishonest men will engage in it, taking any oath or obligation necessary to secure the privilege. Smuggling will at once commence, as it did at Memphis, Helena, and every other place where trade has been allowed within the disloyal states, and the armed enemy will be enabled to procure from northern markets every article they require." On the 13th he wrote to Mr. Mellen, treasury agent, —

"The moment purchasers of cotton are allowed in the market, that moment all the cotton in the Southern States becomes the property of that class of persons who are authorized to sell and receive pay. More than half of the cotton now in the South is the property of the so-called Southern Confederacy, for their benefit. This, of all others, will find its way to market, and will be sold by actual agents of the so-called Confederate government for their benefit. Thus, while we are making such efforts to close their ports, we shall be opening a better market for them. Our money, being always worth a known price in New York city, will have a commercial value in Europe. This will enable the South to ship at much less risk the means of exchange for imported articles, than by sending the bulky article of cotton."

These arguments did not, however, have all the effect they were intended to have upon the policy of the government, and a limited trade was opened, from which the results foreseen and predicted by Grant followed. The government, however, could never be induced to follow out his views in this matter.

The following order, of the 1st of August, will show the policy Grant pursued in his department, to stop all guerrilla fighting, and also to regulate the trade in cotton, to provide for the destitute, and put an end to all plundering by his own soldiers : —

*General Orders, No.* 50.

HEADQUARTERS DEPARTMENT OF THE TENNESSEE,
VICKSBURG, MISS., August 1, 1863.

1. All regularly organized bodies of the enemy having been driven from those parts of Kentucky and Tennessee west of the Tennessee River, and from all of Mississippi west of the Mississippi

Central Railroad, and it being to the interest of those districts not to invite the presence of armed bodies of men among them, it is announced that the most rigorous penalties will hereafter be inflicted upon the following classes of prisoners, to wit: All irregular bodies of cavalry not mustered and paid by the Confederate authorities; all persons engaged in conscripting, enforcing the conscription, or apprehending deserters, whether regular or irregular; all citizens encouraging or aiding the same; and all persons detected in firing upon unarmed transports.

It is not contemplated that this order shall affect the treatment due to prisoners of war captured within the districts named, when they are members of legally organized companies, and when their acts are in accordance with the usages of civilized warfare.

2. The citizens of Mississippi, within the limits above described, are called upon to pursue their peaceful avocations, in obedience to the laws of the United States. While doing so in good faith, *all United States forces are prohibited from molesting them in any way. It is earnestly recommended that the freedom of negroes be acknowledged,* and that, instead of compulsory labor, contracts on fair terms be entered into between the former masters and servants, or between the latter and other persons who may be willing to give them employment. Such a system as this, honestly followed, will result in substantial advantages to all parties.

All private property will be respected, except when the use of it is necessary for the government, in which case it must be taken under the direction of a corps commander, and by a proper detail under charge of a commissioned officer, with specific instructions to seize certain property, and no other. A staff officer of the Quartermaster or Subsistence Department will, in each instance, be designated to receipt for such property as may be seized, the property to be paid for at the end of the war on proof of loyalty, or on proper adjustment of the claim, under such regulations or laws as may hereafter be established. All property seized under this order must be taken up on returns by the officers giving receipts, and disposed of in accordance with existing regulations.

3. Persons having cotton, or other produce not required by the army, will be allowed to bring the same to any military post within

the State of Mississippi, and abandon it to the agent of the Treasury Department at said post, to be disposed of in accordance with such regulations as the Secretary of the Treasury may establish. At posts where there is no such agent, the post Quartermaster will receive all such property, and, at the option of the owner, hold it till the arrival of the agent, or send it to Memphis, directed to Captain A. R. Eddy, Acting Quartermaster, who will turn it over to the properly authorized agent at that place.

4. Within the county of Warren, laid waste by the long presence of contending armies, the following rules, to prevent suffering, will be observed: —

Major General Sherman, commanding the Fifteenth Army Corps, and Major General McPherson, commanding the Seventeenth Army Corps, will each designate *a commissary of subsistence, who will issue articles of prime necessity to all destitute families calling for them*, under such restrictions for the protection of the government as they may deem necessary. Families who are able to pay for the provisions drawn, will in all cases be required to do so.

5. Conduct disgraceful to the American name has been frequently reported to the Major General commanding, particularly on the part of portions of the cavalry. Hereafter, if the guilty parties cannot be reached, the commanders of regiments and detachments will be held responsible, and those who prove themselves unequal to the task of preserving discipline in their commands, will be promptly reported to the War Department for "muster out." Summary punishment must be inflicted upon all officers and soldiers apprehended in acts of violence or lawlessness.

By order of Major General U. S. GRANT.

T. S. BOWERS, *Acting A. A. G.*

The treatment of the negroes being a subject of great importance, Grant issued the following order on the 10th of August: —

*General Orders, No.* 51.

HEADQUARTERS DEPARTMENT OF THE TENNESSEE,
VICKSBURG, MISS., August 10, 1863.

1. At all military posts in states within this department where slavery has been abolished by the proclamation of the President of the United States, camps will be established for such freed people of color as are out of employment.

2. Commanders of posts or districts will detail suitable officers from the army as Superintendents of such camps. It will be the duty of such Superintendents to see that suitable rations are drawn from the Subsistence Department for such people as are confided to their care.

3. All such persons supported by the government will be employed in every practicable way so as to avoid, as far as possible, their becoming a burden upon the government. They may be hired to planters or other citizens, on proper assurance that the negroes so hired will not be run off beyond the military jurisdiction of the United States; they may be employed on any public works, in gathering crops from abandoned plantations, and generally in any manner local commanders may deem for the best interests of the government, in compliance with law and the policy of the administration.

4. It will be the duty of the Provost-marshal at every military post to see that every negro within the jurisdiction of the military authority is employed by some white person, or is sent to the camps provided for freed people.

5. Citizens may make contracts with freed persons of color for their labor, giving wages per month in money, or employ families of them by the year on plantations, &c., feeding, clothing, and supporting the infirm as well as able-bodied, and giving a portion, not less than one twentieth of the commercial part of their crops, in payment for such services.

6. Where negroes are employed under this authority, the parties employing will register with the Provost-marshal their names, occupation, and residence, and the number of negroes so employed. They will enter into such bonds as the Provost-marshal, with the approval of the local commander, may require, for the kind treatment and proper care of those employed, and as security against their being carried beyond the employee's jurisdiction.

7. Nothing of this order is to be construed to embarrass the employment of such colored persons as may be required by the government.

By order of Major General U. S. GRANT.

T. S. BOWERS, *Acting A. A. G.*

He also recognized the value of using the negroes as soldiers, and on the 11th of July, had said to the Adjutant General of the army, "I am anxious to get as many of these negro regiments as possible, and to have them full, and completely equipped. . . . I am particularly desirous of organizing a regiment of heavy artillerists from the negroes, to garrison this place, and shall do so as soon as possible." On the 24th of July, "The negro troops are easier to preserve discipline among than our white troops, and I doubt not will prove equally good for garrison duty. All that have been tried have fought bravely."

On the 9th of August, the President wrote to Grant, "General Thomas has gone again to the Mississippi Valley, with the view of raising colored troops. I have no doubt that you are doing what you reasonably can upon the same subject. I believe it is a resource which, if vigorously applied now, will soon close this contest. It works doubly — weakening the enemy, and strengthening us. We were not fully ripe for it until the river was opened. Now, I think, at least one hundred thousand can, and ought to, be organized along its shores, relieving all the white troops to serve elsewhere. Mr. Davis understands you as believing that the Emancipation Proclamation has helped some in your military operations. I am very glad if this is so."

The Confederates, at first refusing to recognize the

negroes as soldiers, threatened that they and their white officers should be treated, if captured, as runaway slaves, and thieves who had stolen slaves. It having been reported to Grant that a white captain and some negro soldiers captured at Milliken's Bend had been hung, he wrote to General Richard Taylor, then in command of the Confederate forces in Louisiana, "I feel no inclination to retaliate for the offences of irresponsible persons; but if it is the policy of any General intrusted with the command of troops to show no quarter, or to punish with death prisoners taken in battle, I will accept the issue. It may be you propose a different line of policy towards black troops, and officers commanding them, to that practised towards white troops. If so, I can assure you that these colored troops are regularly mustered into the service of the United States. The government, and all officers under the government, are bound to give the same protection to these troops that they do to any other troops."

General Taylor replied that he would punish all such acts, "disgraceful alike to humanity and the reputation of soldiers," but declared that officers of the "Confederate States army" were required to turn over to the civil authorities, to be dealt with according to the laws of the states wherein such were captured, all negroes captured in arms.

## CHAPTER XXIV.

PROPOSES THE CAPTURE OF MOBILE. — VISITS NEW ORLEANS. — MEETS WITH A SEVERE ACCIDENT. — THE POSITION OF ROSECRANS AT CHATTANOOGA. — GRANT'S DEPARTMENT ENLARGED.

ON the 18th of July General Grant announced to Halleck the evacuation of Jackson, and the completion of the Vicksburg campaign, and in the same despatch said, "It seems to me now that Mobile should be captured, the expedition starting from Lake Pontchartrain." But Halleck was of a different opinion. To use his own language, he thought it best, before attempting Mobile, to "clean up a little." The character of the two men's minds was different, and this fact appeared nowhere stronger than in their military conceptions. Halleck would do everything according to the strict rules and precedents heretofore obtaining in the art of war, forgetting that, since these were laid down, the railroad had been invented; while Grant, making the present object in view his only rule and precedent, was so completely a master of the railroad, that he used it as one of the factors in his combinations. On the 24th of July Grant wrote, "It seems to me that Mobile is the point deserving the most immediate attention." On the 1st of August, "Mobile can be taken from the Gulf Department, with only one or two gunboats to protect the debarkation. I can send the necessary force. With your leave I would like to visit New Orleans, particularly if the movement against Mobile is authorized." On the 25th of September, "I am confident that Mobile could now be taken with comparatively a small force. At least a demonstration in that direction would either result in the abandonment of the city, or force the enemy to weaken Bragg's army to hold it." On the 30th, "I regret that I have not got a movable force with which to attack Mobile or the river above. As I am situated, however, I must be content with guarding territory already taken from the enemy. I do not say this complainingly, but simply regret that advantage cannot be taken of so fine an opportunity of dealing the enemy a heavy blow."

The Department at Washington was, however, more impressed at this time with the necessity of reëstablishing, as soon as possible, the national authority in Western Texas. The whole course of the European governments had, from the first, been as open an expression of their desire to see the power of this government overthrown as they dared to make. England had made indecent haste to recognize, almost before there was a rebellion, the Confederacy as a belligerent power. Then came the suggestion to mediate between the contending parties, and finally upon the flimsiest of pretences, but really to gain a foothold from which to interfere with this government, the Mexican expedition was projected, and seemed now in a fair way to succeed. Such a course on the part of the monarchical governments of Europe cannot be wondered at. It was as instinctive an attempt at self-preservation as the rebellion was on the part of the fanatical supporters of slavery. Both conditions of society belong to the barbarism of a past feudal age, and to both of them the democratic idea, as realized in our free republican institutions, gave warning that their days were numbered; that the time had come for a higher and nobler civilization; that the people, having outgrown the need of the leading-strings of their childhood, were now desirous and fitted to obtain and enjoy their prerogative of self-government. The forms of society, and government, are as subject to the laws of development, of growth, of change as is everything in the material universe. The "eternal hills" are not to-day what they were yesterday. The thoughts that form the basis of all governments, are in as constant a condition of evolution and development, as the nations, so governed, are by the constant births and deaths of the individuals who form them. The nineteenth century has raised the great questions of the philosophy of religion, of history, and of philosophy itself, and in science the persistence, the correlation, the identity of force; and how could government expect to avoid being subjected to the application of the same spirit of investigation? In the moral as in the physical world the principle of polarity runs through and pervades all force, and in these two attempts to withstand the energy of the democratic idea, found its natural expression. Therefore, in the larger view, the government was probably right in its opinion of the importance of securing Texas, and thus closing the evident channel through which European interference in Mexico would flow into this country.

On the 7th of August, Grant, having received orders

from Washington, sent the Thirteenth Corps to Banks. He was informed that " General Banks has been left at liberty to select his own objective point in Texas, and may determine to move by sea. If so, your movement will not have his support, and should be conducted with caution. You will confer on this matter freely with General Banks. The government is exceedingly anxious that our troops should occupy some points in Texas with the least possible delay."

On the 30th of August, accordingly, Grant started in person for New Orleans, notifying Halleck of his departure: " General Banks is not yet off, and I am desirous of seeing him before he starts, to learn his plans and see how I may help him."

Before starting upon this visit Grant proposed to Sherman that, as he was the next in command, he should be left in direction during his (Grant's) absence; but Sherman suggesting that the continuance of the present routine would facilitate public business, during Grant's absence all orders were issued in his name with Sherman's concurrence. "With such men," said Grant, "as Sherman and McPherson, commanding corps or armies, there will never be any jealousies or lack of hearty coöperation. Between the two I would have no choice, and the army does not afford an officer superior to either, in my estimation."

Just before this, Grant, on the 25th of August, had paid a visit to Memphis, and was received there with great enthusiasm. A committee of the loyal citizens tendered him the hospitality of the city. In his letter of acceptance he says, —

"In accepting this testimonial, which I do at a great sacrifice of my personal feelings, I simply desire to pay a tribute to the first public exhibition in Memphis of loyalty to the government which I represent in the department of the Tennessee. I should dislike to refuse, for considerations of personal convenience, to acknowledge anywhere, or in any form, the existence of sentiments which I have so long and so ardently desired to see manifested in this department. The stability of this government and the unity of this nation depend solely on the cordial support and the earnest loyalty of the people. While, therefore, I thank you sincerely for the kind expressions you have used towards myself, I am profoundly gratified at this public recognition, in the city of Memphis, of the power and authority of the government of the United States."

On the 2d of September he arrived at New Orleans, and on the 4th assisted at a review of the Thirteenth Corps, at Carrollton, near the city. He was thus described by a correspondent, as he sat out from his hotel for the review: "He was in undress uniform, without sword, sash, or belt; coat unbuttoned, a low-crowned black felt hat, without any mark upon it of military rank; a pair of kid gloves, and a cigar in his mouth."

On the return to his hotel his horse became frightened by the letting off of steam, with a shrill whistle, by a railroad locomotive, and sprang wildly with such violence against a carriage that was coming in an opposite direction, that both horse and rider were thrown upon the street. The result was a most serious accident. His hip was temporarily paralyzed by the tremendous concussion, and he was for a time quite helpless; nor, indeed, did he recover so as to walk without crutches, or mount his horse without assistance, until after he had reached Chattanooga, near the end of October. There really seemed to be danger that his services would be lost to the country.

On the 16th of September, he, however, returned to Vicksburg, being carried on a litter to the steamboat, and was compelled to keep his bed until the 25th of September.

At this time Rosecrans was operating in Tennessee and Northern Georgia, and had possession of Chattanooga, upon the Tennessee River, a strategical point, which is perhaps the most important between Richmond and the Mississippi, since it is the centre of the great southern railroads. His base of supplies was Nashville, and the Confederate army under Bragg was apparently attempting to move west of him, through Northern Alabama, in order to cut off his base of supplies. On the 13th of September Halleck telegraphed Grant, "All of Major General Grant's available force should be sent to Memphis, thence to Corinth and Tuscumbia, to coöperate with General Rosecrans." At this time there was telegraphic communication from Washington only as far as Cairo, and thence by boat to Memphis and Vicksburg. The messenger to whom this despatch was intrusted failed to deliver it promptly. On the 15th the order was repeated, and on the 22d, when Grant received it, he immediately forwarded the required reënforcements, and gave orders to detain all steamers then at Vicksburg, or which should arrive there, in order to afford transportation. Within forty-eight hours after the receipt of the order, the troops were on their way. On the 25th Grant wrote, "I am just out of bed, and find that I can write only with great difficulty. During the twenty days that I have been confined to one position, on my back, I have apparently been in the most perfect health, but now that

I am up on crutches, I find myself very weak;" and on that day he notified Sherman to hold himself in readiness to go to support Rosecrans, and on the 27th the column set out. In order to divert the attention of the enemy, and prevent their interfering with Sherman's march, Grant ordered McPherson to send an expedition to Canton and Jackson.

On the 19th and 20th of September Rosecrans had been severely repulsed on the Chickamauga River, nine miles from Chattanooga, and forced to fall back upon that place, with heavy loss. Here he was nearly surrounded by the Confederate army, which was larger than his, and his only line of communication nearly cut off.

On the 10th of October Grant received orders to report at Cairo, and leaving on the same day, and arriving there on the 16th, telegraphed, "I have just arrived. My staff and headquarters are with me." He was in reply ordered to proceed to Louisville, Kentucky, taking his staff with him, for immediate operations in the field, and that there he would meet an officer of the War Department, with his orders. Starting immediately, he met at Indianapolis, on his way, the Secretary of War, Mr. Stanton, with an order he had brought from Washington, giving Grant a new command — the Military Division of the Mississippi, including all the territory between the Alleghanies and the Mississippi, except such territory as might be occupied by Banks. The three departments of the Tennessee, the Cumberland, now under Rosecrans, and the Ohio, now under Burnside, were made subordinate to him. The advantage of some such change had been suggested by

Grant nearly a year before, and its necessity had become painfully apparent to the government. The three armies had been acting apparently without reference to each other's operations. For some time Halleck had been trying to make Rosecrans coöperate with Grant, but without success, and his last disaster had determined the government to concentrate the command of all the western forces under one head, and Grant had been selected to occupy this position. The operations in the west would now be planned for mutual support, and tend towards a single result. We shall see that eventually the government concluded that it would be best to pursue this course with the military operations of the whole country.

The Secretary brought with him also two other orders, one relieving Rosecrans, and substituting General Thomas in his place, and the other continuing Rosecrans in command. Grant was offered his choice, and preferred the one removing Rosecrans. Great anxiety was felt for the safety of the army under him. Proceeding together to Louisville, the Secretary directed Grant to assume his new position at once, and to relieve Rosecrans by telegraph. This was done, and on the 19th of October he started for Chattanooga.

## CHAPTER XXV.

THE CONDITION AT CHATTANOOGA. — THE MEANS TAKEN TO IMPROVE IT. — THE RESULT OF A WEEK'S WORK.

CHATTANOOGA, while it is the key of the Tennessee River, is also the junction of the railways leading from Memphis to Charleston, from Richmond to Nashville, and south to Atlanta, from whence again the numerous branches supplying the South meet. The railway lines converging here were the interior strategic lines of the Confederacy, enabling them to transport their troops with promptness and facility from one part of the theatre of the war to another, as the necessity arose, and also made their lines of transportation by which the supplies were forwarded from the rich regions of the south-west to their armies in the field. Besides these considerations, situated as this point was at the junction of several states, and at the end of the mountain range of the Alleghanies, it was the centre of the population which remained, all throughout the war, loyal to the national government. The people of East Tennessee, of West Virginia, and North Carolina, and of Northern Alabama and Georgia, had never been false to the Union. The nature of their soil had prevented slavery from becoming a profitable system of labor, and they had not therefore become corrupted by its influence. The record of the sufferings and persecutions they endured for their devotion to the Union cause has not yet been fully written, and probably never will be. The gallows and the bullet did their work so thoroughly, that until the grave yields up its dead, we can never know how many brave hearts perished in this region of country for their loyalty to the Union. The possession of Chattanooga would secure safety for this population, and the reëstablishment of the national authority would be the realization of their daily prayers for years.

In May, 1862, after the evacuation of Corinth, Halleck had sent Buell, with more than forty thousand men, across the States of Alabama and Tennessee, to Chattanooga; but Bragg, having started for the same point, finally forced Buell to fall back towards the Ohio; and when, after months of marching and fighting, Buell was further from Chattanooga than when he started, he was relieved, and Rosecrans placed in command of this army of the Cumberland, with the same object — the possession of Chattanooga — as its aim.

After finally fighting the battle of Murfreesboro', in which the Union army remained in possession of the field, Rosecrans remained stationary until the 24th of June, 1863, when he moved out with about seventy thousand men. During Grant's operations at Vicksburg he had tried to have Rosecrans make at least a sufficient demonstration against Bragg to prevent him from sending reënforcements to Johnston. But though ordered to do so from the Department at Washington, he would not budge, but held a council of war, and decided that it was a maxim in war not to fight two decisive battles at the same time. When, however, he moved out, Bragg was still before him, with an inferior force, and retreated. Continuing to advance, Rosecrans outgeneralled Bragg, and finally, on the 9th of September, occupied Chattanooga. Bragg, however, being largely reënforced, his army numbered about sixty thousand men, while Rosecrans, having been obliged to garrison the places he had left in his rear, had about forty-five thousand, divided into three corps, commanded by Thomas, McCook, and Crittenden. Crittenden held Chattanooga, while the other corps were in the mountains, separated by about twenty miles. Being threatened by Bragg, the army was brought together with difficulty at Chickamauga Creek, about nine miles from Chattanooga, and on the 19th of September was attacked by Bragg, who, after two days' fighting, pierced the centre and scattered the right wing. Rosecrans himself hastened to Chattanooga in order to prepare it for defence, and McCook and Crittenden also left the field. Thomas, however, remained firm, and resisted the attempt of the entire Confederate army to get between him and Chattanooga, until, finding it useless, Bragg desisted from the attempt.

Withdrawing all his army into Chattanooga, Rosecrans determined to hold it if possible; and a formidable line of works was thrown up just outside of the town. Having, however, abandoned Lookout Mountain, which commands the river and the Nashville and Chattanooga Railway, by which all his supplies were brought, Rosecrans found himself besieged, as soon as the Confederates, seeing his error, took possession of the mountain and fortified it. From this point they could throw shells into Rosecrans's camp, and as his only means of communication was by a wagon road over the mountains, which, from the rains, became nearly impassable, the army was soon reduced to half rations.

Here Bragg felt that he had the army of the Cumberland secure, and that starvation would soon make them surrender both Chattanooga and themselves. He says in his report, "These dispositions, faithfully sustained, insured the speedy evacuation of Chattanooga, for want of food and forage. Possessed of the shortest route to his depot, and the one by which reënforcements must reach him, we held him at our mercy, and his destruction was only a question of time."

When, on the 19th of October, 1863, Grant took command of the army, it was reduced to worse straits than any other of our armies was during the war. The men, suffering from insufficient food and insufficient clothing, seeing nothing before them but starvation and surrender, were dispirited and listless; the camp was filled with animals, dead or dying for want of forage, and the stock of ammunition was enough for only one battle.

After the battle of Chickamauga, two corps from the army of the Potomac, under the command of Hooker, had been sent to protect Rosecrans's line of railroad between Nashville and Bridgeport, and were ordered to stop at this last place, since their presence at Chattanooga would only have been a further tax upon the already scanty stock of supplies. Burnside, who was in command of the department of the Ohio, had also been operating in East Tennessee, and had taken Knoxville, on the Tennessee River, about one hundred and ten miles above Chattanooga, and after the defeat at Chickamauga, Bragg had despatched a column to hold him in check.

When Grant telegraphed Thomas, from Louisville, to assume command of the army of the Cumberland, he sent him also the following message: "Hold Chattanooga at all hazards. I will be there as soon as possible." Thomas replied at once, "I will hold the town till we starve."

On the morning of the 20th Grant started by rail from Louisville, and that night arrived at Nashville, where he telegraphed Burnside, "I will be in Stevenson to-morrow night, and Chattanooga the next night." He also telegraphed Admiral Porter at Cairo, "General Sherman's advance was at Eastport on the 15th. The sooner a gunboat can be got to him, the better. Boats must now be on the way from St. Louis, with supplies, to go up the Tennessee, for Sherman."

Sherman's army, it will be remembered, had started from Memphis, to go across the country to the aid of Rosecrans. At Eastport they had reached the Tennessee River. Grant also telegraphed Thomas, "Should not large working parties be put upon the road between Bridgeport and Chattanooga at once?" We see that he was busy with all the various interests of the several armies in his extended command, and was combining them to work towards a single purpose. At Stevenson he met Rosecrans and Hooker, the former on his way north. He was cordial in his behavior, and gave Grant all the information he could concerning the condition of affairs. At Bridgeport Grant telegraphed to Nashville, "Send to the front, as speedily as possible, vegetables for the army. Beans and hominy are especially required."

From Bridgeport to Chattanooga the party travelled on horseback. The mountain roads, which at best are not the easiest, were now in a dreadful state from the rains, and were strewn with the wrecks of wagons and bodies of horses, the remains of the attempts to supply the army after the railroad communications had been cut. Frequently the whole party had to dismount and lead their horses over the most difficult parts. At such times Grant, who was still too lame to walk, had to be carried in the arms of soldiers. But despite all obstacles he pressed on, and reached Chattanooga just at dark, during a heavy rain, the whole party being wet, hungry, and tired. Grant went immediately to Thomas's headquarters, and at half past nine, on the night of the 23d, telegraphed to Halleck, "Have just arrived. I will write to-morrow. Please approve order placing Sherman in command of department of the Tennessee, with headquarters in the field."

The next morning Grant, with Thomas and W. F. Smith, the chief engineer of the department of the Cumberland, made a reconnoissance of the territory, with a view of opening a line for supplies, by obtaining command of Brown's Ferry. Rosecrans had had an idea of some such plan. Smith had proposed it; so had Halleck; and Thomas had resolved upon it even before Grant came. The details of the movement were as follows: Smith was to take a party of four thousand men down the river to Brown's Ferry, on the river, six miles below Chattanooga, at night, past the pickets of the enemy without alarming them, and seize the range of steep hills at the mouth of Lookout Valley, three miles below Lookout Mountain, and which were held in small force by the enemy, and which were of value to him, since they offered him the means of bringing at any time an overwhelming force to blockade the river. This attempt was to be a surprise, and, if successful, would force the enemy between Lookout Creek and Shell Mountain to fall back behind the creek, and would thus open the way for Hooker to bring up his force from Bridgeport into Lookout Valley.

The plan was successfully carried out. On the night of the 26th Smith sent sixty pontoon boats, each containing thirty men, down the river from Chattanooga, and secured the position almost before the enemy were aware that any attempt was made to secure it. On the morning of the same day Hooker started, and at six in the evening of the 28th the command went into camp within a mile of Brown's Ferry.

The enemy, finding that the Union army had secured their base of supplies, attacked Hooker the night after his arrival. The attack was made by Longstreet's corps in force; but after a struggle of some hours they were repulsed, and Hooker held Lookout Valley thereafter without opposition.

Thus, in five days after Grant's arrival at Chattanooga, his connection with Nashville, the base of his supplies, was opened, and the danger of starvation removed. Only a week before Jefferson Davis had visited Lookout Mountain, and from its summit gazed upon the Union army encamped below, considering them caged and secure. But the conditions were now changed. Grant had assumed the offensive, — the position he liked, — and Bragg was forced to act on the defensive. Not only had the line of supplies been opened, but the army had also been reënforced by the two corps under Hooker, who from their position threatened the Confederate force on Lookout Mountain. Forage was at once obtained for the starving animals of the army, fresh horses were forwarded, and full rations were issued again.

The men felt the inspiriting effect, and their listlessness disappeared. On the 28th Grant wrote, "If the rebels give us one week more time, I think all danger of losing territory now held by us will have passed away, and preparations may be made for active operations." In the mean time Grant also turned his attention to providing for the wants of Burnside's army, in East Tennessee, and Sherman's army, on the march across the country to join the force at Chattanooga. The supplies for both of these bodies had to be looked after, and Grant was indefatigable, foreseeing what would be required, and urging upon all his subordinates the necessity for promptness and despatch.

When Grant had sent Sherman from Vicksburg to Memphis, on his way to reënforce Rosecrans, he said, "I hope you will be in time to aid in giving the rebels the worst, or best, thrashing they have had in this war. I have constantly had the feeling that I shall lose you from this command entirely. Of course I do not object to seeing your sphere of usefulness enlarged, and think it should have been enlarged long ago, having an eye to the public good alone. But it needs no assurance from me, General, that, taking a more selfish view, while I would heartily approve such a change, I would deeply regret it on my own account."

It was then supposed that Sherman would relieve Rosecrans in the command of the army of the Cumberland. While he was at Memphis, however, Sherman heard that Grant was ordered north, and suspecting what was about to occur, he wrote, on the 14th of October, nearly a week before the new division was created, or Grant placed at its head, "Accept the command of the great army of the centre; don't hesitate. By your presence at Nashville you will unite all discordant elements, and impress the enemy in proportion. All success and honor to you!" And again, on the 15th, "I am very anxious you should go to Nashville, as foreshadowed by Halleck, and chiefly as you can harmonize all conflicts of feeling that may exist in that vast crowd. Rosecrans, and Burnside, and Sherman, with their subordinates, would be ashamed of petty quarrels, if you were behind and near them, between them and Washington. Next, the union of such armies, and the direction of it, is worthy your ambition. I shall await news from you with great anxiety."

About the middle of October, Sherman, in his advance from Memphis, struck the Tennessee at Eastport, where, it will be remembered, one of Grant's first orders, after taking his present command, was to order supplies to be sent him. On the 24th, the day after his arrival at Chattanooga, Grant sent the following to Sherman, who received it on the 27th: "Drop everything east of Bear Creek, and move with your entire force towards Stevenson, until you receive further orders. The enemy are evidently moving a large force towards Cleveland, and may break through our lines and move on Nashville, in which event your troops are the only forces at command that could beat them there."

Following this order, on the 1st of November, Sherman passed to the front at Florence. On the 7th Grant sent him the following: "The enemy have moved a great part of their force from this front towards Burnside. I have to make an immediate move from here towards their lines of communication, to bring them back if possible. I am anxious to see your old corps here at the earliest moment." When Sherman reached Fayetteville, he received still further instructions: "Come on to Stevenson and Bridgeport, with your four divisions. I want your command to aid in a movement to force the enemy back from their present position, and to make Burnside secure in his."

On the 13th the army arrived at Bridgeport, and from this point Sherman telegraphed to Grant, and was summoned in person to Chattanooga. Grant's anxiety for Sherman's advance was caused by Burnside's position, against whom Bragg had sent a force detached from his army. On the 3d of November, Longstreet was also sent by Bragg, with orders to drive Burnside out of East Tennessee, or, if possible, to capture or destroy him; and the force given Longstreet for this purpose was about fifteen thousand men, with, also, about five thousand cavalry and eighty guns. Longstreet had asked for twenty thousand men, but could not obtain them, and says, in his report, "As my orders were to drive the enemy out of East Tennessee, or, if possible, capture him, I determined that the only possible chance of succeeding in either or both, was to move and act as though I had a sufficient force to do either. I endeavored, therefore, to do as I should have done, had the twenty thousand men that I asked for been given me."

Grant had foreseen the possibility of this move, and on the 5th, the day after Longstreet had started, he sent to Burnside the following: "I will endeavor, from here, to bring the enemy back from your right flank as soon as possible. Should you discover him leaving, you should annoy him all you can with your cavalry, and in fact with all the troops you can bring to bear. Sherman's advance will be at Bridgeport about Monday next. Whether Thomas makes any demonstration before his arrival, will depend upon advices of the enemy's movements."

On the 7th Thomas was ordered to attack Bragg's army. "The news," said Grant, "is of such a nature, that it becomes an imperative duty for your force to draw the attention of the enemy from Burnside to your own front. I deem the best movement to attack the enemy to be, an attack on the northern end of Missionary Ridge, with all the force you can bring to bear against it; and, when that is carried, to threaten and even attack, if possible, the enemy's line of communication between Dalton and Cleveland. Rations should be ready to issue a sufficiency to last four days the moment Missionary Ridge is in our possession; rations to be carried in haversacks. Where there are not horses to move the artillery, mules must be taken from the teams, or horses from ambulances; or, if necessary, officers dismounted, and their horses taken. Immediate preparations should be made to carry these directions into execution. The movement should not be made a moment later than to-morrow morning." On the same day Grant said to Burnside, "I have ordered an immediate move from here to carry Missionary Ridge, and to threaten or attack the railroad between Cleveland and Dalton. This must have the effect to draw the enemy back from your western front."

Thomas, however, declared himself utterly unable to move before Sherman's force came up. He had no horses to drag his artillery, and therefore Grant was forced to leave Burnside to take care of himself. The government at this juncture was more anxious concerning Burnside than Grant was, and its despatches show they felt great alarm lest his army should be forced to surrender or else destroyed. All that could be done, however, in the emergency, Grant did. It was impossible for Thomas to attack; so he had to content himself with exhorting Burnside to keep firm, and with seeing that Sherman was kept furnished with supplies at the various points he reached in his advance, and with preparing the means for supplying the entire army, when it should concentrate, with supplies and material, so that it would be able to take the offensive when the time came for so doing. It was annoying, however, to be forced to remain stationary while Bragg had detached a force from his command; yet there was nothing else to be done.

There was, however, no fault to be found with any one. Thomas's army was temporarily tied by causes that were beyond his control. It required time, whatever means were now at his disposal, to put it again in a condition to take the initiative. Sherman also was completing a march over land of four hundred miles, through an enemy's country. He had been forced to skirmish, to build bridges, to ford streams, to repair the railroads, and had here acquired the experience, and displayed the qualities, which fitted him for his subsequent march to the sea.

The reader, who quietly at home, enjoying the repose of peace, reads of the operations of an army in the field, can hardly realize, without an effort, the enormous amount of labor, of careful preparation, of far-seeing combination and accurate performance, requisite in the active operations of war. Here for this battle of Chattanooga, which was a struggle between the contending parties for the possession of the stand-point from which to arrange and realize still more far-reaching combinations, and which, if the Union army was successful, would be made the base for penetrating the very heart of the Confederacy, or, if the Confederates were successful, would form the point for driving the armies of the government back to the limits of the territory claimed for secession, and perhaps for even carrying the war into the loyal states, — for this battle half the whole continent was laid under contribution, and a hundred centres of industry were resounding with the busy hum of preparation. From St. Louis to Pittsburg, the Mississippi, the Ohio, and their tributaries, were crowded with steamers, bringing supplies of food, of clothes, to feed and clothe, and ammunition and arms to defend and destroy, these hostile armies. From the Lakes to the Gulf, from Maine to Missouri, the workshops of the country were occupied in preparing material for the armies to be soon engaged in the fierce struggle. Two hundred thousand armed men were by the North alone kept in the field, either concentrating or guarding the supplies for this battle-field. Over all this bustle of preparation Grant was the ruling spirit. Grasping at once the main features, as well as the minutest details, he kept control of them all, and, by ceaseless activity and care, kept the whole vast and complicated machinery working evenly and harmoniously towards one object.

# CHAPTER XXVI.

BURNSIDE'S POSITION. — SHERMAN'S ARRIVAL. — THE ARMY PREPARING FOR ACTIVELY OFFENSIVE MEASURES. — THE BATTLE OF CHATTANOOGA.

On the 14th of November Halleck telegraphed, "Advices received from East Tennessee indicate that Burnside intends to abandon the defence of Little Tennessee River, and fall back before Longstreet towards Cumberland Gap and the upper valley. Longstreet is said to be near the Little Tennessee, with from twenty to forty thousand men; Burnside has about thirty thousand in all, and can hold his position; he ought not to retreat. I fear further delay may result in Burnside's abandonment of East Tennessee. This would be a terrible misfortune, and must be averted if possible." To this Grant replied, reassuringly, "Burnside certainly can detain Longstreet in the Tennessee Valley until we can make such moves here as will entirely free him from present dangers. I have asked him if he could hold the Knoxville and Clinton line for one week; if so, we can make moves here that will save all danger in East Tennessee. . . . Sherman is now at Bridgeport. He will commence moving to-morrow or next day, throwing one brigade from Whiteside into Trenton, thus threatening the enemy's left flank. The remainder of his force will pass over by Kelly's Ferry, evading view from Lookout, and march up to the mouth of Chickamauga. Pontoons are made, and making, to throw across at that point, over which it is intended that Sherman's force and one division of Thomas's shall pass. This force will attack Missionary Ridge, with the left flank of Thomas supporting, from here. In the mean time Hooker will attack Lookout, and carry it, if possible. If Burnside can hold the line from Knoxville to Clinton, as I have asked him, for six days, I believe Bragg will be started back for the south side of Oostanaula, and Longstreet cut off."

On the 16th, again, despatches of about the same tenor were sent. On the 14th Grant sent to Burnside the following: "Sherman's advance has reached Bridgeport. His whole force will be ready to move from there by Tuesday at farthest. If you can hold Longstreet in check until he gets up, or, by skirmishing and falling back, can avoid serious loss to yourself, and gain time, I will be able to force the enemy back from here, and place a force between Longstreet and Bragg that must inevitably make the former take to the mountain-passes by every available road, to get to his supplies. Sherman would have been here before this but for high water on Elk River driving him some thirty miles up that river to cross." On the same day he again telegraphed to Burnside, "Can you hold the line from Knoxville to Clinton for seven days? If so, I think the whole Tennessee Valley can be secured from present danger." And again, at ten o'clock that night, "It is of the most vital importance that East Tennessee should be held. Take immediate steps to that end. Evacuate Kingston if you think best. As I said in a previous despatch,

I think seven days more will enable us to make such movements as to make the whole valley secure, if you hold on that time."

On the 17th he said, "I have not heard from you since the 14th. What progress is Longstreet making, and what are your chances for defending yourself? Sherman's forces have commenced their movement from Bridgeport, threatening the enemy. This alone may turn Longstreet back, and if it does not, the attack will be prosecuted until we reach the roads over which all their supplies have to pass, while you hold East Tennessee." Later on the same day, "Your despatch received. You are doing exactly what appears to me to be right. I want the enemy's progress retarded at every point all it can be, only giving up each place when it becomes evident that it cannot longer be held without endangering your force to capture. I think our movements here must cause Longstreet's recall within a day or two, if he is not successful before that time. Sherman moved this morning from Bridgeport, with one division. The remainder of his command moves in the morning. There will be no halt until a severe battle is fought, or the railroads cut supplying the enemy."

On the 18th Grant telegraphed Halleck, "Despatches from General Burnside received at ten P. M. yesterday. Troops had got back from Knoxville. Sherman's advance reached Lookout Mountain to-day. Movements will progress, threatening enemy's left flank, until forces can be got up and thrown across the river, to attack their right flank and Missionary Ridge. A battle or a falling back of the enemy is inevitable by Saturday, at the farthest. Burnside speaks hopefully."

This day also the written orders for the battle were given to Thomas and Sherman. The instructions given to Thomas were as follows: "All preparations should be made for attacking the enemy's position on Missionary Ridge by Saturday morning, at daylight. . . . The general plan is for Sherman, with the force brought with him, strengthened by a division from your command, to effect a crossing of the Tennessee River just below the mouth of the Chickamauga; his crossing to be protected by artillery from the heights of the north bank of the river (to be located by your chief of artillery), and to secure the heights (Missionary Ridge) from the northern extremity to about the railroad tunnel, before the enemy can concentrate against him. You will coöperate with Sherman. The troops in Chattanooga Valley should all be concentrated on your left flank, leaving only the necessary force to defend fortifications on the right and centre, and a movable column of one division, in readiness to move wherever ordered. This division should show itself, as threateningly as possible, on the most practicable line for making an attack up the valley. Your effort, then, will be to form a junction with Sherman, making your advance well towards the northern end of Missionary Ridge, and moving as near simultaneously with him as possible. The junction once formed, and the Ridge carried, connection will be at once established between the two armies by roads on the south bank of the river. Further movements will then depend on those of the enemy.

"Lookout Valley, I think, will be easily held by Geary's division, and what troops you may still have there of the old army of the Cumberland. Howard's corps can then be held in readiness to act, either with you at Chattanooga, or with Sherman. It should be marched, on Friday night, to a position on the north side of the river, not lower down than the first pontoon bridge [at Chattanooga], and then held in readiness for such orders as may become necessary. All these troops will be provided with two days' cooked rations, in haversacks, and one hundred rounds of ammunition, on the person of each infantry soldier."

A copy of these instructions was forwarded to Sherman, for his guidance, and he was also informed —"It is particularly desirable that a force should be got through to the railroad, between Cleveland and Dalton, and Longstreet thus cut off from communication with the South; but, being confronted by a large force here, strongly located, it is not easy to tell how this is to be effected, until the result of our first effort is known."

As was Grant's constant practice, he gave only general orders, since he knew that emergencies would constantly arise, and that plans must be formed then to meet them. It is impossible to foresee all the chances of war, and the part of a commander is to be ready, as the unexpected emergencies arise, to be able to meet them and turn them to his advantage.

On the 20th Sherman reached Hooker's headquarters, in his advance, and there found Grant's orders for a general attack the next day. But as only one division had got into position, and the roads were so wretched, and were made worse just at this time by continuous rains, Sherman was obliged to notify Grant that it was impossible for him to take part in the attack; and so it was again postponed.

On the 20th Grant wrote to Sherman, "To-morrow morning I had set for your attack. I see now it cannot possibly be made then; but can you not get up for the following morning? Every effort must be made to get up in time to attack on Sunday morning." On the 20th Grant received the following communication from Bragg:—

HEADQUARTERS ARMY OF TENNESSEE,
IN THE FIELD, NOV. 20, 1863.

MAJOR GENERAL U. S. GRANT,
*Commanding United States Forces at Chattanooga.*

GENERAL: As there may still be some non-combatants in Chattanooga, I deem it proper to notify you that prudence would dictate their early withdrawal.

I am, General, very respectfully, your obedient servant,
BRAXTON BRAGG, *General commanding.*

This message did not deceive Grant, and, instead of leading him to fear an immediate attack, suggested to him that Bragg was about to evacuate his position, and made him the more anxious to attack him before he should get an opportunity to do so. On the 21st, however, he was forced to again notify Thomas—"I have just received a report of the position of Sherman's forces. The rain, last night, has thrown them back so much, that it will be impossible to get into position for action to-morrow morning. He will be up, however, against all calamities that can be foreseen, to commence on Monday morning."

The next day, however, the rise in the river having carried away the bridge, he was obliged again on the 22d to write to Thomas, "The bridges at Brown's

Ferry being down to-day, and the excessively bad roads since the last rain, will render it impossible for Sherman to get up either of his remaining two divisions in time for the attack to-morrow morning. . . . You can make your arrangements for this delay."

In his despatch to Sherman, on this day, Grant said, "Let me know, to-morrow, at as early an hour as you can, if you will be entirely ready for Tuesday morning."

On this day, the 22d, a deserter from the rebel army came into the lines, and gave information that Bragg was falling back from Missionary Ridge. The next day, therefore, Thomas advanced. From an early hour of the morning our artillery had opened on the enemy, and his replies woke the echoes of the mountains. At the given signal, however, at about two P. M., the dispositions being completed, the troops marched out in such order and precision that the enemy thought it was a review, and from their heights looked down upon their evolutions as upon a pageant. Finally, however, a few shots from the line of skirmishers scattered the Confederate pickets, and the troops, advancing despite the heavy fire from the enemy, now aware of our intentions, carried the whole of the enemy's advanced line, securing Orchard Knoll, and a low range of hills about half way between Chattanooga and Missionary Ridge, and about a mile within the outposts occupied by the enemy before the movement. That night the advanced position was fortified, the artillery placed in position, and pickets thrown out in front. That night Sherman's third division arrived opposite the mouth of the South Chickamauga, about four miles above Chattanooga, and that night and next morning crossed the river, and at half past three in the afternoon had secured a position upon the end of Missionary Ridge, crossing it in a general direction, facing south-east. The same day, at Lookout Mountain Hooker's division had carried that position by a charge, and thus secured the other end of the enemy's line, and at four Hooker reported that his line was impregnable.

Thus from Hooker's original position at Wauchatchie, to the mouth of the North Chickamauga, a distance of thirteen miles, the enemy had been attacked at the same time, and so successfully that on the night of the 24th the national army held an unbroken line from the north end of Lookout Mountain, through Chattanooga Valley, to the farther end of Missionary Ridge. The day had been foggy and rainy, and this had favored our movements. While Hooker's men were scaling Lookout Mountain, the clouds which hung about its sides concealed their advance from the spectators below, so that it was only from the flashes of fire through the clouds, the thunder-like roar of battle, and occasional glimpses of the advancing standards, as the shifting clouds for a moment rose and fell, that his position could be followed. During the night, firing still continued on the mountain, and the signal lights of the rebels remaining on the topmost summit revealed to Bragg, on Missionary Ridge, the extent of the defeat of his army. At times, too, sharp discharges of musketry, or jets of flame from cannon, seemed to issue from the mountain side, while the cries of battle and defeat seemed, to those below, to come from armies contending in the air.

At midnight the Generals received orders to press forward the attack early in the morning. Hooker was to try and cut off Bragg's retreat. At half past five on the afternoon of the 24th Grant telegraphed to Washington, "The fight to-day progressed favorably. Sherman carried the end of Missionary Ridge, and his right is now at the tunnel, and left at Chickamauga Creek. Troops from Lookout Valley carried the point of the mountain, and now hold the eastern slope and point high up. Hooker reports two thousand prisoners taken, besides which a small number have fallen into our hands from Missionary Ridge." The President replied in person to this, on the morning of the 25th, "Your despatches as to fighting on Monday and Tuesday are here. Well done! Many thanks to all. Remember Burnside." Halleck also telegraphed, "I congratulate you on the success thus far of your plans. I fear that Burnside is hard pushed, and that any further delay may prove fatal. I know that you will do all in your power to relieve him."

That night the rebels evacuated Lookout Mountain, retreating to Missionary Ridge.

The morning of the 25th the sun shone brilliantly. Grant's main line faced south and east, towards Missionary Ridge, and about a mile from it. Hooker was marching down the side of Lookout Mountain, towards Rossville Gap. Sherman was in possession of the extreme left of Missionary Ridge, but there were immense natural difficulties in his way for further advance, while the rebel works were also in his front. Bragg's headquarters on the ridge, in the centre of his force, were plainly in sight, while Grant's position was on Orchard

Hill, overlooking the whole field. Early in the morning Sherman advanced, carried and held a ridge about eighty yards from the enemy's intrenchments, and also the extreme edge of the work itself. He also made a threatening move against the enemy's right flank, and also his stores and line of communications at Chickamauga Station. Though he could not push his advance any farther, yet, as he held the ground he had gained firmly, and threatened the enemy's rear, the object of his attack was fully gained, since this was to force Bragg to weaken his centre in order to support this threatened flank, and thus weaken the resistance Thomas would meet in his assault upon this portion of the rebel line.

Grant, from his commanding position, soon saw that his plan was succeeding — that Bragg was drawing troops from his centre to concentrate them in front of Sherman—and though Hooker had been detained by the necessity of constructing the bridge over Chattanooga Creek, which the rebels had destroyed in their retreat from Lookout Mountain, and did not, therefore, on the left, arrive at his proposed position as soon as was expected, yet Grant, having received information that he was safely on his way there, he ordered Thomas, in the centre, to advance.

Thomas's force now consisted of four divisions, under Johnson, Sheridan, Wood, and Baird. His orders were to carry the rifle-pits at the foot of the Ridge, and then to re-form in them, with a view to carry the top of the Ridge.

The men had become impatient at remaining within sight of the battle, and taking no active part in it; and so, when ordered to advance, they started on the run, with fixed bayonets. The artillery from the Ridge poured in a heavy fire upon them, as they crossed the open plain, varying from four to nine hundred yards in width, from their cover of timber, where they started, to the first line of rifle-pits; but the line never wavered, and, charging through, captured the pits, and a thousand men in them, and then kept on up the Ridge. Their enthusiasm could not be checked, and up the whole five hundred yards of the steep and rugged ascent, under a heavy fire of canister and musketry, climbing steadily, if slowly, they pressed on, carried the second line of rifle-pits, about midway in the ascent, and, without stopping, pressed on to the top. The whole ascent was a friendly race between the regiments. As many as five or six color-bearers were successively shot down; but others took the flag, and still pressed on. During the last half of the ascent, from the second line of pits to the crest, a fire of thirty pieces of artillery and a storm of musketry were flung full in their faces. But nothing could stop them. Pushing the enemy up before them, they gained the crest, poured over the works that crowned it, and at the same moment breaking through at six points, captured crowds of the enemy in the very trenches. The rout was overwhelming. Whole regiments of the enemy threw down their arms, and others fled down the eastern slope, pelted by our men with stones. The cannon which crowned the summit were turned upon the retreating enemy, and in fifty-five minutes from the time the charge commenced the place was ours.

Bragg had believed the position so secure, that as he said, "a line of skirmishers should have maintained it against any assaulting column." He at first thought the attack had been repulsed, and was riding along the Ridge, congratulating his troops, when the facts were made plain to him, and proceeding to the rear he tried to rally his retreating men, but could not. "A panic," as he says in his report, "which I had never before witnessed, seemed to have seized upon officers and men, and each seemed to be struggling for his personal safety, regardless of his duty or his character." Orders were given to retire to Chickamauga; and as the roads were familiar to the rebels and equally unknown to us, the remains of the army retired. Grant rode up upon the Ridge immediately, to direct the pursuit, and followed it himself a mile or two. The approach of night, however, put an end to it, though Sheridan pushed on as far as Mission Mills, about seven miles.

The success was complete, and at seven P. M. Grant telegraphed to Washington, "Although the battle lasted from early dawn until dark this evening, I believe I am not premature in announcing a complete victory over Bragg. Lookout Mountain-top, all the rifle-pits in Chattanooga Valley, and Missionary Ridge entire, have been carried, and are now held by us. I have no idea of finding Bragg here to-morrow." A half hour later he despatched again: "I have heard from Burnside, to the 23d, when he had rations for ten or twelve days, and expected to hold out that time. I shall move a force from here on to the railroad between Cleveland and Dalton, and send a column of twenty thousand men up the south side of the Tennessee, without wagons, carrying four days' rations, and taking a steamer loaded with rations, from which to draw, on the route. If

Burnside holds out until this force gets beyond Kingston, I think the enemy will fly, and with the present state of the roads, must abandon almost everything. I believe Bragg will lose much of his army by desertion, in consequence of his defeat in the last three days' fight." On the 26th Halleck replied to Grant's announcement of success, "I congratulate you and your army on the victories of Chattanooga. This is truly a day of thanksgiving."

To Sherman, on the night of the 25th, Grant said, "My plan is to move your forces out gradually, until they reach the railroad between Cleveland and Dalton. Granger will move up the south side of the Tennessee. . . . We will push Bragg with all our strength, to-morrow, and try if we cannot cut off a good portion of his new troops and trains. His men have manifested a strong desire to desert for some time past, and we will now give them a chance. . . . Move the advance force on the most easterly road taken by the enemy." The same night Thomas was ordered—"You will start a strong reconnoissance in the morning at seven A. M., to ascertain the position of the enemy. If it is ascertained that the enemy are in full retreat, follow them with all your force, except that which you intend Granger to take to Knoxville. . . . Four days' rations should be got up to the men between this and morning, and also a supply of ammunition. I shall want Granger's expedition to get off by the day after to-morrow."

At Ringgold, in their retreat, Cleburne, who had been covering the rear of the Confederate army, was ordered to take up a naturally very strong position in the gorge of the mountains, and check the pursuit. Here a severe struggle took place. The enemy, however, were chiefly contending to preserve their train of supplies, and when they had done this, fell back. Here Grant ordered the pursuit to be discontinued, since it was absolutely necessary to move to the aid of Burnside.

Of Grant's bearing in action, the following notice by Colonel E. S. Parker, one of his staff, is interesting: "It has been a matter of universal wonder in this army that General Grant himself was not killed, and that no more accidents occurred to his staff; for the General was always in the front (his staff with him, of course), and perfectly heedless of the storm of hissing bullets and screaming shell flying around him. His apparent want of sensibility does not arise from heedlessness, heartlessness, or vain military affectation, but from a sense of the responsibility resting upon him when in battle. When at Ringgold, we rode for half a mile in the face of the enemy, under an incessant fire of cannon and musketry; nor did we ride fast, but upon an ordinary trot; and not once, do I believe, did it enter the General's mind that he was in danger. I was by his side, and watched him closely. In riding that distance we were going to the front, and I could see that he was studying the positions of the two armies. Another feature in General Grant's personal movements is, that *he requires no escort beyond his staff, so regardless of danger is he.* Roads are almost useless to him, for he takes short cuts through fields and woods, and will swim his horse through almost any stream that obstructs his way. Nor does it make any difference to him whether he has daylight for his movements, for *he will ride from breakfast until two o'clock in the morning, and that too without eating. The next day he will repeat the dose, until he finishes his work.* Now, such things come hard upon the staff, but they have learned how to bear it."

The Union loss in the battle of Chattanooga was seven hundred and fifty-seven killed, four thousand five hundred and twenty-nine wounded, and three hundred and thirty missing; a total of five thousand six hundred and sixteen. Six thousand one hundred and forty-two prisoners were captured, forty pieces of artillery, and seven thousand stands of arms, though the reported loss was less than ours. The Union force engaged was over sixty thousand men, and the Confederate force about forty-five thousand; but these last had an advantage of position, which more than counterbalanced the disparity. Taken all together, the battle was the grandest, and the victory the most brilliant, gained during the war.

At Fort Donelson, the victory was gained by hard fighting and the intuitive knowledge of when to take the initiative; at Shiloh, it had been gained by dogged perseverance and hard fighting; at Vicksburg, it had been by strategy; and here at Chattanooga, by skilful dispositions of the troops, by manœuvring in the face of the enemy, and by the instinct of success. A General is of course unable to carry out his plans without the aid of an army to execute them; but the spirit of his army is in a great measure dependent upon his own. It is of course impossible to make heroes of poltroons, or poltroons of heroes, but it is quite possible to infuse into an army a confidence in themselves, and in their leader, which will make them capable of great deeds, as it is also possible to so break the spirit of true men, as to make them down-hearted and indisposed to take the initiative. We have seen in this campaign instances of both these effects. The army of the Cumberland, when Grant took its command, was listless and dispirited; it felt that it was in a trap, and its tenure of Chattanooga was dependent upon the forbearance of the blockading army. The duties of every day kept thrusting the dangers of the position before the men: their rations were short; their artillery was practically useless on account of the wretched condition of their animals from want of food; an exultant enemy was strongly posted in their front; their retreat was almost as impossible as their advance; and the situation was growing daily and hourly more precarious. In five days, however, from the time Grant personally assumed the command, he had secured their lines of supplies; a bountiful supply of food had again become a part of the daily routine; reënforcements had been brought up; the initiative had been taken, and the result of this common sense applied to war was shown in the final struggle: the men who, a month before had been listless, on that day, with an enthusiasm of victory and a confidence of success which could not be restrained, had scaled, in the face of a furious fire, heights which it would be a task to scale in times of peace. In this faculty of inspiring masses lies one of the chief qualities of the leader; and here at Chattanooga, Grant showed that he possessed it in a most eminent degree. Still suffering from his accident, and hardly able to walk alone, when he took command, yet his indomitable will, his constant energy, made him almost ubiquitous, and set in motion, while he supervised their working, the arrangements which organized success.

Of the technical skill displayed in the plan, and the operations of the battle, the following commendations by Halleck were strictly just and well deserved. In a supplementary report this officer said, "Considering the strength of the rebel position, and the difficulty of storming his intrenchments, the battle of Chattanooga must be regarded as one of *the most remarkable in history.* Not only did the officers and men exhibit great skill and daring in their operations on the field, but the highest praise is also due to the commanding General for his admirable dispositions for dislodging the enemy from a position apparently impregnable. Moreover, by turning his right flank, and throwing him back upon Ringgold and Dalton, Sherman's forces were interposed between Bragg and Longstreet, so as to prevent any possibility of their forming a junction."

## CHAPTER XXVII.

THE RELIEF OF BURNSIDE. — LONGSTREET'S ATTACK ON KNOXVILLE. — HE IS ALLOWED TO FALL BACK UNPURSUED.

On the 28th of November Grant returned to Chattanooga, from the front of the pursuit of Bragg, and found that Granger had not started with his force upon the expedition for the relief of Burnside, and hurried him off.

In the mean while General Foster had been sent to supersede Burnside, but Knoxville was so closely besieged that he could not approach it nearer than Cumberland Gap, where a force of about three thousand national soldiers were posted. On this day Grant telegraphed Foster, "The Fourth Corps, Major General Granger commanding, left here to-day, with orders to push with all possible speed through to Knoxville. Sherman is already in motion for Hiawassee, and will go all the way, if necessary. Communicate this information to Burnside as soon as possible, and at any cost, with directions to hold to the very last moment, and we shall not only relieve him, but destroy Longstreet." The next day he wrote to Granger at length, "On the 23d instant, General Burnside telegraphed that his rations would hold out ten or twelve days; at the end of this time, unless relieved from the outside, he must surrender or retreat. The latter will be an impossibility. You are now going for the purpose of relieving this garrison. You see the short time in which relief must be afforded or be too late, and hence the necessity for forced marches. I want to urge upon you, in the strongest possible manner, the necessity of reaching Burnside in the shortest possible time."

Not satisfied, however, with Granger's promptness, Grant on the 29th sent to Sherman, "Granger is on the way to Burnside's relief; but I have lost all faith in his energy and capacity to manage an expedition of the importance of this one. I am inclined to think, therefore, that I shall have to send you. Push, as rapidly as you can, to the Hiawassee, and determine for yourself what force to take with you from that point. Granger has his corps with him, from which you will select, in conjunction with the forces now with you. In plain words, you will assume command of all the forces now moving up the Tennessee."

On the 2d of December Sherman arrived at Loudon, but, finding the bridge destroyed, turned east, to cross the Little Tennessee at Morgantown, while a cavalry force was sent to ford the Little Tennessee, and push into Knoxville, a distance of forty miles, at any expense, and notify Burnside of Sherman's approach. At Morgantown it was found impossible to ford the river, as was intended; and so a bridge was built, by using houses in the vicinity for material, and on the evening of the 4th the principal portion of the army crossed, when, the bridge having broken down, the balance had to be left on the other side. Here information was received from Burnside that, having become aware of

Longstreet's advance against him, he had resolved to fall back upon Knoxville, condensing all his forces there, and thus drawing Longstreet farther from Bragg's army.

On the 15th he was attacked, on his way, at Campbell's Station, but fell back the next day to Knoxville, and fortified that place immediately. Burnside's force consisted of about fifteen thousand men, of whom about three thousand were loyal Tennesseeans from the surrounding country. Longstreet's forces, before the end of the siege, consisted of about twenty-two thousand. By the 20th of November Burnside's line of defence was considered so strong that he had no fear of his ability to hold the place; yet still the position was further strengthened, while Longstreet did nothing actively to take it. When Longstreet heard of the defeat of Bragg, he determined to attempt to carry the place by assault, though against the opinion of his subordinate officers; and at dark, on the 28th, an attack was commenced on Fort Sanders, one of the strongest points of the defensive works about Knoxville, but also the commanding position to be taken. Early next morning a furious cannonade was opened upon the fort, and then an assault was commenced. . The first column was repulsed, and a second, pushed forward as desperately as the first, met with the same fate. In this attack Longstreet lost over a thousand men, while Burnside lost only thirteen. This disparity arose from the protection afforded the besieged by their works, while the Confederates had to advance to the attack about two hundred and fifty yards without cover.

About half an hour after this repulse, Longstreet

received an order from Jefferson Davis, announcing Bragg's defeat, and ordering Longstreet to coöperate with his retreating army, and at once commenced to move with this purpose; but soon after getting reports of the advance of Sherman's army to prevent this junction, he resolved to return and continue the siege, arguing correctly that by this process he would most effectually prevent Grant from following Bragg.

On the 2d Burnside received intelligence of Sherman's approach, and the next day Longstreet commenced a retreat in the direction of Virginia, withdrawing the last of his troops on the night of the 4th, unmolested by Burnside. On the 5th Sherman, at Marysville, communicated with Burnside — "I am here, and can bring twenty-five thousand men into Knoxville to-morrow; but Longstreet having retreated, I feel disposed to stop, for a stern chase is a long one. But I will do all that is possible. Without you specify that you want troops, I will let mine rest to-morrow, and ride to see you."

At the meeting of the Generals, Burnside said that he required no aid, except Granger's command, and advised that Sherman should return. The next day, therefore, Granger moved into Knoxville, and a force being sent out after Longstreet, Sherman commenced his return.

On the 8th the President sent the following despatch to Grant. "Understanding that your lodgment at Chattanooga and at Knoxville is now secure, I wish to tender you, and all under your command, my more than thanks, my profoundest gratitude, for the skill, courage, and perseverance with which you and they, over so great difficulties, have effected that important object. God bless you all."

Grant's orders had been to drive Longstreet from the limits of his department, or else annihilate his force; but, as it was, Burnside, who was Sherman's superior officer, having ordered his return, and making the mistake of supposing that without the aid of his command his own forces were sufficient, Grant's intentions were not carried out. Longstreet retired to Russelville, and remained there for the winter, living off the country, rendering the occupation of Knoxville insecure, and causing a great deal of anxiety to both the government and to Grant. The following despatch of the 20th of January, from Grant to Halleck, will show what course Grant had intended should have been pursued, and also his consideration for the reputation of his subordinate officers: "It was a great oversight, in the first place, to have ever permitted Longstreet to come to a stop within the State of Tennessee, after the siege was raised. My instructions were full and complete on this subject. Sherman was sent with forces sufficient, alone, to defeat Longstreet, and, notwithstanding the long distance the troops had marched, proposed to go on, and carry out my instructions in full. General Burnside was sanguine that no stop would be made by the enemy in the valley. Sherman then proposed to leave any amount of force Burnside thought might be necessary to make his position perfectly secure. He deemed two divisions ample. . . . I write this now particularly to show that the latter named officer [Sherman] is in nowise to blame for the existing state of affairs in East Tennessee."

The position at Chattanooga being now secure, on the

7th of December Grant, in a despatch to Washington, writes as follows: "The country south of this is extremely mountainous, affording but little for the support of an army; the roads are bad at all times, and the season is so far advanced that an effective campaign from here, this winter, may be looked upon as impossible. Our supplies and means of transportation would not admit of a very early campaign, if the season did. . . . I propose, with the concurrence of higher authority, to move by way of New Orleans and Pascagoula, on Mobile. I would hope to secure that place, or its investment, by the last of January."

The government, however, did not favor this suggestion, and Longstreet's remaining in Tennessee led Grant's thoughts in another direction, so that on the 17th he writes, "I feel deeply interested in moving the enemy beyond Saltville this winter, so as to be able to select my own campaign in the spring, instead of having the enemy dictate it for me."

On the 10th of December Grant issued the following congratulatory order to his troops:—

*General Orders, No.* 9.

HEADQUARTERS MILITARY DIVISION OF THE MISSISSIPPI,
IN THE FIELD, CHATTANOOGA, TENN., December 10, 1863.

The General commanding takes this opportunity of returning his sincere thanks and congratulations to the brave armies of the Cumberland, the Ohio, the Tennessee, and their comrades from the Potomac, for the recent splendid and decisive successes achieved over the enemy. In a short time, you have recovered from him the control of the Tennessee River from Bridgeport to Knoxville. You dislodged him from his great stronghold upon Lookout Mountain; drove him from Chattanooga Valley; wrested from his determined grasp the possession of Missionary

Ridge; repelled, with heavy loss to him, his repeated assaults upon Knoxville, forcing him to raise the siege there; driving him at all points, utterly routed and discomfited, beyond the limits of the state. By your noble heroism and determined courage, you have most effectually defeated the plans of the enemy for regaining possession of the States of Kentucky and Tennessee. You have secured positions from which no rebellious power can drive or dislodge you. For all this, the General commanding thanks you, collectively and individually. The loyal people of the United States thank and bless you. Their hopes and prayers for your success against this unholy rebellion are with you daily. Their faith in you will not be in vain. Their hopes will not be blasted. Their prayers to Almighty God will be answered. You will yet go to other fields of strife; and with the invincible bravery and unflinching loyalty to justice and right which have characterized you in the past, you will prove that no enemy can withstand you, and that no defences, however formidable, can check your onward march.

By order of Major General U. S. GRANT.

T. S. BOWERS, *A. A. G.*

After the defeat at Chattanooga, General Bragg, at his own request, was relieved from the command of the army on the 2d of December, and Hardee put in his place. When Grant heard this, he is reported to have said, "He is just my choice." Bragg was "charged with the conduct of the military operations of the armies of the Confederacy;" and his last appearance on the public stage was as commander in North Carolina, when Fort Fisher fell.

## CHAPTER XXVIII.

PLANS FOR THE NEXT CAMPAIGN. — SHERMAN'S EXPEDITION. — GRANT VISITS ST. LOUIS. — HIS SPEECHES THERE.

ABOUT Christmas Grant went in person to Knoxville, to inspect the condition of the army there, and found the men in great want of clothing, particularly of shoes. The difficulties of the route, and the season of the year, rendered it almost impossible to remedy this, but all that could be done was done. On the 11th he wrote to McPherson, who had been left in command of Vicksburg, concerning a cavalry expedition to move through Mississippi, and "clean out the state entirely of all rebels." On the 13th he returned to Nashville, where his headquarters were now established, coming by way of Cumberland Gap, which had been a point so frequently contested. On the 15th he wrote to Halleck, "Sherman has gone down the Mississippi to collect, at Vicksburg, all the force that can be spared for a separate movement from the Mississippi. He will probably have ready, by the 24th of this month, a force of twenty thousand men. . . . I shall direct Sherman, therefore, to move out to Meridian, with his spare force, the cavalry going from Corinth, and destroy the roads east and south of there so effectually, that the enemy will not attempt to rebuild them during the rebellion. He will then return, unless opportunity of going into Mobile with the force he has appears perfectly plain. Owing to the large number of veterans furloughed, I will not be able to do more, at Chattanooga, than to threaten an advance, and try to detain the force now in Thomas's front. Sherman will be instructed, whilst left with these large discretionary powers, to take no extra hazard of losing his army, or of getting it crippled too much for efficient service in the spring."

The same letter contained an exposition of Grant's plan of campaign for the following spring. "I look upon the next line for me to secure to be that from Chattanooga to Mobile; Montgomery and Atlanta being the important intermediate points. To do this large supplies must be secured on the Tennessee River, so as to be independent of the railroad from here [Nashville] to the Tennessee for a considerable length of time. Mobile would be a second base. The destruction which Sherman will do to the roads around Meridian will be of material importance to us in preventing the enemy from drawing supplies from Mississippi, and in clearing that section of all large bodies of rebel troops. . . . I do not look upon any points, except Mobile in the south, and the Tennessee River in the north, as presenting practicable starting-points from which to operate against Atlanta and Montgomery. They are objectionable, as starting-points, to be all under one command, from the fact that the time it will take to communicate from one to the other will be so great. But Sherman or McPherson, either one of whom could be intrusted with the distant command, are officers of such experience and reliability, that the objections on this score, except that of enabling the two armies to act as a unit, would be removed."

A copy of this letter was sent to Sherman with the following remarks: "The letter contains all the instructions I deem necessary in your present move. . . . Nearly all the troops in Thomas's and Dodge's command, having less than one year to serve, have re-enlisted, and many of them have been furloughed. This, with the fact that Longstreet's force in East Tennessee makes it necessary for me to keep ready a force to meet them, will prevent my doing much more than is indicated in my letter to General Halleck. I will have, however, both Dodge and Logan ready, so that, if the enemy should weaken himself much in front, they can advance."

On the 19th Thomas was informed of this contemplated movement, and directed to coöperate with it as follows: "To coöperate with this movement," said Grant, "you want to keep up the appearance of preparation for an advance from Chattanooga. It may be necessary even to move a column as far as La Fayette. Logan will also be instructed to move at the same time what force he can from Bellefontaine towards Rome. We will want to be ready at the earliest possible moment in the spring for a general advance. I look upon the line for this army to secure, in its next campaign, to be that from Chattanooga to Mobile; Atlanta and Montgomery being the important intermediate points."

On the 23d he wrote to Halleck, "I am now collecting as large a cavalry force as can be spared, at Savannah, Tennessee, to cross the Tennessee River, and coöperate with the cavalry from Hurlbut's command in clearing out entirely the forces now collecting in West

Tennessee, under Forrest. It is the design that the cavalry, after finishing the work they first start upon, shall push south, through East Mississippi, and destroy the Mobile road as far south as they can. Sherman goes to Memphis and Vicksburg in person, and will have Grenada visited, and such other points on the Mississippi Central Railroad as may require it. I want the State of Mississippi so visited that large armies cannot traverse it this winter."

Sherman left Vicksburg on the 3d of February; on the 14th he entered Meridian, a railroad centre, between Vicksburg and Montgomery, and for five days ten thousand men were engaged in destroying the railroads centring here; and the injury they suffered now did good service, the next year, in preventing Hood from conveying his troops quickly against Thomas in the battle at Nashville, so that Thomas had time to prepare for his reception, by bringing together his reenforcements even from as far as Missouri.

On the 28th Sherman returned to Vicksburg, having destroyed the railroads of the state, so as to render it impossible for the Confederates to make use of them in maintaining an army in Mississippi, or in operating against our possession of the Mississippi River. He had also maintained his army principally from the enemy's country, and had learned the secret he was afterwards to display so brilliantly. He had brought away four hundred prisoners, five thousand negroes, about a thousand white refugees, and three thousand animals. He had marched about four hundred miles in a month, and his army was in better health and condition than when they started. His loss was twenty-one killed, sixty-eight wounded, and eighty-one missing, and he had terrified the country. Never before in the war had an army penetrated the enemy's country so far without a base. Their finally interior lines of communication were cut; the places that had fancied themselves most secure were visited with the ruthless scourge of war, and troops were even sent from Johnston's army, lying in front of Thomas, to check him.

On the 24th of January Grant obtained leave to visit St. Louis, to see his son, who was lying there sick, and before leaving gave orders to Thomas to keep up a show of advancing, in order to prevent Johnston, who had succeeded Hardee in command of the Confederate army in his front, from sending troops to interfere with Sherman. He travelled quickly and quietly, without any display, and on the 26th arrived at St. Louis, having given no notice of his intention, and registered his name upon the hotel book simply as U. S. Grant, Chattanooga. The news of his arrival spread quickly through the city, and the next day he was tendered a public reception; the following extract from the invitation will show the spirit which prompted this honor: "As citizens of a republic consecrated to constitutional liberty, and duly appreciating the destinies of the future for our own and other lands which hang upon the results of the present conflict, we glory in the brilliant deeds and unparalleled triumphs of yourself, officers, and men. To you and the gallant soldiers whom you have led a nation's honor and gratitude are due."

The invitation was numerously signed, and was accepted by General Grant in the following letter:—

ST. LOUIS, MO., January 27, 1864.

COLONEL JOHN O'FALLAN, HON. JOHN HOW,
And Citizens of St. Louis.

GENTLEMEN: Your highly complimentary invitation "to meet old acquaintances and make new ones," at a dinner to be given by citizens of St. Louis, is just received.

I will state that I have only visited St. Louis on this occasion to see a sick child. Finding, however, that he has passed the crisis of his disease, and is pronounced out of danger by his physicians, I accept the invitation. My stay in this city will be short — probably not beyond the 1st proximo. On to-morrow I shall be engaged. Any other day of my stay here, and any place selected by the citizens of St. Louis, it will be agreeable for me to meet them.

I have the honor to be, very respectfully,
Your obedient servant,
U. S. GRANT, *Major General U. S. A.*

On the 29th the reception was given in the Lindell Hotel, and the enthusiasm with which the leader of the western armies was greeted was heartfelt and sincere. During the evening, in answer to a toast, "Our Distinguished Guest, Major General Grant," the General rose amid a perfect storm of applause, and said, "Gentlemen, in response, it will be impossible for me to do more than to thank you."

During the evening an immense crowd gathered outside, and the General was greeted with a serenade. When he appeared upon the balcony, he was received with enthusiastic cheers, and called upon for a speech. Nothing else would seem to satisfy the multitude; so that, finally, in self-defence, he took off his hat, and, amid profound silence, said: —

Gentlemen, I thank you for this honor. I cannot make a speech. It is something I have never done, and never intend to do, and I beg you will excuse me.

Loud cheers followed this brief address, at the conclusion of which the General replaced his hat, took a cigar from his pocket, lit it, and stood on the balcony in the presence of the crowd, puffing his Havana and watching the rockets as they ascended and burst in the air.

"Speech! speech!" vociferated the multitude; and several gentlemen near him urged the General to say something to satisfy the people, but he declined. Judge Lord, of the Land Court, appeared very enthusiastic, and, placing his hand on General Grant's shoulder, said, "Tell them you can fight for them, but can't talk to them — do tell them that!"

"I must get some one else to say that for me," replied the General; but the multitude continuing to cry out, "Speech! speech!" he leaned over the railing, blew a wreath of smoke from his lips, and said, "Gentlemen, making speeches is not my business. I never did it in my life, and never will. I thank you, however, for your attendance here;" and with that the General retired.

On the 5th of February Grant had returned to Nashville, and, receiving information the next day that Johnston had forwarded reënforcements to Longstreet, ordered Thomas to send a detachment of troops to East Tennessee. This department had now been transferred to the command of Schofield, at Grant's desire. Foster had requested to be relieved, an old wound, received in the Mexican war, having reopened. Schofield was informed of this action, and that it was Grant's desire to drive Longstreet out of the state, so as to "prepare for a spring campaign of our own choosing, instead of permitting the enemy to dictate it for us." At the same time he wrote, "We will have some sharp fighting in the spring, and, if successful, I believe the war will be ended within the year."

On his way north, Foster stopped at Nashville, and consulted with Grant, and argued that the contemplated campaign against Longstreet would not have a decided effect, since that portion of the country was exhausted, and Schofield's position was secure, without the necessity of further fighting; while Longstreet, if driven back, had only to retreat into Virginia, and the difficulties of following him were greatly increased by the necessity of carrying all supplies. These views decided Grant, and he turned his attention towards Dalton, which he desired to make a point of value in the southern campaign, in the spring, and also at present to create a diversion in favor of Sherman.

## CHAPTER XXIX.

### THE EXTRA MILITARY DUTIES OF THE DEPARTMENT, AND THE MEANS TAKEN TO PERFORM THEM.

IT will be well to return a little from the narrative of the active military operations, and consider Grant's action in the interests other than military which came naturally under his supervision. After the victory at Chattanooga, deserters from the Confederate army began to come into our lines in great numbers. To meet their case, and to protect them should they be recaptured by the Confederates after being paroled, the following order was issued: —

*General Orders, No.* 10.

HEADQUARTERS MILITARY DIVISION OF THE MISSISSIPPI,
IN THE FIELD, CHATTANOOGA, TENN., December 12, 1863.

To obtain uniformity in the disposition of deserters from the Confederate armies coming within this military division, the following order is published: —

1. All deserters from the enemy coming within our lines will be conducted to the commander of division or detached brigade who shall be nearest the place of surrender.

2. If such commander is satisfied that the deserters desire to quit the Confederate service, he may permit them to go to their homes, if within our lines, on taking the following oath: —

THE OATH.

"I do solemnly swear in the presence of Almighty God, that I will henceforth faithfully support, protect, and defend the Constitution of the United

States, and the Union of States thereunder, and that I will in like manner abide by and faithfully support all acts of Congress passed during the existing rebellion with reference to slaves, so long and so far as not yet repealed, modified, or held void by Congress or by decision of the Supreme Court, and that I will in like manner abide by and faithfully support all proclamations of the President made during the existing rebellion having reference to slaves, so long and so far as not modified or declared void by decision of the Supreme Court. So help me God.

"Sworn and subscribed to before me at —— this —— day of —— 186 ."

3. Deserters from the enemy will at once be disarmed, and their arms turned over to the nearest ordnance officer, who will account for them.

4. Passes and rations may be given to deserters to carry them to their homes, and free passes over military railroads and on steamboats in government employ.

5. Employment at fair wages will, when practicable, be given to deserters by officers of the Quartermaster and Engineer Departments.

To avoid the danger of recapture of such deserters by the enemy, they will be exempt from the military service in the armies of the United States.

By order of Major General U. S. GRANT.

T. S. BOWERS, *A. A. G.*

He also ordered that "no encouragement will be given to traders or army followers, who have left their homes to avoid enrolment or the draft, and to speculate upon the soldiers' pay; and this class of persons will not be tolerated in the armies of the military division of the Mississippi."

The country in which his military operations were at this time carried on contained a great many persons who had remained loyal to the government; and the following orders show the course of treatment he adopted for their protection, and also for placing, as far as possible, the burden incidental to the military occupation of a country upon those whose disloyalty had caused the war:—

HEADQUARTERS MILITARY DIVISION OF THE MISSISSIPPI,
IN THE FIELD, CHATTANOOGA, TENN., December 13, 1863.

All Quartermasters within the military division of the Mississippi who now have, or may hereafter receive, moneys for rents accruing from abandoned property, or property known to belong to secessionists within this military division, are hereby directed to pay such moneys into the hands of the nearest treasury agent, taking his receipt therefor, excepting such sums out of said moneys so collected as may be requisite to pay the necessary expenses of collection, and the taxes due the United States upon the same.

Any property now held by any Quartermaster, and upon which rents are collected by him, shall, when satisfactorily proven to belong to loyal citizens, be restored to the possession of the owners, together with all moneys collected for rents upon the same, excepting only such sums as may be required to pay the necessary expenses of collection, and the taxes due to the United States upon the same.

Department and corps commanders and commandants of military posts and stations within this military division are hereby required and directed, whenever called upon by proper authority, to promptly afford all necessary assistance in enforcing the collection of the taxes due upon all property within this command.

Corps commanders within this military division are directed to immediately seize, or cause to be seized, all county records and documents showing titles and claims to property within the revolted states in their respective districts, and hold the same until they can be delivered to an authorized tax commissioner of the United States.

Where property is used by the government without paying rent, the collection of taxes on it will be suspended until further orders.

By order of Major General U. S. GRANT.

HEADQUARTERS MILITARY DIVISION OF THE MISSISSIPPI,
IN THE FIELD, CHATTANOOGA, TENN., December 16, 1863.

1. All seizures of private buildings will be made by the Quartermaster's department, on the order of the commanding officer. The buildings of disloyal persons alone will be taken to furnish officers with quarters, and the need for public offices and storehouses must be supplied in preference.

2. When the urgent exigencies of the service require it, the buildings of loyal persons may be taken for storehouses and offices, but only after all suitable buildings belonging to disloyal persons have been seized.

3. In the seizure of buildings, the owner will be allowed to retain all movables except the means of heating.

4. All officers will remain in the immediate vicinity of their commands, and if having a less command than a division or a post, when the command is in tents they will occupy tents themselves.

5. Commanding officers are prohibited from quartering troops in houses without the special written authority of the General commanding the corps or department to which they belong.

6. In furnishing quarters to officers not serving with troops, the Quartermaster's department will be governed by existing regulations.

7. Ten days after the receipt and distribution of this order, corps commanders will cause an inspection of their commands to be made by their Assistant Inspectors General, and will arrest and perfer charges against every officer who may be occupying quarters not assigned to him by the Quartermaster's department, or in violation of paragraph 4 of this order.

By order of Major General U. S. GRANT.

His care for the comfort of his soldiers prompted the following order, giving authority to secure the transportation of their supplies: —

All requisitions made by Captain J. A. Potter, Assistant Quartermaster United States army, for military supplies, will be immediately and promptly filled.

In case of delay or refusal on the part of any railroad, Captain Potter is authorized to take such means as may be necessary to enforce compliance.

By order of Major General U. S. GRANT.

ROBERT ALLEN,
*Brigadier General and Chief Quartermaster.*

Very soon after his arrival at Chattanooga, the subject of the practice of guerrilla warfare having attracted his attention, and the damage done to the Unionists who lived in this district of country having assumed proportions which required immediate action, he issued the following order, which, by his strict adherence to its provisions, went very far towards having the desired effect: —

*General Orders, No.* 4.

HEADQUARTERS MILITARY DIVISION OF THE MISSISSIPPI,
IN THE FIELD, CHATTANOOGA, TENN., November 5, 1863.

The habit of raiding parties of rebel cavalry visiting towns, villages, and farms where there are no Federal forces, and pillaging Union families, having become prevalent, department commanders will take immediate steps to stop the evil, or make the loss by such raids fall upon secessionists and secession sympathizers in the neighborhood where such acts are committed. For every act of violence to the person of an unarmed Union citizen, a secessionist will be arrested and held as hostage for the delivery of the offender. For every dollar's worth of property taken from such citizens, or destroyed by raiders, an assessment will be made upon secessionists of the neighborhood, and collected by the nearest military forces, under the supervision of the commander thereof, and the amount thus collected paid over to the sufferers. When such assessments cannot be collected in money, property useful to the government may be taken at a fair valuation, and the amount paid in money by a disbursing officer of the government, who will take such property upon his returns. Wealthy secession citizens will be assessed in money and provisions for the support of Union refugees who have been and may be driven from their homes and into our lines by the acts of those with whom secession citizens are in sympathy. All collections and payments under this order will be through disbursing officers of the government, whose accounts must show all money and property received under it, and how disposed of.

By order of Major General U. S. GRANT.

T. S. BOWERS, *A. A. G.*

The result of Grant's administration in his department was such, that in February of this year it was publicly stated, "that all through the country to the rear of the Union lines, a Union officer, in his uniform, can ride unmolested to any portions of Mississippi, Tennessee, and Alabama, halting at farm-houses along the road for such refreshments and shelter as he may desire."

The gratitude of the country for Grant's services and those of the brave men under him, found expression in Congress by the following motion to present him with a gold medal. The resolution was introduced in the house by Mr. Washburne, and was put upon the military record by a general order from the War Department dated December 21, 1863, as follows: —

*General Orders, No.* 398.

JOINT RESOLUTION of thanks to Major General Ulysses S. Grant and the officers and soldiers who have fought under his command during this rebellion; and providing that the President of the United States shall cause a medal to be struck, to be presented to Major General Grant in the name of the United States of America.

*Be it resolved, by the Senate and House of Representatives of the United States of America, in Congress assembled,* That the thanks of Congress be, and they hereby are, presented to Major General Ulysses S. Grant, and through him to the officers and soldiers who have fought under his command during this rebellion, for their gallantry and good conduct in the battles in which they have been engaged; and that the President of the United States be requested to cause a gold medal to be struck, with suitable emblems, devices, and inscriptions, to be presented to Major General Grant.

SEC. 2. *And be it further resolved,* That, when the said medal shall have been struck, the President shall cause a copy of this joint resolution to be engrossed on parchment, and shall transmit the same, together with the said medal, to Major General Grant, to be presented to him in the name of the people of the United States of America.

SEC. 3. *And be it further resolved,* That a sufficient sum of money to carry this resolution into effect is hereby appropriated out of any money in the Treasury not otherwise appropriated.

SCHUYLER COLFAX,
*Speaker of the House of Representatives.*

H. HAMLIN,
*Vice-President of the United States and President of the Senate.*

Approved, December 17, 1863: ABRAHAM LINCOLN.

The design for this medal was made by Leutze, and is thus described: On one side was the profile of Grant, surrounded by a wreath of laurels, with his name, the year 1863, and a galaxy of stars; on the reverse, a figure of Fame, with a trump, and a scroll bearing the names of his victories. The motto was, "Proclaim Liberty throughout the Land."

## CHAPTER XXX.

THE GRADE OF LIEUTENANT GENERAL REVIVED. — GRANT SELECTED TO FILL IT. — CORRESPONDENCE BETWEEN GRANT AND SHERMAN. — VISITS, WASHINGTON AND RECEIVES HIS COMMISSION.

On the 2d of March Grant received the intelligence, through rebel sources, of Sherman's successful return from his raid upon the railroads of Mississippi, and on the 3d was himself ordered to report to Washington in person, in the following despatch: "The Secretary of War directs that you report in person to the War Department as early as practicable, considering the condition of your command. If necessary, you will keep up telegraphic communication with your command while *en route* for Washington." The next day Grant started for the East, and before setting out sent his instructions to Sherman, directing him to use the negro troops, as far as practicable, in guarding the Mississippi, and to assemble the remainder of his command at Memphis, in order to "have them in readiness to join your column on this front, in the spring campaign." This was the campaign against Atlanta, which Grant intended to lead in person. His purpose was from there to advance against either Mobile or Savannah, as should seem best; and in this despatch to Sherman he says, "I am ordered to Washington; but as I am directed to keep up telegraphic communication with this command, I shall expect in the course of ten or twelve days to return to it."

He was, however, to be called to another field of action. The necessity of some one commanding mind to combine the operations of all our armies had been for some time growing more and more evident. The approaching presidential nomination had increased and heightened the political dissensions, which, during the whole of the war, had been a hinderance in the way of the government, and had made too many military appointments wear a political aspect. There was wanting some one commanding mind to overlook the varied offensive operations of our armies, and direct them with a unity of purpose. Heretofore most of our armies had operated independently, and frequently to each other's injury. The advantage of some such arrangement, in a partial field, had been already seen in the successive enlargements of Grant's command, and it was proposed to carry out the same course of action, by putting all the armies under one control, and giving this control to Grant.

At the session of Congress during the winter of 1863–'64, Mr. Washburne, the representative of Illinois from Galena, Grant's place of residence, introduced a bill "to revive the grade of Lieutenant General of the army;" and the intention was, of course, to give the position to Grant. This grade in the army was created in 1798, for Washington, who held it but one year before his death. In 1855 it was bestowed, by brevet, upon General Scott. The debate upon the bill lasted some time, and finally on the 26th of February, 1864, received the sanction of both Houses of Congress, was approved on the 1st of March by the President, who nominated Grant for the position, and on the 2d the nomination was approved by the Senate. In the debate upon the bill in the House, before it was brought to a vote, Mr. Washburne, in the course of his remarks, spoke as follows: —

"I have spoken of the interest I feel in this bill, but, if I know myself, it is a feeling that rises far above the considerations of personal friendship which I entertain for the distinguished soldier whose name has been connected with it. I am not here to speak for General Grant. No man with his consent has ever mentioned his name in connection with any position. I say what I know to be true when I allege that every promotion he has received since he first entered the service to put down this rebellion, was moved without his knowledge or consent; and in regard to this very matter of Lieutenant General, after the bill was introduced and his name mentioned in connection therewith, he wrote me, and admonished me that he had been highly honored already by the government, and did not ask or deserve anything more in the shape of honors or promotion; and that a success over the enemy was what he craved above everything else; that he only desired to hold such an influence over those under his command, as to use them to the best advantage to secure that end. Such is the language of this patriotic and single-minded soldier, ambitious only of serving his country and doing his whole duty. Sir, whatever this House may do, the country will do justice to General Grant. We can see that. I think I can appreciate that myself."

The bill, as finally passed, was worded as follows: —

*Be it enacted by the Senate and House of Representatives of the United States of America in Congress assembled,* That the grade of Lieutenant General be, and the same is hereby, revived in the army of the United States of America; and the President is hereby authorized, whenever he shall deem it expedient, to appoint, by and with the advice and consent of the Senate, a commander of the army, to be selected, during war, from among those officers in the military service of the United States, not below the grade of Major General, most distinguished for courage, skill, and ability; and who, being commissioned as Lieutenant General, *shall be authorized, under the direction of the President, to command the armies of the United States.*

SEC. 2. *And be it further enacted*, That the Lieutenant General, appointed as hereinbefore provided, shall be entitled to the pay, allowances, and staff specified in the fifth section of the act approved May 28, 1798; and also the allowances described in the sixth section of the act approved August 23, 1842, granting additional rations to certain officers: *Provided*, That nothing in this bill contained shall be construed in any way to affect the rank, pay, or allowances of Winfield Scott, Lieutenant General by brevet, now on the retired list of the army.

Mr. Badeau, who was on Grant's staff at the time the debate upon the bill was in progress, writes, concerning Grant's behavior during this time, as follows: —

"Grant himself used no influence, wrote no line, spoke no word to bring about the result. I was with him while the bill was being debated, and spoke to him more than once on the subject. He never manifested any anxiety, or even desire, for the success of the bill; nor did he ever seem to shrink from the responsibilities it would impose upon him. If the country chose to call him to higher spheres and more important services, whatever ability or energy he possessed he was willing to devote to the task. If, on the contrary, he had been left at the post which he then held, he would not have felt a pang of disappointed pride."

The day Grant left his department to report personally at Washington, he sent the following letter to Sherman: —

DEAR SHERMAN: The bill reviving the grade of Lieutenant General in the army has become a law, and my name has been sent to the Senate for the place. I now receive orders to report to Washington immediately, *in person*, which indicates a confirmation, or a likelihood of confirmation. I start in the morning to comply with the order.

Whilst I have been eminently successful in this war, in at least gaining the confidence of the public, no one feels more than I how much of this success is due to the energy, skill, and the harmonious putting forth of that energy and skill, of those whom it has been my good fortune to have occupying subordinate positions under me.

There are many officers to whom these remarks are applicable to a greater or less degree, proportionate to their ability as soldiers; but what I want is, to express my thanks to you and McPherson, as the men to whom, above all others, I feel indebted for whatever I have had of success.

How far your advice and assistance have been of help to me, you know. How far your execution of whatever has been given to you to do, entitles you to the reward I am receiving, you cannot know as well as I.

I feel all the gratitude this letter would express, giving it the most flattering construction.

The word *you* I use in the plural, intending it for McPherson also. I should write to him, and will some day; but starting in the morning, I do not know that I will find time just now.

Your friend, U. S. GRANT, *Major General.*

Sherman received this letter near Memphis, on the 10th of March, and immediately replied, —

DEAR GENERAL: I have your more than kind and characteristic letter of the 4th instant. I will send a copy to General McPherson at once.

You do yourself injustice, and us too much honor, in assigning to us too large a share of the merits which have led to your high advancement. I know you approve the friendship I have ever professed to you, and will permit me to continue, as heretofore, to manifest it on all proper occasions.

You are now Washington's legitimate successor, and occupy a position of almost dangerous elevation; but if you can continue, as heretofore, to be yourself, — simple, honest, and unpretending, — you will enjoy through life the respect and love of friends and the homage of millions of human beings that will award you a large share in securing to them and their descendants a government of law and stability.

I repeat, you do General McPherson and myself too much honor. At Belmont you manifested your traits — neither of us being near. At Donelson, also, you illustrated your whole character. I was not near, and General McPherson in too subordinate a capacity to influence you.

Until you had won Donelson, I confess I was almost cowed by the terrible array of anarchical elements that presented themselves at every point; but that admitted a ray of light I have followed since. I believe you are as brave, patriotic, and just as the great prototype Washington — as unselfish, kind-hearted, and honest as a man should be; but the chief characteristic is the simple faith in success you have always manifested, which I can liken to nothing else than the faith a Christian has in the Saviour.

This faith gave you victory at Shiloh and Vicksburg. Also, when you have completed your best preparations, you go into battle without hesitation, as at Chattanooga — no doubts — no reserves; and I tell you it was this that made us act with confidence. I knew, wherever I was, that you thought of me, and if I got in a tight place you would help me out, if alive.

My only point of doubt was in your knowledge of grand strategy, and of books of science and history; but, I confess, your common sense seems to have supplied all these.

Now, as to the future. Don't stay in Washington. Come West: take to yourself the whole Mississippi Valley. Let us make it dead sure — and I tell you the Atlantic slopes and Pacific shores will follow its destiny, as sure as the limbs of a tree live or die with the main trunk. We have done much, but still much remains. Time, and time's influences, are with us. We could almost afford to sit still, and let these influences work.

Here lies the seat of the coming empire; and from the West, when our task is done, we will make short work of Charleston and Richmond, and the impoverished coast of the Atlantic.

Your sincere friend, W. T. SHERMAN.

On the 29th of December, Sherman had written to Grant, "In relation to the conversation we had in

General Granger's office, the day before I left Nashville, I repeat, you occupy a position of more power than Halleck or the President. There are similar instances in European history, but none in ours. For the sake of future generations, risk nothing. Let *us* risk — and when you strike, let it be as at Vicksburg and Chattanooga. Your reputation as a General is now far above that of any man living, and partisans will manœuvre for your influence; but, if you can escape them, as you have hitherto done, you will be more powerful for good than it is possible to measure. You said that you were surprised at my assertion on this point; but I repeat that, from what I have seen and heard here, I am more and more convinced of the truth of what I told you. Do as you have heretofore done — preserve a plain military character; and let others manœuvre as they will, you will beat them, not only in fame, but in doing good in the closing scenes of this war, when somebody must heal and mend up the breaches made by war."

The journey to Washington was made rapidly and as privately as possible; but wherever it was known that Grant was coming, the people gathered in eager crowds to see and to welcome him. On the 8th of March he arrived at Washington, and proceeded quietly to the hotel. At dinner he was recognized by some one who had seen him before, and it was quickly buzzed about the room that the Lieutenant General was present. A member of Congress who was at the table, rising, announced, "The hero of Vicksburg is among us," and proposed his health, which was the signal for enthusiastic cheering. Rising to his feet, Grant simply bowed his acknowledgments and resumed his seat. His honors he receives as he does his appointments; he seeks and schemes for neither, but does his duty, and if they come to him, receives them calmly, with no feigned modesty, and no hypocritical self-abasement. That evening he attended, unannounced, a reception at the White House. President Lincoln had never seen him before, but, when he was presented, received him with great cordiality, and he soon became the centre of attraction. In the course of the evening he escorted Mrs. Lincoln round the East Room, and is said to have remarked afterwards that it was his "warmest campaign during the whole war."

The next day, the 9th of March, 1864, at one P. M., Grant was received by the President in his cabinet chamber, and formally presented with his commission as Lieutenant General. At this ceremony there were present all the members of the cabinet, Major General Halleck, Brigadier General Rawlins, and Lieutenant Colonel Comstock, both members of General Grant's staff, the President's private secretary, Mr. Lovejoy, a member of the House of Representatives, Grant's eldest son, a boy of about thirteen, President Lincoln, and General Grant. At his entrance the President presented Grant to the members of the cabinet, and then read the following remarks: —

"GENERAL GRANT: The nation's appreciation of what you have done, and its reliance upon you for what still remains to be accomplished in the existing great struggle, are now presented with this commission, constituting you Lieutenant General in the army of the United States. With this high honor devolves upon you, also, a corresponding responsibility. As the coun-

GRANT RECEIVING HIS COMMISSION AS LIEUTENANT-GENERAL.

try herein trusts you, so, under God, it will sustain you. I scarcely need to add, that with what I here speak for the nation goes my own hearty personal concurrence."

In reply, Grant read the following from a slip of paper: —

"MR. PRESIDENT: I accept the commission, with gratitude for the high honor conferred. With the aid of the noble armies that have fought on so many fields for our common country, it will be my earnest endeavor not to disappoint your expectations. I feel the full weight of the responsibilities now devolving on me, and I know that if they are met, it will be due to those armies, and, above all, to the favor of that Providence which leads both nations and men."

The next day, the 10th, Grant, in company with General Meade, the commander of the army of the Potomac, made a brief visit to that army, and the next day, in the morning, started for the West, and was at Nashville when he received the despatch from President Lincoln, which he embodied in the following order: —

HEADQUARTERS OF THE ARMIES OF THE UNITED STATES,
NASHVILLE, TENN., March 17, 1864.

In pursuance of the following order of the President, —

EXECUTIVE MANSION, WASHINGTON, March 10, 1864.

Under the authority of the act of Congress to appoint to the grade of Lieutenant General in the army, of March 1, 1864, Lieutenant General Ulysses S. Grant, United States army, is appointed to the command of the armies of the United States.

ABRAHAM LINCOLN.

I assume command of the armies of the United States. Headquarters will be in the field, and, until further orders, will be with the army of the Potomac. There will be an office-headquarters in Washington, to which all official communications will be sent, except those from the army where the headquarters are at the date of their address.

U. S. GRANT, *Lieutenant General.*

The following order from the War Department was issued the day after Grant left Washington: —

WAR DEPARTMENT, ADJUTANT GENERAL'S OFFICE,
WASHINGTON, March 12, 1864.

The President of the United States orders as follows: —

1. Major General Halleck is, at his own request, relieved from duty as General-in-chief of the army, and Lieutenant General U. S. Grant is assigned to the command of the armies of the United States. The headquarters of the army will be in Washington, and also with Lieutenant General Grant in the field.

2. Major General Halleck is assigned to duty in Washington, as Chief of Staff of the army, under the direction of the Secretary of War and the Lieutenant General commanding. His orders will be obeyed and respected accordingly.

3. Major General W. T. Sherman is assigned to the command of the military division of the Mississippi, composed of the departments of the Ohio, the Cumberland, the Tennessee, and the Arkansas.

4. Major General J. B. McPherson is assigned to the command of the department and army of the Tennessee.

5. In relieving Major General Halleck from duty as General-in-chief, the President desires to express his approbation and thanks for the zealous manner in which the arduous and responsible duties of that position have been performed.

By order of the Secretary of War.

E. D. TOWNSEND, *Assistant Adjutant General.*

## CHAPTER XXXI.

A REVIEW OF THE SITUATION. — HEADQUARTERS IN THE FIELD. — THE NEW CAMPAIGN — THE ARMY OF THE POTOMAC CROSSES THE RAPIDAN.

WE had at this time about eight hundred thousand men in the field. The Mississippi River was opened from its source to its mouth, and garrisoned at various points, principally by negro troops. General Banks commanded at the south-west, with his headquarters at New Orleans, and a portion of his force was in Texas. The army in Arkansas was under the command of General Steele, while the department of Missouri was under General Rosecrans. Sherman was preparing for his March to the Sea. McPherson was in command of the army of the Tennessee, Schofield was in command at Knoxville, and Thomas of the army of the Cumberland. In Virginia, the army of the Potomac was under the command of General Meade. Along the coast the navy was keeping an almost perfect blockade, and on the main land we had footholds at various points. West of the Mississippi the Confederate army was estimated at about eighty thousand men; but it was scattered, partially disbanded, and disintegrated from want of an opposing force to hold it together. Yet still it could easily be called together, should occasion arise. In front of Chattanooga lay an army under

Johnston, while in Virginia Lee held command of the army there, which, with his troops in West Virginia and North Carolina, was estimated at over a hundred thousand men. The Confederates held the advantage of the inside of the circle, while we had the outside. The task of combining the action of our armies, of looking after their supplies, was so vast and so complicated that it required great self-confidence for any one who could appreciate the difficulties to assume it. Grant had, however, never hesitated during the war to assume any position to which his duty called him, and accepted with the same modest self-confidence the position now given him.

The main question of the war was the overthrow of the military power of the Confederacy. Upon this its entire organization depended, and to do this only the armies of Lee and Johnston need be considered. Sherman, in whose military capacity Grant had a confidence which the results show was well founded, was given the task of operating against Johnston, while Grant himself, with the army of the Potomac, commanded by Meade, should operate against Lee. Each of them was to hold his antagonist so fast as to prevent the interchange of reënforcements from one to the other. Grant had consulted frequently and fully with Sherman; they each knew the plan, and they each had confidence in the other's ability to carry out his respective part of it. Grant's attention had been directed to the subject before he had accepted his present position, and he saw that the military operations must be continuous and aggressive. The question was one partly of resources; and, if not possible in any other way, it was by continued attrition that the armies of the Confederacy were to be worn out. The Confederacy had lapsed into so definite a military despotism, that it was useless to have any longer any hope of the people expressing their opinion, and forcing the government to regard their wishes.

In the history of nations, considered philosophically, we find that the system of slavery in labor, as it is a characteristic of barbarism, presupposes always slavery in government; and the history of the despotism established in the Confederacy during their foolish attempt to found a nationality, in the nineteenth century, upon slavery, would add a further proof, if further proof were necessary, that the form of a people's government is an evidence and a test of their development.

The army in Virginia under Lee, and which Grant was now to meet, was posted along the south bank of the Rapidan, governing the advance upon Richmond. This army had as its commander a leader who had skilfully used its valor and determination in defending all approach to the Confederate capital for three years, and in many fierce engagements. Lee was a graduate of West Point, and during the war was the only general, on either side, who had enjoyed the advantage of commanding substantially the same army in the same section of country during the entire continuance of the war. He and his men had become thoroughly acquainted with every foot of the territory they were to defend; they had also the prestige of success to inspirit them, and besides this the sense of responsibility that upon them especially the existence of the Confederacy depended. By their years of active operation in the field, they had also become thoroughly inured to war, and were probably as formidable a body of men as ever were gathered together in an army.

On the other hand, the army of the Potomac had not as yet been successful, despite the persistent bravery they had always shown; and they had suffered further by having their commanders changed frequently. The army, however, despite its long-continued series of disappointments, had undergone its long drill in active service, and was a *real* army, able to march, to manœuvre, to fight, to persist, and endure with the best, and its spirit was strong; while the fact announced in the Lieutenant General's order, that his headquarters would be in the field with them, tended the more to inspirit them, and gratified them as a recognition of their importance.

On the 23d of March Grant returned to Washington, and on the 24th the army was reorganized. The corps were consolidated and reduced to three, the Second, Fifth, and Sixth. The Second was placed under Hancock, the Fifth under Warren, and the Sixth under Sedgwick, while the combined command was kept in the hands of Meade. The command of the cavalry was given to Sheridan, who at Chattanooga, under Grant's own supervision, had displayed the qualities of a leader, and who in his first campaign justified the selection.

Before active operations commenced the army was reënforced by the Ninth Corps, under Burnside, which had returned from East Tennessee. The entire strength of this army was about one hundred and forty thousand men. On the 3d of May the order was given for the advance. The army at this time occupied a position along the north bank of the Rapidan, while Lee's army was upon the southern bank of the river, with its front strongly protected by field-works, its left flank covered by the river, and its right by intrenchments.

The first question that arose in taking command of the army of the Potomac was, which route should be taken for the advance upon Richmond. Should it be the overland route, over the Peninsula? or should it be that south of the James? The first had been repeatedly tried, and had failed as often as it had been tried. The distance to Richmond from any position upon either the Rappahannock or the Rapidan is between sixty and seventy miles, through a country peculiarly fitted for defence, and as full of difficulties in the way of keeping open the communications for supplies. Its advantage, however, was, that by this route the attacking army, while it pressed towards Richmond, at the same time served to cover and defend Washington. The route from the south of the James, while it saved all the difficulties of this advance through a hostile country, since the army could move down the coast, presented, however, the great and seemingly insuperable objection that it uncovered Washington. This objection might be met, however, by having two armies in the field, one to take the route south of the James, and the other to protect Washington.

It is known that before his elevation to his present position General Grant had expressed his opinion as in favor of the route from below the James. On taking command of the army, however, by some means he was forced to abandon his plan, and by a sort of compromise, an independent force was to operate south of the James, while the main army should follow the overland route. The command of this coöperating force was intrusted to General Butler, who, starting from Fortress Monroe, with about thirty thousand men, was to go up the James River, and intrenching himself near City Point, was to operate against Richmond, either investing the city on the south, or getting into a position to join the army of the Potomac, coming down from the north. Besides this, Richmond was to be threatened from the west by a force which should operate against the Virginia and East Tennessee Railway, and another which should advance up the Shenandoah Valley, and force Lee to weaken himself in order to protect his western line of supplies. These forces were respectively under the command of General Cook and General Siegel, and numbered ten thousand and seven thousand men.

The immediate commander of the army of the Potomac was General Meade; and Grant says of him in his report, "Commanding all the armies, as I did, I tried, as far as possible, to leave General Meade in independent command of the army of the Potomac. My instructions for that army were all through him, and were general in their nature, leaving all the details and execution to him. The campaigns that followed proved him to be the right man in the right place. His commanding always in the presence of an officer superior to him in rank, has drawn from him much of that public attention which his zeal and ability entitled him to, and which he would otherwise have received."

On the 3d of May the army moved at midnight, and crossed the Rapidan in two columns. The right, composed of Warren's and Sedgwick's corps, crossed at the Germania Ford, and the other, of Hancock's corps, at Ely's Ford, six miles below.

The following letters, which passed between the President and the Lieutenant General just before the resumption of active operations, will show the relations existing between these two representative men:—

EXECUTIVE MANSION, WASHINGTON, April 30, 1864.

LIEUTENANT GENERAL GRANT: Not expecting to see you before the spring campaign opens, I wish to express, in this way, my entire satisfaction with what you have done up to this time, so far as I understand it. The particulars of your plans I neither know nor seek to know.

You are vigilant and self-reliant; and, pleased with this, I wish not to obtrude any restraints or constraints upon you. While I am very anxious that any great disaster or capture of our men in great numbers shall be avoided, I know that these points are less likely to escape your attention than they would be mine. If there be anything wanting which is within my power to give, do not fail to let me know it. And now, with a brave army and a just cause, may God sustain you.

Yours very truly, A. LINCOLN.

HEADQUARTERS ARMIES UNITED STATES,
CULPEPPER C. H., VIRGINIA, May 1, 1864.

THE PRESIDENT: Your very kind letter of yesterday is just received. The confidence you express for the future, and satisfaction for the past, in my military administration, is acknowledged with pride. It shall be my earnest endeavor that you and the country shall not be disappointed. From my first entrance into the voluntary service of the country to the present day, I have never had cause of complaint, have never expressed or implied a complaint against the Administration or the Secretary of War, for throwing any embarrassment in the way of my vigorously prosecuting what appeared to be my duty. Indeed, since the promotion which placed me in command of all the armies, and in view of the great responsibility and importance of success, I have been astonished at the readiness with which everything asked for has been yielded, without even an explanation being asked.

Should my success be less than I desire and expect, the least I can say is, the fault is not with you.

Very truly, your obedient servant,

U. S. GRANT, *Lieutenant General.*

## CHAPTER XXXII.

### THE CAMPAIGN COMMENCED. — THE BATTLE OF THE WILDERNESS.

ON the 4th, the crossing having been successfully accomplished without resistance, it appeared as though Lee's right flank was turned. The value of this passage of the Rapidan is evident from the estimate Grant gives of it in his report. He says, " This I regarded as a great success, and it removed from my mind the most serious apprehensions I had entertained—that of crossing the river in the face of an active, large, well-appointed, and ably-commanded army, and how so large a train was to be carried through a hostile country and protected."

From the Rapidan southward and westward extends the country known as the Wilderness. The character of this country is expressed in its name. It is a mining region, and rests on a bed of mineral rock. The forests having been cut away for mining purposes, the whole region is covered with a dense new undergrowth, which prevents all military operations, while the roads through it are simple paths, such as are always found in such a country. The use of artillery or cavalry in this thicket of scrub oaks and stunted pines is impossible, and the nature of the ground will be most apparent when it is realized that the movements of the army could be directed only by the use of the compass. It was not here, however, that Grant expected to meet the enemy. The orders for May 5, as the extract given below will show, prove that it was not here that he expected to fight.

HEADQUARTERS ARMY OF THE POTOMAC,
May 4, 1864 — 6 P. M.

The following movements are ordered for the 5th of May, 1864: 1. Major General Sheridan, commanding cavalry corps, will move with Gregg's and Torbert's divisions against the enemy's cavalry in the direction of Hamilton's Crossing. General Wilson, with the Third Cavalry Division, will move at five A. M. to Craig's Meeting-house, on the Catharpin Road. He will keep out parties on the Orange Court-house pike and plank road, the Catharpin Road, Pamunkey Road (road to Orange Springs), and in the direction of Troyman's Store and Andrews's Store, or Good Hope Church. 2. Major General Hancock, commanding Second Corps, will move at five A. M. to Shady Grove Church, and extend his right towards the Fifth Corps at Parker's Store. 3. Major General Warren, commanding Fifth Corps, will move at five A. M. to Parker's Store on the Orange Court-house plank road, and extend his right towards the Sixth Corps at Old Wilderness Tavern. 4. Major General Sedgwick, commanding Sixth Corps, will move to Old Wilderness Tavern on the Orange Court-house pike as soon as the road is clear.

By such a movement it was expected that the army, having turned Lee's right by the passage of the Rapidan, would be able to pass the Wilderness, and then, by a rapid advance towards Gordonsville, place itself between Lee and Richmond. But Lee, having received timely notice of the crossing, instead of falling back, took the offensive, and from Orange Court-house, which was the centre of his position, marched by two parallel roads, the Orange plank road and the Fredericksburg turnpike, so as to strike Grant's advance at right angles, and force him to fight in the Wilderness.

On the morning of the 5th, when Grant and Meade reached the Old Wilderness Tavern, they found Warren's corps in position there, and Sedgwick's coming up, and received information that the enemy were advancing upon them by the turnpike. It was at first supposed that this was merely a diversion to prevent any interference with Lee's design of retiring to take up another position; and it was resolved to push this force away. This movement was at first successful; the enemy's advance was driven back, but soon, being reënforced by the main body, the Confederates resumed the offensive. This was the opening of the battle, which soon became general, and raged all day with great fury, neither party gaining a decided advantage; and at night the troops of both armies passed the long hours until morning where darkness had found them.

The complicated nature of the ground, and the impossibility of manœuvring large bodies of men through the narrow roads, and the dense underbrush, made the contest a confused struggle, more like an old Indian battle, than a modern one, and renders any clear account of it next to impossible. It was a test of the enduring valor of both sides, and nobly both sides bore the test.

Both armies the next morning assumed the offensive. By dawn of the 6th, the Union line was formed. It extended about five miles, facing westward, with Sedgwick on the right next Warren, and Burnside and Hancock on the left. With the Confederates, Longstreet's corps, which had the day before been marching up from Gordonsville, arrived so as to be present the second day, while the army held the same ground as the day before — Ewell on the left, covering the turnpike, and Hill on the right, covering the plank road, and meeting so as to form a continuous line.

The orders for the Union army were to make a general attack along the line, while Lee determined, by threatening the Union right, to distract Grant's attention, and then, by an overwhelming attack upon his left, as soon as Longstreet should come up, to force him back to the Rapidan. The Confederates commenced the battle upon our extreme right, and the contest raged again almost continuously that whole day, swaying backwards and forwards with changing success, but neither army gaining any decisive advantage.

The next morning, Saturday, the 7th of May, neither army seemed inclined to take the offensive. Both had suffered severely, and both remained behind their intrenchments. The following summing up by the historian of the *Army of the Potomac* is the best statement to be given of the results of these two days' terrible fighting. "The battle of the Wilderness is scarcely to be judged as an ordinary battle. It will happen in the course, as in the beginning of every war, that there occur actions in which ulterior purposes and the combinations of a military programme play very little part, but which are simply trials of strength. The battle of the Wilderness was such a mortal combat — a combat in which the adversaries aimed each, respectively, at a result that should be decisive — Lee to crush the campaign in its inception, by driving the army of the Potomac across the Rapidan; Grant to destroy Lee.

"Out of this fierce determination came a close and deadly grapple of the two armies — a battle terrible and indescribable in those gloomy woods. There is something horrible, yet fascinating, in the mystery shrouding this strangest of battles ever fought — a battle which no man could see, and whose progress could only be followed by the ear, as the sharp and crackling volleys of musketry, and the alternate Union cheer and Confederate yell, told how the fight surged and swelled. The battle continued two days; yet such was the mettle of each combatant, that it decided nothing. It was in every respect a drawn battle; and its only result appeared in the tens of thousands of dead and wounded in blue and gray that lay in the thick woods. The Union loss exceeded fifteen thousand, and the Confederate loss was about eight thousand."

## CHAPTER XXXIII.

THE FIRST OF THE SERIES OF FLANK MOVEMENTS. — THE BATTLE OF SPOTTSYLVANIA COURT-HOUSE.

ON Saturday, the 7th of May, Grant resolved to move south from the Wilderness, and plant himself at Spottsylvania Court-house, between Lee and Richmond. This point is fifteen miles south-east of the battle-field of the Wilderness, and the march was to be begun that night; but the noise of the trains informed Lee that some movement was commenced, though it gave no idea of what it was. The routes to this point for both armies, from their present position, were about the same length. The Fifth Corps was to lead and seize the Court-house. The advance began at nine P. M. on the 7th. At the same time Longstreet's division of the Confederate army set out for the same spot; and early the next morning, when Warren's troops reached the ground, they were met by the advance of Longstreet's division, and the day was occupied with each army hastening to its position; and in so doing every one of the corps of our army was more or less engaged during this day. The 9th was spent in taking up positions and strengthening them, and on the 10th the attack upon the enemy was ordered along the line, to carry his intrenchments, but failed. The next day, the 11th, was spent in preparation for another attack against the enemy's right centre, and at early dawn on the 12th Hancock's division marched to the assault, and carried a point in the first line of intrenchments, which we held that day despite all the enemy's attempts to recapture it. Five separate times fresh troops were led by the enemy up to the assault, and each time they were forced to retire. The struggle here was of the fiercest and most deadly character. Frequently the rival standards were planted on opposite sides of the breastworks. So continuous and dense was the fire, that there is now in Washington the trunk of a tree, eighteen inches in diameter, which was actually cut in two by the bullets. At midnight Lee withdrew to his inner line of defence. Our loss this day was above eight thousand, and that of the Confederates quite as much.

On the 11th Grant sent his first despatch to Washington since the advance. It was as follows: —

HEADQUARTERS IN THE FIELD, May 11, 1864 — 8 A. M.

We have now ended the sixth day of very heavy fighting. The result, to this time, is much in our favor.

Our losses have been heavy, as well as those of the enemy. I think the loss of the enemy must be greater.

We have taken over five thousand prisoners by battle, while he has taken from us but few, except stragglers.

I PROPOSE TO FIGHT IT OUT ON THIS LINE, IF IT TAKES ALL SUMMER.

U. S. GRANT, *Lieutenant General,*
*Commanding the Armies of the United States.*

And again on the 12th: —

SPOTTSYLVANIA C. H., May 12, 1864.

The eighth day of battle closes, leaving between three and four thousand prisoners in our hands for the day's work, including two general officers and over thirty pieces of artillery.

The enemy is obstinate, and seems to have found the last ditch. We have lost no organization, not even a company, while we have destroyed and captured one division, one brigade, and one regiment entire of the enemy.

U. S. GRANT, *Lieutenant General.*

As the result of the fighting of the 12th was Lee's retiring to his inner line of works, the succeeding week was spent in endeavoring to find some spot in which his line could be pierced; and to this end movements were made from flank to flank, but were skilfully met at every point, the Confederates extending their line to meet every new attempt, so that in ten days the position had changed from a line extending four or five miles to the north-west of Spottsylvania Court-house to a position almost due east of that place. The amount of labor in marching and fighting, the amount of privation and suffering, that our army underwent in these ten days, was enormous, and can hardly be estimated. At the end of these attempts, finding, however, that carrying the position was hopeless, Grant resolved to turn it, and commenced preparations for this movement on the afternoon of the 19th; but the enemy, discovering them, attacked our right, and delayed the movement until the following night, that of the 20th of May, when, moving by the left, the army took up its march again for Richmond.

## CHAPTER XXXIV.

### THE COÖPERATING MOVEMENTS IN THE SHENANDOAH VALLEY, AND SOUTH OF THE JAMES.

It will be well now to glance at the coöperating movements of Sheridan, of Butler, and in West Virginia. On the 9th of May, Sheridan set out from Spottsylvania Court-house, with a portion of his cavalry force, with orders to engage the enemy's cavalry, to destroy the Virginia Central and the Richmond and Fredericksburg Railroads, to threaten Richmond, and finally to communicate and draw his supplies from Butler's army on the James. To deceive the enemy, this force set out at first towards Fredericksburg, and then, turning southward, pushed to the North Anna River, which it crossed by Anderson's bridge, and the next day reaching Beaver Dam Station, on the Virginia Central Railroad, destroyed two locomotives, three trains of cars, ten miles of the track, and a million and a half of rations, and recaptured four hundred Union prisoners, on their way to the horrors of the Libby Prison in Richmond.

Here Sheridan was attacked by the enemy in flank and rear, but repulsed them with inconsiderable loss, and continued on his route. The South Anna was crossed at Ground Squirrel Bridge, and at daylight on the 11th Ashland Station, on the Richmond and

Fredericksburg Railroad, was captured by a brigade detached from the main body, and the depot, six miles of the road, a train of cars, and quantities of stores, destroyed, when, uninjured, this brigade rejoined the main body, which had been pushing southward towards Richmond.

At Yellow Tavern, a few miles from this city, Stuart, in command of the enemy's cavalry, had managed to interpose himself, by a *détour* between Sheridan's force and the Confederate capital, with all the troops he could gather. Sheridan promptly attacked him on the 11th, and after an obstinate contest, in which Stuart, the most brilliant cavalry leader of the Confederates, was killed, finally drove the enemy back, gained possession of the turnpike, and forced his opposers across the north fork of the Chickahominy. Continuing his course, Sheridan dashed boldly upon the outer defences of Richmond, and, with a rush, carried the first line. Finding, however, that the second line was too strong to be carried by assault, and that the garrison was rallying for its defence, he retired to the Chickahominy, at Meadow Bridge. Here he found that the enemy had partially destroyed the bridge, and were posted so as to prevent his crossing. Rebuilding the bridge, however, under a heavy fire, he drove the opposing force away, and repulsing an attack upon his rear, made by infantry from the garrison at Richmond, he destroyed the railway bridge over the Chickahominy, proceeded to Haxell's Landing, where he arrived on the 14th, and sent a messenger to Butler, and after remaining here three days to recuperate, set out again, by way of Hanover Court-house, and rejoined the army of the

Potomac on the 25th of May, in the position it then held on the Pamunkey River. The raid had been eminently successful, and established the fitness of the command to which Grant had elevated Sheridan; while the boldness and dashing valor with which the whole affair was conducted astonished and dismayed the enemy.

Butler's coöperative force, which was to act offensively upon the southern approach to Richmond, consisted of the Eighteenth Corps, commanded by General W. F. Smith, and the Tenth, commanded by General Gillmore, who had gained a reputation in the operations at Charleston, South Carolina, while General Smith had so distinguished himself at Chattanooga, that Grant, in his report, recommending him for promotion, said that he "felt under more than ordinary obligations to the masterly manner in which he had discharged his duties." With these forces, and his cavalry under General Kautz, Butler's army numbered something more than thirty thousand men.

During the month of April his forces assembled at Yorktown and Gloucester Point; and here the route was open towards Richmond, either up the Peninsula or by the line of the James, threatening that capital from the south side. This last course was the one it really was intended to take; but to deceive the enemy as to our real intention, a feint was made in the other direction.

On the 4th of May, the troops being embarked in transports, Butler moved at night, unobserved by the enemy, down the York and up the James, and took up a position on its south bank, the major portion of his force being stationed at Bermuda Hundred, a strong position, situated in a bend of the river, three miles above the mouth of the Appomattox, and here rapidly intrenched, while the fleet of gunboats which had convoyed the transports served to guard the flanks. This point is between the cities of Richmond and Petersburg, about ten miles north of the last, and twenty miles south of the first. The landing was a complete surprise to the enemy, and was conducted cleverly and without interference, for, in fact, at this time the enemy's force about Richmond and Petersburg was quite inconsiderable.

By the 6th the debarkation was finished, and the position strengthened. In front of Butler's line, about three miles distant, ran the Petersburg and Richmond Railroad, and its destruction was the first thing which attracted his attention, and the same day a brigade was sent out to perform this duty. Meeting a small force of the enemy, they retired, after a slight skirmish. That night the advance of Beauregard's army, drawn from Charleston, Savannah, and Florida, reached Petersburg, and the next day (the 7th) when a larger column was sent to destroy the railroad, the enemy were found in a position covering it, and an engagement commenced. At first the Union forces were successful; but the enemy, rallying, regained the position they had lost, and both parties withdrew.

The next day (the 9th) another advance was made in this direction, the position carried, the railroad destroyed, and the enemy driven back to within three miles of Petersburg, at Swift Creek, where his position was strongly defended by earth-works. Butler determined the next day to drive him back to Petersburg, but that night having received from Washington accounts of Lee's being in "full retreat to Richmond," resolved to turn northward and aid in the investment of that capital. On the 12th this advance was made, and the enemy driven back, until they were found, on the 15th, in a strong position on the left bank of Proctor's Creek, their left resting on Drury's Bluff. It was designed to assault this position the next day; but that night, the enemy, taking advantage of a dense fog, which rose just before morning, and was so thick as to make it impossible to see ten yards in advance, sallied out and attacked the Union forces with such desperate bravery, that at one time it seemed as though we would be overwhelmed. The army, however, stood firm, but was finally forced to withdraw again to its position at Bermuda Hundred, and the Confederates following, took up an intrenched position in our front, so that, as Butler said, his army was "bottled up and hermetically sealed," and was powerless for any operation against Richmond, while at the same time reënforcements for Lee could be spared from Beauregard's army.

In this last engagement our loss was about four thousand, while that of the Confederates was about three thousand. While thus rendered inactive, it was still possible for Butler to cross to the south bank of the Appomattox and seize Petersburg, and he was preparing for this important move, when he was ordered to detach the greater part of his army, in order to reenforce the army of the Potomac, which was then approaching the Chickahominy.

The coöperative movements in Western Virginia were commenced on the 1st of May. The forces were divided into two columns. One under Crook was to move by the Kanawha, and operate against the East Tennessee and Virginia Railroad, and the other, under Siegel, to penetrate as far as possible up the Shenandoah Valley. Siegel advanced up the Valley, and on the 15th met an opposing force under Breckinridge, which had been hastily collected. A severe engagement followed, in which Siegel was defeated with severe loss, and retired behind Cedar Creek. At Grant's request Siegel was then relieved, and General David Hunter put in command, and, under Grant's instructions, took the offensive, meeting the enemy on the 5th of June at Piedmont, and there, after an action of several hours, defeating him, capturing fifteen hundred prisoners and three pieces of cannon. Before this engagement, however, Lee had recalled Breckinridge's division to reenforce his own army.

On the 8th Hunter formed a junction with Crook's column, which had destroyed the railway as far as Newbern from Dublin, and moved towards Lynchburg, by way of Lexington. Finding that this place was, however, strongly defended, and that reënforcements were arriving there from Lee's army, he determined to return, and did so through the mountains, suffering great privations, but in no way coöperating with the movements of the army of the Potomac.

## CHAPTER XXXV.

ANOTHER FLANK MOVEMENT.—THE POSITION ON THE NORTH ANNA.

THUS the design of having the coöperating armies aid the army of the Potomac in the realization of its purpose, by cutting the communications, distracting the attention, and preventing reënforcements from reaching the army covering Richmond, had not succeeded. The impossibility of carrying the enemy's position at Spottsylvania was also apparent, and it was determined to flank the position, and, by a movement similar to that performed in the Wilderness, to get the Union army between Richmond and Lee's army.

Such a movement is always difficult and hazardous in the presence of an active and vigilant foe; but in this case it was conducted with skill, and was a complete success. On the night of the 20th the movement began. In a movement such as this, the flanking army of course lays itself open, during its motion, to the favorable attack of the enemy. Lee, however, did not attempt this; but becoming immediately aware of Grant's movements, he contented himself with moving along the interior line, and stationing his army in a favorable position for again resisting the Union advance; but still the military possibilities of the situation obliged the Lieutenant General, during the whole of the movement, to keep his troops well together, and always ready to form in line, to receive any attack that might be made upon them.

Wellington once said that there were very few generals in Europe who could march one hundred thousand men through Hyde Park Gate in perfect order and without interfering with or jostling each other. Here, however, the task was very much more difficult: the country was hostile, and an active enemy was vigilantly on the watch to take immediate advantage of any favorable opportunity that should offer itself for attack. On the 23d of May, in the afternoon, the entire Union army, with the exception of Burnside's corps, which was still on the march, had reached the north bank of the South Anna River. The route to the present position of the army, from that they recently held at Spottsylvania, led them through a rich agricultural country, which was at the time in the full beauty of spring. It had never been overrun with hostile armies, and in place of the bare and barren fields, which war had for three years laid ruthlessly waste, here was the tender green of young vegetation, and all the rich glory of Nature in her most generous mood.

On the 20th, not more than half an hour after the movement of Grant's army commenced, Lee had also set his troops in motion, and following the subsequent moves of his antagonist, withdrew his troops from their lines at Spottsylvania as fast as Grant did his from their lines, and having the advantage of moving on the chord of the arc while Grant was obliged to use the arc itself, he had reached and posted himself upon the south bank of this stream, when our forces came up to the opposite bank. This position was one he would of course defend, since it covered the Virginia Central Railroad, by which he was receiving reënforcements from the Shenandoah Valley.

In its advance Grant's army struck the North Anna near the point at which the Fredericksburg and Richmond Railroad crosses that stream; the left, consisting of Hancock's corps, which led the advance, at a point one mile above where the telegraph road crosses this stream on a wooden bridge, while the right, under Warren, touched the river four miles higher up, at Jericho Ford. Hancock, on his arrival, found the bridge strongly guarded and protected by works which were built the year before, and prepared to carry it by assault. While the column was getting into position, the artillery prepared their way, and an hour before sunset the assault was made. On the approach of our men on the double quick, the enemy deserted their defensive works and retreated across the river, and we took possession of the bridge. During that night the enemy tried several times to burn the bridge, but were prevented by our vigilance; and the next morning, it being found that they had also deserted their defensive works on the other side, the corps crossed the bridge and took up their position on the other side. Warren found no opposition in crossing, and the head of the column waded over, formed on the other side, and protected the building of a pontoon bridge, over which the remainder of the corps passed, and formed in line of battle, but met only slight opposition, and about five had begun intrenching, when they were furiously attacked by a force which had been sent against them, and a severe struggle ensued in which we were finally successful in holding the position, and in capturing nearly a thousand prisoners, while our loss was about three hundred and fifty.

Thus both wings of our army had crossed the North Anna, at points distant from each other about four miles, and made their positions good; but Lee's centre still extended to the stream, and when our centre attempted to cross the river, they were prevented, and suffered severely in the attempt, and Lee, holding his position, divided the right wing of the Union army from the left, necessitating a double crossing of the stream in order for one to support or reënforce the other.

Grant therefore resolved to withdraw his force, and in his report gives his reason for so doing: "Finding the enemy's position on the North Anna stronger than either of his previous ones, I withdrew, on the night of the 26th, to the north bank of the North Anna." After remaining, therefore, two days in their position, which were occupied in making reconnoissances and in destroying some miles of the Virginia Central Railroad, the withdrawal commenced on the evening of the 26th of May, and the army retired by the bridges to the opposite bank. The movement was made secretly and with perfect success, and it was nearly daylight before the last of the long columns had crossed, and the army took up its march to its next position, on the Pamunkey.

This river is formed by the confluence of the North and South Anna, and in its turn unites with the Mattapony, forming the York, and empties into Chesapeake Bay.

By this move Grant avoided the necessity of driving Lee from the strong position he had taken on the North Anna, and prevented his making the same use of what would have been the same advantages upon the South Anna, while, in addition, he secured for himself a base of supplies by water carriage, which, in anticipation of this move, had been sent to White House, on the Pamunkey.

## CHAPTER XXXVI.

THE BATTLE OF COLD HARBOR.—THE MOVEMENT TO THE SOUTH SIDE OF THE JAMES.

ON the 23d, Sheridan, on the cavalry expedition we have already spoken of, had reached White House, and on the 25th rejoined the army of the Potomac, and that same night was sent down the Pamunkey, and on the 27th, by noon, had seized the ferry crossing at Hanovertown, fifteen miles from Richmond, and thrown a pontoon bridge across. On this day and the next, the 28th of May, the army crossed the river, the Fifth and Ninth Corps at Hanover Ferry, and the Second and Sixth at Huntley's Ford, above. On Sunday, the 29th, the Union army was across the river and three miles beyond it, and continued the advance next day, with Hancock in the centre, Warren on the left, and Wright on the right. The flanks and rear were protected by cavalry, and at two P. M. the cavalry pickets on our left, which were advancing on the Cold Harbor road, were driven in, and, Warren was attacked in force about five. As soon as it was known that the enemy had been met, an attack was ordered along the line; but the orders were received too late, except by Hancock, who carried the enemy's advanced line, but found the main position too strong to be carried. It was evident that the enemy was here in force, and in a strong position covering the advance to the Chickahominy, and that to drive him away in order to force our advance would cost another battle.

To cover the Chickahominy, and prevent our advance upon Richmond, Lee had taken up a position parallel to our front, exending on his left from Hanover Courthouse to Bottom's Bridge on his right; and it being evident that to attempt to force a passage directly in front would be attended with the severe loss incident to a desperate battle, Grant resolved to attempt a passage by his left, at Cold Harbor, a spot which, as it was the point of convergence for the roads leading both to Richmond and to White House, our base of supplies, was as important for us to gain as it was necessary for the enemy to guard. On the afternoon of the 31st, this place had been secured by Sheridan with a force of cavalry, after a spirited contest, and the same night the Sixth Corps was directed to the same place. They arrived in time, on the afternoon of June 1, to support Sheridan, who was hard pressed by the enemy, the importance of the place having become so evident that strong efforts had been made to recapture it. The result of the contest here, which was quite severe, costing us the loss of some two thousand men, was that we held Cold Harbor, and thus protected our base of supplies at White House.

Finding that Butler's force was useless at Bermuda Hundred, Grant had ordered him to send all the troops he could spare to join the army of the Potomac; and accordingly, on the 29th of May, a column of sixteen thousand men embarked on transports, and, passing down the James, ascended the York and the Pamunkey, and disembarked the next day at White House. Owing to some error in the orders received by General W. F. Smith, their commander, it was not until the afternoon of the 1st of June that the column reached Cold Harbor, and took up its position on the right of the Sixth Corps, ready to coöperate in the battle which was imminent.

The headquarters of the Union army was established at Cold Harbor, which is simply a locality, designating the convergence of the roads at this point, and is quite inland, with the Chickahominy running behind, and near Gaines's Mills, the place where McClellan fought the first of his battles in his retrograde movement over the Peninsula, though in the present action the positions of the armies were reversed, Grant holding the position the Confederate army held then.

Lee's army was admirably posted for defence, on this side of the Chickahominy, with its front obstructed by marshes and thickets; while the right of the Union army rested on Tolopotomy Creek, and its left across the Despatch Station road, making a line of about six miles, Hancock occupying the left, Warren and Burnside the right, the Sixth Corps and Smith's command the centre. The order was a general assault along the whole line, at half past four in the morning.

At the appointed hour, in the dim gray of the early morning, the line advanced, and the lingering darkness was lit up with the lurid gleams of battle. There was a rush, a bitter struggle, a rapid interchange of deadly fire, and the army became conscious that the task was more than it could do. Hancock, on the left, carried, with severe loss, the first line of the enemy's defence, but his corps was in turn forced back, and intrenching themselves in a wonderfully short space of time, kept their ground in advance of where they started, and about one to two hundred feet from the enemy.

This was the result along the whole line; the assault was everywhere repulsed; the men everywhere showed themselves brave to rashness; but the most that could be done was to take a position more or less close to the enemy's line, according to the varying nature of the ground, and holding the positions thus taken against the enemy, who in his turn tried by assault to drive us from them, and at half past one all offensive operations were stopped. The loss was very severe, and in this respect, as the attacking party, we suffered much more severely than the enemy, having lost about seven thousand five hundred men, all told. Again, it was found impossible to drive the opposing army away, or to break through its opposition; and again Grant determined to flank the position, and, by passing round Lee's right, lay siege to the southern defences of Richmond. During the next few days the armies remained substantially as they were, our position being strengthened by intrenchments, and the lines being so close that the sharpshooters, on both sides, could pick off the men and officers at work in the trenches.

Meanwhile Sheridan was sent with the cavalry to destroy the Virginia Central Railroad thoroughly, to join Hunter, and then return to the army of the Potomac, all railroad communication between Richmond and the Shenandoah Valley and Lynchburg being thus destroyed. The first part of this programme was successfully accomplished. Moving rapidly up the railroad, destroying it as he went, he encountered the enemy's cavalry, under Wade Hampton, at Trevillian Station, on the 11th of June, and defeated them severely. The next day, continuing, he met Hampton again about five miles from Gordonsville, in an intrenched position, and also reënforced with infantry. Our first assault was repulsed, and night coming on, Sheridan, finding his supplies giving out, and hearing nothing of Hunter, who, it will be remembered, was withdrawing over the mountains, he himself withdrew to White House, which he reached on the 19th, at an opportune moment for driving away the enemy's cavalry, who were preparing to attack this place. Here his orders were to break up the depot of supplies, and escort the garrison to the James, which he did, keeping off the enemy and repelling his attacks, and on the 25th of June reached the James, and, crossing it, joined the army of the Potomac.

The next move was to transfer the army to the south side of the James, and approach Richmond from this quarter. The overland route had been tried—tried with persistence and vigor; but it had been found impossible to cut through or to destroy the opposing army. At every advance Lee had been able to meet the army of the Potomac, and with the advantage of position in his favor. The loss had been enormous in this month of battles. From the Wilderness to Cold Harbor, the aggregate, all told, amounts to about sixty thousand men, killed, wounded, and missing. The record looks ghastly, but the work was to be done. War is at best a ghastly butchery, a "stupendous imbecil ity," and an evidence of the want of development of the interests of productive industry. This was the debt we had to pay for our national connivance during more than sixty years in the injustice of slavery. Had the rights of labor, the first claim of mankind to the product of their toil, been recognized by the nation, slavery would have been impossible, and the rebellion would never have occurred. The law of retributive justice is as inexorable in its workings with nations as it is with individuals. To support the individual in health, he must preserve the conditions necessary for health, and must be free to choose them. Bad food, bad air, confinement, oppression, must produce their ill results. And as the law of liberty, the freedom of development, which is the basis of the democratic idea, is found to be absolutely necessary for the individual, so is it the law for nations. And further, too, as we know that we can judge easier of the causes of ill health in others than we can in our own cases, as we see easier the motes in the eyes of our friends than the beams in our own, since our prejudices, our vanity, our self-esteem, and our pride obscure our vision in this respect, we find the same rule holds with nations. Though there may be still some who deny that slavery was the cause of the war, and that the suffering and death it entailed upon this nation was in requital for our maintenance of that gigantic system of oppression of labor, yet few of us can fail to see that in the case of England, her centuries of oppression of Ireland have caused her present condition, when she presents to the world the ludicrously tragic aspect of a nation quaking with fear before a cause which does not boast an armed man in its defence, and in her terror the cabinet calling upon Parliament to repeal the *habeas corpus*. As it is the part of the wise man to know himself, and if his right eye offends to pluck it out and cast it from him, so too with nations; and while with gratitude and grief we cherish the memory of those whose lot it was to offer themselves a sacrifice for our sin, let the lesson the necessity has taught us not be lost upon us, and let us further recognize the decisive firmness of the man who with all modesty, but with the self-reliance of genius, took upon himself the responsibility, and carried us through suffering to victory.

It is questioned still by many whether much of this loss could not have been avoided by a different course; but all such suggestions depend upon an *if* for their conclusions, and can only be answered in the same way. If this had not been done, would the war not have lasted longer than it did, and would not the suffering and loss have been much greater than it was? But to rise from the discussion of probabilities, in which anything is possible to ingenuity, let us look at the facts. The victory was gained; to gain it, fighting, severe, deadly, persistent fighting, was necessary; and this being so, —

> "If it were done when 'tis done, then 'twere well
> It were done quickly."

And in this view of the case, — which, though apparently unfeeling, is that of the surgeon who amputates the limb in order to save the patient's life, — the justification of the result is complete and full.

Sherman's criticism upon the battle at Shiloh may also, with slight modifications, be applied to this case. These reflections are perhaps necessary here, when we consider the amount of objurgation which was heaped upon Grant at the time for his course, and the remains of which are still occasionally met with. But it is a noticeable fact that most of the tender delicacy which was horrified at this disregard of human life came, as a rule, from the men whose sympathies were principally with the rebellion; to whom the wrongs which were to be redressed by this lavish expenditure excited simply contempt and derision; who excused everything to the slaveholders in rebellion, but had, and have, no pity or sympathy for the slave — the men who stand in the nineteenth century as representatives of the seventeenth, and whose value is principally that of a species of moral fossils, serving as specimens to show the eras through which the world has passed in its progress to the evolution of the democratic era.

During this month of continuous battles Grant was in constant receipt of reënforcements; and though the loss of experienced officers could not be replaced immediately, yet the spirit and temper of his army had not suffered as severely as it would be natural to expect that it would.

The loss in Lee's army is estimated at twenty thousand men; and though this difference appears too great, yet it must be remembered that it had generally had the great advantage of position, and of being the attacked and not the attacking force. Its spirit is also said to have been high; in fact, that it was never better than after the battle of Cold Harbor; and this opinion, it is claimed, is founded upon the "unanimous and emphatic testimony of its officers."

The movement to transfer the army of the Potomac to

the south side of the James necessitated the apparent uncovering of Washington. In the series of movements from the Rapidan to the James, the army of the Potomac had been constantly interposed to prevent any offensive movement, on the part of the enemy, having Washington as its object; and to the army of politicians and office-seekers who make Washington the field and base of their campaigns against the national purse, this protection of their precious persons in the undisturbed pursuit of their favorite art, seemed to be the chief occupation of the army of the Potomac. It was naturally to be expected, therefore, that such a movement should excite their extremest fear and disgust, and that they should express their disapprobation of it in no measured terms, and in so far as they could, by influencing at once both the government and public opinion, prevent it.

The changing by an army of its base is also an operation which Napoleon has pronounced to be "the ablest manœuvre taught by military art," and requires great skill to be performed successfully and well.

In disregarding, therefore, the objections of ignorance of military affairs and of self-interest, Grant showed the moral firmness which he has displayed in his whole course. Being resolved to do only his duty, as he best understands it, and to the best of his ability, having once come to a conclusion concerning his course of action, his only object is to carry it out, regardless of all other considerations, in the promptest and most efficacious way. His conception of the necessity of the move was as accurate and comprehensive as the ability he showed in the manner of its execution. Gradually withdrawing the right, and extending his left flank, the army was brought within easy distance of the lower crossings of the Chickahominy, and on the night of the 12th the movement began. Warren's corps, preceded by a division of cavalry, took the lead, and crossing the Chickahominy at Long Bridge, threatened an advance on Richmond, and covered the movement of the army. The distance across the Peninsula was here fifty-five miles, and it was marched by the army in two days. The movement was, therefore, a perfect success.

On the morning of the 13th Lee discovered that the army had withdrawn, and retired towards Richmond. The points at which Grant's army should cross had been selected by Brigadier General Weitzel, and a pontoon bridge, which was a triumph of engineering skill, being over two thousand feet long, and the channel boats being anchored in water thirteen fathoms deep, was commenced under the direction of Brigadier General Benham, on the forenoon of the 14th, and completed by midnight. Over this and in ferry boats the army crossed, and on the 16th was entirely on the south side of the stream. During this movement Smith's command had returned to Bermuda Hundred, and on landing, on the 14th, was sent by Butler to take Petersburg. This city is situated on the south bank of the Appomattox, twenty-two miles from Richmond, and about ten from City Point, where the Appomattox empties into the James, and is a centre of the Lynchburg, Weldon, and the Norfolk Railways.

The Appomattox is navigable to the wharves of Petersburg for vessels of one hundred tons, while six miles below the city, at a place called Walthall's, vessels of a larger size unload. It is the third city of Virginia, but obtained now, as an outpost of Richmond, a great strategic value, and was strongly fortified by the enemy, whose lines were admirably constructed to defend it, and protect its valuable railroads.

Grant had gone in person to superintend the operations which were to capture this place, and on the 10th, before the works had been greatly strengthened, and before its importance had become so manifest, Butler had sent Gillmore, with thirty-five hundred men, over the Appomattox, to move by the river turnpike and capture the city if possible. This movement was supported by an attack made by gunboats upon Fort Clinton, below the city, and by a cavalry expedition under Kautz, which was to move across the Norfolk Railroad and enter the city from the south. Gillmore advanced, drove in the enemy's skirmishers, and penetrated to within two miles of the city, and then retired, finding the enemy's works too strong and his own force too weak. Meanwhile, Kautz, with cavalry, crossed the railroad, and rapidly penetrated into the town, but was repulsed by the enemy, who, unengaged by Gillmore, concentrated to resist this rear attack.

## CHAPTER XXXVII.

THE POSITION BEFORE PETERSBURG. — THE ATTEMPTS TO CAPTURE THIS CITY.

After this failure, Grant again returned to Bermuda Hundred, and gave Butler verbal instructions to use Smith's command in another attack, engaging to return to the army of the Potomac, and send them down as speedily as possible to take part in the attack, or to support those engaged in it. As we have seen, Smith's column arrived at Bermuda Hundred on the night of the 14th, and during that night passed over the Appomattox, and the next morning was pushed towards Petersburg, distant seven miles. After advancing two miles, a line of rifle trenches was encountered, which were captured by the colored division in a spirited charge, and the forces advanced to the line of fortifications. The day was occupied in these operations and in bringing up the troops, and at seven P. M. a line of skirmishers was thrown out, and the outposts of the defences were carried. This statement is based upon the report of General Smith, which differs in some minor points with Grant's report, but is probably the more exact of the two, since it was made by one who was on the spot. It seems, however, decided that a great mistake was made in not pushing forward, since at this time the works were but weakly defended, and might have been easily carried. Meanwhile the army of the Potomac was crossing the James, Hancock having crossed this same day, and Lee was also bringing his army to the south side of the James, crossing near Drury's Bluff. On the 16th, Burnside, with the Ninth Corps, reached Petersburg about noon. Warren reached the same spot in the evening, and Hancock, with two divisions, the evening before. The army remained, however, in the position it had gained on the night of the 15th, and was found there by Burnside and Warren. This day also General Meade, after consultation with General Grant, proceeded from City Point to Petersburg, and taking command, ordered an assault that night. During the day, the enemy, however, had reenforced the garrison, and were ready for the attack, which commenced at six in the evening and lasted until next morning, and resulted in our gaining only a temporary advantage. During the 16th and 17th, the attack was continued with further reënforcements, and the fighting was of the severest description; yet the result was not what had been hoped. Our movements were too slow, and the enemy, by celerity of movement, was enabled to reënforce the place and keep it against our repeated assaults, and it became evident that it would be necessary to reduce the place by a siege.

The few following days brought our intrenched lines to such a state of forwardness, that the front of our position could be held by only a portion of the army, leaving the rest of the troops free for offensive operations, in extending the line of investment, and threatening to cut the railroad lines of communication by which the enemy obtained his supplies.

On Monday, the 20th of June, preparations were made for a movement in the direction of the enemy's right, the object of which was to extend our lines so as to cover the Weldon Railroad, which was a very important branch of the enemy's lines of communication, both for Petersburg and Richmond. On the morning of the 21st, therefore, the Second and Sixth Corps were moved rapidly out, across the Norfolk Railroad, then across the Jerusalem plank road, to which the lines of the Fifth Corps already extended. The movement, however, advanced only to a point known as Davis's Farm, on the plank road, between the two railroads, where they encountered the enemy in such force, that after a severe but brief action, they were compelled to retire. On the 22d and the 23d, the attempt was renewed, but without success. We were able to advance only about half way to the point desired; for the possession of the road was felt by the enemy to be of such vital importance to him, that he made every effort to retain its possession.

During the time spent in these unsuccessful attempts, the rest of the army did not remain idle. In every part of the line, each day had its battle, and every hour was marked by the restless energy which the spirit of the commander infused into the operations of the army. During the two weeks thus passed, the losses of the army amounted to about fifteen thousand men, while the enemy, by a vigilance which was as untiring as our attacks, had finally succeeded in surrounding Petersburg with a line of defences which made it impossible to take the place by assault. This line, beginning at the south bank of the Appomattox, surrounded Petersburg on the east and south, extending westward beyond the left flank of our army, while a continuation of the same series of defensive works upon the north side of the Appomattox defended the city and the railroad to Richmond from any attack by Butler with the force at Bermuda Hundred.

On the night of the 20th, Deep Bottom, a place only ten miles from Richmond, and on the north bank of the James, had been occupied by a force sent by General Butler, under the command of Brigadier General Foster, and connected with Bermuda Hundred by a pontoon bridge, while at the same time the force at this last place was strengthened by the withdrawal from the army of the Potomac of the balance of the Eighteenth Corps. At Deep Bottom an intrenched camp was formed, and by thus holding this position Grant was enabled at any time to threaten Richmond by an approach from the north bank of the James, upon which side of this stream Richmond itself is situated. To meet this possibility, Lee laid a pontoon bridge over the James, near Drury's Bluff, between Richmond and Deep Bottom, which would enable him to make a counter move with the same ease. In protecting his lines of communication, and preventing access to Richmond, the line to be guarded by Lee was about thirty miles long, so that the opportunities were offered to Grant to keep him busily engaged in varying the position of his troops, in order to meet any threatened attack, until a weak point should be found at which his line could be broken through. The energy of the army was devoted to the erection of a strong line of defence, so that the position could be kept with a small force, and a column could be spared for active operations to the above ends, and this work was completed about the end of July.

The army of the Potomac, thus in its position before Petersburg, protected Washington from any threatening attack from the army in its front, while, at the same time, itself threatening Richmond. But owing to the comparative failure of Hunter's expedition in the Shenandoah Valley, this route was open for the Confederates to threaten an invasion of the north, and the possible capture of Washington; and we shall see presently that they did not fail to avail themselves of it.

## CHAPTER XXXVIII.

### THE MINE, AND WHY IT FAILED.

BEFORE, however, looking to this part of the theatre of war, let us follow the army of the Potomac in its doings; and the next important occurrence which engages our attention is the famous mine. A spot in front of General Burnside's lines, where a hollow occurred just behind a deep cut in the City Point Railroad, was selected for the mine. The idea was started originally by Lieutenant Colonel Pleasants, of the Forty-eighth Pennsylvania Volunteers, who was a practical miner, and whose regiment was recruited in the mining districts of Pennsylvania. When the idea was broached to General Burnside, he warmly approved it, and Colonel Pleasants was set to work with his regiment, but found the greatest difficulty was caused by the want of proper tools. At first the plan elicited nothing but derision, but finally excited more attention. The work was begun on the 25th of June, and completed, despite the obstacles arising from the want of proper appliances, on the 23d of July, and charged with four tons of powder on the 25th of July.

The main gallery extended five hundred and ten feet, ending directly under the parapet of one of the enemy's redoubts, and though the line here reëntered, exposing the position to an enfilading fire from both sides, yet it was seen that if a crest just behind it could be carried, Petersburg might be secured. The morning of the 30th of July was fixed for the explosion and assault, and the operations of the army just at this juncture were auspicious auguries of success. On the 26th of July, General Hancock with the Second Corps, and two divisions of the cavalry under Sheridan, had been sent to Deep Bottom, with instructions to proceed to Chapin's Bluff to prevent reënforcements from Lee's army crossing on his pontoon bridge at this place, while Sheridan was to proceed to the Virginia Central Railroad and operate against Richmond, the defensive force in which was supposed to be small. Foster's position at Deep Bottom had caused Lee to send a force against him, which held a position in his front. On the 27th, Hancock turned the right flank of this force, while Foster threatened its front, and obliged it to fall back to another line of works, behind Bailey's Creek, where it checked Hancock's further advance. Meanwhile the cavalry had attempted to get at the enemy's rear, but were unsuccessful, and Lee, hearing of the attack, sent heavy reënforcements to oppose Hancock, detaching for this purpose five out of the eight divisions of his army.

Grant, becoming aware of how Lee had weakened his force, ordered Hancock to retain a defensive position, and secretly to return on the night of the 29th, in order to take part in the assault of the next morning. This was done. The plan was to explode the mine at half past four in the morning, and then, through the breach thus made, to assault. The assaulting party was chosen by lot, and it fell to the first division, under

Brigadier General Ledlie. The following order was issued by General Meade on the night of the 29th, for the disposition of the forces and their duty: —

The following instructions are issued for the guidance of all concerned: —

1. As soon as it is dark, Major General Burnside, commanding Ninth Corps, will withdraw his two brigades, under General White, occupying the intrenchments between the plank and Norfolk roads, and bring them to his front. Care will be taken not to interfere with the troops of the Eighteenth Corps, moving into their position in rear of the Ninth Corps. General Burnside will form his troops for assaulting the enemy's works at daylight on the 30th, prepare his parapets and abatis for the passage of the columns, and have the pioneers equipped for work in opening passages for artillery, destroying enemy's abatis, and the intrenching tools distributed for effecting lodgment, &c., &c.

2. Major General Warren, commanding Fifth Corps, will reduce the number of his troops holding the intrenchments of his front to the minimum, and concentrate all his available force on his right, and hold them prepared to support the assault of Major General Burnside. The preparations in respect to pioneers, intrenching tools, &c., &c., enjoined upon the Ninth Corps, will also be made by the Fifth Corps.

3. As soon as it is dark, Major General Ord, commanding Eighteenth Corps, will relieve his troops in the trenches by General Mott's division of the Second Corps, and form his corps in rear of the Ninth Corps, and be prepared to support the assault of Major General Burnside.

4. Every preparation will be made for moving forward the field artillery of each corps.

5. At dark, Major General Hancock, commanding Second Corps, will move from Deep Bottom to the rear of the intrenchments now held by the Eighteenth Corps, resume the command of Mott's division, and be prepared at daylight to follow up the assaulting and supporting columns, or for such other operations as may be found necessary.

6. Major General Sheridan, commanding cavalry corps, will

proceed at dark from the vicinity of Deep Bottom to Lee's Mill, and at daylight will move with his whole corps, including Wilson's division, against the enemy's troops defending Petersburg on the right, by the roads leading to that town from the southward and westward.

7. Major Duane, acting chief engineer, will have the pontoon trains parked at convenient points in the rear, prepared to move. He will see that supplies of sand-bags, gabions, fascines, &c., &c., are in depot near the lines, ready for use.

He will detail engineer officers for each corps.

8. At half past three ($3\frac{1}{2}$) in the morning of the 30th, Major General Burnside will spring his mine, and his assaulting columns will immediately move rapidly upon the breach, seize the crest in the rear, and effect a lodgment there. He will be followed by Major General Ord, who will support him on the right, directing his movement to the crest indicated, and by Major General Warren, who will support him on the left.

Upon the explosion of the mine, the artillery of all kinds in battery will open upon those points of the enemy's works whose fire covers the ground over which our columns must move, care being taken to avoid impeding the progress of our troops. Special instructions respecting the direction of fire will be issued through the chief of artillery.

9. Corps commanders will report to the commanding General when their preparations are complete, and will advise him of every step in the progress of the operation, and of everything important that occurs.

10. Promptitude, rapidity of execution, and cordial coöperation, are essential to success; and the commanding General is confident that this indication of his expectations will insure the hearty efforts of the commanders and troops.

11. Headquarters, during the operations, will be at the headquarters of the Ninth Corps.

By command of Major General MEADE.

At the appointed hour the fuse was lighted, but the mine did not explode. Lieutenant Colonel Pleasants, who had superintended the work, knew that the difficulty arose from a splice he had been forced to make in the fuse, and Lieutenant Jacob Douty and Sergeant Henry Reese, of the Forty-eighth Pennsylvania, volunteered to enter the mine and relight it. To do so they went along the gallery one hundred feet before coming to the place where the fuse had gone out, and having relighted it, the mine exploded at forty-two minutes past four.

The earth above the excavation rose, by the force of the explosion, in a solid mass, some two hundred feet in the air, like a dense and heavy cloud, through which the burning powder flashed like lightning. The quiver of the explosion shook the earth like an earthquake. The entire mass seemed to rest poised a moment in mid-air, and then, as it broke to pieces and fell, a thick, black cloud of smoke floated away, the wrecks of men and guns returned, with the mingled earth, back to the ground, and the artillery fire opened rapidly from every gun we had bearing upon the position. The assaulting column then marched out, but as sufficient openings had not been prepared for them in our own lines, the advance was very slow.

The explosion had made a crater two hundred feet long, sixty wide, and thirty deep, and opened the enemy's line for an assault, and had so paralyzed them that their artillery was silent. In this crater the troops halted, though there was nothing to prevent their going forward, since the enemy remained inactive for half an hour. The other troops, sent forward to support the first, were also forced to remain in the crater; and a scene of hopeless confusion ensued, as disgraceful as it was disastrous, for the enemy, recovering from his surprise, commenced to plant his artillery so as to command the crater, and to mass his infantry in a ravine to the right. At seven, two hours after his first advance, Ledlie was still in the crater, his men in a state of confused entanglement, and in the way of others. A division of colored troops was then sent forward, and passing beyond the crater, advanced towards the crest, but were driven back. The crater now became a slaughter-pen, in which whites and blacks were confusedly mingled, and into which the enemy rained every kind of deadly missile. To remain was certain death, to advance was impossible, and to retreat almost as dangerous as to remain. Above four thousand men were killed or captured in "this miserable affair," as Grant termed it.

This failure led to a great deal of crimination and recrimination, and finally was examined by a Congressional Investigating Committee, who found that the failure was due to the following causes: 1. The fact that the charge was led by white instead of black troops. This they considered "the first and great cause of disaster." 2. The fact that General Meade directed that the assaulting column should push at once for the crest of Cemetery Hill, instead of first clearing the enemy's lines to the right and left of the mine. This last opinion appears to be a conclusion drawn from an acquaintance with the tactics of party politics, and applied to military affairs. A military court of inquiry which was instituted soon after, and composed of Generals Hancock, Ayres, and Miles, found as follows: —

The causes of failure are, —

1. The injudicious formation of the troops in going forward, the movement being mainly by flank instead of extended front.

General Meade's order indicated that columns of assault should be employed to take Cemetery Hill, and that proper passages should be prepared for those columns. It is the opinion of the court that there were no proper columns of assault. The troops should have been formed in the open ground in front of the point of attack, parallel to the line of the enemy's works. The evidence shows that one or more columns might have passed over at and to the left of the crater, without any previous preparation of the ground.

2. The halting of the troops in the crater instead of going forward to the crest, when there was no fire of any consequence from the enemy.

3. No proper employment of engineer officers and working parties, and of materials and tools for their use, in the Ninth Corps.

4. That some parts of the assaulting columns were not properly led.

5. The want of a competent common head at the scene of the assault, to direct affairs as occurrences should demand.

Had not failure ensued from the above causes, and the crest been gained, the success might have been jeoparded by the failure to have prepared in season proper and adequate debouches through the Ninth Corps' lines for troops, and especially for field artillery, as ordered by Major General Meade.

The reasons why the attack ought to have been successful are, —

1. The evident surprise of the enemy at the time of the explosion of the mine, and for some time after.

2. The comparatively small force in the enemy's works.

3. The ineffective fire of the enemy's artillery and musketry, there being scarcely any for about thirty minutes after the explosion, and our artillery being just the reverse as to time and power.

4. The fact that some of our troops were able to get two hundred yards beyond the crater, towards the crest, but could not remain there or proceed farther for want of supports, or because they were not properly formed or led.

That the colored troops engaged in this affair showed

the bravery they showed constantly whenever they were employed, appears from the following report of the casualties they met with; but it is also said that the rebels, infuriated at seeing them employed in the army, singled them out for slaughter whenever it was possible, and did so in this case with especial savageness, while they were helplessly involved in the crater:—

Twenty-third U. S. Colored — Fifteen officers killed and wounded; four hundred men, including the missing.

Twenty-eighth U. S. Colored — Eleven officers, and about one hundred and fifty men killed, wounded, and missing.

Twenty-seventh U. S. Colored — Six officers, and about one hundred and fifty men killed, wounded, and missing.

Twenty-ninth U. S. Colored — Eight officers, and about two hundred and seventy-five men killed, wounded, and missing.

Thirty-first U. S. Colored — Seven officers, and about two hundred men killed, wounded, and missing.

Forty-third U. S. Colored — Six officers, and a large number of men killed, wounded, and missing.

Thirty-ninth U. S. Colored — Several officers, and about two hundred and fifty men killed, wounded, and missing.

## CHAPTER XXXIX.

### OPERATIONS IN THE SHENANDOAH VALLEY.—EARLY'S ADVANCE AGAINST WASHINGTON.

LET us now turn to the operations in the Shenandoah Valley. Hunter, as will be remembered, had retreated by way of Western Virginia, so as to leave the path open for the enemy to advance upon the loyal states, and advantage was taken of this condition of things by Lee, who sent General Jubal Early, with about twenty-five thousand men, down the Shenandoah Valley, to threaten Washington, and make a diversion in favor of Lee's army, held tightly at Petersburg by the army of the Potomac. On the 3d of July Early was before Martinsburg, and Siegel, who held this place with a small force, retreated across the Potomac at Shepherdstown. Harper's Ferry, in the possession of General Weber, was also evacuated, the force retiring to the Maryland Heights.

Hunter, who was in Western Virginia, had been ordered to move as rapidly as possible to Harper's Ferry, but the obstacles and difficulties in his way had delayed him. The river was low, and the railroad was broken in several places. The way being thus open to him, Early crossed the Potomac at Williamsport, and on the 6th of July was at Hagerstown, and on the 7th at Frederick, from which point he threatened both Washington and Baltimore.

Early in July, as soon as he heard that the enemy was on the way, Grant sent troops from the army of the Potomac to protect Washington. This force consisted of the Sixth Corps, which was forwarded on transports to Washington. At this time, also, the Nineteenth Corps, which had been ordered to return from New Orleans, had just arrived at Hampton Roads, and was sent, without landing, after the Sixth. Besides these reënforcements, the only troops available for opposing Early were those under General Wallace, who had command of the department of Annapolis, with his headquarters at Baltimore, and consisted of a few thousand foot artillerists, the hundred days' men, and the invalids. With these, and the advance of the Sixth Corps, which had fortunately arrived, Wallace moved promptly forward, and took a position on the Monocacy, near the railroad crossing, where, on the 8th of July, he fought the advancing enemy, and though driven back, and forced to retreat to Baltimore, yet the stand he had made delayed the enemy, and gave time for the rest of the reënforcements from the army of the Potomac and the Nineteenth Corps to arrive at Washington.

Elated by their success, on the 8th Early's troops advanced upon Washington, on the 10th were at Rochville, fourteen miles from that capital, and on the next day approached the fortifications of the city, and by the afternoon showed a strong line in front of Fort Stevens. During this day the remainder of the Sixth Corps arrived at Washington, and soon after the Nineteenth Corps. During the 12th the Confederates held their position, and there was skirmishing during that whole day, though the enemy did not show great vigor. Had he attacked with promptness and energy as soon as he had arrived, it is hardly questionable but that he might have captured the capital, though, if he had carried off the majority of the politicians, who are generally to be found there in great numbers, he would have done the nation more service than injury. Perhaps the consciousness of this fact had some influence in causing the feebleness of Early's action; but, be this as it may, that night Early withdrew his troops, and retired across the Potomac. His expedition had certainly been successful, if it was undertaken for the purpose of frightening the entire population of Washington, or if for the purpose of gathering booty of all kinds; for his troops retired laden with this, and had, in addition, destroyed quite a long piece of the Northern Central Railroad, burned bridges, and also collected money from some of the towns they passed through, under the threat of burning them if their demands were not complied with

On the night of the 12th Grant telegraphed to have General Wright take command, and urged a pursuit of the retreating Confederates, which was commenced next day; but the enemy were not overtaken until they had reached the Shenandoah Valley, at Snicker's Ferry, where, after a sharp skirmish with the rear-guard, the Confederates retired, and the Union troops returned to Washington.

One of the main objects of this expedition of the enemy had been to force Grant to transfer his army from the James to the defence of Washington; and during the successful progress of Early, the pressure brought to bear upon Grant by the administration, in order to induce him to do this, was so severe, that any one having less than his firmness and persistence would have succumbed. To do so would have been to give up all that had been gained by the whole campaign; and it is fortunate for the country that we had at the time a man at the head of our armies, who, like Grant, could take a comprehensive military view of the situation, and see that the important thing was holding his army where it was, since the whole expedition was a confession on the part of the enemy that this was so.

It was evident, however, that something must be done to prevent a recurrence of such an affair; and finding that Early designed staying in the valley of the Shenandoah, and that this rich country was made the chief resource of Lee's army for its supplies, he felt the importance of some plan which should forever stop this condition of things. On the 24th, Early, again advancing, drove Hunter's forces through Winchester and across the Potomac, and the next day, threatening to cross himself, Grant ordered the Sixth Corps to Harper's Ferry, and on the 2d of August ordered Sheridan to Washington, in order to have him ready to take command of the Middle Military Division, which he designed forming. On the 4th of August Grant left City Point, and on the 5th had a consultation with General Hunter, and finding him desirous of being relieved, sent for Sheridan to come up to Harper's Ferry from Washington, and gave him command of the Middle Military Division, in which were united the departments of Western Virginia, Washington, and the Susquehanna, which, up to this time, had been separate commands, and strengthened his force with two cavalry divisions from the army of the Potomac. Giving then his instructions to Sheridan, Grant returned to City Point. The result soon showed the excellence of this arrangement, and the merits of this selection. Our disgraceful failures in the Shenandoah Valley, as in some larger fields of action, had been caused as much by the petty jealousies of the rival commanders as by anything else. Many of our Generals, during the war, showed themselves as contemptible, by their selfish ambition for personal aggrandizement and jealous intrigues against each other, as any set of politicians, not, perhaps, excepting the local rings of New York city, or the lobby interests that gather about Washington. In this respect Grant's military record is most admirable. Prompt and generous as he has always been in fully recognizing the merits of others, he has, when slighted himself, been man enough to rise above the personal pique of rank, and being anxious only to see the rebellion put down, has been willing to do any duty assigned him, and to do it in any position. In so far he is the best representative of the democratic idea which has appeared in our army, for the spirit of this idea tends to replace the isolation of barbarism, where all men are enemies, by the union of civilization, where the interests of all are bound together, since those of all and each are identical. It is this spirit which is uniting Europe, which fought the battles of the Union, and which is influencing all societies. As, in all social movements, the upper classes, or those who call themselves by this invidious name, are the last to be influenced, we cannot wonder that the officers of the army were more backward than the men in displaying this new spirit. The enlisted men from any section fraternized, and even accepted the coöperation of the negro as readily as though there was no tradition of a curse laid upon all of Ham's hypothetical descendants. But the officers were inclined to be as punctilious concerning technicalities of rank, and all such petty conventions, as we find the doctors are concerning the various schools of practice in their profession — as though it were better the patient should die by allopathy than be cured by homœopathy, and vice versa; or as the preachers are jealous of each other's creeds — as though the important thing is not that men should be made better and happier by whatever means; or as the lawyers, the politicians, the diplomatists, who are all engaged in nullifying each other's work, instead of combining to extend the rule of justice in all individual, party, and national concerns.

Sheridan's force consisted of the troops Hunter had brought from Western Virginia, the Nineteenth Corps and the Sixth Corps, with the cavalry from the army of the Potomac. This force he posted in front of Berryville, while the enemy was on the west bank of Opequan Creek, covering Winchester. Here, with constant skirmishing, he kept Early stationary until his own troops should be prepared. Assuming the command on the 7th of August, and in September feeling confident of success, and receiving on the 15th a personal visit from General Grant, he obtained permission to assume the offensive. In his report Grant says, "He was off promptly to time; and I may here add, that I have never since deemed it necessary to visit General Sheridan before giving him orders."

On the 19th Sheridan, therefore, advanced, and met the enemy at Winchester, and drove them through the town, night stopping the pursuit. Early, however, retreated to Fisher's Hill, thirty miles south of Winchester, and Sheridan arrived in front of this position on the morning of the 22d, and attacking again, drove him back; nor did Early stop until he had reached the passes of the Blue Ridge, with the loss of half his army. Sheridan pushed the pursuit as far as Staunton, destroyed the Virginia Central Railroad, and returned to Strasburg, laying the country completely waste on his return. This course has been thought to be indefensible, and can be justified only on the grounds that anything in war can be justified. Certain it was, that this course, by beggaring the inhabitants, laying waste the fields, destroying the crops, burning the mills, and so on, prevented the people in this region from continuing to aid the enemy on every occasion, as they had repeatedly done before. It is difficult, if not impossible, to draw a line that shall accurately divide the allowable from the unallowable in war; the entire system is one of violence and injury, and if these are necessary, who shall say how far they shall go? Of course there is a difference between a love of carnage and destruction for their own sake, such as the savage displays, and severity for the purpose of accomplishing the object which every civilized nation engaged in war has, that is, of putting a stop to the war; and it cannot be said that Sheridan here overstepped the bounds allowed to this last.

The next month, while Sheridan still occupied a position on the north bank of Cedar Creek, Early,

SHERIDAN'S RIDE AT WINCHESTER.

having been reënforced from Lee's army, assumed the offensive, and having made his dispositions at Fisher's Hill, moved forward, on the night of the 18th of October, to surprise the Union force. Fording the north fork of the Shenandoah, and under the cover of a fog, they attacked our forces early in the morning of the 19th, while Sheridan was absent at Winchester, and came very near causing a most serious disaster. When daylight came, the whole of our left and centre was a confused mass; the Sixth Corps stood, however, firm, and protected the retreat, which now seemed the only course left, and it was not until a position was reached between Middletown and Newtown, and the pursuit of the enemy slackened, that the line could be re-formed. At about half past ten A. M., Sheridan, who had heard the guns at Winchester, came riding up post haste, and, inspiriting his men, led them back, and routed the enemy entirely, and finished the war forever in the Shenandoah Valley, so that most of his troops returned to the army of the Potomac, and the scattered remnants of Early's force to Lee's army, since the want of forage in the valley rendered it impossible for the Confederates to support an armed force there.

There is no doubt that it was Sheridan's personal bearing, and his magnetic influence over men which enabled him to thus pluck victory from the jaws of defeat; but it must not be forgotten that General Wright had already stayed the rout, and formed the line anew. General Early afterwards ascribed the rout of his army to the men, and some commissioned officers yielding "to a disgraceful propensity for plunder," and leaving their ranks in order to "appropriate" the "abandoned property of the enemy."

For this action Sheridan was made a Major General in the regular army, in the following order from the President, to fill the place resigned by McClellan, the order to take effect on the 8th of November: —

"That for personal gallantry, military skill, and just confidence in the courage and patriotism of his troops, displayed by Philip H. Sheridan on the 19th of October, at Cedar Run, whereby, under the blessing of Providence, his routed army was reorganized, a great national disaster averted, and a brilliant victory achieved over the rebels for the third time in pitched battle within thirty days, Philip H. Sheridan is appointed Major General in the United States army, to rank as such from the 8th day of November, 1864."

The operations in the Shenandoah being thus brought to a happy conclusion, let us return to the army of the Potomac in its position before Petersburg.

## CHAPTER XL.

THE SIEGE OF PETERSBURG.—THE ACTIVE OPERATIONS OF THE ARMY OF THE POTOMAC DURING THE SUMMER AND WINTER MONTHS.

DURING the summer and autumn months of 1864, the army of the Potomac remained in its position before Petersburg, but not lying idly in its trenches. The restless activity and indomitable perseverance of its commander kept it constantly employed, either in attempts to cut the enemy's lines of communication, and thus completely invest the city, or else, by diversions upon the north side of the James, to threaten Richmond itself directly. The first of the movements of this latter class was begun on the 12th of August. In order to deceive the enemy as to the destination of the expeditionary force, the transports upon which it embarked were sent ostentatiously down the river, as though they were destined for Fortress Monroe or Washington. During the night of the 12th, however, they returned up the river, and landed the troops at Deep Bottom, where General Foster still continued to hold his intrenched camp.

The task of embarkation was found so difficult, from the ill-adapted character of the boats used in this movement, and the want of proper appliances, that it was not completed until the morning of the 13th. The force sent on this expedition consisted of the Second and the Tenth Corps, with a cavalry division, the whole under the command of General Hancock. General Grant in person visited the field of operations. On the 13th, the force moved against the enemy, encountering but little opposition until they reached Bailey's Creek, the point where a similar advance, some little time ago, had been arrested. It had been supposed that the enemy's force on the north side of the James had been weakened by the sending of three divisions to the Shenandoah Valley; but the result proved that only one had gone, the two others, which were under marching orders when the movement began, being retained to resist it. The advantage gained on this day was slight, the enemy's lines being pierced in one spot, and four guns captured. On the 14th Hancock manœuvred for a better position, and another slight success was gained, six guns being captured. The next day new dispositions were made, and on the 16th a direct attack was made, and the line was carried, but recaptured by the enemy. The 17th, 18th, and 19th were passed in unimportant skirmishes, though on the night of the 18th a sally by the enemy upon our line was repulsed, and on the 20th the force returned to their position before Petersburg, the loss during this series of engagements being about fifteen hundred.

While this expeditionary force was engaged in the movement we have just described, and the enemy's attention was thus attracted to the north of the James, a movement was also made against the Weldon Railroad, the principal line of communication with the South and Petersburg. On the 18th, Warren was sent to take possession of it, and did so without encountering any serious opposition. In the afternoon the enemy attacked the forces in possession of the railroad, and gained a temporary advantage, but were finally driven back, leaving us in possession of the road. The position was strengthened, and the next afternoon, the 19th, another attack was made by the enemy, with an increased force, but again unsuccessfully. During this attack, the enemy had pressed our troops severely, and the result appeared doubtful, when the opportune arrival of reënforcements enabled the Union force to assume the offensive, and the enemy was driven back in confusion to his intrenchments, leaving us in full possession of the coveted position. Supposing that the importance of the road, as a means of communication for supplies, would lead to a renewal of the attempt to regain it, Warren busied himself with posting his artillery advantageously to defend the position, and waited the attack. His expectations were not disappointed, for on the morning of the 21st, the enemy opened with some thirty pieces of artillery, and then attacked in front, while at the same time they attempted to turn our left. Both these attacks were repulsed, and the second with such success that the result was the capture of five hundred prisoners. The position, being thus held, was made perfectly secure, and this line of supplies cut off permanently. The loss sustained in this struggle reached an aggregate in killed, wounded, and missing of nearly five thousand, while that of the enemy was much greater.

As soon as Warren's position was made secure, the Second Corps, under Hancock, was sent down the Weldon road on the 21st, to the rear of Warren, and destroyed the road as far as Reams's Station, and in this work the troops employed two days. As Hancock's instructions were to destroy the road as far as Rowanty Creek, eight miles farther south than Reams's Station, the troops were sent upon this mission on the 25th, but had hardly moved out when they encountered the enemy in force, who advanced to the attack, and after a severe struggle obtained an advantage, breaking a portion of our defensive line, which had been constructed some time before, by another corps, and was faulty in its location. Reënforcements, which had been sent to Hancock upon receipt of the intelligence that he was hard pressed, did not arrive until the engagement was over; and that night both parties retired from the field of action.

The possession of the Weldon road remained, however, in our hands, and our position here was connected by intrenchments with the Jerusalem plank road, and by the 12th of September, a railroad was completed from our position on the Weldon road to City Point, thus insuring the constant and easy distribution of supplies along the whole of the line, and the army rested for a time.

Grant being resolved, however, to cut all the lines of communication, and the next in order being the Southside Railroad, a movement was prepared for this purpose; but before actively commencing the advance upon this left flank, an advance was made upon the right flank, on the north side of the James. On the 28th of September, the first move was made in this direction, in order to test whether the force of the enemy was weak in this portion of his line, and if so to take advantage of it, or at least to prevent his massing to prevent the extension of our lines upon the left.

This force sent on this duty moved under the command of General Ord, and was composed of the Tenth and Eighteenth Corps. Crossing on the night of the 28th, they moved against the enemy's intrenched lines just below Chapin's Farm, carried these, took Fort Harrison, and secured a strong position, having possession of the New Market road, with the works defending it. An assault was also made upon Fort Gilmer, but without success, while the cavalry penetrated to within two or three miles of Richmond itself, but were forced to retire. The enemy made several determined attempts to dislodge the menacing position thus secured, but without success, and with severe loss to themselves.

On the 30th, the movement to extend our left began. Two divisions of the Fifth Corps under Warren, and two of the Ninth under Parke, moved towards Poplar Spring Church and Peeble's Farm, at which points the enemy were strongly intrenched, in order to cover our advance upon the Southside Railway, and with success. The next day the enemy attacked during the afternoon, but were repulsed with considerable loss. The advanced positions thus gained led to an advance along the whole line on the 2d of October, when the enemy was found to have withdrawn to his main intrenchments, and preparations were made to advance our lines, so as to cover the ground thus gained.

The season was now approaching when active operations would have to be discontinued; but before settling down to winter quarters, Grant resolved to make another attempt to gain the Boydton plank road, which, since the capture of the Weldon Railroad, had become doubly valuable and necessary to the enemy for his supplies. At this time our line upon the left extended two miles west of the Weldon Railroad, and three miles farther was this plank road, running to Petersburg, and protected by an extension of the enemy's line, which covered that road for some distance below the point where it crosses Hatcher's Run. These defences also covered the Southside Railroad, which was two miles farther, running at this point parallel with the plank road. The country to be operated in here was so thickly wooded that the movement became a confused one; the coöperating columns failing to support each other, and it becoming manifest that the enemy's flank could not be reached, the troops were withdrawn without having attained the object of the movement.

From this time until the opening of the spring campaign, the operations of the army of the Potomac were principally confined to extending and defending the lines, until they reached Hatcher's Run, which was brought into our lines on the 5th of February, after a severe struggle. On the 1st of January, also, the Dutch Gap Canal was opened. This was an experiment made by General Butler to cut a canal, which it was hoped would make a passage for our iron-clads, through a peninsula formed by a bend in the James River, and known as Farrer's Island, and which is only half a mile wide in its narrowest part. The work was commenced on the 10th of August, and was done principally by negroes, though Butler, with his characteristic ingenuity, used it also as a means for retaliating upon the rebels for the outrageous cruelty they showed in the treatment of our prisoners, by making those we captured work in the ditch, within range of the rebel fire. The canal was not, however, a success, since it was raked from end to end by the enemy's guns.

During the month of December, a movement was made to destroy entirely, for a distance of twenty-five miles, the Weldon Railway. The possession we had of it did not entirely prevent the enemy from making it of service, since they brought their supplies up to a certain point, and then wagoned them the remainder of the way. The force started on the 7th, under Warren, and completely destroyed the road for about twenty miles, returning as successfully as they had advanced. They started with four days' rations, and besides thus injuring the road, were almost constantly engaged in conflict with the enemy.

Let us now give a hasty glance at the military operations in other portions of the country, and see what success Grant's plans for the overthrow of the rebellion, by the destruction of its military power, have met with; for as he sits in his wooden hut at City Point during this winter, upon these, in great measure, will depend his action in the coming spring.

## NOTE.

[The tabular statements given below are made from data furnished by a staff officer of General Grant.]

*Tabular Statement of Casualties in the Army of the Potomac from May* 5, 1864, *to November* 1, 1864.

| BATTLES. | DATES. | KILLED. | | WOUNDED. | | MISSING. | | Aggregate. |
|---|---|---|---|---|---|---|---|---|
| | | Officers. | Enlisted Men. | Officers. | Enlisted Men. | Officers. | Enlisted Men. | |
| Wilderness . . . | May 5 to 12 . . . | 269 | 3,019 | 1,017 | 18,261 | 177 | 6,667 | 29,410 |
| Spottsylvania . . | May 12 to 21 . . . | 114 | 2,032 | 259 | 7,697 | 31 | 248 | 10,381 |
| North Anna . . . | May 21 to 31 . . . | 12 | 138 | 67 | 1,063 | 3 | 324 | 1,607 |
| Cold Harbor . . . | June 1 to 10 . . . | 144 | 1,561 | 421 | 8,621 | 51 | 2,355 | 13,153 |
| Petersburg. . . . | June 10 to 20. . . | 85 | 1,113 | 361 | 6,492 | 46 | 1,568 | 9,665 |
| Ditto. . . . . . . . | June 20 to July 30 | 29 | 576 | 120 | 2,374 | 108 | 2,109 | 5,316 |
| Ditto. . . . . . . . | July 30 . . . . . | 47 | 372 | 124 | 1,555 | 91 | 1,819 | 4,008 |
| Trenches. . . . . | Aug. 1 to 18 . . . | 10 | 128 | 58 | 626 | 1 | 45 | 868 |
| Weldon RR. . . | Aug. 18 to 21 . . | 21 | 191 | 100 | 1,055 | 104 | 3,072 | 4,543 |
| Reams's Station . | Aug. 25 . . . . . | 24 | 93 | 62 | 484 | 95 | 1,674 | 2,432 |
| Peeble's Farm . . | Sept. 30 to Oct. 1 . | 12 | 129 | 50 | 738 | 56 | 1,700 | 2,685 |
| Trenches. . . . . | Aug. 18 to Oct. 30 | 13 | 284 | 91 | 1,214 | 4 | 800 | 2,406 |
| Boydton Pl'k r'd. | Oct. 27 to 28 . . . | 16 | 140 | 66 | 981 | 8 | 619 | 1,830 |
| | | 796 | 9,776 | 2,796 | 51,161 | 775 | 23,000 | 88,304 |

*Statement showing the Number of Colors captured from the Enemy during the Operations of the Army of the Potomac, from May* 4, 1864, *to November* 1, 1864.

Number of Colors captured . . . . . . . . . . 67

Captured by Cavalry Corps . . . . . . . 3
Captured by Second Corps . . . . . . . 40
Captured by Fifth Corps . . . . . . . 10
Captured by Sixth Corps . . . . . . . 3
Captured by Ninth Corps . . . . . . . 11
—— 67

NOTE.—The foregoing statement is made up from the reports of captured colors that had been received at this time.

Two divisions of the Cavalry Corps and the Sixth Corps having been transferred from the army of the Potomac, it is not certainly known that all the colors captured by these troops prior to their transfer are here reported.

*Statement showing the Number of Prisoners captured by the Army of the Potomac, during the Operations from May* 4, 1864, *to November* 1, 1864.

| | |
|---|---|
| From May 1 to May 12 | 7,078 |
| From May 12 to July 31 | 6,506 |
| From July 31 to August 31 | 573 |
| From August 31 to September 30 | 78 |
| From September 30 to October 31 | 1,138 |
| Total | 15,373 |

*Statement showing the Number of Guns captured from the Enemy, also the Number of Guns lost during the Operations of the Army of the Potomac, from May* 4, 1864, *to November* 1, 1864. *Thirty-two guns were captured, and twenty-five guns lost, as follows:* —

| DATE. | CORPS. | NUMBER. | | WHERE. | REMARKS. |
|---|---|---|---|---|---|
| | | Capt'd. | Lost. | | |
| May 5 | Fifth. | — | 2 | Wilderness. | Winslow's battery "D," First N. Y. Artillery. |
| " 10 | Second. | — | 1 | South of the Po River. | Brown's battery "B," First R. I. Light Artillery. |
| " 11 | Cavalry. | 2 | — | Yellow Tavern. | |
| " 12 | Second. | 20 | — | Spottsylvania. | |
| June 17 | Ninth. | 4 | — | Petersburg. | |
| " 22 | Second. | — | 4 | Ditto. | McKnight's Twelfth N. Y. battery. |
| " 29 | Cavalry. | — | 8 | Reams's Station. | Maynadier's, "K," First U. S. 4; Fitzhugh's, "C" and "E," 4. |
| July 28 | Second. | 4 | — | Jones's Neck. | |
| " 28 | Cavalry. | — | 1 | Deep Bottom. | Denison's, "A," Second U. S. |
| Aug. 15 | Second. | 1 | — | | |
| " 25 | Second. | — | 9 | Reams's Station. | Sleeper's Tenth Mass. battery, 4. McKnight's, Twelfth N. Y., 1. |
| Sept. 30 | Fifth. | 1 | — | Poplar Gr. Ch. | |
| | | 32 | 25 | | |

## CHAPTER XLI.

OPERATIONS ELSEWHERE IN THE FIELD. — SHERMAN ON HIS MARCH TO THE SEA. — THOMAS AT NASHVILLE. — THE ATTACK ON FORT FISHER. — SHERIDAN ON A RAID.

As Grant now held the position of General of all our armies, it comes of course naturally in the record of his influence during the war to describe the military actions which in other parts of the country, and under his general though not under his personal supervision, put an end to the rebellion, and vindicated the theory of the progress of nations, of the spread of the democratic idea, of the recognition of the dignity of labor, and that justice should and must be the foundation of all social organization.

The principal coöperating army was that led by Sherman, which gathered at Chattanooga, and on the 1st of May, 1864, reached an aggregate of nearly one hundred thousand men, with two hundred and fifty-four guns, and commenced to move on the 6th of May. In and about Dalton, Georgia, lay the opposing army, under the command of Johnston, and numbering about sixty thousand men.

To give a minute account of the brilliant manœuvres by which Sherman forced his antagonist to fall back constantly in order to maintain his lines of communication, would occupy us too long, and would hardly be in place here. On the 10th of July, however, after a most brilliant series of movements, varied with fierce fighting, Sherman and his army found themselves "undisputed masters north and west of the Chattahoochie," and within eight miles of Atlanta. Here the Confederate government relieved Johnston from the command, and gave it to Hood, who met with no better success than his predecessor; since a furious attack on the Union forces, with which he inaugurated his command, did more injury to his own army than to that of his antagonist, while Sherman, by again threatening its base of supplies, forced the rebel army to evacuate Atlanta, which thus fell into our hands on the 2d of September. Here the army rested to recruit and prepare for its march to the sea, while Hood, abandoning the South, which Sherman was now preparing to invade, advanced to cut Sherman's lines of communication, which Sherman himself was now about to abandon.

Leaving, therefore, Thomas to look after Hood, on the 14th of November Sherman commenced his southern march, and, living off the country, met hardly any opposition until he reached Savannah, where Fort McAllister was carried by storm, while the garrison of the city, under Beauregard and Hardee, escaped, and the army entered Savannah without further opposition, and communicated with the fleet.

The plan of this march Sherman had submitted to General Grant, and received his sanction for attempting it. Fort McAllister was carried on the 13th of December, just one month after the army had cut loose from Atlanta, a distance of over three hundred miles, and Savannah was occupied on the 21st of the same month.

During this time, Hood, in his march north, had, on the 30th of November, been checked at Franklin by a corps of observation under Schofield, which had been watching his advance, and made a stand here to protect the trains of the army gathering under Thomas, at Nashville.

After this battle, which fulfilled all it was intended to do, Schofield fell back to Nashville, and Hood, pressing on, commenced the establishment of his line before that city on the 2d of December. On the 15th of this month, Thomas, having matured his preparations, attacked Hood in his position, and, after a battle of two days, routed him thoroughly, and drove his army away as a confused, unorganized crowd. Hood had advanced into Tennessee with fifty thousand men, and left it with one half that number, and these in such a condition that they never again were of any value as an organized military force.

From Savannah Sherman's army could have been brought up by sea to coöperate with the army of the Potomac before Petersburg, or could take the over land route, marching through the Carolinas until it formed a junction with Grant's. This last course was decided upon, and on the 19th of January, 1865, all preparations being complete, the orders for marching were given, and the army set out, expecting to reach Goldsboro', North Carolina, by the 15th of March, and then, by the extension of the railroad from Newbern, again communicate with the sea.

Thus, at the commencement of the year 1865, the entire military operations of the country were working together towards a single object, and that was the overthrow of the armed resistance of the rebellion, and this resistance was centred about Richmond. By his superior military skill, by the character of the men forming his army, and by the combination of fortuitous circumstances, Lee had been enabled to prolong the resistance at this point, which was almost an outpost of the Confederacy. Had it not been for this, the course of the war would have demonstrated, even more decidedly than it has, the absolute necessity, from the geographical character of the country, that the interests of its inhabitants are interdependent upon each other, and that Nature herself had preordained, by a law as inexorable as that by which water seeks its level, that the portion of mankind inhabiting this section of the world should be united, and not divided. A map of the country, showing the principal features of its physical geography, the course of its rivers, the lines of its mountain ranges, and the various modifications of surface and production, which physical geography treats, would prove as conclusively as the bitter experience of civil war has proved, that it would be impossible to draw division lines, and would have made the theory of secession as absurd as the attempt has been futile and disastrous.

While the army of the Potomac remained quiet but watchful before Petersburg during the winter months, various movements were planned and executed, having the object of preparing for the spring campaign, or co-operating with Sherman's advance. One of these movements was the expedition against Fort Fisher, which was prepared in November and started early in December. The capture of this place would close the port of Wilmington, which was the most important port remaining for the blockade runners. The arrangements were completed during a personal visit from Grant to Hampton Roads, and detailed in the following order to General Butler, from whose department the troops were drawn, and in which it is shown that General Weitzel was to command the expedition: —

CITY POINT, VA., December 6, 1864.

GENERAL: The first object of the expedition under General Weitzel is to close to the enemy the port of Wilmington. If successful in this, the second will be to capture Wilmington itself. There are reasonable grounds to hope for success, if advantage can be taken of the absence of the greater part of the enemy's forces now looking after Sherman in Georgia. The directions you have given for the numbers and equipment of the expedition are all right, except in the unimportant matter of where they embark, and the amount of intrenching tools to be taken. The object of the expedition will be gained by effecting a landing on the main land between Cape Fear River and the Atlantic, north of the north entrance to the river. Should such landing be effected whilst the enemy still holds Fort Fisher and the batteries guarding the entrance to the river, then the troops should intrench themselves, and by coöperating with the navy, effect the reduction and capture of those places. These in our hands, the navy could enter the harbor, and the port of Willmington would be sealed. Should Fort Fisher and the point of land on which it is built fall into the hands of our troops immediately on landing, then it will be worth the attempt to capture Wilmington by a forced march and surprise. If time is consumed in gaining the first object of the expedition, the second will become a matter of after consideration.

The details for execution are intrusted to you and the officer immediately in command of the troops.

Should the troops under General Weitzel fail to effect a landing at or near Fort Fisher, they will be returned to the armies operating against Richmond without delay.

U. S. GRANT, *Lieutenant General.*

MAJOR GENERAL B. F. BUTLER.

On the 13th of December the fleet of transports got under way, but from various delays the expeditionary force did not disembark until the 25th, and after a bombardment of the fort by the fleet, returned without making an assault. The fleet, however, remained, and the expedition was sent back with General Terry in command, with the following instructions from Grant: —

CITY POINT, VA., January 3, 1865.

GENERAL: The expedition intrusted to your command has been fitted out to renew the attempt to capture Fort Fisher, N. C., and Wilmington, ultimately, if the fort falls. You will then proceed, with as little delay as possible, to the naval fleet lying off Cape Fear River, and report the arrival of yourself and command to Admiral D. D. Porter, commanding North Atlantic Blockading Squadron. It is exceedingly desirable that the most complete understanding should exist between yourself and the naval commander. I suggest, therefore, that you consult with Admiral Porter freely, and get from him the part to be performed by each branch of the public service, so that there may be unity of action. It would be well to have the whole programme laid down in writing. I have served with Admiral Porter, and know that you can rely on his judgment and his nerve to undertake what he proposes. I would, therefore, defer to him as much as is consistent with your own responsibilities. The first object to be attained is, to get a firm position on the spit of land on which Fort Fisher is built, from which you can operate against that fort. You want to look to the practicability of receiving your supplies, and to defending yourself against superior forces sent against you by any of the avenues left open to the enemy. If such a position can be obtained, the siege of Fort Fisher will not be abandoned until its reduction is accomplished, or another plan of campaign is ordered from these headquarters.

My own views are, that if you effect a landing, the navy ought to run a portion of their fleet into Cape Fear River, whilst the balance of it operates on the outside. Land forces cannot invest Fort

Fisher, or cut it off from supplies or reënforcements whilst the river is in possession of the enemy.

A siege-train will be loaded on vessels, and sent to Fort Monroe, in readiness to be sent to you if required. All other supplies can be drawn from Beaufort as you need them.

Keep the fleet of vessels with you until your position is assured. When you find they can be spared, order them back, or such of them as you can spare, to Fort Monroe, to report for orders.

In case of failure to effect a landing, bring your command back to Beaufort, and report to these headquarters for further instructions. You will not debark at Beaufort until so directed.

General Sheridan has been ordered to send a division of troops to Baltimore, and place them on sea-going vessels. These troops will be brought to Fort Monroe, and kept there on the vessels until you are heard from. Should you require them, they will be sent to you.

U. S. GRANT, *Lieutenant General.*

BREVET MAJOR GENERAL A. H. TERRY.

On the 6th of January the expedition started from Fortress Monroe, on the 13th and 14th the troops were landed, and on the 15th the fleet commenced a bombardment at a quarter before seven in the morning, which lasted until the guns of the fort were silenced in the early afternoon, when an assault was made, and the fort captured, with a total loss of about nine hundred men. A portion of this loss was in an assaulting column made up of sailors from the fleet, who behaved with the greatest gallantry. The next day the defences on the opposite side of the river were taken, and Wilmington was sealed. The necessity of the capture was shown in the fact that two or three blockade-runners ran in and were captured after we had taken the fort.

On the 15th of February General Schofield, who had

been detached from Thomas's army after Hood's defeat at Nashville, was put in command of the department of North Carolina, and, having arrived, took command of the troops, in obedience to the following order: —

City Point, Va., January 31, 1865.

General: . . . Your movements are intended as coöperative with Sherman's through the States of South and North Carolina. The first point to be attained is to secure Wilmington. Goldsboro' will then be your objective point, moving either from Wilmington or Newbern, or both, as you deem best. Should you not be able to reach Goldsboro', you will advance on the line or lines of railway connecting that place with the sea-coast, as near to it as you can, building the road behind you. The enterprise under you has two objects: the first is, to give Sherman material aid, if needed, in his march north; the second, to open a base of supplies for him on his line of march. As soon, therefore, as you can determine which of the two points, Wilmington or Newbern, you can best use for throwing supplies from, to the interior, you will commence the accumulation of twenty days' rations and forage for sixty thousand men and twenty thousand animals. You will get of these as many as you can house and protect to such point in the interior as you may be able to occupy. I believe General Palmer has received some instructions direct from General Sherman on the subject of securing supplies for his army. You can learn what steps he has taken, and be governed in your requisitions accordingly. A supply of ordnance stores will also be necessary.

Make all requisitions upon the chiefs of their respective departments in the field with me at City Point. Communicate with me by every opportunity, and should you deem it necessary at any time, send a special boat to Fortress Monroe, from which point you can communicate by telegraph.

The supplies referred to in these instructions are exclusive of those required for your own command.

The movements of the enemy may justify you, or even make it your imperative duty, to cut loose from your base, and strike for the interior to aid Sherman. In such case, you will act on your own judgment, without waiting for instructions. You will report, however, what you propose doing. The details for carrying out these instructions are necessarily left to you. I would urge, however, if I did not know that you are already fully alive to the importance of it, prompt action. Sherman may be looked for in the neighborhood of Goldsboro' any time from the 22d to the 28th of February. This limits your time very materially.

If rolling-stock is not secured in the capture of Wilmington, it can be supplied from Washington. A large force of railroad-men has already been sent to Beaufort, and other mechanics will go to Fort Fisher in a day or two. On this point I have informed you by telegraph.

U. S. GRANT, *Lieutenant General.*

MAJOR GENERAL J. M. SCHOFIELD.

On the 16th Schofield advanced against Fort Anderson, and on the 18th prepared for an assault, which the enemy made needless by evacuating that work early the next morning, and, pushing forward, on the 22d the army entered the city of Wilmington, from which the enemy had also retreated.

The following orders, sent to Thomas, will show how the force under his command was to be occupied: —

CITY POINT, VA., February 14, 1865.

General Canby is preparing a movement from Mobile Bay against Mobile and the interior of Alabama. His force will consist of about twenty thousand men, besides A. J. Smith's command. The cavalry you have sent to Canby will be debarked at Vicksburg. It, with the available cavalry already in that section, will move from there eastward in coöperation. Hood's army has been terribly reduced by the severe punishment you gave it in Tennessee, by desertion consequent upon their defeat, and now by the withdrawal of many of them to oppose Sherman. (I take it a large portion of the infantry has been so withdrawn. It is so asserted in the Richmond papers; and a member of the rebel Congress said a few days since, in a speech, that one half of it had been brought to South Carolina to oppose Sherman.) This being true, or even if it is not true, Canby's movement will attract all the attention of the enemy, and leave an advance from your stand-point easy. I think it advisable, therefore, that you prepare as much of a cavalry force as you can spare, and hold it in readiness to go south. The object would be threefold: First, to attract as much of the enemy's force as possible, to insure success to Canby; second, to destroy the enemy's line of communications and military resources: third, to destroy or capture their forces brought into the field. Tuscaloosa and Selma would probably be the points to direct the expedition against. This, however, would not be so important as the mere fact of penetrating deep into Alabama. Discretion should be left to the officer commanding the expedition to go where, according to the information he may receive, he will best secure the objects named above.

Now that your force has been so much depleted, I do not know what number of men you can put into the field. If not more than five thousand men, however, all cavalry, I think it will be sufficient. It is not desirable that you should start this expedition until the one leaving Vicksburg has been three or four days out, or even a week. I do not know when it will start, but will inform you by telegraph as soon as I learn. If you should hear through other sources before hearing from me, you can act on the information received.

To insure success, your cavalry should go with as little wagon-train as possible, relying upon the country for supplies. I would also reduce the number of guns to a battery, or the number of batteries, and put the extra teams to the guns taken. No guns or caissons should be taken with less than eight horses.

Please inform me by telegraph, on receipt of this, what force you think you will be able to send, under these directions.

U. S. GRANT, *Lieutenant General.*

MAJOR GENERAL GEORGE H. THOMAS.

About this time also Sheridan was sent to encircle the Confederate position at Richmond and Petersburg, thus cutting all their connections, and finally make a junction with Sherman coming up from the South.

Starting, therefore, from Winchester on the 27th of February, Sheridan rode through the Valley of the Shenandoah, scattering the remnants of an army which still remained with Early, and, striking Charlottesville, destroyed the Richmond and Lynchburg Railroad. His orders were to reach Lynchburg, destroy the railroad and canal, and then, passing west of Danville, join Sherman when he should arrive. While waiting, however, at Charlottesville for his trains, the James River became so swollen that he could not cross, and, therefore, changing his plan, he destroyed the canal, and sought a crossing of the James between Lynchburg and Richmond. The destruction of the bridges having, however, made this also impossible, he resolved to turn in the direction of White House, and from thence make a junction with the army of the Potomac. This plan was successfully carried out, and reaching White House on the 19th of March, he finally pushed across the peninsula, and joined the army before Petersburg on the 26th of March. The following order contains the instructions under which Sheridan acted during this most successful expedition: —

CITY POINT, VA., February 20, 1865 — 1 P. M.

GENERAL: As soon as it is possible to travel, I think you will have no difficulty about reaching Lynchburg with a cavalry force alone. From there you could destroy the railroad and canal in every direction, so as to be of no further use to the rebellion. Sufficient cavalry should be left behind to look after Mosby's gang. From Lynchburg, if information you might get there would justify it, you could strike south, heading the streams in Virginia, to the westward of Danville, and push on and join Sherman. This additional raid, with one now about starting from East Tennessee, under Stoneman, numbering four or five thousand cavalry; one from Vicksburg, numbering seven or eight thousand cavalry; one from Eastport, Mississippi, numbering ten thousand cavalry; Canby, from Mobile Bay, with about thirty-eight thousand mixed troops, — these three latter pushing for Tuscaloosa, Selma, and Montgomery, and Sherman with a large army eating out the vitals of South Carolina, — is all that will be wanted to leave nothing for the rebellion to stand upon. I would advise you to overcome great obstacles to accomplish this. Charleston was evacuated on Tuesday last.

U. S. GRANT, *Lieutenant General.*

MAJOR GENERAL P. H. SHERIDAN.

## CHAPTER XLII.

### THE OPENING OF THE LAST CAMPAIGN.—PETERSBURG AND RICHMOND EVACUATED.

THE day appointed for the movement of the army of the Potomac was the 29th of March, 1865. This was now the position of affairs. Lee was sorely beset by his indomitable antagonist. Sherman had arrived at Goldsboro', and the army opposing him, under Johnston, made up as it was of all the various small detachments of men the Confederacy could gather, was unable to resist his further advance. Thomas had sent out two cavalry expeditions, one into Northern Alabama, and the other into Eastern Tennessee, while Pope was taking care of the west of the Mississippi; and Hancock was in the Valley of the Shenandoah, at Winchester, ready to coöperate with Grant's army by a march against Richmond. The real difficulty now was to prevent Lee from leaving his position, and, by hastening south, form a junction with Johnston's army, and then, thus reënforced, prolong the war by retreating to the mountainous portions of West Virginia and East Tennessee.

On the 24th the following orders for the movement on the 29th were given to the various commanders:—

CITY POINT, VA., March 24, 1865.

GENERAL: On the 29th instant the armies operating against Richmond will be moved by our left, for the double purpose of turning the enemy out of his present position around Petersburg, and to insure the success of the cavalry under General Sheridan, which will start at the same time, in its efforts to reach and destroy the Southside and Danville Railroads. Two corps of the army of the Potomac will be moved, at first, in two columns, taking the two roads crossing Hatcher's Run nearest where the present line held by us strikes that stream, both moving towards Dinwiddie Court-house.

The cavalry under General Sheridan, joined by the division now under General Davies, will move, at the same time, by the Weldon road and the Jerusalem plank road, turning west from the latter before crossing the Nottoway, and west with the whole column reaching Stony Creek. General Sheridan will then move independently under other instructions, which will be given him. All dismounted cavalry belonging to the army of the Potomac, and the dismounted cavalry from the middle military division not required for guarding property belonging to their arm of service, will report to Brigadier General Benham, to be added to the defences of City Point. Major General Parke will be left in command of all the army left for holding the lines about Petersburg and City Point, subject, of course, to orders from the commander of the army of the Potomac. The Ninth Army Corps will be left intact to hold the present line of works so long as the whole line now occupied by us is held. If, however, the troops to the left of the Ninth Corps are withdrawn, then the left of the corps may be thrown back so as to occupy the position held by the army prior to the capture of the Weldon road. All troops to the left of the Ninth Corps will be held in readiness to move at the shortest notice by such route as may be designated when the order is given.

General Ord will detach three divisions, two white and one colored, or so much of them as he can, and hold his present lines, and march for the present left of the army of the Potomac. In the absence of further orders, or until further orders are given, the white divisions will follow the left column of the army of the

Potomac, and the colored division the right column. During the movement Major General Weitzel will be left in command of all the forces remaining behind from the army of the James.

The movement of troops from the army of the James will commence on the night of the 27th instant. General Ord will leave behind the minimum number of cavalry necessary for picket duty in the absence of the main army. A cavalry expedition from General Ord's command will also be started from Suffolk, to leave there on Saturday, the 1st of April, under Colonel Sumner, for the purpose of cutting the railroad about Hicksford. This, if accomplished, will have to be a surprise, and, therefore, from three to five hundred men will be sufficient. They should, however, be supported by all the infantry that can be spared from Norfolk and Portsmouth, as far out as to where the cavalry crosses the Blackwater. The crossing should probably be at Uniten. Should Colonel Sumner succeed in reaching the Weldon road, he will be instructed to do all the damage possible to the triangle of roads between Hicksford, Weldon, and Gaston. The railroad bridge at Weldon being fitted up for the passage of carriages, it might be practicable to destroy any accumulation of supplies the enemy may have collected south of the Roanoke. All the troops will move with four days' rations in haversacks, and eight days' in wagons. To avoid as much hauling as possible, and to give the army of the James the same number of days' supplies with the army of the Potomac, General Ord will direct his Commissary and Quartermaster to have sufficient supplies delivered at the terminus of the road to fill up in passing. Sixty rounds of ammunition per man will be taken in wagons, and as much grain as the transportation on hand will carry, after taking the specified amount of other supplies. The densely wooded country in which the army has to operate making the use of much artillery impracticable, the amount taken with the army will be reduced to six or eight guns to each division, at the option of the army commanders.

All necessary preparations for carrying these directions into operation may be commenced at once. The reserves of the Ninth Corps should be massed as much as possible. Whilst I would not now order an unconditional attack on the enemy's line by them, they should be ready, and should make the attack, if the enemy weakens his line in their front, without waiting for orders. In case they carry the line, then the whole of the Ninth Corps could follow up so as to join or coöperate with the balance of the army. To prepare for this, the Ninth Corps will have rations issued to them the same as the balance of the army. General Weitzel will keep vigilant watch upon his front, and if found at all practicable to break through at any point, he will do so. A success north of the James should be followed up with great promptness. An attack will not be feasible unless it is found that the enemy has detached largely. In that case, it may be regarded as evident that the enemy are relying upon their local reserves principally for the defence of Richmond. Preparations may be made for abandoning all the line north of the James, except enclosed works; only to be abandoned, however, after a break is made in the lines of the enemy.

By these instructions, a large part of the armies operating against Richmond is left behind. The enemy, knowing this, may, as an only chance, strip their lines to the merest skeleton, in the hope of advantage not being taken of it, whilst they hurl everything against the moving column, and return. It cannot be impressed too strongly upon commanders of troops left in the trenches not to allow this to occur without taking advantage of it. The very fact of the enemy coming out to attack, if he does so, might be regarded as conclusive evidence of such a weakening of his lines. I would have it particularly enjoined upon corps commanders, that in case of an attack from the enemy, those not attacked are not to wait for orders from the commanding officer of the army to which they belong, but that they will move promptly, and notify the commander of their action. I wish also to enjoin the same action on the part of division commanders, when other parts of their corps are engaged. In like manner, I would urge the importance of following up a repulse of the enemy.

U. S. GRANT, *Lieutenant General.*

MAJOR GENERALS MEADE, ORD, AND SHERIDAN.

It appears to be certain that Lee at this time had formed the intention to retreat, and, leaving both Petersburg and Richmond, make a junction with Johnston somewhere on the Danville Railroad; and it is asserted that arrangements were made for carrying out this design: the line of retreat was chosen, and supplies were ordered to be sent beforehand, early in March, to meet the retreating army at Amelia Court-house. In this plan Lee designed taking the south bank of the Appomattox, which would be the shortest route to Amelia Court-house; but as the extension of the left of the army of the Potomac interfered with the roads by which the retreat was to be effected, Lee resolved by making an attack upon the right flank of the army, to force the weakening of the left flank to support the right, and thus open the desired road for him. The point at which it was evidently best that such a bold stroke should be directed was Fort Steadman, one of the works of our line, the capture of which would give the victor control of the railroad to City Point, and thus threaten the supplies. The morning of the 25th of March was selected for this attack, and at early dawn the assaulting column charged and carried the fort. It was a surprise, and the majority of the garrison were taken prisoners. The guns of the fort were immediately turned upon the other adjacent points of our line to the right and left, and batteries nine, ten, and eleven were consequently abandoned also.

Thus far the success of the Confederate commander's plan was most perfect, but its continuance was short-lived. The assaulting column was to be supported with a large body of troops, in fact by all that could be gathered for this duty, since such was the construction of the Union lines, that the capture of any single isolated point in them, if not supported by the capture of the contiguous parts of the line, was of no avail, since the point would be commanded by those contiguous. This support, for some reason or other, the assaulting column did not have, and so they soon found that their success was their misfortune. The fort they had taken they could not expect to hold isolated and alone, while retreat was equally impossible, since the ground over which it must be made was swept by such a murderous fire that to pass through it was certain death. Thus they were caged, and forced to surrender, and about two thousand of them did so. This attack also served to awaken our army; and a general advance being ordered, the advance picket lines of the enemy, which were strongly intrenched, were carried, and held, and were of service subsequently.

On the 27th of March, Sherman, whose army had arrived on the 21st at Goldsboro', where it was resting for a few days and receiving supplies, paid a visit to Grant at City Point, and a conference was held, at which President Lincoln was present, with Sheridan, Meade, and other Generals. Sherman said he would be ready to move on the 10th of April against Johnston, with twenty days' supplies, and having been informed of the plan of action decided upon for the army of the Potomac, returned to Goldsboro'.

On the 28th the following instructions were given to Sheridan.

CITY POINT, VA., March 28, 1865.

GENERAL: The Fifth Army Corps will move by the Vaughan road at three A. M. to-morrow morning. The Second moves at about nine A. M., having but about three miles to march to reach the first point designated for it to take on the right of the Fifth Corps, after the latter reaching Dinwiddie Court-house. Move your cavalry at as early an hour as you can, and without being confined to any particular road or roads. You may go out by the nearest roads in rear of the Fifth Corps, pass by its left, and passing near to or through Dinwiddie, reach the right and rear of the enemy as soon as you can. It is not the intention to attack the enemy in his intrenched position, but to force him out if possible. Should he come out and attack us, or get himself where he can be attacked, move in with your entire force in your own way, and with the full reliance that the army will engage or follow, as circumstances will dictate. I shall be on the field, and will probably be able to communicate with you. Should I not do so, and you find that the enemy keeps within his main intrenched line, you may cut loose and push for the Danville road. If you find it practicable, I would like you to cross the Southside road, between Petersburg and Burkesville, and destroy it to some extent. I would not advise much detention, however, until you reach the Danville road, which I would like you to strike as near to the Appomattox as possible. Make your destruction on that road as complete as possible. You can then pass on to the Southside road, west of Burkesville, and destroy that in like manner.

After having accomplished the destruction of the two railroads, which are now the only avenues of supply to Lee's army, you may return to this army, selecting your road farther south; or you may go on into North Carolina, and join General Sherman. Should you select the latter course, get the information to me as early as possible, so that I may send orders to meet you at Goldsboro'.

U. S. GRANT, *Lieutenant General.*

MAJOR GENERAL P. H. SHERIDAN.

The force under Sheridan's command amounted to about nine thousand men, and on the afternoon of the 29th he was at Dinwiddie Court-house, thus forming the extreme left of our line. At the same time the left of the army had been also advanced, and on the 29th, Grant, who was with the advance at Gravelly Run, sent the following despatch to Sheridan: —

GRAVELLY RUN, March 29, 1865.

GENERAL: Our line is now unbroken from the Appomattox to Dinwiddie. We are all ready, however, to give up all from the Jerusalem plank road to Hatcher's Run, whenever the forces can be used advantageously. After getting into line south of Hatcher's, we pushed forward to find the enemy's position. General Griffin was attacked near where the Quaker road intersects the Boydton road, but repulsed it easily, capturing about one hundred men. Humphreys reached Dabney's Mill, and was pushing on when last heard from.

I now feel like ending the matter, if it is possible to do so, before going back. I do not want you, therefore, to cut loose and go after the enemy's roads at present. In the morning, push round the enemy if you can, and get on to his right rear. The movements of the enemy's cavalry may, of course, modify your action. We will act all together as one army here, until it is seen what can be done with the enemy. The signal-officer at Cobb's Hill reported, at 11.30 A. M., that a cavalry column had passed that point from Richmond towards Petersburg, taking forty minutes to pass.

U. S. GRANT, *Lieutenant General.*

MAJOR GENERAL P. H. SHERIDAN.

This movement had been successfully carried out with but very little loss, and with great celerity; yet it had not escaped Lee's observation. It was evident that his vital lines of communication were being cut, and the existence of his army depended upon his preserving these, or else cutting his way out in retreat. At the same time, also, it was necessary that he should preserve his lines, covering Petersburg and Richmond; and from his left to his right these lines extended thirty-five miles. His army, however, had suffered greatly during the last campaign, and the spirit of desertion was now rife among the remainder. The Confederate leaders had shown for the rights of the people of the Confederacy as contemptuous a disregard as they had displayed for their duties to the nation. Every branch of their pretended government was characterized by as mad folly and wickedness as was displayed in the whole conception of secession. Their financial system was conceived and managed in a spirit as contemptuously ignorant of the people's rights, as their attempt to found a nationality based upon slavery was for the rights of labor, and of course resulted in the same disastrous failure. Their system of conscription was marked by the same imbecile spirit of despotism, and while it failed to replete their armies, filled the country with discontent. Their commissary department was a system of organized theft, and in so far was, perhaps, the fairest exposition of the whole movement, since in not even a single state was any attention paid to the law or the people's rights in the passage of the pretended secession ordinances. How, then, can it be wondered at that a movement commenced in treason, carried on by injustice and falsehood, should fail to display these qualities in its every detail?*

While Lee, therefore, could not entirely abandon his lines in front of Richmond, and before Bermuda Hundred, he did not even dare to weaken his effective force there, since he was unaware that Grant had withdrawn the greater portion of his troops threatening the ad-

* Mr. Swinton reports a conversation held, after the war, with the rebel General Johnston, from which we take the following extracts. Speaking of the conscription, he says, "Finally, it resulted that it required as many men to enforce the conscription as it was expected to raise by the operation. Then ensued evasion; those who wished to shirk service, or aid others to do so, opened their ranks, allowed them to slip through, and closed up behind. Supplies also, instead of being honestly raised, were impressed by a band of Commissaries and Quartermasters, who only paid one half the market value. As might have been expected, this was enough to prevent their getting

vance at these points, in order to mass them in his attempt upon our left. It was not until four days afterwards that he found how weak was the force Grant had left threatening Richmond directly. Collecting, however, all the force he could make available, Lee transferred them to protect his threatened right.

The morning of the 30th, a heavy rain-storm, which had set in the night before, and which continued steadily all that day, prevented any active operations, since it made the roads wholly impassable. Nothing could be done but advance the corps of Humphreys and Warren, who held the extreme left, next to Sheridan, close to the Confederate line, while Sheridan moved a body of cavalry to Five Forks, but found it so strongly held by the enemy, that the force sent could not carry it. Friday, the 31st, the ground was still so swampy that it was decided that active operations were impossible, but Warren was advanced still farther upon the left, touching the extreme right of the Confederate position on the White Oak road. Sheridan, at this time, was still some miles farther to the left, and Warren was directed, if he found he could gain possession of the White Oak road, to do so.

The advance in this direction had, however, hardly begun, when, at half past ten in the morning, Lee took

anything. These they took by force, and did it with the greatest injustice. You can imagine what disorganization of labor and discontent this produced. The mismanagement of the Confederate executive in these two regards was enough to ruin the cause."

The cause was not ruined by these systems; they were the direct results of the cause itself. No one but a fool would expect to gather figs from thistles, and the world has advanced to the point where we know, that to expect from men who profess to believe in slavery, and who do really fight for its support, anything but injustice and dishonesty, is an equal folly.

the initiative, and by a heavy attack upon Warren, who held the exposed right flank of the army, sought to prevent our extension in this direction. It was the same move he had often tried before with greater or less success; and in this case all the troops he had been able to collect were put in this attack, in order to make it of sufficient weight to secure success. The attack came suddenly, and at first promised success; but the corps soon rallied, and, holding their own, took, in their turn, the aggressive, and forced the Confederates back to their old line on the White Oak road.

Foiled, therefore, in this attempt, Lee withdrew his troops, and turned them against Sheridan, who, on the morning of the 31st, had taken Five Forks, a position about eight miles north of Didwiddie Court-house, and only four miles east of Lee's intrenched position in front of Warren and Humphreys, and from which position he threatened to turn Lee's right. The attack was made in such force that Sheridan was compelled to fall back upon Dinwiddie Court-house, and the Confederates following up their advantage, pressed the troops heavily; but they held their position until night put an end to the contest. That night reënforcements were sent to Sheridan; but Lee, finding that keeping a strong force at Dinwiddie weakened his line, withdrew the troops, at ten P. M., to Five Forks, leaving only a cavalry picket.

The next day, the 1st of April, Sheridan, with his reenforcements, advanced against Five Forks; and it was evident that this was the important point along the entire line. Here, after a brilliant engagement, in which Sheridan, combining his infantry and cavalry, using the last as a mask for his first, and displaying great skill not only as an impetuous and dashing cavalry officer, but also as a sagacious tactician, finally succeeded in entirely routing the enemy, driving him out of the position, capturing over five thousand prisoners and many guns and standards. It was a complete victory, and broke the line of defence against the advance of the army of the Potomac. The enemy, fleeing west, was pursued until after dark by the cavalry. As soon as the result was known, the guns along the entire line opened upon the enemy's defences, and all night the darkness was made luminous by the bursting of hundreds of shells. The object of this bombardment was to prevent Lee from leaving his works either to retreat or to fall upon Sheridan in his isolated position. The firing began at nightfall on the 1st, and continued until the dawn of the next day, which was Sunday, the 2d of April, when an assault was made along the entire line, from the Appomattox to Hatcher's Run.

This attack was successful in driving the enemy from their intrenchments, and forcing them back to the chain of works immediately about Petersburg, where Lee made a last and desperate stand, in order to prepare for the evacuation of the town as soon as night should come. This design he communicated to Davis at Richmond, about eleven in the morning of this Sunday.

The despatch found the Confederate president at church; reading it, he rose hastily and left the place, while, as he passed down the aisle, the ghastliness of his face told the tale of disaster to all who saw it. Lee was about to abandon Petersburg and Richmond that night, and it behooved the chief conspirator to look out for his own personal safety.

Expecting Lee's retreat, Grant, that night, took measures to prevent it. There was but one safe line opened for the Confederate retreat, and that was up the Appomattox, west of the Danville Railroad ; but on the night of the 2d, Sheridan was at Ford's Station, and this forced Lee to take the north side of the Appomattox. Meanwhile, the lines round Petersburg were closely held, and Weitzel on the north was set to watch Richmond.

That night, however, Lee's army withdrew, marching noiselessly through the town, and filing over to the north bank of the Appomattox. Thence turning towards Chesterfield Court-house, it was joined by the troops withdrawn from in front of Bermuda Hundred, together with whatever force remained on the Richmond side, and started westward.

The retreat was conducted with such celerity that by morning the army, now reduced to twenty-five thousand men, were sixteen miles away. So quietly was this done, that on the morning of the 3d the skirmishers before Petersburg found the town evacuated, while at the same time on the north, Weitzel, startled by the reports and flames of the explosions in Richmond, surmised that the place was being evacuated, and with a body of forty troopers rode in and took possession of the capital, which had for years baffled all our attempts to capture it. The rear-guard, on leaving Richmond, had blown up the iron-clads in the James, and also the bridges on the river; and the government officials appropriately finished their reign of control by setting fire to the store-houses of supplies. From these the fire spread to the houses of the city, and though the energies of the Union troops were immediately devoted to overcoming the conflagration, a large part of the city was consumed before their efforts were successful.

This incident is a fit commentary upon the purposes of the two parties, one maddened by its disappointed ambition, scattering fire and destruction, regardless of consequences, the other hastening to save; and not only was the city preserved by our troops, but, the supplies being destroyed, our army gave food to the inhabitants.

The news of the capture of Richmond was sent to Washington, in the following despatch, and from there spread all over the country: —

CITY POINT, VIRGINIA, April 3 — 11 A. M.

General Weitzel telegraphs as follows: —

"We took Richmond at 8:15 this morning. I captured many guns. The enemy left in great haste.

"The city is on fire in one place. We are making every effort to put it out.

"The people received us with enthusiastic expressions of joy.

"General Grant started early this morning, with the army, towards the Danville road, to cut off Lee's retreating army, if possible."

President Lincoln has gone to the front.

T. S. BOWERS, *Assistant Adjutant General.*

E. M. STANTON, *Secretary of War.*

## CHAPTER XLIII.

### THE PURSUIT. — THE SURRENDER OF LEE. — END OF THE TEN DAYS' CAMPAIGN.

THUS on Monday morning, the 3d of April, 1865, the news of the evacuation of Richmond, and that it was in possession of the Union forces, had spread all over the country, and the day was spent in universal rejoicing. All business was suspended by a tacit universal consent. The nation gave itself up to congratulations and every kind of expression of joy. The long agony of the war was over, and the sight of a nation rejoicing will never be forgotten by those who saw it. In the city of New York, it seemed as though the houses clothed themselves in flags as naturally as the trees put forth their foliage in the spring. The streets were filled with smiling crowds; even the well-known haunts of secession, making a virtue of necessity, put on an air of rejoicing.

But while the country was thus busy in expressing its happiness, Grant lost no time in organizing a vigorous pursuit of the retreating Confederate army. Early on the morning of Monday, the 3d of April, the advance of our skirmishers before Petersburg found the city evacuted, and the pursuit began immediately. Lee's army, as we have seen, retreated by the north bank of the Appomattox. Pursuing this route for a distance of about thirty miles, they then crossed this stream at Goode's Bridge, in order to strike the Danville road at Amelia Court-house. This place is situated about thirty-eight miles west of both Richmond and Petersburg, and was reached by the army on the 4th.

In anticipation of his retreat, Lee had sent a train with supplies to this spot, but an order having met the train when it arrived, on Sunday, from the authorities at Richmond, that the train was wanted there for the purpose of transporting the officers of the Confederate government and their baggage, the train was sent to Richmond without being unloaded, and with its supplies was consumed in the conflagration of the next day. On his arrival, therefore, at Amelia Court-house, on the morning of the 4th, Lee found his army wearied with their forced march, without any supplies, and consequently was forced to remain here the rest of this day and the following one, while foraging parties were sent out through the neighboring country to obtain the needed food. This accidental delay gave an opportunity for the advance of the pursuing army under Sheridan to strike Peterson, on the Danville Railroad, seven miles south-west of Amelia Court-house on the afternoon of the 4th, and thus interpose themselves and cut off the line of retreat Lee had selected. On the 4th General Grant telegraphed the following report to Washington: —

WILSON'S STATION, VIRGINIA, April 4, 1865.

HON. E. M. STANTON, *Secretary of War.*

The army is pushing forward, in the hope of overtaking or dispersing the remainder of Lee's army.

Sheridan, with his cavalry and the Fifth Corps, is between this and the Appomattox, General Meade, with the Second and Sixth, following; General Ord following the line of the Southside Railroad. All of the enemy that retain anything like organization have gone north of the Appomattox, and are apparently heading for Lynchburg, their losses having been very heavy.

The houses through the country are nearly all used as hospitals for wounded men. In every direction I hear of rebel soldiers pushing for home, some in large and some in small squads, and generally without arms. The cavalry have pursued so closely that the enemy have been forced to destroy, probably, the greater part of their transportation, caissons, and munitions of war.

The number of prisoners captured yesterday will exceed two thousand. From the 28th of March to the present time, our loss, in killed, wounded, and captured, will probably not reach seven thousand, of whom from fifteen hundred to two thousand are captured, and many but slightly wounded.

I shall continue the pursuit as long as there appears to be any use in it.

U. S. GRANT, *Lieutenant General.*

The next day he also sent the following despatch to General Sherman: —

WILSON'S STATION, April 5, 1865.

GENERAL: All indications now are, that Lee will attempt to reach Danville with the remnant of his force. Sheridan, who was up with him last night, reports all that is left — horse, foot, and dragoons — at twenty thousand, much demoralized. We hope to reduce this number one half. I shall push on to Burkesville, and if a stand is made at Danville, will in a few days go there. If you can possibly do so, push on from where you are, and let us see if we cannot finish the job with Lee's and Johnston's armies. Whether it will be better for you to strike for Greensboro', or nearer to Danville, you will be better able to judge when you receive this. Rebel armies now are the only strategic points to strike at.

U. S. GRANT, *Lieutenant General.*

MAJOR GENERAL W. T. SHERMAN.

In the afternoon of the 5th, General Meade, with the

Second and Sixth Corps, joined Sheridan at Jettersville, where Sheridan, well intrenched, had held his position that day, keeping his cavalry operating well to his left, in order to see that Lee made no move in that direction to escape. Early in the afternoon of this day Sheridan sent the following despatch to Grant:—

JETTERSVILLE, April 5, 1865—3 P. M.

TO LIEUTENANT GENERAL U. S. GRANT.

GENERAL: I send you the enclosed letter, which will give you an idea of the condition of the enemy and their whereabouts. I sent General Davies's brigade this morning around on my left flank. He captured at Fame's Cross five pieces of artillery, about two hundred wagons, and eight or nine battle-flags, and a number of prisoners. The Second Army Corps is now coming up. I wish you were here yourself. I feel confident of capturing the army of Northern Virginia, if we exert ourselves. I see no escape for Lee. I will send all my cavalry out on our left flank, except McKenzie, who is now on the right.

P. H. SHERIDAN, *Major General.*

AMELIA COURT HOUSE, April 5, 1865.

DEAR BRAMMIA: Our army is ruined, I fear. We are all safe as yet. Theodore left us sick. John Taylor is well; saw him yesterday. We are in line of battle this evening. General Robert Lee is in the field near us. My trust is still in the justice of our cause. General Hill is killed. I saw Murray a few moments since. Bernard Perry, he said, was taken prisoner, but may get out. I send this by a negro I see passing up the railroad to Michlenburg. Love to all. Your devoted son,

W. B. TAYLOR, *Colonel.*

On the morning of the 5th a heavy train of supplies for the Confederate army had been intercepted at a place called Paine's Cross-roads, and destroyed, and both parties being reënforced, a somewhat severe engagement ensued, in which the Confederates were worsted.

The next morning (the 6th) the whole army of the Potomac, having concentrated at Jettersville, advanced towards Amelia Court-house, to attack the Confederate army, but found that during the night Lee had again retreated, and was hurrying to Farmville, thirty-five miles farther west, where, by crossing the Appomattox again, destroying the bridges after him, he could escape into the mountains beyond Lynchburg. The course of the army was then changed, and hurried in pursuit of the retreating foe, in three columns, one upon the road taken by Lee, and the others upon parallel roads to the north and south. The army of the James, which was also on the road, having reached Burkseville, was, on the morning of the 6th, directed towards Farmville, the point to which Lee was hastening, and an advance-guard, pressing vigorously forward, consisting of two regiments of infantry and a squadron of cavalry under Brigadier General Theodore Read, met the advance of Lee's army near Farmville, and, despite the disparity of their numbers, heroically determined to hold their position in the way of the retreating army, and thus detain them until the army of the James should arrive. In this heroic attempt, which was successful, General Read lost his life, and his command was overwhelmed; but the point was gained, and, the army of the James coming up, the Confederates immediately intrenched themselves.

On the same day (the 6th) Sheridan, with the cavalry forming the advance of the army of the Potomac, came up near Deatonsville, with the wagon train of the retreating army, guarded by a strong escort, and immediately attacked and finally captured it, destroying four hundred wagons, and capturing sixteen pieces of artillery, and a great many prisoners. Ewell's corps, which was following the train, being thus cut off from its line of retreat, was also, after a sharp engagement, forced to surrender. Meanwhile Lee, with the remains of his army, withdrew that night to the north bank of the Appomattox, by the bridges near Farmville, and continued his retreat. The sufferings of this fragment of his army during these last few days were terribly intense. On the 5th and the 6th, hundreds dropped to the ground from exhaustion, and thousands had not strength enough to carry their muskets. The retreat had been commenced with one day's rations, and the accident which deprived them of the supplies forwarded to Amelia Court-house forced them to depend upon the exhausted country through which their race for life was held, and the young twigs of the trees, just blooming in spring, was all that many of them could find to serve as food. Meanwhile the Union forces were pressing closer and closer upon them, and all hope in the future was fading fast away. On the night of the 6th a council of officers, at which General Lee was not present, consulted informally as to what should be their course of action, and the conclusion being that surrender was all that was left to them, one of their number was deputed to acquaint General Lee with the result of their conference. The Confederate commander did not, however, agree with this opinion, though if he had arrived at the same conclusion a month before, and acted upon it, such a course would have been a proof that he was more than simply a skilful soldier. But in the beginning of the war, his course in holding a position of confidence and trust as General Scott's aid, while knowing that he was not loyal to the country whose uniform he wore, and whose cause he professed to serve, until the necessity for active service forced him to declare himself a partisan of secession, the principles and objects of which he professed were abhorrent to him, show that he was not a man to follow principle regardless of personal consequences, or of a nature large enough and grand enough to take the initiative. During also the whole continuance of the war, his course had been the same. While our soldiers were starving and rotting with disease in the southern prison pens, a word from him would have removed this disgrace from the cause he was serving as the military head; but no such word was ever spoken. And now, in these last scenes of the war, he appears as unable to grasp the large military necessities of the occasion, the considerations which a large-hearted humanity would have dictated, as he had ever shown himself during the whole four years of the conflict. He was a skilful soldier, but the soldier of slavery, in the last armed conflict which this organized system of injustice and disregard for human labor, human happiness, and human life, will ever maintain upon this soil

The whole of the Confederate army had not crossed the Appomattox until nearly daylight on the 7th, and were engaged in burning the bridges over which they had crossed, when the Second Corps of the army of the Potomac, under Humphreys, coming up, prevented their destruction, and, crossing, hurried on in the pursuit towards Farmville, where a portion of the enemy was found burning the bridges, but who retired and joined the main body. The pursuit being continued, the remainder of Lee's army was found intrenched about five miles north of Farmville, covering the roads to Lynchburg. The advance of the army of the Potomac consisted of the Second Corps, and finding the position held by the enemy was very strong, and that they were not numerous enough to take it, halted in position until the rest of the army should come up; and when they did, it was too late that day to commence active operations. This night of the 7th, Grant sent the following note from Farmville to Lee:—

April 7, 1865.

GENERAL R. E. LEE, *Commander C. S. A.*

GENERAL: The result of the last week must convince you of the hopelessness of further resistance on the part of the army of Northern Virginia in this struggle. I feel that it is so, and regard it as my duty to shift from myself the responsibility of any further effusion of blood, by asking of you the surrender of that portion of the Confederate States army known as the army of Northern Virginia.

Very respectfully, your obedient servant.

U. S. GRANT, *Lieutenant General,*
*Commanding Armies of the United States.*

To this Lee responded as follows:—

April 7, 1865.

GENERAL: I have received your note of this date. Though not entertaining the opinion you express on the hopelessness of further resistance on the part of the army of Northern Virginia, I reciprocate your desire to avoid useless effusion of blood, and therefore, before considering your proposition, ask the terms you will offer, on condition of its surrender.

R. E. LEE, *General.*

TO LIEUTENANT GENERAL U. S. GRANT,
*Commanding Armies of the United States.*

This night Lee again retreated, and the next day had put a night's march between his army and his pursurers. Grant, however, on the morning of the 8th wrote him as follows: —

April 8, 1865.

TO GENERAL R. E. LEE,
*Commanding Confederate States Army.*

GENERAL: Your note of last evening, in reply to mine of same date, asking the conditions on which I will accept the surrender of the army of Northern Virginia, is just received.

In reply, I would say that, peace being my first desire, there is but one condition that I insist upon, namely, —

That the men and officers surrendered shall be disqualified for taking up arms again against the government of the United States until properly exchanged.

I will meet you, or will designate officers to meet any officers you may name for the same purpose, at any point agreeable to you, for the purpose of arranging definitely the terms upon which the surrender of the army of Northern Virginia will be received.

Very respectfully, your obedient servant,
U. S. GRANT, *Lieutenant General,*
*Commanding Armies of the United States.*

Lee's retreat, however, upon the night of the 7th, obliged the army of the Potomac to recommence the pursuit upon the morning of the 8th. Lee, however, during the retreat, received Grant's note, and answered it as follows: —

April 8, 1865.

GENERAL: I received, at a late hour, your note of to-day. In mine of yesterday, I did not intend to propose the surrender of the army of Northern Virginia, but to ask the terms of your proposition. To be frank, I do not think the emergency has arisen to call for the surrender of this army; but as the restoration of peace should be the sole object of all, I desired to know whether your proposals would lead to that end. I cannot, therefore, meet you with a view to surrender the army of Northern Virginia; but as far as your proposal may affect the Confederate States forces under my command, and tend to the restoration of peace, I should be pleased to meet you at ten A. M. to-morrow on the old stage road to Richmond, between the picket lines of the two armies.

R. E. LEE, *General.*

LIEUTENANT GENERAL U. S. GRANT.

Lee's line of retreat was up the narrow neck of land enclosed by the Appomattox and James Rivers; and if the outlet towards Lynchburg should be closed by our army, before he had had time to pass through, he would then be caged. This was done by Sheridan on the evening of the 8th, when, after a march of over thirty miles, he reached Appomattox Station, on the Lynchburg Railroad, five miles south of Appomattox Court-house. Here he captured a train of supplies for the Confederate army, and drove the van-guard protecting it back to Appomattox Court-house. Knowing that he was in possession of the line of retreat of the army, he determined to hold his position firmly, keeping the enemy in check until the army of the James, which was hastening to join him, should arrive and strengthen him in the morning, while the army of the Potomac should also arrive to strike the enemy in the rear. But one course remained to Lee, and that was to cut his way through the force that checked his advance. This he attempted to do, and the attempt was made with great vigor and impetuosity, so much so that our troops were forced somewhat back; but Sheridan, at this juncture arriving personally upon the ground from Appomattox Station, where he had been to hasten the advance of the army of the James, ordered his dismounted troopers to retire slowly, so as to give the reënforcements time to form their lines. As soon as this was done, and the Confederates saw the bayonets of the advancing army of the James, they fell back. Sheridan then, ordering his troopers to mount, prepared to charge, when a white flag was seen advancing, bearing a letter requesting a cessation of hostilities.

In answer to Lee's last letter, Grant had written the following, on the 9th:—

April 9, 1865.

GENERAL: Your note of yesterday is received. I have no authority to treat on the subject of peace; the meeting proposed for ten A. M. to-day could lead to no good. I will state, however, General, that I am equally anxious for peace with yourself, and the whole North entertains the same feeling. The terms upon which peace can be had are well understood. By the South laying down their arms they will hasten that most desirable event, save thousands of human lives, and hundreds of millions of property not yet destroyed. Sincerely hoping that all our difficulties may be settled without the loss of another life,

I subscribe myself, &c.,

U. S. GRANT, *Lieutenant General.*

GENERAL R. E. LEE.

The answer to this note, borne by the flag of truce, was as follows, and was received by Grant while on his way to join Sheridan:—

April 9, 1865.

GENERAL: I received your note of this morning, on the picket line, whither I had come to meet you, and ascertain definitely what terms were embraced in your proposal of yesterday, with reference to the surrender of this army. I now ask an interview in accordance with the offer contained in your letter of yesterday, for that purpose.

R. E. LEE, *General.*

LIEUTENANT GENERAL U. S. GRANT.

To this note Grant responded as follows:—

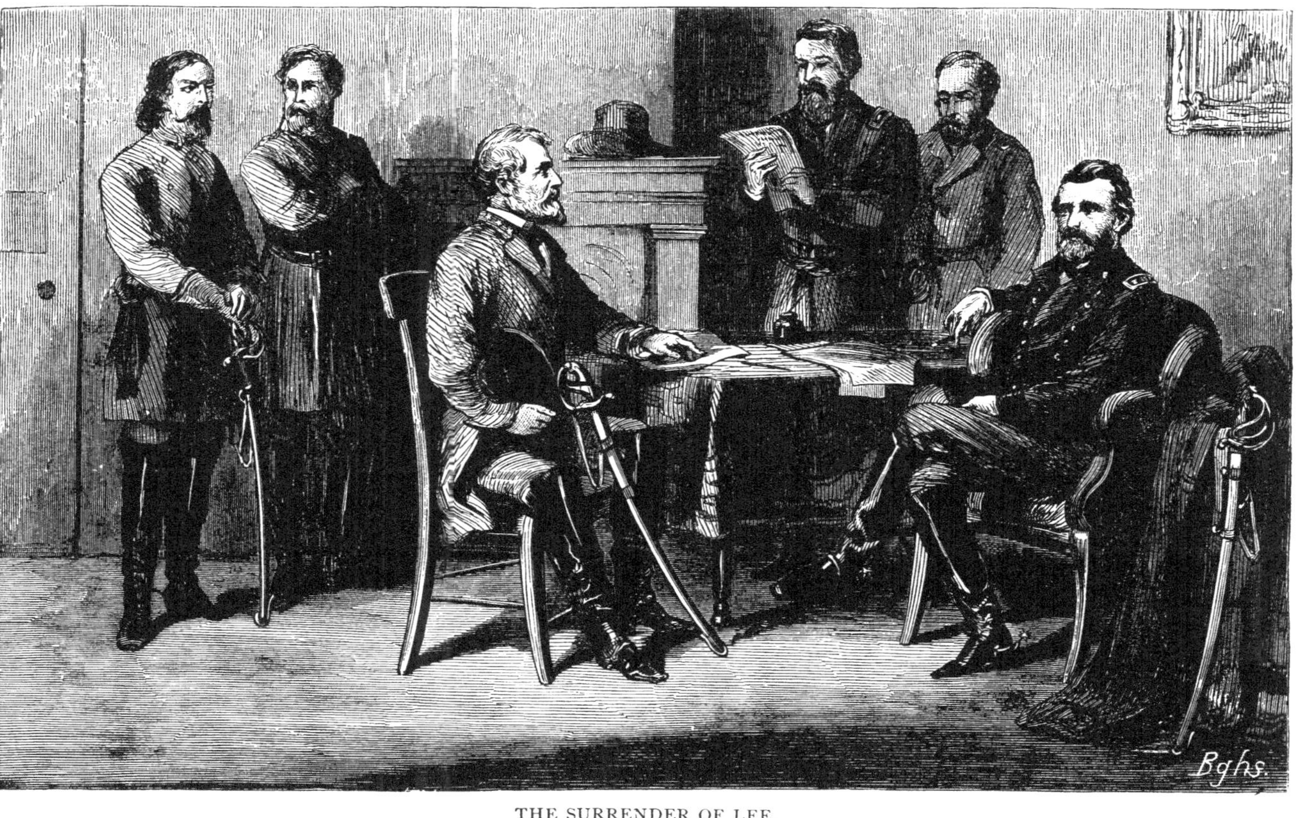


THE SURRENDER OF LEE.

April 9, 1865.

GENERAL R. E. LEE, *Commanding C. S. A.*

Your note of this date is but this moment (11:50 A. M.) received. In consequence of my having passed from the Richmond and Lynchburg road to the Farmville and Lynchburg road, I am at this writing about four miles west of Walter's Church, and will push forward to the front for the purpose of meeting you.

Notice sent to me on this road where you wish the interview to take place will meet me.

Very respectfully, your obedient servant,

U. S. GRANT, *Lieutenant General.*

The meeting was arranged at the residence of Mr. W. McLean, at Appomattox Court-house; and here in a plain room, seated at an ordinary deal table, the two commanders, attended each by members of their respective staffs, reduced to writing the agreement which blotted from existence the army that for years had been the main stay of the Confederacy. The terms of surrender were given and accepted in the following correspondence: —

APPOMATTOX COURT-HOUSE, April 9, 1865.

GENERAL R. E. LEE, *Commanding C. S. A.*

In accordance with the substance of my letter to you of the 8th instant, I propose to receive the surrender of the army of Northern Virginia on the following terms, to wit: —

Rolls of all the officers and men to be made in duplicate, one copy to be given to an officer designated by me, the other to be retained by such officer or officers as you may designate.

The officers to give their individual paroles not to take arms against the United States until properly exchanged, and each company or regimental commander sign a like parole for the men of their commands.

The arms, artillery, and public property to be packed and stacked, and turned over to the officers appointed by me to receive them. This will not embrace the side-arms of the officers, nor their private horses or baggage.

This done, each officer and man will be allowed to return to their homes, not to be disturbed by United States authority so long as they observe their parole and the laws in force where they may reside.

Very respectfully,

U. S. GRANT, *Lieutenant General.*

HEADQUARTERS ARMY OF NORTHERN VIRGINIA,
April 9, 1865.

LIEUTENANT GENERAL U. S. GRANT,
*Commanding U. S. A.*

GENERAL: I have received your letter of this date, containing the terms of surrender of the army of Northern Virginia, as proposed by you; as they are substantially the same as those expressed in your letter of the 8th instant, they are accepted. I will proceed to designate the proper officers to carry the stipulations into effect.

Very respectfully, your obedient servant,

R. E. LEE, *General.*

The campaign of ten days was over, and, like all of Grant's campaigns, was decisive; its result being the complete removal of all armed resistance in the district in which it was actively carried on, by the destruction of all the armed force opposing the legal sway of the government of the United States. The terms accorded by General Grant were as liberal and magnanimous as only a great nation, conscious of the strength and security of its national life,—based as these are upon the principles of freedom and justice,—could grant. There was no vindictiveness, no desire for revenge, but the large charity that Nature gives to all who outrage her laws from ignorance or passion, when, forced by suffering, they acknowledge the error of their ways. The delicacy with which Grant bore himself through this ever-memorable interview, was such as only a great soul naturally displays, and excited the admiration even of his enemies. The interview was short, and as Lee rode back from it, dressed gayer than usual, and wearing his sword, the rumor of immediate surrender ran like wildfire through the Confederate ranks, and the scene that took place is thus described by an eye-witness: "Whole lines of battle rushed up to their beloved old chief, and, choking with emotion, broke ranks and struggled with each other to wring him once more by the hand. Men who had fought throughout the war, and knew what the agony and humiliation of that moment must be to him, strove, with a refinement of unselfishness and tenderness which he alone could fully appreciate, to lighten his burden and mitigate his pain. With tears pouring down both cheeks, General Lee at length commanded voice enough to say, 'Men, we have fought through the war together. I have done the best that I could for you.' Not an eye that looked on that scene was dry. Nor was this the emotion of sickly sentimentalists, but of rough and rugged men, familiar with hardships, danger, and death in a thousand shapes, mastered by sympathy and feeling for another which they never experienced on their own account."

As the armies were now no longer enemies, and the men had learned to respect each other by the rough experience of war, they now fraternized together, and, as was seen at Vicksburg, they could be seen walking and talking together. The necessities of the Confederates were provided for; supplies, which were very welcome after the intense sufferings of the past ten days, were distributed, and the first fruits these men, who had for years been in armed resistance to the government, obtained from their submission to the defenders of law and order was, that their physical needs were amply provided for. It is a pity that all of their leaders and politicians had not been subjected to the same hardships, in order that the practical lesson they thus obtained of the absurdities of secession and the advantages of submission could have taught them the folly and wickedness of their course, and the most mortifying chapter in history of the incompetence of the leading classes of our present condition of society, and the gullibility of the people, would have been not enacted in vain. If the energy and enthusiasm the South had displayed in conducting the war, had been organized in the interests of productive labor, instead of in the destructive work of the four long years; if the treasure wasted in the munitions of destruction to life and property, had been devoted to the construction of the railroads necessary for the free circulation of labor and the products of labor, in manufactories for the application of industry, and schools for the education of labor, how different would have been the condition, physically and morally, of its people after the passage of these four years! The sight of these gaunt and starving men, clothed in rags, penniless, far away from their homes, demoralized by war and defeat, would have cured all enthusiasm for the "pomp, pride, and circumstance of glorious war." Such an ending of the course of action undertaken by these misguided men, by the advice and under the direction of their leaders, would have been so decided and so sad a proof of incapacity on the part of the leaders, that it would seem as though forever after they would keep their peace, nor dare ever again to offer public advice, but with modesty and shamefacedness remain forever silent and retired. That they have not done so, and that the people whom they have once so fatally deceived should ever again listen to them, is a proof that the impudence and folly of men is as infinite for evil, as their energy and knowledge are infinite for good, if properly organized and directed.

Immediately after the surrender, the Fifth Corps was ordered to remain at Appomattox, to guard the public property and be present at the paroling of the Confederate army, while Grant himself, with the remainder of his army, set out for Burkesville, which was, now that Lee's army had surrendered, the point at which the army under Johnston, the last armed body organized in resistance to the government, was opposed to Sherman. The following is the form of the personal parole of officers, copied from the original document given by Lee and a portion of his staff: —

We, the undersigned, prisoners of war, belonging to the army of Northern Virginia, having been this day surrendered by General R. E. Lee, commanding said army, to Lieutenant General Grant, commanding the armies of the United States, do hereby give our solemn parole of honor that we will not hereafter serve in the armies of the Confederate States, or in any military capacity whatever, against the United States of America, or render aid to the enemies of the latter, until properly exchanged in such manner as shall be mutually approved by the respective authorities.

R. E. LEE, *General.*
W. H. TAYLOR, *Lieutenant Colonel and A. A. G.*
CHAS. S. VENABLE, *Lieutenant Colonel and A. A. G.*
CHAS. MARSHALL, *Lieutenant Colonel and A. A. G.*
H. E. PRATON, *Lieutenant Colonel and Ins. General.*
GILES BOOKE, *Major and A. A. Surgeon General.*
H. S. YOUNG, *A. A. General.*

Done at Appomattox Court-house, Va., this ninth (9th) day of April, 1865.

The parole is the same given by all officers, and is countersigned as follows: —

The above-named officers will not be disturbed by United States authorities as long as they observe their parole and the laws in force where they may reside.

GEORGE H. SHARP, *General Assistant Provost Marshal.*

The obligation of officers for the subdivisions under their command is in form as follows: —

I, the undersigned, commanding officer of ——, do, for the within-named prisoners of war, belonging to the army of Northern Virginia, who have been this day surrendered by General Robert E. Lee, Confederate States army, commanding said army, to Lieutenant General Grant, commanding armies of the United States, hereby give my solemn parole of honor that the within-named shall not hereafter serve in the armies of the Confederate States, or in military or any capacity whatever against the United States of America, or render aid to the enemies of the latter, until properly exchanged in such manner as shall be mutually approved by the respective authorities.

Done at Appomattox Court-house, Va., this 9th day of April, 1865.

The within-named will not be disturbed by the United States authorities so long as they observe their parole and the laws in force where they reside.

By the evening of the 12th the paroles were generally distributed, and the army of Northern Virginia was scattered over the country, returning to their homes. With the delicacy he had shown before on similar occasions, Grant was not seen after his interview with Lee. The petty vanity which would be gratified by a display, in the scene of its triumphs, has no part in his composition. He had done his work thoroughly and well, and now was hastening to another part of the country, where, perhaps, his presence was needed.

## CHAPTER XLIV.

THE SURRENDER OF JOHNSTON. — THE DISBANDING OF ALL ARMED AND ORGANIZED OPPOSITION TO THE GOVERNMENT.

It will be remembered that just previous to the commencement of this campaign, Sherman had paid a visit to Grant's headquarters at City Point, and having decided upon the course of action to be pursued by his army, in conjunction with that of the army of the Potomac, as soon as the campaign should actively commence, had returned to Goldsboro', in North Carolina. Upon the receipt of the letter from Grant which we have already given, Sherman moved at once upon Johnston, and entered Raleigh, on the 13th, Johnston retreating before him. The news of Lee's surrender on the 9th was received by Sherman on the 12th, and on the 14th Johnston sent a letter to Sherman, proposing a meeting. The next day Sherman replied, appointing a meeting for the 17th, provided the armies remained in *statu quo* until that time. This delay he felt was of importance in order to repair the railroad in his rear, and put it in running order, so that in case the negotiation failed, he would be able to cut off Johnston's retreat. At the time appointed the two commanders met, and, after consultation, agreed to meet the next day, in order to settle the minutiæ of the terms. On the 18th, therefore, a suspension of hostilities was agreed to, either party to give forty-eight hours' notice before their resumption, in order to give time to submit the memorandum of agreement to the government for approval. On the 17th, the news of President Lincoln's assassination on the 14th reached General Sherman. On the 24th, the officer despatched by General Sherman to Washington, with the memorandum of agreement, returned accompanied by General Grant, and notice was given of the termination of the truce. On the 25th, however, there was another meeting between Generals Sherman and Johnston, the result of which was the surrender of the Confederate army upon the same terms as those granted to Lee. This surrender Sherman received. The military power of the rebellion was now broken and destroyed. The few unimportant small forces still in arms in distant parts of the country, were too insignificant to require our attention here. Suffice it to say that, on the 26th of May, the last of these in Texas surrendered to Sheridan, who had been sent there for the purpose of forcing them to terms, should they prove contumacious.

The final scene in the military drama was the review at Washington, which commenced on the 22d of May, and occupied two days. In it were embraced the armies of the Potomac and those under Sherman, and these fine bodies of men representing all sections of the country passed in review before the executive and military officers of the government, and then, disbanding, doffed the army blue, and were quietly absorbed again in the peaceful pursuits of life. Perhaps the ease and quiet with which this was done gave even a stronger proof of the strength and stability of freedom, than the sudden gathering of armed men, from the bosom of a peaceful nation devoted to productive industry, to defend the sovereignty of law and order against the attacks of those who had been demoralized by living so long upon the oppression of labor.

The war now was over; the new phase of the old contest of freedom against slavery had ended in victory. Those whose first impulse to defend their system of society, founded upon injustice to labor, had been to grasp the sword, had been overthrown by the sword. But the end was not yet. The contest was simply transferred from the field of battle to the field of politics.

If history teaches any one lesson, it is that the safety and security of political institutions are secured only as they rest upon the broad foundation of justice; that what we mortals call our laws must, to be respected, resemble the laws of nature in their universality and freedom from all exceptions. The experience of men, in politics as in science, is rising up to the comprehension of the fact that nature's law is freedom of development, not repression. In physical science we have arrived at the demonstration of the correlation of force, and it now remains for us, in politics and in moral science, to demonstrate, and act upon the demonstration, that the physical and moral laws of the universe are identical; that the wealth, the power, the stability of nations, and consequently the happiness of those constituting them, depend upon the freedom of development, individual and collective, enjoyed by each and every member of the nation. The moral forces are physical forces, and act in the same way, and are as infinite in their might, when repressed, as they are harmonious and beneficent in their results, when allowed freedom of action. As the free circulation of light and air prevents pestilence and disease by removing their causes, so the free circulation of the light of intelligence and the air of liberty will remove the pestilences of the moral world — ignorance, poverty, crime, revolution, and war — by removing their causes. The cities of Europe, by conforming to the laws of physical hygiene, have freed themselves from the recurrence of the black death and the plagues of the middle ages, and it remains for the nations now, by conforming to the laws of moral hygiene, to remove the moral pestilences of mankind. The necessity is equally imperative, and the result is equally certain.

As we see, in the South, that the education of labor, despite the legal, social, and other disabilities of the slave, had yet fitted him better for the comprehension of what the war meant, and what its results must certainly be, than his masters were, than the whole class of persons who believed themselves his superiors in intelligence, as they were in position, so, through the whole world, the producers — the class who create all wealth — are better fitted to judge how best to dispose of it than those who, priding themselves upon their superior intelligence, have, either by trickery, custom, or usurpation, obtained its control.* The universal tes-

* More than a year before the commencement of the war, there was established in Charleston, South Carolina, a sort of club, called the "Association of 1860," the object of which was to prepare the South for secession by the publication of pamphlets and similar means of propaganda. This association had among its members most of those who considered themselves, and were

timony of the Union prisoners who escaped is, that they never hesitated to confide in the negro, and were never betrayed. Despite all the influence of their masters brought in the other direction, the slave was not to be found who did not know that the success of the Union cause meant his freedom; and upon this faith they acted from the firing of the first gun against Fort Sumter, though for years the government failed to see the inevitable conclusion of the logic of events, and tried to compromise with justice.

The war was now over. The four long years of struggle had ended in victory. The barbarism of the old world, represented in slavery, in the oppression of labor, had trusted to the sword for its maintenance, and had been conquered by the sword. The struggle had been most severe, and had assumed the vastest proportions since the system of slavery, though by its nature belonging to the barbarous period of the development of society, had yet in its possession all the appliances of war belonging to the nineteenth century, and fought with the desperation of a dying monster. It had also all the moral support of the aristocratic feeling of Europe, and as far as this feeling controlled the

generally accepted as, the intelligent and cultivated leaders of society in that pseudo aristocratic city. Among the pamphlets they published was one written by W. D. Porter, Esq., a lawyer of considerable local reputation, which will show the whole tendency of the efforts of the Association. Its title ran as follows: "*Slavery, its Doom in the Union, its Safety out of it.*" This was the creed they all held with an unquestioning faith, and the firing on Fort Sumter was hailed by them all as the first step towards the realization of their prophecies. But while this conviction was universal among the whites, the instinctive conviction among the slaves, that secession meant their freedom, was equally universal. This fact is worthy of most serious consideration, and can be either disregarded or applied in the study and the settlement of the labor question, which is *the* question of to-day for the whole world.

various governments of Europe, this sympathy was openly expressed, and backed up by material aid. The twin systems of barbarism, which had thrust themselves forward into the nineteenth century, — slavery and aristocracy, — had of course a brotherly sympathy with each other; since whether the law oppresses one class or elevates another, the result must be the same. In both the class which suffers from injustice is oppressed, while that which gains by such injustice is corrupted. We find, therefore, that while the aristocratic classes of Europe sympathized with the slaveholders in their rebellion, the people of Europe, those who by the education of labor had been fitted to a right comprehension of the logic of events, saw, as shrewdly and as quickly as the slaves of the South saw it, what was the meaning of the war, what must be its result, and steadfastly throughout, despite all the attempts of the so-called leading classes to mystify the question by sophistry, displayed their sympathy with the cause of freedom. The two most notable evidences of this were, first, in England, where the operatives in Lancashire, while suffering most severely themselves from the cotton famine caused by the war, yet at the very point of their highest misery, expressed in public meetings their full sympathy with the Union cause; while second, in Germany, during one of the darkest moments for the cause, the people, despite the penny-wise and pound-foolish wisdom of the financial leaders, invested largely in our bonds, leaving those of the Southern Confederacy to the bankers and moneyed classes, who, as they ape the manners of the aristocracy, followed their lead in their sympathies.

The end of the contest had come in the field of battle, and it is well to look over the record and see what we had gained. In the first place, slavery was abolished. The magnitude of this step in the progress of the nation towards the realization of the democratic idea, of the reign of justice, of the foundation of the national spirit, as expressed in its government, or in the relations of social life, upon the dignity of labor, and of the ample recognition of its rights, since all social advance, as all individual or national wealth, is derived from labor, cannot even now be fully appreciated. In the next place, the spirit of national unity had grown even out of the conflict of sections. If the war had proved anything, it had proved the geographical necessity that this nation must be one; that there are no possible boundaries which can be established in this continent to divide different nations; while out of the necessities of the war, from the strain it caused upon the resources of the government, there had also grown a financial system which gave us a currency circulating at par all over the country. The pecuniary advantage of this system to the business of the country, in facilitating and cheapening the free circulation of the products of its industry, can hardly be estimated, but is second to the benefit it produces in demonstrating and strengthening the principle of national unity. Our armies had also been drawn from all sections of the country, and in their various campaigns had passed in company over all its various sections. The men of the West had met personally those from the East, and opportunities had been offered to both, of seeing and becoming personally aware of the merits and virtues of each; and the result of all free circulation of men among their fellows is to stimulate the germ of the feelings of the unity of the human race, to weaken all sectional prejudices, and prepare the way for the final realization of the universal brotherhood of man. In his last report of the active operations in the field, Grant speaks thus eloquently and truthfully of the result of this feature of the war: "It has been my fortune to see the armies of both the West and East fight battles, and from what I have seen, I know there is no difference in their fighting qualities. All that it was possible for men to do in battle, they have done. The western armies commenced their battles in the Mississippi Valley, and received the final surrender of the remnant of the principal army opposed to them in North Carolina. The armies of the East commenced their battles on the river from which the army of the Potomac derived its name, and received the final surrender of their old antagonist at Appomattox Court-house, Virginia. The splendid achievements of each have nationalized our victories, removed all sectional jealousies, of which we have unfortunately experienced too much, and the cause of crimination and recrimination that might have followed had either section failed in its duty. All have a proud record, and all sections can well congratulate themselves and each other for having done their full share in restoring the supremacy of law over every foot of territory belonging to the United States. Let them hope for perpetual peace and harmony with that enemy whose manhood, however mistaken the cause, drew forth such herculean deeds of valor."

## CHAPTER XLV.

GRANT IN A NEW FIELD.—HIS COURSE AS COMMANDER OF THE ARMIES IN THE MATTER OF RECONSTRUCTION.

THE war was now over, and the practical application of the results of victory passed from the hands of the military commanders into those of the legislators. The entire social system of the South having been violently overturned, there was of course a pressing necessity to reorganize it in accordance with the new condition of things. The labor of the South, the application of its productive energies, by which alone all wealth is produced, was no longer to be performed by slaves; but, as of course the prejudices which the old system had produced, and by which those who had heretofore held the governing power had become demoralized and corrupted, still remained, it was necessary that, for the present at least, the labor of the South should be protected in their new rights by the strong arm of the military power. The rebellion itself was a sufficient proof that the civil officers of the South were not fit to be trusted with the administration of justice, since, when the crisis came, they had been found basely and meanly derelict. In following General Grant through his course in the administration of this extra military authority, we shall find that he has distinguished himself by the application of common sense to the affairs of state,—embroiled as they were by the chicanery of politics and the violence of party feeling,—as he had in the application of the same qualities to war.

As soon as Lee had surrendered, General Grant, before going South, and without stopping to even visit Richmond, hastened to Washington, and feeling the necessity of reducing the expenses of the government, which were necessarily enormous while our vast armies were maintained in the field, busied himself in this important and practical reform. The result of his visit is seen in the following order, issued from the War Department on the 13th of April:—

WAR DEPARTMENT, WASHINGTON,
April 13—6 P. M.

TO MAJOR GENERAL DIX, *New York.*

The Department, after mature consideration and consultation with the Lieutenant General upon the results of the recent campaign, has come to the following determinations, which will be carried into effect by appropriate orders to be immediately issued:—

*First.* To stop all drafting and recruiting in the loyal States.

*Second.* To curtail purchases of arms, ammunition, quartermaster and commissary supplies, and reduce the military establishment in its several branches.

*Third.* To reduce the number of general and staff officers to the actual necessities of the service.

*Fourth.* To remove all military restrictions upon trade and commerce, so far as may be consistent with public safety.

As soon as these measures can be put in operation, it will be made known by public order.

EDWIN M. STANTON, *Secretary of War.*

On the 28th of April, the following order was issued, carrying these suggestions into practice:—

WAR DEPARTMENT, ADJUTANT GENERAL'S OFFICE,
WASHINGTON, April 28, 1865.

*Ordered, First.* That the chiefs of the respective bureaus of this department proceed immediately to reduce the expenses of their respective departments to what is absolutely necessary, in view of an immediate reduction of the forces in the field and garrisons, and the speedy termination of hostilities, and that they severally make out statements of the reductions they deem practicable.

*Second.* That the Quartermaster General discharge all ocean transports not required to bring home troops in remote departments. All river and inland transportation will be discharged, except that required for the necessary supplies of troops in the field. Purchases of horses, mules, wagons, and other land transportation will be stopped; also purchases of forage, except what is required for immediate consumption. All purchases for railroad construction and transportation will also be stopped.

*Third.* That the Commissary General of Subsistence stop the purchase of supplies in his department for such as may, with what is on hand, be required for the forces in the field on the 1st of June next.

*Fourth.* That the Chief of Ordnance stop all purchase of arms, ammunition, and material therefor, and reduce the manufacturing of arms and ordnance stores in government arsenals, as rapidly as can be done without injury to the service.

*Fifth.* That the Chief of Engineers stop work on all field fortifications, and other works, except those for which specific appropriations have been made by Congress for completion, or that may be required for the proper protection of works in progress.

*Sixth.* That all soldiers in hospitals, who require no further medical treatment, be honorably discharged from service, with immediate payment. All officers and enlisted men who have been prisoners of war and are now on furlough or at parole camps, and all recruits in rendezvous, except those for the regular army, will be likewise honorably discharged. Officers whose duty it is, under the regulations of the service, to make out rolls and other final papers connected with the final discharge and payment of soldiers, are directed to make payment without delay, so that the order may be carried into effect immediately.

*Seventh.* The Adjutant General of the army will cause immediate returns to be made by all commanders in the field, garrisons, detachments, and forts, of their respective forces, with a view to their immediate reduction.

*Eighth.* The Quartermasters of Subsistence, Ordnance, Engineers, and Provost Marshal General's departments, will reduce the number of clerks and employees to that absolutely required for closing the business of their respective departments, and will, without delay, report to the Secretary of War the number required of each class or grade. The Surgeon General will make a similar reduction of surgeons, nurses, and attendants in his bureau.

*Ninth.* The chiefs of the respective bureaus will immediately cause proper returns to be made out of public property in their charge, and a statement of property in each that may be sold upon advertisement and public sale, without prejudice to the service.

*Tenth.* That the Commissary of Prisoners will have rolls made out of the name, residence, time and place of capture, and occupation of all prisoners of war, who will take the oath of allegiance to the United States, to the end that such as are disposed to become good and loyal citizens of the United States, and who are proper objects of Executive clemency, may be relieved, upon terms that the President shall deem fit and consistent with the public safety.

By order of the Secretary of War.

W. A. NICHOLS, *A. A. G.*

Official — THOS. M. VINCENT, *A. A. G.*

## CHAPTER XLVI.

A RETROSPECT OF WHAT HAS BEEN DONE DURING THE WAR.—THE ARMY RETURNING TO THE PURSUITS OF PEACE.

THE war was over, and the army thus returned to the peaceful industries of life. A few statements from the report of the Secretary of War, presented in November of 1865, at the first meeting of Congress after the termination of the war, will give an accurate idea of the magnitude of the struggle in which we had been engaged. On May 1, 1865, the army numbered, all told, one million five hundred and sixteen men, while the aggregate of men put in the service from April 15, 1861, to April 14, 1865, was two million six hundred and fifty-six thousand five hundred and fifty-three. This aggregate embraces, of course, all the enlistments for short terms. The promptness with which this enormous body of soldiers had been organized ready for action, from citizens engaged in the peaceful avocations of daily life, will appear from the following statements, which show at the same time the admirable organization of the War Department, as well as the enthusiasm of the people in support of the war.

In 1862, after the disasters on the Peninsula, in Virginia, over eighty thousand troops were enlisted, organized, armed, equipped, and sent to the field in less than a month. During the continuance of the war, sixty thousand men had repeatedly been sent into the field within four weeks, while ninety thousand infantry wei sent to the armies from the five States of Ohio, Indiana, Illinois, Iowa, and Wisconsin, within ninety days.

But however assuring such an exhibition of the stability of republican institutions may be, showing as it does the promptness and enthusiasm with which the people rush to the support of a government which they feel is their own, and which they have formed for their own purposes, and must therefore maintain, when its existence is imperilled, a still greater test, according to the experience of all European governments, was to be made of the stability, the inherent strength and morality of democratic institutions, in the disbanding of this force. The experience of all the governments in Europe had shown that the disbanding of an army was always attended with serious demoralizing effects upon society. The reason of this lies not in the simple fact of the disbanding of the army, but further back, in the organization of the army itself.

We have seen, during the continuance of the war, that our army differed entirely in its composition from those of Europe. It was anything but a hired set of mercenaries: but, as we have seen, was drawn from the industrious producers of the country. Grant himself, in one of his reports, speaks of the fact, that whatever branch of industry was rendered necessary by the varied and multifarious duties resulting from the anomalous position of our army in the field, he could find among the enlisted men in the ranks experts ready and capable of performing it. It is certain that an army composed of such materials is not either a demoralizing or easily demoralized body of men. And therefore, notwithstanding the predictions of the European press, who, judging from the evils arising from the disbanding of armies in their own countries, and unaware of or unable to comprehend the essential difference between the constitution of our army as a part and parcel of the industry of the country, from that of their own, we find the army disbanding, and returning to the peaceful occupations it had left temporarily, to engage in the pressing duty of defending its own government, without producing any of the evils prophesied by those to whom the realization of the democratic idea seems to be only the realization of discord and anarchy. The war ended in April, and on November the 15th of the same year, eight hundred thousand nine hundred and sixty-three men had been mustered out of the service. Never before in the world has such a sight been seen as this number of men, who had been for so long a time accustomed to the excitement and violence of war, returning to the peaceful pursuits of labor, and becoming again citizens engaged in productive industry.

That such a sight has been seen in this country, is as legitimate a cause for confidence in the stability and persistence of a government based upon the practical realization of the democratic idea, as was the equally new and glorious spectacle of a nation turning its attention away from its ordinary pursuits, and taking up arms to defend its government from the attacks of those who, reared in a system which educated them in a contempt of productive industry, sought finally, in the madness of their scorn, to rebel against the government in order to sustain and perpetuate a system of slavery. It cannot be wondered at that a people so deluded as to take up arms in such a monstrous cause, should be ignorant enough of the spirit of the northern army to suppose that they were a set of mercenaries. This term, we have found, was frequently applied to them by the leaders in the proclamations they issued for the purpose of "firing the southern heart;" but one fact is very noticeable — that whatever influence such epithets had in exciting the ignorant portion of the white population south, they never for a moment deceived the negro; but on all occasions, wherever the opportunity offered, he recognized the "boys in blue" as his friends. The unanimous testimony of the Union prisoners who escaped from the slaughter and starvation pens, which the South called its prisons, is, that the negro was always their friend, and that in no case did he fail to assist them on their road. At the same time, despite all that had been told them by their masters of the terrible purposes for which the "mercenary hoards of Yankees" invaded "the sunny south," the negroes welcomed the advent of our armies with confidence and joy. The simple education of labor had given them intelligence enough to comprehend their own interest in freedom, better than their brethren whose social degradation was as great as their own, and who differed from them only in the color of their skins and in their contempt for industry; or even than the educated classes of the South, who prided themselves upon their culture and refinement, but who were equally wanting in the recognition of the truth that industry is the only foundation of the well-being of a state, and that justice to labor is the only means of giving stability to its social arrangements, or of making their play harmonious.

Besides the amount of strictly warlike energy the army had displayed in the field, it had also performed an enormous amount of productive work. The roads it had constructed, the railroads it had built and kept in order, the fortifications it had thrown up, the intrenchments it had raised, may be estimated from the fact that fifteen thousand miles of military telegraph had been laid during the war. The amount of physical energy expended upon both sides during the war, would have sufficed, had it been valued according to the present standard of wages, and had it been directed in the interest of production, instead of in the interest of destruction, to have purchased, at the highest valuation, the entire negro population of the South, and have set them free, while such an application of the energies of both sections of the country, would have left the South, at the end of the four years, with its railway system perfected, instead of destroyed, with its roads built, its swamps drained, and its lands in a high state of culture, instead of being laid desolate with fire and sword.

It is at present considered utopian to suppose that wars will ever cease; but certainly, if ever reason and a wise self-interest, instead of subverted passions, shall come to govern men's actions, this result will be obtained. Whenever the industry of a country, which produces all its wealth, shall retain in its own possession the wealth it creates, and shall have thus in its own hands the disposition of its own energies, then war, since it is evidently never an aid, but always an injury to productive industry, will come to be classed among the follies of the world's childhood. That this result must inevitably arrive, and that it will arrive by the diffusion and practical realization of the democratic idea, is as evident, as that the war was inaugurated by the class at the South who lived by the spoliation of industry, and that if the labor of the South had for the last sixty years been treated with justice, slavery would have been abolished long ago, and the war would have become impossible for want of a moving cause.

Thus it is seen that the spread of the democratic idea, and its practical realization in our social arrangements, is the growth of all real conservatism, if this word has the meaning of its derivation,—which is, to *preserve*,—since justice alone can guarantee that stability and peace, in which society moves forward to its ultimate destiny of freedom, by the gradual and persistent process of development which runs uninterruptedly through all nature. Change is the necessary condition of growth, and growth is the necessity of existence. As the Latin poet says,—

> "——— Immota labescunt,
> Et quæ perpetuo sunt agitata manent."

Or, expressing the same idea, the quaint old English poet,—

> "That which is motionless decays;
> Only in constant change is length of days."

## CHAPTER XLVII.

THE FIRST YEAR OF RECONSTRUCTION, AND GRANT'S COURSE AS HEAD OF THE MILITARY AUTHORITY.—HIS ANSWER TO GENERAL LEE'S PETITION FOR PARDON.—THE TESTIMONIALS GIVEN HIM BY THE PEOPLE.

During the summer of 1865, Grant made a tour through the North, and was everywhere received with enthusiasm. Continuing his tour through the West, he visited at Springfield, Illinois, the tomb of Abraham Lincoln, where reposes the body of the President, to whose firm confidence in his ability Grant was indebted for the opportunity for its display, and whose assassination, at the moment when victory came to reward his four years of care and anxiety, turned a nation's rejoicing to tears. At Galena, Illinois, Grant was presented by his fellow-townsmen with a furnished house, situated just out of the town, and commanding a fine view of the river and surrounding country. Early in November, having remained for some time in Washington after his return from the West, Grant paid a visit to New York, and was tendered a splendid reception by the citizens. The banquet was given at the Fifth Avenue Hotel, and the enthusiasm with which his entrance was greeted was such as rarely finds genuine expression in fashionable society, where the conventional restraints of respectability repress the expression of every natural feeling, on the supposition that such conduct is vulgar. Though he was the centre of attraction, Grant remained as impassive and apparently unconcerned as he always does. Such ovations he receives, as he gains his victories, without surprise and without elation.

On his return to Washington, Grant resolved to pay a visit to the South, and carried out his resolution as quietly and unostentatiously as he had made it. His first stopping-place was Richmond; and though the capture of this place will ever be connected with his name, yet this was the first visit he had paid to it, and now he entered with no flourish or display, but simply as an officer of the government, whose duty led him South on a tour of observation. On the 1st of December, he arrived in Charleston, South Carolina, the cradle of secession, and was received there with enthusiasm. The Union League, composed of colored citizens, honored his presence with a torchlight procession and a serenade.

The object of Grant's tour through the South was to inform himself by personal observation concerning the workings of the military government and of the Freedmen's Bureau, and also to observe the condition, physically and morally, of the people. Though the time devoted to this trip was but short, yet Grant made the best use of it, and by freely conversing with the people he met, and by investigating for himself the workings of the new system of things in the South, was able to report on his return. He arrived at Washington from this southern tour on the 11th of December, 1865, and on the 18th reported to the President the result of his observations. This report was a short one, and the following extract from it will show the result of his observations concerning the most important matter at this period, which was the harmonious working of the military authority and the Freedmen's Bureau. The evident necessity was to introduce a unity of action between these; and upon the want of this unity Grant writes, —

"It seems to me that this could be corrected by regarding every officer on duty with troops in the Southern States as an agent of the Freedmen's Bureau, and then have all orders from the head of the Bureau sent through the department commanders. This would create a responsibility that would cause uniformity of action throughout the South, and cause the orders and instructions from the head of the Bureau being carried out, and would relieve from duty and pay a large number of employees of the government."

It is a pity that this practical suggestion was not then carried out, since it is evident that such an application of common sense to the new condition of affairs in the South could not fail to have produced the effects desired, and which are certainly most necessary. Economy and efficiency — these are the needed reforms; and these would have been secured by the adoption of this common-sense suggestion.

On the 12th of January, 1866, the following order was issued from the War Department: —

*General Orders, No. 3.*

WAR DEPARTMENT, ADJUTANT GENERAL'S OFFICE,
WASHINGTON, January 12, 1866.

Military division and department commanders whose commands embrace or are composed of any of the late rebellious states, and who have not already done so, will at once issue and enforce orders protecting from prosecution or suits, in the state or municipal courts of such states, all officers and soldiers of the armies of the United States, and all persons thereto attached, or in any way thereto belonging, subject to military authority, charged with offences for acts done in their military capacity, or pursuant to orders from military authority, and to protect from suit or prosecution all loyal citizens or persons charged with offences done against the rebel forces, directly or indirectly, during the existence of the rebellion, and all persons, their agents or employees, charged with the occupancy of abandoned lands or plantations, or the possession or custody of any kind of property whatever, who occupied, used, possessed, or controlled the same, pursuant to the order of the President or any of the civil or military departments of the government, and to protect them from any penalty or damages that may have been, or may be, pronounced or adjudged in said courts in any of such cases, and also protecting colored persons from prosecutions in any of said states, charged with offences for which white persons are not prosecuted or punished in the same manner or degree.

By command of Lieutenant General GRANT.

E. D. TOWNSEND, *Assistant Adjutant General.*

The simple fact that the necessity should exist for such an order would serve to show that the injustice with which the negroes had been treated while slavery existed, and the foolish hatred which the South had cherished as a virtue against northern or loyal men, had not yet died out. The records of the time are, however, full of instances in which persecution, violence, robbery, and murder had been exercised against both these classes of persons, while among those to whom these means of revenge were distasteful, or when opportunities to exercise them did not exist, the ordinary plan was to invoke the aid of the civil courts, and, under the guise of law, fine, imprison, or otherwise punish, those whose loyalty or whose complexion made them objectionable to the "chivalry." While this condition of things remained in the South, and were so flagrant that the above order was felt to be a necessity, Governor Parsons, of Alabama, had, however, the effrontery to write to Grant asking for the withdrawal from the state of the United States troops, and for permission to arm the militia. To this request Grant responded as follows: "For the present, and until there is full security for equitably maintaining the right and safety of all classes of citizens in the states lately in rebellion, I would not recommend the withdrawal of the United States troops from them. The number of interior garrisons might be reduced, but a movable force sufficient to insure tranquillity should be retained. While such a force is retained in the South, I doubt the propriety of putting arms in the hands of the militia."

The whole theory and practice of a wise reconstruction could not be better stated than in this letter. The rebellion had arisen from the fact that the "rights and safety of *all* classes" in the South had not been maintained: those who, by the accident of birth, had been placed in the position of rulers, had ignored and despised the rights of the labor of the South, and, to maintain the system which enabled them to continue in this course, had rebelled. Now that their rebellion had been put down, they had not learned the lesson that justice is the only foundation for a stable condition of society. It is the repetition of all the lessons of history. As with every aristocracy the world has seen, founding their power upon tyranny and their wealth upon the oppression of industry, the rulers of the South had supposed that they were all of society, and that the realization of justice was the maintenance of their peculiar privileges and immunities, and in support of these had finally taken up arms. The history of all wars is the same. War is the natural method by which oppression seeks either to maintain or to increase its power. There is yet in the history of mankind the first instance to be found where productive industry has sought this means of extending its sway, since peace, good will, and justice are the necessary conditions for its well being. If the result of the war had not been enough to teach the late ruling classes of the South their error, it is hardly to be expected that they would learn immediately from any other source the lesson of the necessity of justice. A course of life-long oppression cannot be compensated for in a day. Time must enter as a necessary element into all the processes of moral as of physical growth and development. It is the part of a wise statesman, however, by the application of common sense to the condition of things brought under his observation, to influence and stimulate this growth as much as possible. With men, as with children, the sense of responsibility is one of the best educational influences. This wise course was pursued by Grant in showing the rulers of the South that the matter was in their own hands; that, when the rights and safety of all classes were "equitably" maintained, then, but not until then, could their wishes be met. It is a pity that the same intelligent application of common sense to the circumstances of the present condition could not be equally found in all the departments of the government.

In February, 1866, the following order was issued by Grant to the various department commanders: —

HEADQUARTERS ARMIES OF THE UNITED STATES,
WASHINGTON, February 17, 1866.

You will please send to these headquarters, as soon as practicable, and from time to time thereafter, such copies of newspapers, published in your department, as contain sentiments of disloyalty and hostility to the government in any of its branches, and state whether such paper is habitual in its utterance of such sentiments. The persistent publication of articles calculated to keep up an hostility of feeling between the people of different sections of the country cannot be tolerated. This information is called for with a view to their suppression, which will be done from these headquarters only.

By command of Lieutenant General GRANT.

T. S. BOWERS, *Assistant Adjutant General.*

This order was issued on account of the suppression of the Richmond Examiner, on the 13th of February, by General Terry, who was in command of the department of Virginia. On the 19th of this month this journal was, however, given permission to continue its issue. The press of the South, which had used all its influence in "firing the southern heart," and in bringing on the rebellion, had, in the large majority, learned apparently nothing from the events of the past few years, and the undoubted evils which arise from the license of printing were never more fully manifested than here. It is a fault of the journalism all over the civilized world that it does not fulfil the possibilities of its mission, but degenerates from its rightful position into merely an organ of party. The best corrective of its faults is the education of the people, from whom it obtains its readers and supporters. The question of the freedom of the press is like that of the freedom of the ballot: no restrictions upon either can be justified logically, while at the same time the freedom of neither can be practically realized unless the people are sufficiently educated to be their own masters, not the slaves of ignorance or the followers of demagogues. While, then, the people are in a transitional condition, it is the duty of a wise government to remove all obstacles in their way of improvement, and to foster all their attempts to develop themselves towards self-reliance and the freedom of self-government. In pursuing this course it is manifestly one of the main duties of the government, to restrain the open expression of impassioned appeals, tending to excite the mean prejudices of class hatred and to foster the love of injustice and tyranny. This is evidently the course necessary in the education of children, and "men are but children of a larger growth;" and this has been the course pursued by Grant in the performance of his duties as commander-in-chief of the armies while the necessity remains for maintaining a military power in the South. This order, however, was revoked in August, 1866.

In September, 1866, the following letter, which had been written more than a year before, and very soon after the surrender of Lee, was made public, and shows conclusively the opinion Grant then entertained concerning the position of those who had surrendered and been paroled. We shall have, further on, other proofs of his opinions upon this subject:—

HEADQUARTERS ARMIES OF THE UNITED STATES,
WASHINGTON, D. C., June 20, 1865.

GENERAL R. E. LEE, *Richmond, Va.*

GENERAL: Your communication, of date 13th instant, stating the steps you had taken after reading the President's proclamation of the 29th ult., with the view of complying with its provisions, when you learned that, with others, you were to be indicted for treason by the grand jury at Norfolk; that you had supposed that the officers and men of the army of Northern Virginia were, by the terms of their surrender, protected by the United States government from molestation so long as they conformed to its conditions; that you were ready to meet any charges that might be preferred against you, and did not wish to avoid trial; but that if you were correct as to the protection granted by your parole, and were not to be prosecuted, you desired to avail yourself of the President's Amnesty Proclamation, and enclosing an application therefor, with the request that in that event it be acted upon, — has been received and forwarded to the Secretary of War, with the following opinion indorsed thereon: —

"In my opinion, the officers and men paroled at Appomattox Court-house, and since upon the same terms given to Lee, cannot be tried for treason so long as they observe the terms of their parole. This is my understanding. Good faith, as well as true policy, dictates that we should observe the condition of that convention. Bad faith on the part of the government, or a construction of that covenant subjecting the officers to trial for treason, would produce a feeling of insecurity in the minds of the officers and men. If so disposed, they might even regard such an infraction of terms by the government as an entire release from all obligations on their part. I will state further, that the terms granted by me met with the hearty approval of the President at the time, and of the country generally. The action of Judge Underwood, in Norfolk, has already had an injurious effect, and I would ask that he be ordered to quash all indictments found against paroled prisoners of war, and to desist from the further prosecution of them.

U. S. GRANT, *Lieutenant General.*

HEADQUARTERS ARMIES OF THE UNITED STATES,
June 16, 1865."

This opinion, I am informed, is substantially the same as that entertained by the government. I have forwarded your application for amnesty and pardon to the President, with the following indorsement thereon: —

"Respectfully forwarded through the Secretary of War to the President, with the earnest recommendation that this application of General R. E. Lee for amnesty and pardon be granted him. The oath of allegiance required by recent order of the President does not accompany this, for the reason, I am informed by General Ord, the order requiring it had not reached Richmond when this was forwarded.

U. S. GRANT, *Lieutenant General.*

HEADQUARTERS ARMIES OF THE UNITED STATES,
June 16, 1865."

Very respectfully,

U. S. GRANT, *Lieutenant General.*

During the month of February, 1866, Grant visited New York, and was received with great enthusiasm wherever he appeared. One of the pleasantest incidents of his visit at this time was a reception given him by the leather dealers of that city, in the warerooms of Messrs. Armstrong and Sons, No. 19 Ferry Street, in what is called the "Swamp," which is the seat of the extensive leather business of the city. The warehouse was handsomely decorated with flags, and an elegant banquet was prepared. Grant, on his appearance, was greeted with enthusiasm, and in response to repeated calls for a speech, said, "Gentlemen, you know I never make speeches. I am happy to meet my old friends of the leather trade."

During this visit to New York he also visited the rooms of the Union Relief Committee, and inspected the specimens of writing executed with their left hands by soldiers who had lost their right arms in the war. There were on exhibition two hundred and seventy specimens of such work; and, looking at them, Grant remarked, "These boys write better with their left hands than I do with my right." Before leaving the rooms, he wrote the following upon the visitors' book: —

NEW YORK, February 24, 1866.

I have examined the large and exceedingly interesting collection of the left hand manuscripts written by our disabled soldiers, who have lost their right arms. They are eminently honorable to the authors, and from the excellence of the penmanship, it would require a task I should be sorry to accept, to decide on the merits of the competitors.

U. S. GRANT, *Lieutenant General U. S. Army.*

On the evening of the 26th he was given a public reception at the Brooklyn Academy of Music, and left that night, after the reception, on a special train for Washington.

During this visit to New York a purse of one hundred thousand dollars was contributed by a few of the capitalists of New York, and offered to Grant. The presentation was made quite informally, and was received in the same way. Up to this time Grant had been the recipient of the following testimonials from the people of various parts of the country: The citizens of Philadelphia had presented him with thirty thousand dollars; the citizens of Galena, Illinois, with a house and furniture; some citizens of Boston had given him a library, and besides these he had been presented with various swords, horses, pistols, and other similar gifts. The pecuniary value of all of these was, however, inconsiderable, in comparison with the rewards voted by the British Parliament to Wellington after his victory at Waterloo, or to Marlborough for his victories, and to both of these soldiers these rewards were given in the shape of estates and titles. This species of reward, since the money to furnish it is raised by taxation, is of course really given by the productive labor of the country; but as their will is not consulted in England, and as the credit of such generosity accrues to those who vote it, but do not bear their share in paying it, such lavishness might naturally be expected. There is no such easy generosity as that which is practised with other people's money. The theory and practice of such rewards in this country are entirely different. The gratitude and admiration of the American people are not to be measured by a pecuniary standard. To the great men of our country, from Washington down, this course has never been pursued. The Washington Monument, despite even the assistance of Everett's "made-to-order" oratory, is to-day in no more imminent danger of completion than it has ever been. It is not in such modes, copied and adopted from the self-glorifications of aristocratical monopolies, that the American people desire to express their gratitude and admiration; and though in the present transitional condition, the method of expressing the national gratitude is not yet entirely developed, yet it is a great step in advance to have discarded the pecuniary form, and it is equally certain that, with the social elevation of productive labor, this spread of justice in the daily distribution of the rewards for service performed, will find the fit means for its expression in all such exceptional cases, for exceptional services.

## CHAPTER XLVIII.

THE SECOND YEAR OF RECONSTRUCTION. — THE BLOCK IN THE ADMINISTRATION OF AFFAIRS. — GRANT'S POSITION AND ACTION.

In April, 1866, Grant, accompanied by Mrs. Grant, paid a visit to Richmond, and was received there with great cordiality. In September of this year he accompanied the President in a tour through the country to Chicago, undertaken for the purpose of assisting at the laying of the corner-stone of a monument to Stephen A. Douglas. The presence of Grant and Farragut on this trip was a piece of political diplomacy, upon the part of its originators, which, though apparently successful at first, turned finally, as all such petty tricks must, to the confusion of those who had designed it. The question of reconstruction at this time had commenced to assume great importance. When the armed resistance of the Confederacy was overthrown, the southern people were ready to accept any terms. The system of slavery being, however, abolished, manifestly the most important thing for them to do was to accept the change in good faith, and busy themselves in removing the traces of the ravages of war, and in developing, by a system of free labor, in which justice should be the foundation-stone, the wonderful agricultural and other resources of their territory. But in time the old political leaders of the South found that they had in Washington a "humble individual," who would aid them in attempting to regain, by the tricks of politics, the dominion which they had lost by an appeal to the sword. This change in the spirit of the administration finally culminated in July, 1866, in a riot in New Orleans, in which, under the form of law, the members of a state convention were murdered by the police, and their meeting dispersed. It was a display of the old spirit of slavery, exercising its natural manner of killing out freedom of discussion by violence. General Sheridan, who was in command of the Department of the Gulf, wrote thus to General Grant, from New Orleans, under date of the 12th of August. Sheridan had been absent from the city at the time the massacre occurred. "The more information I obtain of the affair of the 30th in this city, the more revolting it becomes. It was no riot. It was an absolute massacre by the police, which was not excelled in murderous cruelty by that of Fort Pillow. It was a murder which the mayor and police of the city perpetrated without the shadow of a necessity. I recommend the removing of this bad man. I believe it would be hailed with the sincerest gratification by two thirds of the population of the city. There has been a feeling of insecurity on the part of the people here, on account of this man, which is now so much increased that the safety of life and property does not rest with the civil authority, but the military."

In his report before Congress of November of this year, Sheridan further says, "My own opinion is, that the trial of a white man for the murder of a freedman in Texas would be a farce; and in making this statement, I make it because truth compels me, and for no other reason. It is strange that over a white man killed by Indians on our extensive frontier the greatest excitement takes place; but over the killing of many freedmen in the settlements nothing is done. I cannot help but see this, and I cannot but tell it to my superiors, no matter how unpleasant it may be to the authorities of Texas."

In July of this year the grade of General was created in the army, and Grant was nominated and confirmed for the position on the 25th of July, 1866. It was soon after this that Grant's good nature was prevailed upon to accompany the President in his tour. But, as it became evident, during its continuance, that his presence was used as a sort of indorsement for the policy which led to the New Orleans riot, and which was drifting the South back to its old position, where "the right and safety of all classes" were not "equitably maintained," he took the first occasion to leave the party, and returned to Washington. During the balance of this year, and until the meeting of Congress in December, the course of events continued drifting in the same direction. As chief of the armies, Grant presided over the military departments, and the tenor of his instructions continued the same. In September of this year, his correspondence with General Lee, which we have already given, was first made public.

29

## CHAPTER XLIX.

THE DIVERGENCE BETWEEN THE PRESIDENT AND CONGRESS.—GRANT'S POSITION IN THIS CONTEST.

IN March, 1867, the Fortieth Congress assembled, and the necessity for a more definite line of action became more apparent. It is neither the place, nor have we the space, to enter into a lengthy examination of the disagreement between the Executive and Congress; all we can do is to show the course Grant took officially, and how far his acts gave indication of what his opinions were, and upon which side his sympathies lay, in this transference of the contest between the "equitable" maintenance of the "rights" and "safety of all classes," and the injustice of class oppression, from the field of battle to the arena of political intrigue and chicanery. It is not Grant's place, nor is it his nature, to express himself in any other way than by his acts. There can be but little doubt of the position he occupied during the time that this question was settled on the battle-field, and those who have followed him there, could have but little doubt concerning what his course would be in the more tortuous labyrinth of politics. So accustomed, however, have we become to the perpetual prattle of men who, filling public positions, are either called, or feel themselves called, on to declare their position, that Grant's reticence was construed by many into a denial of his own course of action, or an indorsement of the Executive, according to the malice or the obtuseness of those inquiring into it.

On the 12th of July, 1867, in answer to a call from Congress, the following document was laid before it. It was a circular issued on the 22d of May previous, by the Secretary of War, addressed to General Grant, and by him forwarded to the several district commanders for their guidance. This circular read as follows: "General: Recent occurrences in some of the military districts indicate a necessity of great vigilance, on the part of military commanders, to be prepared for the prevention and prompt suppression of riots and breaches of the public peace, especially in towns and cities; and they should have their forces in hand, and so posted, on all occasions where disturbances may be apprehended, as to promptly check, and if possible to prevent, outbreaks and violence endangering public or individual safety. You will, therefore, call the attention of commanders of military districts to this subject, and issue such precautionary orders as may be found necessary for the purpose indicated."

Grant's indorsement of this order is as follows: "The above conveys all the instructions deemed necessary, and will be acted on by district commanders making special reports of precautionary orders issued by them to prevent the recurrence of mobs or other unlawful violence."

The following official letter to General Ord, in command of the Fourth District, will show most definitely what course of action in the matter of reconstruction he felt it was his duty to pursue:—

WASHINGTON, June 23, 1867.

BREVET MAJOR GENERAL E. O. ORD,
*Commanding Fourth District.*

GENERAL: A copy of your final instructions to the Board of Registration of June 10, 1867, is just received. I entirely dissent from the views contained in paragraph 4. Your views as to the duties of registers to register every man who will take the required oath, though they may know the applicant perjures himself, is sustained by the Attorney General. My opinion is, that it is the duty of the Board of Registration to see, as far as it lies in their power, that no unauthorized person is allowed to register. To secure this end, registers should be allowed to administer oaths and examine witnesses. The law, however, makes District Commanders their own interpreters of their power and duty under it, and, in my opinion, the Attorney General or myself can no more than give our opinion as to the meaning of the law. Neither can enforce their views against the judgment of those made responsible for the faithful execution of the law — the District Commanders.

Very respectfully, your obedient servant,

U. S. GRANT, *General.*

The following correspondence is also of great importance in forming an intelligent opinion concerning Grant's position upon the whole subject of reconstruction. On the 7th of April, General Pope, in command of the Third District, wrote to General Grant, asking his views on the status of officers of the rebel army paroled at the end of the war. He wanted to know whether paroles still held good, or whether they were set aside by the proclamation of the President. He asked the question because he desired to know what action he ought to take against rebel officers thus paroled, who should actively and openly counsel the people of their district to resist the action of the Reconstruction Acts passed by Congress. He gave it as his opinion that the provisions of their paroles required them to return to their homes and obey the laws; and also that they refrain from inciting others to neglect or resist the laws of the United States. He also asked whether an attempt on their part to keep up difficulty and prevent the settlement of the southern question in accordance with the recent action of Congress was not a violation of their parole. To this letter Grant replied, on the 13th of April, as follows: —

"Your views on the obligation of a parole are in strict accordance with my own."

On the 6th of August, 1867, Andrew Johnson, the then acting President of the United States, notified Mr. Stanton, then filling the office of Secretary of War, that he was dismissed from his position. Stanton refused to surrender his office, since under the provisions of a bill entitled the Tenure of Office Bill, which had been recently passed by Congress, he could not be removed without the concurrence of the Senate, and that body was not now in session. On the 12th of August Johnson notified Stanton that he should "cease to exercise all the functions pertaining" to the office of Secretary of War, and "transfer to General U. S. Grant, who has this day been authorized and empowered to act as Secretary of War *ad interim*, all records, books, papers, and other public property now in your custody and charge." On the same day Grant was officially notified by the President of his appointment, and Stanton surrendered his position, notifying the President at the same time that, "under a sense of public duty I am compelled to deny your right under the constitution and laws of the United States, without the advice and consent of the Senate, to suspend me from office as

Secretary of War, or the exercise of any or all functions pertaining to the same. But inasmuch as the General commanding the armies of the United States has been appointed Secretary of War *ad interim*, and has notified me that he has accepted the appointment, I have no alternative but to submit, under protest, to superior force."

The official notice given to Stanton by Grant, of his appointment, was sent in the following letter:—

HEADQUARTERS ARMIES OF THE UNITED STATES,
WASHINGTON, August 12, 1867.

THE HON. E. M. STANTON, *Secretary of War*.

SIR: Enclosed herewith I have to transmit to you a copy of a letter just received from the President of the United States, notifying me of my assignment as acting Secretary of War, and directing me to assume those duties at once. In notifying you of my acceptance, I cannot let the opportunity pass without expressing to you my appreciation of the zeal, patriotism, firmness, and ability with which you have ever discharged the duty of Secretary of War.

With great respect, your obedient servant,

U. S. GRANT, *General*.

Grant's acceptance of this position was made the signal and the theme for any amount of the ill-considered and malicious remark in the press, which passes under the dignified name of journalism. Every species of motive was ascribed to him, except the simple one, which his whole previous course should have shown was the only one that influenced him, namely, that of doing his duty, as he best conceived and understood it, for the benefit of the country. The practice of simple, straightforward honesty is so unusual and strange in the cunning and trickery of party politics, that it never occurs to the politicians and their dependants, that any man can be actuated by a motive so curiously anomalous. But here, as in war, Grant has shown that he is trustworthy and reliable. Sherman was right in feeling anxious concerning his remaining in Washington, even after he had proved in war that his "common sense" had supplied all the aids which Sherman feared he needed, since the dangers of politics are greater than those of war; but Grant has shown that with the simple clew of honesty of purpose, he has been able to walk securely through the mazes and pitfalls of political intrigue. To those whose scope of vision is bounded by the petty circle of a mean personal ambition, it seems incredible that any one should rise so far above such limitations, as to lose sight of them entirely for the broader and wider view of a nation's well-being. It is not strange, then, that the politicians should fail to comprehend, and should misrepresent, Grant; but from the people, who in these matters are wiser than their pretended rulers and instructors, he will receive recognition and confidence.

Despite the amount of objurgation which was aimed at him, Grant held his peace; he knew he had done his duty, and did not feel that there was any need to vindicate himself; his record should do that. He had, however, written the following admirable letter to the President, protesting against the removal of Stanton, and also against the removal of Sheridan from the government of the Fifth Military District, which the President had also resolved upon. This letter, which was a private one, was not made public until December 17, 1867, when it formed part of the documents laid before the judiciary committee of the House of Representatives, on a demand made by them for information concerning the action of the President in this matter.

[PRIVATE.]

HEADQUARTERS ARMIES OF THE UNITED STATES,
WASHINGTON, D. C., August 11, 1867.

HIS EXCELLENCY ANDREW JOHNSON,
*President of the United States.*

SIR: I take the liberty of addressing you privately on the subject of the conversation we had this morning, feeling, as I do, the great danger to the welfare of the country should you carry out the designs then expressed.

First. On the subject of the displacement of the Secretary of War. His removal cannot be effected against his will without the consent of the Senate. It was but a short time since the United States Senate was in session, and why not then have asked for his removal, if it was desired? It certainly was the intention of the legislative branch of the government to place a cabinet minister beyond the power of the executive removal; and it is pretty well understood that, so far as cabinet ministers are affected by the Tenure of Office Bill, it was intended specially to protect the Secretary of War, whom the country felt great confidence in. The meaning of the law may be explained away by an astute lawyer; but the common sense and the views of loyal people will give it the effect intended by its framers.

Second. On the subject of the removal of the very able commander of the Fifth Military District, let me ask you to consider the effect it would have upon the public. He is universally and deservedly beloved by the people who sustained this government through its trials, and feared by those who would be still the enemies of the government. It fell to the lot of but few men to do as much against an armed enemy as General Sheridan did during the rebellion, and it is within the scope of the ability of but few in this, or any other country, to do what he has. His civil administration has given equal satisfaction. He has had difficulties to contend with which no other district commander has encountered. Almost, if not quite, from the day he was appointed district commander to the present time, the press has given out that he was to be removed, that the administration was not satisfied with him. This has emboldened the opponents of the laws of Congress within his command, to oppose him in every way in their power, and has rendered necessary measures which otherwise might never have been necessary. In conclusion, allow me to say as a friend, desiring peace and quiet, the welfare of the whole country, north and south, that it is, in my opinion, more than the loyal people of this country (I mean those who supported the government during the great rebellion) will quietly submit to, to see the very man, of all others, in whom they have expressed their confidence, removed.

I would not have taken the liberty of addressing the Executive of the United States thus, but for the conversation on the subject alluded to in this letter, and from a sense of duty, feeling that I know I am right in this matter.

With great respect,

Your obedient servant,

U. S. GRANT, *General.*

Among the documents which were made public at this time, there was also a letter from Sheridan to Grant, dated from New Orleans on the 25th of January, 1867, in which he describes the horrible condition of things in Texas. In it he says that the government is denounced, freedmen are shot, and Union men persecuted if they express their opinions. On the 29th of January Grant forwarded this letter to the Secretary of War, with this indorsement:—

Respectfully forwarded to the Secretary of War. Attention is invited to that portion of the within communication which refers to the condition of the Union men and freedmen in Texas, and to the powerlessness of the military to afford them protection. Even the moral effect of the presence of troops is passing away, and a few days ago, a squad of soldiers on duty were fired on by citizens in Brownsville. In my opinion, the great number of murders of Union men and freedmen in Texas, not only, as a rule, unpunished, but uninvestigated, constitute practically a state of insurrection; and believing it to be the province and duty of every good government to afford protection to the lives, liberty, and property of its citizens, I would recommend the declaration of martial law in Texas to secure these. The necessity of governing any portion of our territory by martial law is to be deplored. If restored to, it should be limited in its authority, and should leave all local authorities and civil tribunals free and unobstructed, until they prove their inefficiency or unwillingness to perform their duties. Martial law would give security, or comparatively so, to all classes of citizens, without regard to race, color, or political opinions, and could be continued until society was capable of protecting itself, or until the state is returned to its full relation to the Union. The application of martial law to one of these states would be a warning to all, and, if necessary, can be extended to others.

U. S. GRANT, *General.*

This document shows that Grant has always held very decided opinions upon the method necessary to be pursued in the matter of reconstruction, and that he foreshadowed the course which Congress has only partially pursued.

Having accepted the position of Secretary of War *ad interim*, Grant, in obedience to an order from the President on the 19th of August, removed Sheridan from the Fifth Military District, and assigned him to the department of Missouri. Before doing so, however, he again protested against such a course of action in the following letter to the President, which, as containing his views upon the duties of those holding office in a representative government, should be transferred to our school books, and thus impressed upon our youth, in order to guide them when they come to take their part in the political management of the country.

Having accepted the position of Secretary of War *ad interim*, Grant, with his characteristic promptness, set himself to work in cutting down the expenditures of the military department of the government, and was here as successful as he has always been. In the administration of civil affairs, as in his practice of war, he directs his energies against the most important points; and now that the war was over, a return to the principles of economy, which, before the war, regulated our military expenditures, was the most important reform. The result of his labors here will be found in his report, in the Appendix.

On the 19th of August, Sheridan was transferred from his command of the Fifth Military District to the Department of the Missouri. The order for this change was issued by the President, through General Grant. The letter from Grant to the President, which has been quoted above, was not the only protest he made against this; but on the first receipt of the order, he also wrote as follows: —

HEADQUARTERS ARMIES OF THE UNITED STATES,
WASHINGTON, D. C., August 17, 1867.

HIS EXCELLENCY ANDREW JOHNSON,
*President of the United States.*

SIR: I am in receipt of your order of this date, directing the assignment of General G. H. Thomas to the command of the Fifth Military District; General Sheridan to the Department of the Missouri, and General Hancock to the Department of the Cumberland; also your note of this date (enclosing these instructions), saying, "Before you issue instructions to carry into effect the enclosed order, I would be pleased to hear any suggestions you may deem necessary respecting the arrangements to which the order refers."

I am pleased to avail myself of this invitation to urge, earnestly urge — urge in the name of a patriotic people who have sacrificed hundreds of thousands of loyal lives and thousands of millions of treasure to preserve the integrity and union of this country — that this order be not insisted on. It is unmistakably the expressed wish of the country that General Sheridan should not be removed from his present command. This is a republic where the will of the people is the law of the land. I beg that their voice may be heard.

General Sheridan has performed his civil duties faithfully and intelligently. His removal will only be regarded as an effort to defeat the laws of Congress. It will be interpreted by the unreconstructed element in the South — those who did all they could to break up this government by arms, and now wish to be the only element consulted as to the method of restoring order — as a triumph. It will embolden them to renewed opposition to the will of the loyal masses, believing that they have the Executive with them.

The services of General Thomas, in battling for the Union, entitle him to some consideration. He has repeatedly entered his protest against being assigned to either of the five military districts, and especially to being assigned to relieve General Sheridan.

General Hancock ought not to be removed from where he is. His department is a complicated one, which will take a new commander some time to become acquainted with.

There are military reasons, pecuniary reasons, why this order should not be insisted on.

I beg to refer to a letter (marked private) which I wrote to the President when first consulted on the subject of the change in the War Department. It bears upon the subject of this removal, and I had hoped would have prevented it.

I have the honor to be, with great respect,

Your obedient servant,

U. S. GRANT, *General U. S. Army, and*
*Secretary of War ad interim.*

In September of this year there was great fear felt lest there should be violence grow out of the political excitement incident to an election in Nashville, Tennessee. Grant ordered General Thomas, with troops, to proceed to this point, and his instructions were strictly to not interfere in any way between the parties, but only to put down violence, if it should break out. Fortunately the election passed off quietly; and the circumstance is not worth mentioning here, except as it affords another instance of the wise, conciliatory, and entirely impartial course Grant has always pursued, in the cases where his military duties have brought him into collision with the civil authorities. His position is plain: violence must be put down promptly; and it is only wanting for the South to show that they are able to conduct their affairs peaceably, and that the presence of the military is not necessary in order to secure and guarantee freedom of action to all parties, to have the military power withdrawn.

On the reassembling of Congress, the Senate refused to acquiesce in the removal of Stanton as Secretary of War, and on the reception of an official notice from that body to this effect, Grant immediately surrendered the office to Stanton, who was thus declared its legal occupant. Shortly after this, a correspondence, which will be found in the Appendix, took place between the President and General Grant, in which the President seeks to show that Grant had not treated him with perfect fairness. This charge Grant repudiates, and the President attempts to further maintain by obtaining and publishing the recollections of the conversation, concerning which the disagreement has arisen, of those members of his cabinet who were present. The whole matter is of very slight importance, except that it shows what are some of the pitfalls which lie in the path of a straightforward man, when he wanders in the company of politicians in Washington. The President and his friends say that their recollection of what Grant said is so and so, while Grant says he said nothing which could mean what they say they remember he said. In such a matter of contradiction, it is not strength of assertion, but the character of the assertor, that must carry the day; and in this view of the case there can be no doubt who was right.

## CHAPTER L.

### PERSONAL APPEARANCE AND CHARACTERISTICS.

WE have thus passed in review the record of Grant's public life, and have found that from the first to the last, as a soldier and a statesman, his chief characteristic is action. Calm, self-reliant, persistent, he accepts any duty laid upon him, and with a singleness of purpose devotes his whole energies to its accomplishment. While singularly free from the narrowness of mind which generally distinguishes men who are only persistent, he is equally free from the personal vanity and self-conceit which passes generally for self-reliance. At the beginning of the war his services in organizing the volunteer troops in Illinois were hardly recognized at first, and it was only when the result of his ability was seen in the discipline and effectiveness of his men, that he began to be appreciated. The same simple straightforward reliableness has characterized his entire career. Paducah, Belmont, Donelson, Shiloh, Vicksburg, Chattanooga, Richmond, Washington, — these names recall the almost uninterrupted course of his victories as a soldier and statesman. While never thrusting himself officiously forward, he is patient under misconception and misrepresentation, as only a man who is conscious of doing his duty, and whose ambition is not a merely personal one, can be.

In person Grant is about the middle height, is solidly and compactly built, can bear great fatigue, and a long-continued strain upon his energies. His hair is light brown and abundant, his eyes are blue, while his beard and mustache are heavy and reddish. These last he keeps trimmed short. His face has become familiar to the people of the country from the numerous portraits of all kinds which have been made of him. The best of these is a steel portrait engraved by Marshall, whose fine likeness of Lincoln is the best we have of him. Both of these engravings are made from likenesses painted by Mr. Marshall himself, who is as skilful with his brush as with his burin. General Sheridan, on seeing this portrait of Grant, pronounced it unquestionably the best ever made of the General. Besides this, there is a life-size wood-cut made by Mr. A. G. Holcomb, which, from its greater cheapness, will be more extensively circulated, and which, in its branch of art, is equally commendable. Both of these portraits represent Grant as he is — a simple and unpretending man, with nothing of the traditional hero about him; but a glance at his face shows that he can be relied upon.

In his manners Grant is mild, even during the moments of greatest excitement, and is readily approached by every one, since he surrounds himself with none of the conventionalities of rank or position. Mr. Marshall, while painting the portrait, in 1866, from which his likeness is engraved, expressed a desire that General Grant should give him a sitting in the uniform of his rank. "Why," said the Lieutenant General, "the fact is, that I have not yet had a coat made according to the regulation; but you can take the old one, and put the necessary changes in it." A correspondent thus described him at the battle of Chattanooga: "He was there to be seen enveloped in a rather huge military coat, wearing a slouching hat, which seemed to have a predisposition to turn up before and down behind, with a gait slightly limping, from his accident at New Orleans, giving his orders with as few words as possible, in a low tone, and with an accent which partook of the slight nervousness, intensity of feeling, yet perfect self-command, seen in all his movements. General Grant might be described best as a little old man — yet not really old — who, with a keen eye, did not intend that anything should escape his observation. At that battle he was not in his usual physical condition, his recent illness, added to his arduous labors, having made him lean in flesh, and given a sharpness to his features which he did not formerly have. Those features, however, go far to define the man of will and self-control that he is. At the critical moment of the day's operations, the muscles appeared to gather tighter and harder over his slightly projecting chin, which seems to have an involuntary way of working, and the lips to contract. There is in what he does or says nothing that has the slightest approach to ostentation or show, but the palpable evidence of a plain man of sense, will, and purpose, who has little idea that more eyes are turned on him than on any other man on the continent."

One of his staff officers writes of him thus, in private life: "If you could see the General as he sits just over beyond me, with his wife and two children, looking more like a chaplain than a General, with that quiet air so impossible to describe, you would not ask me if he drinks. He rarely ever uses intoxicating liquors; more moderate in his habits and desires than any other man I ever knew; *more pure and spotless in his private character than almost any man I ever knew;* more brave than any man I ever saw; with more power to command and ability to plan than any man I ever served under; cool to excess, when others lose nerve, always hopeful, always undisturbed, never failing to accomplish what he undertakes just as he expects to. He is the only General worthy to command Americans fighting for their national salvation."

Of his bravery there can be no doubt, as it has been shown on all occasions. "I was at West Point," said General Sherman at a public dinner at Memphis, in 1864, "with General Grant. The General is not a man of remarkable learning, but *he is one of the bravest I ever saw.* He smokes his cigar with coolness in the midst of flying shot. *He has no fear, because he is an honest man.* I like Grant. I do not say he is a hero; I do not believe in heroes; but I know he is a gentleman, and a good man."

Grant's great passion is horses, and this tendency he has shown from his childhood. He makes friends with them, and they with him. There is a fine touch of quiet sarcastic humor in the facility with which he turns the conversation upon horses, when officious intruders attempt to sound him on political subjects. His taciturnity is a quality which has excited the most surprise and comment from the politicians. This species of man, characterized by Carlyle as "spouting wretches," have increased so marvellously under our free institutions, and are so constantly intent on attracting attention to themselves, by proclaiming and explaining themselves aloud, in season and out of season, by defining their position, and by all the demagogic arts for obtaining notoriety, that they cannot understand a man who can hold his peace; and silence is generally a proof to them that a man has neither opinions nor a mind capable of forming them. But it is not from any such reason that Grant is silent. His forte lies in action, not in words. And any one who will follow carefully his record will find that he has very decided opinions, that they are very decidedly on the side of right, and that he does not hesitate to express them by his actions, in the most decided manner, when the proper occasion for so doing occurs. But a few years ago unknown, he has risen, without the adventitious aid of friends, by the expression of his opinions in action, to the present position which he holds as the foremost man in this nation. That he is the fittest man among us to express in action the spirit of the nineteenth century, here in the United States, seems to be the almost universal opinion. While the country owes him a debt it can neither estimate nor discharge, for his services both in the field and in the cabinet, he has himself been educated by the popular movement during the past few years. It is earnestly to be hoped that this mutual recognition and influence may not be destroyed or diminished, but that in the future, as in the past, this nation may be found in the van of the world's progress towards the realization of the democratic idea, and Grant be found its leader, in this noble task.

# APPENDIX.

## I.

### THE CAPTURE OF FORT DONELSON.

### GENERAL GRANT'S REPORT.

HEADQUARTERS ARMY IN THE FIELD,
FORT DONELSON, February 16, 1862.

GENERAL G. W. CULLUM,
*Chief of Staff, Department of Missouri.*

GENERAL: I am pleased to announce to you the unconditional surrender, this morning, of Fort Donelson, with twelve to fifteen thousand prisoners, at least forty pieces of artillery, and a large amount of stores, horses, mules, and other public property.

I left Fort Henry on the 12th instant, with a force of about fifteen thousand men, divided into two divisions, under the command of Generals McClernand and Smith. Six regiments were sent around by water the day before, convoyed by a gunboat, or rather started one day later than one of the gunboats, with instructions not to pass it.

The troops made the march in good order, the head of the column arriving within two miles of the fort at twelve o'clock M. At this point the enemy's pickets were met and driven in.

The fortifications of the enemy were from this point gradually approached and surrounded, with occasional skirmishing on the line. The following day, owing to the non-arrival of the gunboats and reënforcements sent by water, no attack was made; but the investment was extended on the flanks of the enemy, and drawn closer to his works, with skirmishing all day. The evening of the

13th, the gunboats and reënforcements arrived. On the 14th, a gallant attack was made by Flag-officer Foote upon the enemy's works with his fleet. The engagement lasted, probably, one hour and a half, and bade fair to result favorably to the cause of the Union, when two unlucky shots disabled two of the armored gunboats, so that they were carried back by the current. The remaining two were very much disabled also, having received a number of heavy shots about the pilot-house and other parts of the vessels. After these mishaps, I concluded to make the investment of Fort Donelson as perfect as possible, and partially fortify and await repairs to the gunboats. This plan was frustrated, however, by the enemy making a most vigorous attack upon our right wing, commanded by General J. A. McClernand, with a portion of the force under General L. Wallace. The enemy were repelled after a closely-contested battle of several hours, in which our loss was heavy. The officers, and particularly field-officers, suffered out of proportion. I have not the means yet of determining our loss, even approximately, but it cannot fall far short of one thousand two hundred killed, wounded, and missing. Of the latter, I understand through General Buckner, about two hundred and fifty were taken prisoners. I shall retain enough of the enemy to exchange for them, as they were immediately shipped off, and not left for recapture.

About the close of this action the ammunition in the cartridge-boxes gave out, which, with the loss of many of the field-officers, produced great confusion in the ranks. Seeing that the enemy did not take advantage of this fact, I ordered a charge upon the left — enemy's right — with the division under General C. F. Smith, which was most brilliantly executed, and gave to our arms full assurance of victory. The battle lasted until dark, giving us possession of part of their intrenchments. An attack was ordered upon their other flank, after the charge of General Smith was commenced, by the divisions under Generals McClernand and Wallace, which, notwithstanding the hours of exposure to a heavy fire in the fore part of the day, was gallantly made, and the enemy further repulsed. At the points thus gained, night having come on, all the troops encamped for the night, feeling that a complete victory would crown their labors at an early hour in the morning. This morning, at a very early hour, General S. B. Buckner sent a message to our camp, under a flag of truce, proposing an armistice, &c. A copy of the correspondence which ensued is herewith accompanied.

I cannot mention individuals who specially distinguished themselves, but leave that to division and brigade officers, whose reports will be forwarded as soon as received. To division commanders, however, Generals McClernand, Smith, and Wallace, I must do the justice to say that each of them were with their commands in the midst of danger, and were always ready to execute all orders, no matter what the exposure to themselves.

At the hour the attack was made on General McClernand's command, I was absent, having received a note from Flag-officer Foote, requesting me to go and see him, he being unable to call.

My personal staff, — Colonel J. D. Webster, Chief of Staff; Colonel J. Riggin, Jr., Volunteer Aid; Captain J. A. Rawlins, A. A. General; Captains C. B. Lagow and W. S. Hillyer, Aids, and Lieutenant Colonel V. B. McPherson, Chief Engineer, — all are deserving of personal mention for their gallantry and services.

For full details and reports and particulars, reference is made to the reports of the Engineer, Medical Director, and commanders of brigades and divisions, to follow.

I am, General, very respectfully,

Your obedient servant,

U. S. GRANT, *Brigadier General.*

## REBEL REPORTS.

### JEFF. DAVIS'S MESSAGE ACCOMPANYING THE REPORTS.

EXECUTIVE DEPARTMENT, March 11, 1862.

TO THE SPEAKER OF THE HOUSE OF REPRESENTATIVES.

I transmit herewith copies of such official reports as have been received at the War Department, of the defence and fall of Fort Donelson.

They will be found incomplete and unsatisfactory. Instructions have been given to furnish further information upon the several points not made intelligible by the reports. It is not stated that reënforcements were at any time asked for; nor is it demonstrated to have been impossible to have saved the army by evacuating the position; nor is it known by what means it was found practicable to withdraw a part of the garrison, leaving the remainder to surrender; nor upon what authority or principles of action the senior General abandoned responsibility by transferring the command to a junior officer.

In a former communication to Congress, I presented the propriety of a suspension of judgment in relation to the disaster at Fort Donelson, until official reports could be received. I regret that the information now furnished is so defective. In the mean time, hopeful that satisfactory explanation may be made, I have directed, upon the exhibition of the case as presented by *the two senior Generals, that they should be relieved from command*, to await further orders whenever a reliable judgment can be rendered on the merits of the case.

JEFFERSON DAVIS.

## EXTRACTS FROM THE REPORT OF JOHN B. FLOYD.

CAMP NEAR MURFREESBORO', February 27, 1862.

GENERAL A. S. JOHNSTON.

SIR: Your order of the 12th of this month, transmitted to me by telegraph from Bowling Green to Cumberland City, reached me the same evening. It directed me to repair at once, with what force I could command, to the support of the garrison at Fort Donelson. I immediately prepared for my departure, and effected it in time to reach Fort Donelson the next morning, 13th, before daylight. Measures had been already taken by Brigadier General Pillow, then in command, to render our resistance to the attack of the enemy as effective as possible. He had, with activity and industry, pushed forward the defensive works towards completion.

. . . . . . . .

Soon after my arrival, the intrenchments were fully occupied from one end to the other; and just as the sun rose, the cannonade from one of the enemy's gunboats announced the opening of the conflict, which was destined to continue for three days and nights. In a very short time the fire became general along our whole lines, and the enemy, who had already planted batteries at several points around the whole circuit of our intrenchments, opened a general and active fire from all arms upon our trenches, which continued until darkness put an end to the conflict. They charged with uncommon spirit at several points along on the line, but most particularly at a point undefended by intrenchments, down a hollow which separated the right wing, under Brigadier General Buckner, from the right of the centre, commanded by Colonel Himan.

. . . . . .

The enemy continued their fire upon different parts of our intrenchments throughout the night, which deprived our men of every opportunity of sleep. We lay that night upon our arms in the trenches. We confidently expected, at the dawn of day, a more vigorous attack than ever; but in this we were entirely mistaken. The day advanced, and no preparation seemed to be making for a general onset. But an extremely annoying fire was kept up from the enemy's sharp-shooters throughout the whole length of the intrenchments, from their long-range rifles. Whilst this mode of attack was not attended with any considerable loss, it, nevertheless, confined the men to their trenches, and prevented their taking their usual rest.

. . . . . .

There was no place within our intrenchments but could be reached by the enemy's artillery from their boats or their batteries. It was but fair to infer that, while they kept up a sufficient fire upon our intrenchments, to keep our men from sleep and prevent repose, their object was merely to give time to pass a column above us on the river, both on the right and the left banks, and thus to cut off all our communications, and to prevent the possibility of egress. I thus saw clearly that but one course was left by which a rational hope could be entertained of saving the garrison, or a part of it. That was, to dislodge the enemy from his position on our left, and thus to pass our people into the open country lying southward towards Nashville. I called for a consultation of the officers of divisions and brigades, to take place after dark, when this plan was laid before them, approved and adopted, and at which it was determined to move from the trenches at an early hour on the next morning, and attack the enemy in his position.

. . . . . .

Our troops were completely exhausted by four days and nights of continued conflict. To renew it with any hope of successful result was obviously vain, and such I understood to be the unanimous opinion of all the officers present at the council called to consider what was best to be done. I thought, and so announced, that a desperate onset upon the right of the enemy's forces, on the ground where we had attacked them in the morning, might result in the extrication of a considerable proportion of the command from the position we were in, and this opinion I understood to be concurred in by all who were present. But it was likewise agreed, with the same unanimity, that it would result in the slaughter of nearly all who did not succeed in effecting their escape. The question then arose, whether, in point of humanity and a sound military policy, a course should be adopted from which the probabilities were, that the larger portion of the command would be cut to pieces in an unavailing fight against overwhelming numbers. I understood the general sentiment to be averse to the proposition. I felt that in this contingency, whilst it might be questioned whether I should, as commander of the army, lead it to certain destruction in an unavailing fight, yet I had a right, individually, to determine that I would not survive a surrender there. To satisfy both propositions, I agreed to hand over the command to Brigadier General Buckner, through Brigadier General Pillow, and to make an effort for my own extrication by any and every means that might present themselves to me.

I therefore directed Colonel Forrest, a daring and determined officer, at the head of an efficient regiment of cavalry, to be present for the purpose of accompanying me in what I supposed would be an effort to pass through the enemy's lines. I announced the fact, upon turning the command over to Brigadier General Buckner, that I would bring away with me, by any means I could, my own particular brigade, the propriety of which was acquiesced in on all hands. This, by various modes, I succeeded in accomplishing to a great extent.

. . . . . .

The command was turned over to Brigadier General Buckner, who at once opened negotiations with the enemy, which resulted in the surrender of the place.

JOHN B. FLOYD, *Brigadier General commanding.*

## EXTRACTS FROM GENERAL PILLOW'S REPORT.

COLUMBIA, TENNESSEE, February 18, 1862.

CAPTAIN CLARENCE DERRICK, *A. A. General.*

On the 18th instant General A. S. Johnston ordered me to proceed to Fort Donelson, and take command at that post. On the 19th instant I arrived at that place. In detailing the operations of the forces under my command at Fort Donelson, it is proper to state the condition of that work and of the forces constituting its garrison.

. . . . . .

The armament of the batteries consisted of eight thirty-two-pounders, three thirty-two pound carronades, one eight-inch columbiad, and one rifled gun of thirty-two pound calibre. The selection of the site for the work was an unfortunate one. While its command of the river was favorable, the site was commanded by the hills above and below on the river, and by a continuous range of hills all around the works to its rear.

A field-work of very contracted dimensions had been constructed for the garrison to protect the battery; but this field-work was commanded by the hills already referred to, and lay open to a fire of artillery from every direction except from the hills below. To guard against the effect of fire of artillery from these heights, a line of defence-work, consisting of rifle-pits and abatis for infantry, detached on our right, but continuous on our left, with defences for our light artillery, were laid off by Major Gilmer — engineer of General A. S. Johnston's staff, but on duty with me at the post — around the rear of the battery, and on the heights from which artillery could reach our battery and inner field-work, enveloping the inner work and the town of Dover, where our principal supplies of quartermaster and commissary stores were on deposit.

These works, pushed with the utmost possible energy, were not quite completed, nor my troops all in position, though nearly so, when Brigadier General Floyd, my senior officer, reached that station. The works were laid off with judgment and skill by Major Gilmer; were well executed, and designed for the defence of the rear of the works. . . .

I had placed Brigadier General Buckner in command of the right wing, and Brigadier General Johnson in command of the left.

By extraordinary efforts, we had barely got the works in a defensible condition, when the enemy made an advance in force around and against the entire line of our outer works.

The first assault was commenced by the enemy's artillery against the entire line of our left wing, which was promptly responded to by Captain Green's battery of field artillery. After several hours of firing between the artillery of the two armies, the enemy's infantry advanced to the conflict all along the line, which was kept up and increased in volume from one end of the line to the other for several hours, when at last the enemy made a vigorous assault against the right of our left wing.

. . . . . .

The result of the day's work pretty well tested the strength of our defensive lines, and established, beyond question, the gallantry of our entire command, all of which defended well their portion of the line. The loss sustained by our forces in this engagement was not large, our men being mostly under shelter of their rifle-pits; but we, nevertheless, had quite a number of killed and wounded; but owing to the continued fighting which followed, it was impossible to get any official report of the casualties of the day.

. . . . . .

On the 14th instant the enemy was busy throwing his forces of every arm around us, extending his line of investment around our position, and completely enveloping us. We were now surrounded by immense force, said by persons to amount to fifty-two regiments, and every road and possible avenue of departure were cut off, with the certainty that our sources of supply by the river would soon be cut off by the enemy's batteries placed upon the river above us.

At a meeting of the general officers, called by General Floyd, it was unanimously determined to give the enemy battle next day at daylight, so as to cut open a route of exit for our troops to the interior of the country, and thus to save our army. We had knowledge that the principal portion of the enemy's forces were massed in encampment in front of our extreme left, commanding the two roads leading into the interior, one of which we must take in leaving our position. We knew that he had massed in encampment another large force on the Union Ferry Road, opposite the centre of our left wing. His fresh arrival of troops which encamped on the bank of the river, two and a half miles below us, from which latter encampment a stream of fresh troops was continually pouring around us on his line of investment, and thus strengthening his general encampment on the extreme right. At each of his encampments and on each road he had a position, a battery of field artillery, and twenty-four pound iron guns on siege-carriages.

. . . . . .

The operations of the day had forced the entire command of the enemy around to our right wing, and in front of General Buckner's position in the intrenchments; and when his command reached his position he found the enemy rapidly advancing to take possession of this portion of his work. He had a stubborn conflict, lasting one and a half hours, to regain it, and the enemy actually got possession of the extreme right of his position, and he held it so firmly that he could not dislodge him. The position thus gained by the enemy was a most commanding one, being immediately on the rear of our river battery and field-work for its protection. From it he could readily turn the intrenched work occupied by General Buckner, and attack him in reverse, or advance under cover of an intervening ridge directly upon our battery and field-work. While he held this position, it was manifest we could not hold the main work or battery. Such was the condition of the armies at nightfall, after nine hours of severe conflict on the 15th instant.

. . . . . .

In this condition the general officers held a consultation to determine what we should do. General Buckner gave it as his decided opinion that he could not hold his position one half hour against an assault of the enemy, and said the enemy would attack him next morning at daylight. The proposition was then made by the undersigned to again fight our way through the enemy's line, and cut our way out. General Buckner said his command was so worn out and cut to pieces and demoralized, that he could not make another fight; that it would cost the command three quarters of its present number to cut its way through, and it was wrong to sacrifice three quarters of a command to save a quarter; that no officer had a right to cause such a sacrifice. General

Floyd and Major Gilmer I understood to concur in this opinion.

I then expressed the opinion that we could hold out another day, and in that time we could get steamboats and set the command over the river, and probably save a large portion of it. To this General Buckner replied that the enemy would certainly attack him at daylight, and that he could not hold his position half an hour.

The alternative of these propositions was a surrender of their position and command. General Floyd said that he would neither surrender the command, nor would he surrender himself a prisoner. I had taken the same position. General Buckner said he was satisfied nothing else could be done, and that, therefore, he would surrender if placed in command. General Floyd said he would turn over the command to him if he could be allowed to withdraw his command. To this General Buckner consented. Thereupon General Floyd turned the command over to me. I passed it instantly to General Buckner, saying I would neither surrender the command nor myself a prisoner. I directed Colonel Forrest to cut his way out. Under these circumstances General Buckner accepted the command, and sent a flag of truce to the enemy for an armistice for six hours to negotiate for terms of capitulation. Before this flag and communication were delivered, I retired from the garrison.

. . . . . . .

GID. J. PILLOW, *Brigadier General C. S. A.*

# II.

## LETTER FROM GENERAL SHERMAN CONCERNING THE BATTLE OF SHILOH, OR PITTSBURG LANDING.

HEADQUARTERS MILITARY DIVISION OF THE MISSISSIPPI.

PROFESSOR HENRY COPPEE, *Philadelphia.*

DEAR SIR: In the June number of the United States Service Magazine I find a brief sketch of Lieutenant General U. S. Grant, in which I see you are likely to perpetuate an error, which General Grant may not deem of sufficient importance to correct. To General Buell's noble, able, and gallant conduct you attribute the fact that the disaster of April 6, at Pittsburg Landing, was retrieved, and made the victory of the following day. As General Taylor is said in his later days to have doubted whether he was at the battle of Buena Vista at all, on account of the many things having transpired there, according to the historians, which he did not see, so I begin to doubt whether I was at the battle of Pittsburg Landing of modern description. But I was at the battles of April 6 and 7, 1862. General Grant visited my division in person about ten A. M., when the battle raged fiercest. I was then on the right. After some general conversation, he remarked that I was doing right in stubbornly opposing the progress of the enemy, and, in answer to my inquiry as to cartridges, told me he had anticipated their want, and given orders accordingly; he then said his presence was more needed over at the left. About two P. M. of the 6th, the enemy materially slackened his attack on me, and about four P. M. I deliberately made a new line behind McArthur's drill-field, placing batteries on chosen ground, repelled easily a cavalry attack, and watched the cautious approach of the enemy's infantry, that never dislodged me there. I selected that line in advance of a bridge across Snake Creek, by which we had all day been expecting the approach of Lewis Wallace's division from Crump's Landing. About five P. M., before the sun set, General Grant came again to me, and after hearing my report of matters, explained to me the situation of affairs on the left, which were not as favorable; still, the enemy had failed to reach the landing of the boats. We agreed that the enemy had expended the *furore* of his attack, and we estimated our loss, and approximated our then strength, including Lewis Wallace's fresh division, expected each minute. He then ordered me to get all things ready, and at daylight the next day to assume the offensive. That was before General Buell had arrived, but he was known to be near at hand. General Buell's troops took no essential part in the first day's fight; and Grant's army, though collected together hastily, green as militia, some regiments arriving without cartridges even, and nearly all hearing the dread sound of battle for the first time, had successfully withstood and repelled the first day's terrific onset of a superior enemy, well commanded and well handled. I know I had orders from General Grant to assume the offensive before I knew General Buell was on the west side of the Tennessee. I think General Buell, Colonel Fry, and others of General Buell's staff, rode up to where I was about sunset, about the time General Grant was leaving me. General Buell asked me many questions, and got of me a small map, which I had made for my own use, and told me that by daylight he could have eighteen thousand fresh men, which I knew would settle the matter.

I understood Grant's forces were to advance on the right of the Corinth road, and Buell's on the left; and accordingly, at daylight, I advanced my division by the flank, the resistance being trivial, up to the very spot where the day before the battle had been most severe, and then waited till near noon for Buell's troops to get up abreast, when the entire line advanced and recovered all the ground we had ever held. I know that, with the exception of one or two severe struggles, the fighting of April 7 was easy, as compared with that of April 6.

I never was disposed, nor am I now, to question anything done by General Buell and his army, and know that, approaching our field of battle from the rear, he encountered that sickening crowd of laggards and fugitives that excited his contempt and that of his army, who never gave full credit to those in the front line, who did fight hard, and who had, at four P. M., checked the enemy, and were preparing the next day to assume the offensive. I remember the fact the better from General Grant's anecdote of his Donelson battle, which he told me then for the first time — that at a certain period of the battle he saw that either side was ready to give way, if the other showed a bold front; and he determined to do that very thing — to advance on the enemy, when, as he prognosticated, the enemy surrendered. At four P. M. of April 6, he thought the appearances the same, and he judged, with Lewis Wallace's fresh division, and such of our startled troops as had recovered their equilibrium, he would be justified in dropping the defensive and assuming the offensive in the morning. And, I repeat, I received such orders before I knew General Buell's troops were at the river. I admit that I was glad Buell was there, because I knew his troops were older than ours, and better systematized and drilled; and his arrival made that certain which before was uncertain. I have heard this question much discussed, and must say that the officers of Buell's army dwelt too much on the stampede of some of our raw troops, and gave us too little credit for the fact that for one whole day, weakened as we were by the absence of Buell's army, long expected, of Lewis Wallace's division, only four miles off, and of the fugitives from our ranks, we had beaten off our assailants for the time. At the same time, our army of the Tennessee have indulged in severe criticisms at the slow approach of that army which knew the danger that threatened us from the concentrated armies of Johnston, Beauregard, and Bragg, that lay at Corinth. In a war like this, where opportunities for personal prowess are as plenty as blackberries to those who seek them at the front, all such criminations should be frowned down; and were it not for the military character of your journal, I would not venture to offer a correction to a very popular error.

I will also avail myself of this occasion to correct another very common mistake, in attributing to General Grant the selection of that battle-field. It was chosen by that veteran soldier, Major General Charles F. Smith, who ordered my division to disembark there, and strike for the Charleston Railroad. This order was subsequently modified, by his ordering Hurlbut's division to disembark there, and mine higher up the Tennessee, to the mouth of Yellow Creek, to strike the railroad at Burnsville. But floods prevented our reaching the railroad, when General Smith ordered me in person also to disembark at Pittsburg Landing, and take post well out, so as to make plenty of room, with Snake and Lick Creeks the flanks of a camp for the grand army of invasion.

It was General Smith who selected that field of battle, and it was well chosen. On any other we surely would have been overwhelmed, as both Lick and Snake Creeks forced the enemy to confine his movement to a direct front attack, which new troops are better qualified to resist than where the flanks are exposed to a real or chimerical danger. Even the divisions of that army were arranged in that camp by General Smith's order, my division forming, as it were, the outlying picket, whilst McClernand and Prentiss's were the real line of battle, with W. H. L. Wallace in support of the right wing, and Hurlbut of the left; Lewis Wallace's division being detached. All these subordinate dispositions were made by the order of General Smith, before General Grant succeeded him to the command of all the forces up the Tennessee — headquarters, Savannah. If there were any error in putting that army on the west side of the Tennessee, exposed to the superior force of the enemy also assembling at Corinth, the mistake was not General Grant's; but there was no mistake. It was necessary that a combat, fierce and bitter, to test the manhood of the two armies, should come off, and that was as good a place as any. It was not then a question of military skill and strategy, but of courage and pluck; and I am convinced that every life lost that day to us was necessary, for otherwise at Corinth, at Memphis, at Vicksburg, we would have found harder resistance, had we not shown our enemies that, rude and untutored as we then were, we could fight as well as they.

Excuse so long a letter, which is very unusual from me; but of course my life is liable to cease at any moment, and I happen to be a witness to certain truths which are now beginning to pass out of memory, and form what is called history.

I also take great pleasure in adding, that nearly all the new troops that at Shiloh drew from me official censure, have more than redeemed their good name; among them, that very regiment which first broke, the Fifty-third Ohio, Colonel Appen. Under another leader, Colonel Jones, it has shared every campaign and expedition of mine since, is with me now, and can march, and bivouac, and fight as well as the best regiment in this or any army. Its reputation now is equal to that of any from the State of Ohio.

I am, with respect, yours truly,

W. T. SHERMAN, *Major General.*

# III.

EXTRACTS FROM THE REMARKS OF HON. E. B. WASHBURNE, OF ILLINOIS, MADE IN THE HOUSE OF REPRESENTATIVES, MAY 2, 1862.

IN time came the operations up the Cumberland and Tennessee Rivers, and I state what I know. By a singular coincidence, on the 29th day of January last, without any suggestion from any source, General Grant and Commodore Foote, always acting in entire harmony, applied for permission to move up those rivers, which was granted. The gunboats and land forces moved up to Fort Henry. After that fort was taken, it was determined to attack Fort Donelson. The gunboats were to go round and up the Cumberland River, while the army was to move over land from Fort Henry to Fort Donelson.

The roads were the worst ever known, and almost any other general or any other troops would have despaired of moving. But they did move. If General Grant had been told that it was impossible to move his army there, he would have made a reply like to that of the royal Pompey, when he was told that his fleet could not sail: "It is necessary to sail, not necessary to live." It was necessary for this western army to march, but it was not necessary to live. The country knows the result — Donelson fell. The enemy, twenty thousand strong, behind his intrenchments, succumbed before the unrelenting bravery and vigor of our troops, no more than twenty-eight thousand engaged. We took there, not twelve thousand, nor fifteen thousand, but more than *sixteen thousand* prisoners. I have it from General Halleck, that we have actually paid transportation for more than sixteen thousand prisoners. That, in most countries, would have been called a most brilliant military achievement. Napoleon surrounded old Mack at Ulm, and captured twenty thousand or more prisoners, and that exploit has filled a great space in history.

While the capture of Donelson filled the country with joy, there was a cruel disposition to withhold from the commanding General the meed of gratitude and praise so justly his due. Captious criticisms were indulged in, that he did not make the attack properly, and that if he had done differently the work might have been better accomplished. It was not enough that he fought and gloriously conquered, but he ought to have done it differently, forsooth. Success could be no test of merit with him. That was the way the old Generals spoke of the young Napoleon when he was beating them in every battle, and carrying his eagles in triumph over all Europe. He did not fight according to the rules of war. But there was a more grievous suggestion touching the General's habits. It is a suggestion that has infused itself into the public mind everywhere. There never was a more cruel and atrocious slander upon a brave and noble-minded man. There is no more temperate man in the army than General Grant. He never indulges in the use of intoxicating liquors at all. He is an example of courage, honor, fortitude, activity, temperance, and modesty, for he is as modest as he is brave and incorruptible. To the bravery and fortitude of Lannes he adds the stern republican simplicity of Guvion St. Cyr. It is almost vain to hope that full justice will ever be done to men who have been thus attacked. Truth is slow upon the heels of falsehood. It has been well said that "falsehood will travel from Maine to Georgia while truth is putting on its boots."

Let no gentleman have any fears of General Grant. He is no candidate for the Presidency. He is no politician. Inspired by the noblest patriotism, he only desires to do his whole duty to his country. When the war shall be over he will return to his home, and sink the soldier in the simple citizen. Though living in the same town with myself, he has no political claims on me, for, so far as he is a politician, he belongs to a different party. He has no personal claims upon me more than any other constituent. But I came here to speak as an Illinoisian, proud of his noble and patriotic state; proud of its great history now being made up; proud, above all earthly things, of her brave soldiers, who are shedding their blood upon all the battle-fields of the republic. If the laurels of Grant shall ever be withered, it will not be done by the Illinois soldiers who have followed his victorious banner.

But to the victory at Pittsburg Landing, which has called forth such a flood of denunciation upon General Grant. When we consider the charges of bad generalship, incompetency, and surprise, do we not feel that "even the joy of the people is cruel"? As to the question of whether there was, or not, what might be called a surprise, I will not argue it; but even if there had been, General Grant is nowise responsible for it, for *he* was not surprised. He was at his headquarters at Savannah when the fight commenced. Those headquarters were established there, as being the most convenient point for all parts of his command. Some of the troops were at Crump's Landing, between Savannah and Pittsburg, and all the new arrivals were coming to Savannah. That was the proper place for the headquarters of the commanding General at that time. The General visited Pittsburg Landing and all the important points every day. The attack was made Sunday morning by a vastly superior force. In five minutes after the first firing was heard, General Grant and staff were on board a steamboat on the way to the battle-field; and instead of not reaching the field till ten o'clock, or, as has been still more falsely represented, till noon, I have a letter before me from one of his aids who was with him, and who says he arrived there at eight o'clock in the morning, and immediately assumed command. There he directed the movements, and was always on that part of the field where his presence was most required, exposing his life, and evincing in his dispositions the genius of the greatest commanders. With what desperate bravery that battle of Sunday was fought! What display of prowess and courage! What prodigies of valor! Our troops, less than forty thousand, attacked by more than eighty thousand of the picked men of the rebels, led by their most distinguished Generals!

But it is gravely charged by these military critics who sit by the fireside while our soldiers are risking their lives on the field of conflict, that Grant was to blame in having his troops on the same side of the river with the enemy. I suppose they would have the river interpose between our army and the enemy, and permit that enemy to intrench himself on the other side, and then undertake to cross in his face. It was, in the judgment of the best military men, a wise disposition of his forces, placing them where he did. To have done otherwise would have been like keeping the entire army of the Potomac on this side of the river, instead of crossing it when it could be done, and advancing on the other side.

After fighting all day with immensely superior numbers of the enemy, they only drove our forces back two and one half miles, and then it was to face the gunboats and the terrible batteries so skilfully arranged and worked by the gallant and accomplished officers, Webster and Callender, and which brought the countless host of the enemy to a stand. And when night came, this unconquerable army stood substantially triumphant on that bloody field. I am not here to speak disparagingly of the troops of any other state, but I will speak in praise of the troops of my own state. No Illinois regiment, no Illinois company, no Illinois soldier, fled from the battle-field. If any did flee, they were not from Illinois; and they would be the ones who, after their own flight, would seek to cover up their own disgrace, but only add to it by attacks upon an Illinois General.

Now, sir, I have something to say about the Generals and the soldiers who fought in the battle. I have a word to say about the brave McClernand, so lately our colleague here, who, as I learn from a man who was on the battle-field on that Sunday, was seen riding at the head of his division, holding his flag in the face of the enemy, daring them to come on. I would say something in relation to the bravery and skill of Hurlbut, from my own district, who commanded another division there, and won great glory. I would say something in defence of another man, who has been charged with having his division surprised, and having been taken prisoner at the time. I mean General Prentiss. I have a letter upon my desk which says, that instead of being surprised on Sunday morning, the writer saw him at half past two o'clock of that day fighting most gallantly at the head of his division. I rejoice to have this opportunity to make that statement in justice to a brave man and true soldier.

Sir, if I had time I would like to speak of others; I would speak of General Wallace, of my state, who fell nobly fighting at the head of his division, a soldier by nature, a pure and noble man, whose memory will be ever honored in Illinois. I would speak of the gallant Colonel Ellis, falling at the head of the Fifteenth, and of Major Goddard, of the same regiment, also killed; of Davis, of the Forty-sixth, terribly wounded while gallantly bearing in his own hands the colors of his regiment. I would speak of the deeds of valor of the lead-mine Forty-fifth, covering itself with undying honor; of Captains Connor and Johnson, falling at the head of their companies; of the genial and impetuous young Irishman, Lieutenant George Moore, mortally wounded; of Captains Wayne, and Nase, and Brownell, all killed. Nor would I fail to mention Brigadier-General McArthur and Acting Brigadier General Kirk, who boldly led their brigades everywhere where duty called and danger threatened, and were at last carried from the field badly wounded; and of Colonel Chetlain, of the old Twelfth, rising from a sick bed and entering into the thickest of the fight; and, too, I would like to speak of the dauntless valor of Rawlins, and Rowley, and Campbell, and of many others who distinguished themselves on that field.

I see before me my friend from Pennsylvania [Mr. McPherson], which reminds me of a friend of us both — young Baugher, a Lieutenant in the lead-mine regiment, who, wounded six times, refused to leave the field; and, when finally carried off, waved his sword in defiance to the enemy. But who shall attempt to do justice to the bravery of the soldiers and the daring and skill of the officers? Who shall describe all the valor exhibited on those days? Who shall presume to speak of all the glory won on that blood-stained field? I have spoken of those more particularly from my own part of the state; but it is because I know them best, and not because I claim more credit for them than I know to be due to the troops from all parts of the state. They all exhibited the same bravery, the same unbounded devotion, the same ardor in vindicating the honor and glory of the flag, and maintaining the prestige of our state.

Mr. WILSON. I desire to ask the gentleman whether he denies that the army was surprised at Pittsburg on the morning of Sunday.

Mr. WASHBURNE. I state that I have the fullest authority for making a substantial denial of that charge. I said, however, that I did not intend to argue that question; that it was not necessary for the defence of General Grant. But I say, whether there was a surprise or not, the manner in which all those gallant troops fought on that day has conferred upon them and upon the country imperishable renown.

Mr. WILSON. I desire to ask, admitting that it was a surprise, whose fault it was.

Mr. WASHBURNE. I suppose, if there had been a surprise, it would have been the fault of the man who commanded the division surprised. I come not here, however, to speak of the faults of anybody, but to do justice.

Mr. WILSON. I desire the gentleman to follow that a little further.

Mr. KELLOGG, of Illinois. I want to say a word before the gentleman from Iowa proceeds. My colleague [Mr. Washburne] has defended his friend well. I regret the disposition to find fault with our Generals in the field, who have done so nobly, so bravely, and so well. Let us remember only their prowess and their glory, and let there not be crimination and recrimination. Let us rather glory in the success of our arms in our brilliant achievements on the well-fought field, and say all have done well. I regret that this matter of crimination of officers in the field should be brought up.

Mr. WILSON. I will state that I fully concur in the remark of the gentleman from Illinois [Mr. Kellogg] last on the floor, that this matter ought not to have been brought up here; and I for one do not intend to join in any crimination or recrimination. I have thought the whole thing out of taste. I have thought it improper and uncalled for. There was no occasion for it at all that I can discover. No charge has been made here against General Grant or any other officer engaged in that contest, although there are very grave differences of opinion in relation to certain matters connected with the fight.

Mr. WASHBURNE. I cannot yield further. Whatever may be my friend's opinion on the subject, I say to him that whenever I find a General from my own state at the head of an army attacked as General Grant has been, I will feel myself called upon, in all places and upon all occasions, to defend him; and I think this is the best occasion I shall have, and I intend to avail myself of it. I believe, notwithstanding the desperate fighting on Sunday, and the partial repulse of our troops, that, aided by the fresh troops of the brave Lew. Wallace, that army could have whipped the enemy on Monday without further reënforcements. That army could never have been conquered. But I would not detract from the glorious fighting of Buell's troops on Monday, for they behaved with great gallantry, and fought bravely, successfully, and well. Justice must be done to all.

# IV.

## AN ESTIMATE OF THE NUMBER OF MEN IN PEMBERTON'S COMMAND DURING AND BEFORE THE SIEGE OF VICKSBURG.

THE records of the Commissary General of Prisoners show a total of forty-two thousand and fifty-nine prisoners captured during the Vicksburg campaign, after the 1st of May. As Grant lost in that time nearly nine thousand men in killed and wounded, it is fair to suppose that Pemberton and Johnston, so repeatedly and disastrously beaten, lost twelve thousand. Any one who has seen war is aware how small an estimate six thousand is for the stragglers in an unsuccessful campaign. The calculation is simple.

| | |
|---|---|
| Prisoners, . . . . . . . . . | 42,000 |
| Killed and wounded, . . . . . . | 12,000 |
| Stragglers, . . . . . . . . . | 6,000 |
| Total, . . . . . . . . . | 60,000 |

This estimate is proof of Pemberton's force at the beginning of the campaign. He surrendered thirty-two thousand men at Vicksburg; three thousand were captured at Champion's Hill; nearly two thousand at the Big Black Bridge; and at least two thousand others at Port Gibson and Raymond, and during the campaign and siege; while those who escaped with Loring from Champion's Hill could not have been fewer than four thousand.

| | |
|---|---|
| Surrendered at Vicksburg, . . . . . | 32,000 |
| Captured at Champion's Hill, . . . . | 3,000 |
| " " Big Black Bridge, . . . . | 2,000 |
| " " Port Gibson, &c., . . . . | 2,000 |
| Loring, . . . . . . . . . . | 4,000 |
| Killed and wounded in Pemberton's command, | 10,000 |
| Stragglers, . . . . . . . . . | 3,000 |
| Total, . . . . . . . . . | 56,000 |

There can no longer be a doubt that many rebel officials persistently and designedly misstated the numbers and losses in their armies. Doubtless in this they persuaded themselves that the end justified the means. But the possession of the records of both parties to the contest makes the fact plain. In this very instance, Pemberton stated in his official report, that his effective strength at the beginning of the siege was eighteen thousand five hundred men; and (May 14) that his whole available force, at the time of the battle of Champion's Hill, was sixteen thousand in the field, while seven thousand eight hundred were left to hold Vicksburg. He lost at least fifteen thousand men after this, and had thirty-two thousand to surrender two months later. — BADEAU, *Military History*.

---

## V.

### REPORT OF LIEUTENANT GENERAL GRANT, 1864-65.

HEADQUARTERS ARMIES OF THE UNITED STATES,
WASHINGTON, D. C., July 22, 1865.

SIR: I have the honor to submit the following report of the operations of the armies of the United States from the date of my appointment to command the same: —

From an early period in the rebellion I had been impressed with the idea that active and continuous operations of all the troops that could be brought into the field, regardless of season and weather, were necessary to a speedy termination of the war. The resources of the enemy and his numerical strength were far inferior to ours; but as an offset to this, we had a vast territory, with a population hostile to the government, to garrison, and long lines of river and railroad communications to protect, to enable us to supply the operating armies.

The armies in the east and west acted independently and without concert, like a balky team, no two ever pulling together, enabling the enemy to use to great advantage his interior lines of communication for transporting troops from east to west, reenforcing the army most vigorously pressed, and to furlough large numbers, during seasons of inactivity on our part, to go to their homes and do the work of producing for the support of their armies. It was a question whether our numerical strength and resources were not more than balanced by these disadvantages and the enemy's superior position.

From the first, I was firm in the conviction that no peace could be had that would be stable and conducive to the happiness of the people, both north and south, until the military power of the rebellion was entirely broken.

I therefore determined, first, to use the greatest number of troops practicable against the armed force of the enemy; preventing him from using the same force at different seasons against first one and then another of our armies, and the possibility of repose for refitting and producing necessary supplies for carrying on resistance. Second, to hammer continuously against the armed force of the enemy and his resources, until by mere attrition, if in no other way, there should be nothing left to him but an equal submission with the loyal section of our common country to the constitution and laws of the land.

These views have been kept constantly in mind, and orders given and campaigns made to carry them out. Whether they might have been better in conception and execution is for the people, who mourn the loss of friends fallen, and who have to pay the pecuniary cost, to say. All I can say is, that what I have done has been done conscientiously, to the best of my ability, and in what I conceived to be for the best interests of the whole country.

At the date when this report begins, the situation of the contending forces was about as follows: The Mississippi River was strongly garrisoned by Federal troops from St. Louis, Missouri, to its mouth. The line of the Arkansas was also held, thus giving us armed possession of all west of the Mississippi, north of that stream. A few points in Southern Louisiana, not remote from the river, were held by us, together with a small garrison at and near the mouth of the Rio Grande. All the balance of the vast territory of Arkansas, Louisiana, and Texas was in the almost undisputed possession of the enemy, with an army of probably not less than eighty thousand effective men, that could have been brought into the field had there been sufficient opposition to have brought them out. The *let-alone policy* had demoralized this force so that probably but little more than one half of it was ever present in garrison at any one time. But the one half, or forty thousand men, with the bands of guerrillas scattered through Missouri, Arkansas, and along the Mississippi River, and the disloyal character of much of the population, compelled the use of a large number of troops to keep navigation open on the river and to protect the loyal people to the west of it. To the east of the Mississippi we held substantially with the line of the Tennessee and Holston Rivers, running eastward to include nearly all of the State of Tennessee. South of Chattanooga, a small foothold had been obtained in Georgia, sufficient to protect East Tennessee from incursions from the enemy's force at Dalton, Georgia. West Virginia was substantially within our lines. Virginia, with the exception of the northern border, the Potomac River, a small area about the mouth of James River covered by the troops at Norfolk and Fort Monroe, and the territory covered by the army of the Potomac lying along the Rapidan, was in the possession of the enemy. Along the sea-coast footholds had been obtained at Plymouth, Washington, and Newbern, in North Carolina; Beaufort, Folly and Morris Islands, Hilton Head, Fort Pulaski, and Port Royal, in South Carolina; Fernandina and St. Augustine, in Florida. Key West and Pensacola were also in our possession, while all the important ports were blockaded by the navy. The accompanying map, a copy of which was sent to General Sherman and other commanders in March, 1864, shows by red lines the territory occupied by us at the beginning of the rebellion and at the opening of the campaign of 1864, while those in blue are the lines which it was proposed to occupy.

Behind the Union lines there were many bands of guerrillas, and a large population disloyal to the government, making it necessary to guard every foot of road or river used in supplying our armies. In the South a reign of military despotism prevailed, which made every man and boy capable of bearing arms a soldier, and those who could not bear arms in the field acted as provosts for collecting deserters and returning them. This enabled the enemy to bring almost his entire strength into the field.

The enemy had concentrated the bulk of his forces east of the Mississippi into two armies, commanded by Generals R. E. Lee and J. E. Johnston, his ablest and best Generals. The army commanded by Lee occupied the south bank of the Rapidan, extending from Mine Run westward, strongly intrenched, covering and defending Richmond, the rebel capital, against the army of the Potomac. The army under Johnston occupied a strongly intrenched position at Dalton, Georgia, covering and defending Atlanta, Georgia, a place of great importance as a railroad centre, against the armies under Major General W. T. Sherman. In addition to these armies, he had a large cavalry force under Forrest, in North-east Mississippi; a considerable force, of all arms, in the Shenandoah Valley, and in the western part of Virginia, and extreme eastern part of Tennessee; and also confronting our sea-coast garrisons, and holding blockaded ports where we had no foothold upon land.

These two armies, and the cities covered and defended by them, were the main objective points of the campaign.

Major General W. T. Sherman, who was appointed to the command of the military division of the Mississippi, embracing all the armies and territory east of the Mississippi River to the Alleghanies, and the department of Arkansas, west of the Mississippi, had the immediate command of the armies operating against Johnston.

Major General George G. Meade had the immediate command of the army of the Potomac, from where I exercised general supervision of the movements of all our armies.

General Sherman was instructed to move against Johnston's army, to break it up, and to go into the interior of the enemy's country as far as he could, inflicting all the damage he could upon their war resources; if the enemy in his front showed signs of joining Lee, to follow him up to the full extent of his ability, while I would prevent the concentration of Lee upon him if it was in the power of the army of the Potomac to do so. More specific written instructions were not given, for the reason that I had talked over with him the plans of the campaign, and was satisfied that he understood them, and would execute them to the fullest extent possible.

Major General N. P. Banks, then on an expedition up Red River against Shreveport, Louisiana (which had been organized previous to my appointment to command), was notified by me, on the 15th of March, of the importance it was that Shreveport should be taken at the earliest possible day, and that if he found that the taking of it would occupy from ten to fifteen days' more time than General Sherman had given his troops to be absent from their command, he would send them back at the time specified by General Sherman, even if it led to the abandonment of the main object of the Red River expedition, for this force was necessary to movements east of the Mississippi; that should his expedition prove successful, he would hold Shreveport and the Red River with such force as he might deem necessary, and return the balance of his troops to the neighborhood of New Orleans, commencing no move for the further acquisition of territory, unless it was to make that then held by him more easily held; that it might be a part of the spring campaign to move against Mobile; that it certainly would be if troops enough could be obtained to make it without embarrassing other movements; that New Orleans would be the point of departure for such an expedition; also, that I had directed General Steele to make a real move from Arkansas, as suggested by him (General Banks), instead of a demonstration, as Steele thought advisable.

On the 21st of March, in addition to the foregoing notification and directions, he was instructed as follows: —

1st. If successful in your expedition against Shreveport, that you turn over the defence of the Red River to General Steele and the navy.

2d. That you abandon Texas entirely, with the exception of your hold upon the Rio Grande. This can be held with four thousand men, if they will turn their attention immediately to fortifying their positions. At least one half of the force required for this service might be taken from the colored troops.

3d. By properly fortifying on the Mississippi River, the force to guard it from Port Hudson to New Orleans can be reduced to ten thousand men, if not to a less number. Six thousand more would then hold all the rest of the territory necessary to hold until active operations can be resumed west of the river. According to your last return, this would give you a force of over thirty thousand effective men, with which to move against Mobile. To this I expect to add five thousand men from Missouri. If, however, you think the force here stated too small to hold the territory regarded as necessary to hold possession of, I would say, concentrate at least twenty-five thousand men of your present command for operations against Mobile. With these and such additions as I can give you from elsewhere, lose no time in making a demonstration, to be followed by an attack upon Mobile. Two or more iron-clads will be ordered to report to Admiral Farragut. This gives him a strong naval fleet with which to coöperate. You can make your own arrangements with the admiral for his coöperation, and select your own line of approach. My own idea of the matter is, that Pascagoula should be your base; but, from your long service in the Gulf department, you will know best about the matter. It is intended that your movements shall be coöperative with movements elsewhere, and you cannot now start too soon. All I would now add is, that you commence the concentration of your forces at once. Preserve a profound secrecy of what you intend doing, and start at the earliest possible moment.

U. S. GRANT, *Lieutenant General.*

MAJOR GENERAL N. P. BANKS.

Major General Meade was instructed that Lee's army would be his objective point; that wherever Lee went he would go also. For his movement two plans presented themselves: one, to cross the Rapidan below Lee, moving by his right flank; the other, above, moving by his left. Each presented advantages over the other, with corresponding objections. By crossing above, Lee would be cut off from all chance of ignoring Richmond or going north on a raid. But if we took this route, all we did would have to be done whilst the rations we started with held out; besides, it separated us from Butler, so that he could not be directed how to coöperate. If we took the other route, Brandy Station could be used as a base of supplies until another was secured on the York or James River. Of these, however, it was decided to take the lower route.

The following letter of instruction was addressed to Major General B. F. Butler: —

FORT MONROE, VA., April 2, 1864.

GENERAL: In the spring campaign, which it is desirable shall commence at as early a day as practicable, it is proposed to have coöperative action of all the armies in the field, as far as this object can be accomplished.

It will not be possible to unite our armies into two or three large ones, to act as so many units, owing to the absolute necessity of holding on to the territory already taken from the enemy. But, generally speaking, concentration can be practically effected by armies moving to the interior of the enemy's country from the territory they have to guard. By such movement they interpose themselves between the enemy and the country to be guarded, thereby reducing the number necessary to guard important points, or at least occupy the attention of a part of the enemy's force, if no greater object is gained. Lee's army and Richmond being the greater objects towards which our attention must be directed in the next campaign, it is desirable to unite all the force we can against them. The necessity of covering Washington with the army of the Potomac, and of covering your department with your army, makes it impossible to unite these forces at the beginning of any move. I propose, therefore, what comes nearest this of anything that seems practicable. The army of the Potomac will act from its present base, Lee's army being the objective point. You will collect all the forces from your command that can be spared from garrison duty — I should say not less than twenty thousand effective men — to operate on the south side of James River, Richmond being your objective point. To the force you already have will be added about ten thousand men from South Carolina, under Major General Gillmore, who will command them in person. Major General W. F. Smith is ordered to report to you, to command the troops sent into the field from your own department.

General Gillmore will be ordered to report to you at Fortress Monroe, with all the troops on transports, by the 18th instant, or as soon thereafter as practicable. Should you not receive notice by that time to move, you will make such disposition of them and your other forces as you may deem best calculated to deceive the enemy as to the real move to be made.

When you are notified to move, take City Point with as much force as possible. Fortify, or rather intrench, at once, and concentrate all your troops for the field there as rapidly as you can. From City Point directions cannot be given at this time for your further movements.

The fact that has already been stated — that is, that Richmond is to be your objective point, and that there is to be coöperation between your force and the army of the Potomac — must be your guide. This indicates the necessity of your holding close to the south bank of the James River as you advance. Then, should the enemy be forced into his intrenchments in Richmond, the army of the Potomac would follow, and by means of transports the two armies would become a unit.

All the minor details of your advance are left entirely to your direction. If, however, you think it practicable to use your cavalry south of you, so as to cut the railroad about Hick's Ford about the time of the general advance, it would be of immense advantage.

You will please forward for my information, at the earliest practicable day, all orders, details, and instructions you may give for the execution of this order.

U. S. GRANT, *Lieutenant General.*

MAJOR GENERAL B. F. BUTLER.

On the 16th these instructions were substantially reiterated. On the 19th, in order to secure full coöperation between his army and that of General Meade, he was informed that I expected him to move from Fort Monroe the same day that General Meade moved from Culpeper. The exact time I was to telegraph him as soon as it was fixed, and that it would not be earlier than the 27th of April; that it was my intention to fight Lee between Culpeper and Richmond, if he would stand. Should he, however, fall back into Richmond, I would follow up and make a junction with his (General Butler's) army on the James River; that, could I be certain he would be able to invest Richmond on the south side, so as to have his left resting on the James above the city, I would form the junction there; that circumstances might make this course advisable anyhow; that he should use every exertion to secure footing as far up the south side of the river as he could, and as soon as possible after the receipt of orders to move; that if he could not carry the city, he should at least detain as large a force as possible.

In coöperation with the main movements against Lee and Johnston, I was desirous of using all other troops necessarily kept in departments remote from the fields of immediate operations, and also those kept in the background for the protection of our extended lines between the loyal states and the armies operating against them.

A very considerable force under command of Major General Sigel was so held for the protection of West Virginia, and the frontiers of Maryland and Pennsylvania. Whilst these troops could not be withdrawn to distant fields without exposing the north to invasion by comparatively small bodies of the enemy, they could act directly to their front, and give better protection than if lying idle in garrison. By such movement they would either compel the enemy to detach largely for the protection of his supplies and lines of communication, or he would lose them.

General Sigel was therefore directed to organize all his available force into two expeditions, to move from Beverly and Charleston, under command of Generals Ord and Crook, against the East Tennessee and Virginia Railroad. Subsequently, General Ord having been relieved at his own request, General Sigel was instructed, at his own suggestion, to give up the expedition by Beverly and to form two columns, one under General Crook, on the Kanawha, numbering about ten thousand men, and one on the Shenandoah, numbering about seven thousand men; the one on the Shenandoah to assemble between Cumberland and the Shenandoah, and the infantry and artillery advanced to Cedar Creek with such cavalry as could be made available at the moment, to threaten the enemy in the Shenandoah Valley, and advance as far as possible; while General Crook would take possession of Lewisburg with part of his force, and move down the Tennessee Railroad, doing as much damage as he could, destroying the New River Bridge and the salt-works at Saltville, Virginia.

Owing to the weather and bad condition of the roads, operations were delayed until the 1st of May, when, everything being in readiness and the roads favorable, orders were given for a general movement of all the armies not later than the 4th of May.

My first object being to break the military power of the rebellion and capture the enemy's important strongholds, made me desirous that General Butler should succeed in his movement against Richmond, as that would tend more than anything else, unless it were the capture of Lee's army, to accomplish this desired result in the east. If he failed, it was my determination, by hard fighting, either to compel Lee to retreat or to so cripple him that he could not detach a large force to go north and still retain enough for the defence of Richmond. It was well understood, by both Generals Butler and Meade, before starting on the campaign, that it was my intention to put both their armies south of the James River, in case of failure to destroy Lee without it.

Before giving General Butler his instructions, I visited him at Fort Monroe, and in conversation pointed out the apparent importance of getting possession of Petersburg and destroying railroad communication as far south as possible. Believing, however, in the practicability of capturing Richmond unless it was reenforced, I made that the objective point of his operations. As the army of the Potomac was to move simultaneously with him, Lee could not detach from his army with safety, and the enemy did not have troops elsewhere to bring to the defence of the city in time to meet a rapid movement from the north of James River.

I may here state that, commanding all the armies as I did, I tried, as far as possible, to leave General Meade in independent command of the army of the Potomac. My instructions for that army were all through him, and were general in their nature, leaving all the details and the execution to him. The campaigns that followed proved him to be the right man in the right place. His commanding always in the presence of an officer superior to him in rank, has drawn from him much of that public attention that his zeal and ability entitle him to, and which he would otherwise have received.

The movement of the army of the Potomac commenced early on the morning of the 4th of May, under the immediate direction and orders of Major General Meade, pursuant to instructions. Before night the whole army was across the Rapidan (the Fifth and Sixth Corps crossing at Germania Ford, and the Second Corps at United States Ford, the cavalry, under Major General Sheridan, moving in advance), with the greater part of its trains, numbering about four thousand wagons, meeting with but slight opposition. The average distance travelled by the troops that day was about twelve miles. This I regarded as a great success, and it removed from my mind the most serious apprehension I had entertained — that of crossing the river in the face of an active, large, well-appointed and ably-commanded army, and how so large a train was to be carried through a hostile country and protected. Early on the 5th, the advance corps (the Fifth, Major General G. K. Warren commanding) met and engaged the enemy outside his intrenchments near Mine Run. The battle raged furiously all day, the whole army being brought into the fight as fast as the corps could be got upon the field, which, considering the density of the forest and narrowness of the roads, was done with commendable promptness.

General Burnside, with the Ninth Corps, was, at the time the army of the Potomac moved, left with the bulk of his corps at the crossing of the Rappahannock River and Alexandria Railroad, holding the road back to Bull Run, with instructions not to move until he received notice that a crossing of the Rapidan was secured, but to move promptly as soon as such notice was received. This crossing he was apprised of on the afternoon of the 4th. By six o'clock of the morning of the 6th he was leading his corps into action near the Wilderness Tavern, some of his troops having marched a distance of over thirty miles, crossing both the Rappahannock and Rapidan Rivers. Considering that a large proportion, probably two thirds of his command, was composed of new troops, unaccustomed to marches and carrying the accoutrements of a soldier, this was a remarkable march.

The battle of the Wilderness was renewed by us at five o'clock on the morning of the 6th, and continued with unabated fury until darkness set in, each army holding substantially the same position that they had on the evening of the 5th. After dark the enemy made a feeble attempt to turn our right flank, capturing several hundred prisoners and creating considerable confusion. But the promptness of General Sedgwick, who was personally present and commanded that part of our line, soon reformed it and restored order. On the morning of the 7th, reconnoissances showed that the enemy had fallen behind his intrenched lines, with pickets to the front, covering a part of the battle-field. From this it was evident to my mind that the two days' fighting had satisfied him of his inability to further maintain the contest in the open field, notwithstanding his advantage of position, and that he would wait an attack behind his works. I therefore determined to push on, and put my whole force between him and Richmond; and orders were at once issued for a movement by his right flank. On the night of the 7th the march was commenced towards Spottsylvania Court-house, the Fifth Corps moving on the most direct road. But the enemy, having become apprised of our movement, and having the shorter line, was enabled to reach there first. On the 8th General Warren met a force of the enemy which had been sent out to oppose and delay his advance, to gain time to fortify the line taken up at Spottsylvania. This force was steadily driven back on the main force, within the recently constructed works, after considerable fighting, resulting in severe loss to both sides. On the morning of the 9th General Sheridan started on a raid against the enemy's lines of communication with Richmond. The Ninth, Tenth, and Eleventh were spent in manœuvring and fighting, without decisive results. Among the killed on the 9th was that able and distinguished soldier Major General John Sedgwick, commanding the Sixth Army Corps. Major General H. G. Wright succeeded him in command. Early on the morning of the 12th a general attack was made on the enemy in position. The Second Corps, Major General Hancock commanding, carried a salient of his line, capturing most of Johnston's division of Ewell's corps and twenty pieces of artillery. But the resistance was so obstinate that the advantage gained did not prove decisive. The 13th, 14th, 15th, 16th, 17th, and 18th were consumed in manœuvring and awaiting the arrival of reënforcements from Washington. Deeming it impracticable to make any further attack upon the enemy at Spottsylvania Court-house, orders were issued on the 18th with a view to a movement to the North Anna, to commence at twelve o'clock on the night of the 19th. Late in the afternoon of the 19th Ewell's corps came out of its works on our extreme right flank; but the attack was promptly repulsed, with heavy loss. This delayed the movement to the North Anna until the night of the 21st, when it was commenced. But the enemy, again having the shorter line, and being in possession of the main roads, was enabled to reach the North Anna in advance of us, and took position behind it. The Fifth Corps reached the North Anna on the afternoon of the 23d, closely followed by the Sixth Corps. The Second and Ninth Corps got up about the same time, the Second holding the railroad bridge and the Ninth lying between that and Jericho Ford. General Warren effected a crossing the same afternoon, and got a position without much opposition. Soon after getting into position he was violently attacked, but repulsed the enemy with great slaughter. On the 25th General Sheridan rejoined the army of the Potomac from the raid on which he started from Spottsylvania, having destroyed the depots at Beaver Dam and Ashland Stations, four trains of cars, large supplies of rations, and many miles of railroad track; recaptured about four hundred of our men, on their way to Richmond as prisoners of war; met and defeated the enemy's cavalry at Yellow Tavern; carried the first line of works around Richmond, but finding the second line too strong to be carried by assault, recrossed to the north bank of the Chickahominy at Meadow's Bridge, under heavy fire, and moved by a detour to Haxall's Landing, on the James River, where he communicated with General Butler. This raid had the effect of drawing off the whole of the enemy's cavalry force, and making it comparatively easy to guard our trains.

General Butler moved his main force up the James River, in pursuance of instructions, on the 4th of May, General Gillmore having joined him with the Tenth Corps. At the same time he sent a force of eighteen hundred cavalry, by way of West Point, to form a junction with him wherever he might get a foothold, and a force of three thousand cavalry, under General Kautz, from Suffolk, to operate against the roads south of Petersburg and Richmond. On the 5th he occupied, without opposition, both City Point and Bermuda Hundred, his movement being a complete surprise. On the 6th he was in position with his main army, and commenced intrenching. On the 7th he made a reconnoissance against the Petersburg and Richmond Railroad, destroying a portion of it after some fighting. On the 9th he telegraphed as follows:—

HEADQUARTERS NEAR BERMUDA LANDING, May 9, 1864.

Our operations may be summed up in a few words. With seventeen hundred cavalry we have advanced up the Peninsula, forced the Chickahominy, and have safely brought them to our present position. These were colored cavalry, and are now holding our advance pickets towards Richmond.

General Kautz, with three thousand cavalry from Suffolk, on the same day with our movement up James River, forced the Blackwater, burned the railroad bridge at Stony Creek, below Petersburg, cutting in two Beauregard's force at that point.

We have landed here, intrenched ourselves, destroyed many miles of railroad, and got a position which, with proper supplies, we can hold out against the whole of Lee's army. I have ordered up the supplies.

Beauregard, with a large portion of his force, was left south by the cutting of the railroads by Kautz. That portion which reached Petersburg under Hill I have whipped to-day, killing and wounding many, and taking many prisoners, after a severe and well-contested fight.

General Grant will not be troubled with any further reënforcements to Lee from Beauregard's force.

BENJAMIN F. BUTLER, *Major General.*

HON. E. M. STANTON, *Secretary of War.*

On the evening of the 13th and morning of the 14th he carried a portion of the enemy's first line of defences at Drury's Bluff, or Fort Darling, with small loss. The time thus consumed from the 6th lost to us the benefit of the surprise and capture of Richmond and Petersburg, enabling, as it did, Beauregard to collect his loose forces in North and South Carolina, and bring them to the defence of those places. On the 16th the enemy attacked General Butler in his position in front of Drury's Bluff. He was forced back, or drew back, into his intrenchments between the forks of the James and Appomattox Rivers, the enemy intrenching strongly in his front, thus covering his railroads, the city, and all that was valuable to him. His army, therefore, though in a position of great security, was as completely shut off from further operations directly against Richmond as if it had been in a bottle strongly corked. It required but a comparatively small force of the enemy to hold it there.

On the 12th General Kautz, with his cavalry, was started on a raid against the Danville Railroad, which he struck at Coalfield, Powhatan, and Chola Stations, destroying them, the railroad track, two freight trains, and one locomotive, together with large quantities of commissary and other stores; thence crossing to the Southside road, struck it at Wilson's, Wellsville, and Black and White Stations, destroying the road and station-houses; thence he proceeded to City Point, which he reached on the 18th.

On the 19th of April, and prior to the movement of General Butler, the enemy, with a land force under General Hoke, and an iron-clad ram, attacked Plymouth, N. C., commanded by General H. W. Wessels, and our gunboats there; and after severe fighting the place was carried by assault, and the entire garrison and armament captured. The gunboat Smithfield was sunk and the Miami disabled.

The army sent to operate against Richmond having hermetically sealed itself up at Bermuda Hundred, the enemy was enabled to bring the most, if not all, the reënforcements brought from the South by Beauregard against the army of the Potomac. In addition to this reënforcement, a very considerable one, probably not less than fifteen thousand men, was obtained by calling in the scattered troops under Breckinridge from the western part of Virginia.

The position at Bermuda Hundred was as easy to defend as it was difficult to operate from against the enemy. I determined, therefore, to bring from it all available forces, leaving enough only to secure what had been gained; and accordingly, on the 22d, I directed that they be sent forward, under command of Major General W. F. Smith, to join the army of the Potomac.

On the 24th of May the Ninth Army Corps, commanded by Major General A. E. Burnside, was assigned to the army of the Potomac, and from this time forward constituted a portion of Major General Meade's command.

Finding the enemy's position on the North Anna stronger than either of his previous ones, I withdrew on the night of the 26th to the north bank of the North Anna, and moved via Hanovertown to turn the enemy's position by his right.

Generals Torbert's and Merritt's divisions of cavalry, under Sheridan, and the Sixth Corps, led the advance; crossed the Pamunkey River at Hanovertown, after considerable fighting, and on the 28th the two divisions of cavalry had a severe but successful engagement with the enemy at Haw's Shop. On the 29th and 30th we advanced, with heavy skirmishing, to the Hanover Courthouse and Cold Harbor road, and developed the enemy's position north of the Chickahominy. Late on the evening of the last day the enemy came out and attacked our left, but was repulsed with very considerable loss. An attack was immediately ordered by General Meade along his whole line, which resulted in driving the enemy from a part of his intrenched skirmish line.

On the 31st General Wilson's division of cavalry destroyed the railroad bridges over the South Anna River, after defeating the enemy's cavalry. General Sheridan on the same day reached Cold Harbor, and held it until relieved by the Sixth Corps and General Smith's command, which had just arrived, via White House, from General Butler's army.

On the 1st day of June an attack was made at five P. M. by the Sixth Corps and the troops under General Smith, the other corps being held in readiness to advance on the receipt of orders. This resulted in our carrying and holding the enemy's first line of works in front of the right of the Sixth Corps and in front of General Smith. During the attack the enemy made repeated assaults on each of the corps not engaged in the main attack, but were repulsed with heavy loss in every instance. That night he made several assaults to regain what he had lost in the day, but failed. The 2d was spent in getting troops into position for an attack on the 3d. On the 3d of June we again assaulted the enemy's works, in the hope of driving him from his position. In this attempt our loss was heavy, while that of the enemy, I have reason to believe, was comparatively light. It was the only general attack made from the Rapidan to the James which did not inflict upon the enemy losses to compensate for our own losses. I would not be understood as saying that all previous attacks resulted in victories to our arms, or accomplished as much as I had hoped from them; but they inflicted upon the enemy severe losses, which tended, in the end, to the complete overthrow of the rebellion.

From the proximity of the enemy to his defences around Richmond, it was impossible by any flank movement to interpose between him and the city. I was still in a condition to either move by his left flank and invest Richmond from the north side, or continue my move by his right flank to the south side of the James. While the former might have been better as a covering for Washington, yet a full survey of all the ground satisfied me that it would be impracticable to hold a line north and east of Richmond that would protect the Fredericksburg Railroad — a long, vulnerable line, which would exhaust much of our strength to guard, and that would have to be protected to supply the army, and would leave open to the enemy all his lines of communication on the south side of the James. My idea, from the start, had been to beat Lee's army north of Richmond if possible; then, after destroying his lines of communication north of the James River, to transfer the army to the south side, and besiege Lee in Richmond, or follow him south if he should retreat. After the battle of the Wilderness it was evident that the enemy deemed it of the first importance to run no risks with the army he then had. He acted purely on the defensive behind breastworks, or feebly on the offensive immediately in front of them, and where, in case of repulse, he could easily retire behind them. Without a greater sacrifice of life than I was willing to make, all could not be accomplished that I had designed north of Richmond. I therefore determined to continue to hold substantially the ground we then occupied, taking advantage of any favorable circumstances that might present themselves, until the cavalry could be sent to Charlottesville and Gordonsville, to effectually break up the railroad connection between Richmond and the Shenandoah Valley and Lynchburg; and, when the cavalry got well off, to move the army to the south side of the James River, by the enemy's right flank, where I felt I could cut off all his sources of supply except by the canal.

On the 7th two divisions of cavalry, under General Sheridan, got off on the expedition against the Virginia Central Railroad, with instructions to Hunter, whom I hoped he would meet near Charlottesville, to join his forces to Sheridan's, and after the work laid out for them was thoroughly done, to join the army of the Potomac by the route laid down in Sheridan's instructions.

On the 10th of June General Butler sent a force of infantry under General Gillmore, and cavalry under General Kautz, to capture Petersburg, if possible, and destroy the railroad and common bridges across the Appomattox. The cavalry carried the works on the south side, and penetrated well in towards the town, but were forced to retire. General Gillmore, finding the works which he approached very strong, and deeming an assault impracticable, returned to Bermuda Hundred without attempting one.

Attaching great importance to the possession of Petersburg, I sent back to Bermuda Hundred and City Point General Smith's command by water, via the White House, to reach there in advance of the army of the Potomac. This was for the express purpose of securing Petersburg before the enemy, becoming aware of our intention, could reënforce the place.

The movement from Cold Harbor commenced after dark on the evening of the 12th; one division of cavalry (under General Wilson) and the Fifth Corps crossed the Chickahominy at Long Bridge, and moved out to White Oak Swamp, to cover the crossings of the other corps. The advance corps reached James River, at Wilcock's Landing and Charles City Court-house on the night of the 13th.

During three long years the armies of the Potomac and Northern Virginia had been confronting each other. In that time they had fought more desperate battles than it probably ever before fell to the lot of two armies to fight, without materially changing the vantage-ground of either. The southern press and people, with more shrewdness than was displayed in the North, finding that they had failed to capture Washington and march on to New York, as they had boasted they would do, assumed that they only defended their capital and southern territory. Hence Antietam, Gettysburg, and all the other battles that had been fought, were by them set down as failures on our part, and victories for them. Their army believed this. It produced a *morale* which could only be overcome by desperate and continuous hard fighting. The battles of the Wilderness, Spottsylvania, North Anna, and Cold Harbor, bloody and terrible as they were on our side, were even more damaging to the enemy, and so crippled him as to make him wary ever after of taking the offensive. His losses in men were probably not so great, owing to the fact that we were, save in the Wilderness, almost invariably the attacking party; and when he did attack, it was in the open field. The details of these battles, which for endurance and bravery on the part of the soldiery have rarely been surpassed, are given in the report of Major General Meade, and the subordinate reports accompanying it.

During the campaign of forty-three days, from the Rapidan to James River, the army had to be supplied from an ever-shifting base, by wagons, over narrow roads, through a densely-wooded country, with a lack of wharves at each new base from which to conveniently discharge vessels. Too much credit cannot, therefore, be awarded to the quartermaster and commissary departments for the zeal and efficiency displayed by them. Under the general supervision of the chief Quartermaster, Brigadier General R. Ingalls, the trains were made to occupy all the available roads between the army and our water base, and but little difficulty was experienced in protecting them.

The movement of the Kanawha and Shenandoah Valleys, under General Sigel, commenced on the 1st of May. General Crook, who had the immediate command of the Kanawha expedition, divided his forces into two columns, giving one, composed of cavalry, to General Averill. They crossed the mountains by separate routes. Averill struck the Tennessee and Virginia Railroad, near Wytheville, on the 10th, and proceeding to New River and Christiansburg, destroyed the road, several important bridges and depots, including New River Bridge, forming a junction with Crook at Union on the 15th. General Sigel moved up the Shenandoah Valley, met the enemy at New Market on the 15th, and, after a severe engagement, was defeated with heavy loss, and retired behind Cedar Creek. Not regarding the operations of General Sigel as satisfactory, I asked his removal from command, and Major General Hunter was appointed to supersede him. His instructions were embraced in the following despatches to Major General H. W. Halleck, chief of staff of the army: —

NEAR SPOTTSYLVANIA COURT-HOUSE, VA., May 20, 1864.

. . . . .

The enemy are evidently relying for supplies greatly on such as are brought over the branch road running through Staunton. On the whole, therefore, I think it would be better for General Hunter to move in that direction; reach Staunton, and Gordonsville, or Charlottesville, if he does not meet too much opposition. If he can hold at bay a force equal to his own, he will be doing good service. . . .

U. S. GRANT, *Lieutenant General.*

MAJOR GENERAL H. W. HALLECK.

JERICHO FORD, VA., May 25, 1864.

If Hunter can possibly get to Charlottesville and Lynchburg, he should do so, living on the country. The railroads and canal should be destroyed beyond possibility of repairs for weeks. Completing this, he could find his way back to his original base, or from about Gordonsville join this army.

U. S. GRANT, *Lieutenant General.*

MAJOR GENERAL H. W. HALLECK.

General Hunter immediately took up the offensive, and moving up the Shenandoah Valley, met the enemy on the 5th of June at Piedmont, and after a battle of ten hours routed and defeated him, capturing on the field of battle fifteen hundred men, three pieces of artillery, and three hundred stand of small arms. On the 8th of the same month he formed a junction with Crook and Averill at Staunton, from which place he moved direct on Lynchburg, via Lexington, which place he reached and invested on the 16th day of June. Up to this time he was very successful; and but for the difficulty of taking with him sufficient ordnance stores over so long a march, through a hostile country, he would, no doubt, have captured that (to the enemy) important point. The destruction of the enemy's supplies and manufactories was very great. To meet this movement under General Hunter, General Lee sent a force, perhaps equal to a corps, a part of which reached Lynchburg a short time before Hunter. After some skirmishing on the 17th and 18th, General Hunter, owing to a want of ammunition to give battle, retired from before the place. Unfortunately, this want of ammunition left him no choice of route for his return but by way of Kanawha. This lost to us the use of his troops for several weeks from the defence of the North.

Had General Hunter moved by way of Charlottesville, instead of Lexington, as his instructions contemplated, he would have been in a position to have covered the Shenandoah Valley against the enemy, should the force he met have seemed to endanger it. If it did not, he would have been within easy distance of the James River Canal, on the main line of communication between Lynchburg and the force sent for its defence. I have never taken exception to the operations of General Hunter, and I am not now disposed to find fault with him, for I have no doubt he acted within what he conceived to be the spirit of his instructions and the interests of the service. The promptitude of his movements and his gallantry should entitle him to the commendation of his country.

To return to the army of the Potomac: The Second Corps commenced crossing the James River on the morning of the 14th, by ferry-boats, at Wilcox's Landing. The laying of the pontoon bridge was completed about midnight of the 14th, and the crossing of the remainder of the army was rapidly pushed forward by both bridge and ferry.

After the crossing had commenced, I proceeded by a steamer to Bermuda Hundred, to give the necessary orders for the immediate capture of Petersburg.

The instructions to General Butler were verbal, and were for him to send General Smith immediately, that night, with all the troops he could give him without sacrificing the position he then held. I told him that I would return at once to the army of the Potomac, hasten its crossing, and throw it forward to Petersburg by divisions as rapidly as it could be done; that we could reënforce our armies more rapidly there than the enemy could bring troops against us. General Smith got off as directed, and confronted the enemy's pickets near Petersburg before daylight next morning, but, for some reason that I have never been able to satisfactorily understand, did not get ready to assault his main lines until near sundown. Then, with a part of his command only, he made the assault, and carried the lines north-east of Petersburg from the Appomattox River, for a distance of over two and a half miles, capturing fifteen pieces of artillery and three hundred prisoners. This was about seven P. M. Between the line thus captured and Petersburg there were no other works, and there was no evidence that the enemy had reënforced Petersburg with a single brigade from any source. The night was clear — the moon shining brightly — and favorable to further operations. General Hancock, with two divisions of the Second Corps, reached General Smith just after dark, and offered the service of these troops as he (Smith) might wish, waiving rank to the named commander, who, he naturally supposed, knew best the position of affairs, and what to do with the troops. But instead of taking these troops, and pushing at once into Petersburg, he requested General Hancock to relieve a part of his line in the captured works, which was done before midnight.

By the time I arrived the next morning the enemy was in force. An attack was ordered to be made at six o'clock that evening by the troops under Smith and the Second and Ninth Corps. It required until that time for the Ninth Corps to get up and into position. The attack was made as ordered, and the fighting continued with but little intermission until six o'clock the next morning, and resulted in our carrying the advance and some of the main works of the enemy to the right (our left) of those previously captured by General Smith, several pieces of artillery, and over four hundred prisoners.

The Fifth Corps having got up, the attacks were renewed and persisted in with great vigor on the 17th and 18th, but only resulted in forcing the enemy to an interior line, from which he could not be dislodged. The advantages in position gained by us were very great. The army then proceeded to envelop Petersburg towards the Southside Railroad, as far as possible, without attacking fortifications.

On the 6th, the enemy, to reënforce Petersburg, withdrew from a part of his intrenchment in front of Bermuda Hundred, expecting, no doubt, to get troops from north of the James to take the place of those withdrawn before we could discover it. General Butler, taking advantage of this, at once moved a force on the railroad between Petersburg and Richmond. As soon as I was apprised of the advantage thus gained, to retain it I ordered two divisions of the Sixth Corps, General Wright commanding, that were embarking at Wilcox's Landing, under orders for City Point, to report to General Butler, at Bermuda Hundred, of which General Butler was notified, and the importance of holding a position in advance of his present line urged upon him.

About two o'clock in the afternoon General Butler was forced back to the line the enemy had withdrawn from in the morning. General Wright, with his two divisions, joined General Butler on the forenoon of the 17th, the latter still holding with a strong picket line the enemy's works. But instead of putting these divisions into the enemy's works to hold them, he permitted them to halt and rest some distance in the rear of his own line. Between four and five o'clock in the afternoon the enemy attacked and drove in his pickets, and reoccupied his old line.

On the night of the 20th and morning of the 21st a lodgment was effected by General Butler, with one brigade of infantry, on the north bank of the James, at Deep Bottom, and connected the pontoon bridge with Bermuda Hundred.

On the 19th, General Sheridan, on his return from his expedition against the Virginia Central Railroad, arrived at the White House just as the enemy's cavalry was about to attack it, and compelled it to retire. The result of this expedition was, that General Sheridan met the enemy's cavalry near Trevillian Station on the morning of the 11th of June, whom he attacked, and after an obstinate contest drove from the field in complete rout. He left his dead and nearly all his wounded in our hands, and about four hundred prisoners and several hundred horses. On the 12th he destroyed the railroad from Trevillian Station to Louisa Courthouse. This occupied until three o'clock P.M., when he advanced in the direction of Gordonsville. He found the enemy reënforced by infantry, behind well-constructed rifle-pits, about five miles from the latter place, and too strong to successfully assault. On the extreme right, however, his reserve brigade carried the enemy's works twice, and was twice driven therefrom by infantry. Night closed the contest. Not having sufficient ammunition to continue the engagement, and his animals being without forage (the country furnishing but inferior grazing), and hearing nothing from General Hunter, he withdrew his command to the north side of the North Anna, and commenced his return march, reaching White House at the time before stated. After breaking up the depot at that place, he moved to the James River, which he reached safely after heavy fighting. He commenced crossing on the 25th, near Fort Powhatan, without further molestation, and rejoined the army of the Potomac.

On the 22d General Wilson, with his own division of cavalry of the army of the Potomac, and General Kautz's division of cavalry of the army of the James, moved against the enemy's railroads south of Richmond. Striking the Weldon Railroad at Ream's Station, destroying the depot and several miles of the road, and the Southside Road, about fifteen miles from Petersburg, to near Nottoway Station, where he met and defeated a force of the enemy's cavalry, he reached Burkesville Station on the afternoon of the 23d, and from there destroyed the Danville Railroad to Roanoke Bridge, a distance of twenty-five miles, where he found the enemy in force, and in a position from which he could not dislodge him. He then commenced his return march, and on the 28th met the enemy's cavalry in force at the Weldon Railroad crossing of Stony Creek, where he had a severe but not decisive engagement. Thence he made a detour from his left, with a view of reaching Ream's Station (supposing it to be in our possession). At this place he was met by the enemy's cavalry, supported by infantry, and forced to retire, with the loss of his artillery and trains. In this last encounter, General Kautz, with a part of his command, became separated, and made his way into our lines. General Wilson, with the remainder of his force, succeeded in crossing the Nottoway River and coming in safely on our left and rear. The damage to the enemy in this expedition more than compensated for the losses we sustained. It severed all connection by railroad with Richmond for several weeks.

With a view of cutting the enemy's railroad from near Richmond to the Anna Rivers, and making him wary of the situation of his army in the Shenandoah, and, in the event of failure in this, to take advantage of his necessary withdrawal of troops from Petersburg, to explode a mine that had been prepared in front of the Ninth Corps, and assault the enemy's lines at that place, on the night of the 26th of July the Second Corps and two divisions of the Cavalry Corps and Kautz's Cavalry were crossed to the north bank of the James River, and joined the force General Butler had there. On the 27th the enemy was driven from his intrenched position, with the loss of four pieces of artillery. On the 28th our lines were extended from Deep Bottom to New Market road, but in getting this position were attacked by the enemy in heavy force. The fighting lasted for several hours, resulting in considerable loss to both sides. The first object of this move having failed, by reason of the very large force thrown there by the enemy, I determined to take advantage of the diversion made, by assaulting Petersburg before he could get his force back there. One division of the Second Corps was withdrawn on the night of the 28th, and moved during the night to the rear of the Eighteenth Corps, to relieve that corps in the line, that it might be foot-loose in the assault to be made. The other two divisions of the Second Corps and Sheridan's cavalry were crossed over on the night of the 29th, and moved in front of Petersburg. On the morning of the 30th, between four and five o'clock, the mine was sprung, blowing up a battery and most of a regiment, and the advance of the assaulting column, formed of the Ninth Corps, immediately took possession of the crater made by the explosion, and the line for some distance to the right and left of it, and a detached line in front of it, but for some cause failed to advance promptly to the ridge beyond. Had they done this, I have every reason to believe that Petersburg would have fallen. Other troops were immediately pushed forward, but the time consumed in getting them up enabled the enemy to rally from his surprise (which had been complete), and get forces to this point for its defence. The captured line thus held being untenable, and of no advantage to us, the troops were withdrawn, but not without heavy loss. Thus terminated in disaster what promised to be the most successful assault of the campaign.

Immediately upon the enemy's ascertaining that General Hunter was retreating from Lynchburg by way of the Kanawha River, thus laying the Shenandoah Valley open for raids into Maryland and Pennsylvania, he returned northward, and moved down that valley. As soon as this movement of the enemy was ascertained, General Hunter, who had reached the Kanawha River, was directed to move his troops without delay, by river and railroad, to Harper's Ferry; but owing to the difficulty of navigation, by reason of low water and breaks in the railroad, great delay was experienced in getting there. It became necessary, therefore, to find other troops to check this movement of the enemy. For this purpose the Sixth Corps was taken from the armies operating against Richmond, to which was added the Nineteenth Corps, then fortunately beginning to arrive in Hampton Roads from the Gulf Department, under orders issued immediately after the ascertainment of the result of the Red River expedition. The garrisons of Baltimore and Washington were at this time made up of heavy artillery regiments, hundred-days men, and detachments from the invalid corps. One division, under command of General Ricketts, of the Sixth Corps, was sent to Baltimore, and the remaining two divisions of the Sixth Corps, under General Wright, were subsequently sent to Washington. On the 3d of July the enemy approached Martinsburg; General Sigel, who was in command of our forces there, retreated across the Potomac at Shepardstown; and General Weber, commanding at Harper's Ferry, crossed the river and occupied Maryland Heights. On the 6th the enemy occupied Hagerstown, moving a strong column towards Frederick City. General Wallace, with Ricketts's division and his own command, — the latter mostly new and undisciplined troops, — pushed out from Baltimore with great promptness, and met the enemy in force on the Monocacy, near the crossing of the railroad bridge. His force was not sufficient to insure success, but he fought the enemy nevertheless, and although it resulted in a defeat to our arms, yet it detained the enemy, and thereby served to enable General Wright to reach Washington with two divisions of the Sixth Corps, and the advance of the Nineteenth Corps, before him. From Monocacy the enemy moved on Washington, his cavalry advance reaching Rockville on the evening of the 10th. On the 12th a reconnoissance was thrown out in front of Fort Stevens, to ascertain the enemy's position and force. A severe skirmish ensued, in which we lost about two hundred and eighty in killed and wounded. The enemy's loss was probably greater. He commenced retreating during the night. Learning the exact condition of affairs at Washington, I requested by telegraph, at quarter of twelve P. M., on the 12th, the assignment of Major General H. G. Wright to the command of all the troops that could be made available to operate in the field against the enemy, and directed that he should get outside of the trenches with all the force he could, and push Early to the last moment. General Wright commenced the pursuit on the 13th. On the 18th the enemy was overtaken at Snicker's Ferry, on the Shenandoah, when a sharp skirmish occurred; and on the 20th General Averill encountered and defeated a portion of the rebel army at Winchester, capturing four pieces of artillery and several hundred prisoners.

Learning that Early was retreating south towards Lynchburg or Richmond, I directed that the Sixth and Nineteenth Corps be got back to the armies operating against Richmond, so that they might be used in a movement against Lee before the return of the troops sent by him into the valley; and that Hunter should remain in the Shenandoah Valley, keeping between any force of the enemy and Washington, acting on the defensive as much as possible. I felt that if the enemy had any notion of returning, the fact would be developed before the Sixth and Nineteenth Corps could leave Washington. Subsequently the Nineteenth Corps was excepted from the order to return to the James.

About the 25th it became evident that the enemy was again advancing upon Maryland and Pennsylvania, and the Sixth Corps, then at Washington, was ordered back to the vicinity of Harper's Ferry. The rebel force moved down the valley, and sent a raiding party into Pennsylvania, which, on the 30th, burned Chambersburg and then retreated, pursued by our cavalry, towards Cumberland. They were met and defeated by General Kelly, and with diminished numbers escaped into the mountains of West Virginia. From the time of the first raid the telegraph wires were frequently down between Washington and City Point, making it necessary to transmit messages a part of the way by boat. It took from twenty-four to thirty-six hours to get despatches through and return answers back; so that often orders would be given, and then information would be received showing a different state of facts from those on which they were based, causing a confusion and apparent contradiction of orders that must have considerably embarrassed those who had to execute them, and rendered operations against the enemy less effective than they otherwise would have been. To remedy this evil, it was evident to my mind that some person should have the supreme command of all the forces in the Departments of West Virginia, Washington, Susquehanna, and the Middle Department, and I so recommended.

On the 2d of August I ordered General Sheridan to report in person to Major General Halleck, chief of staff, at Washington, with a view to his assignment to the command of all the forces against Early. At this time the enemy was concentrated in the neighborhood of Winchester, whilst our forces, under General Hunter, were concentrated on the Monocacy, at the crossing of the Baltimore and Ohio Railroad, leaving open to the enemy Western Maryland and Southern Pennsylvania. From where I was, I hesitated to give positive orders for the movement of our forces at Monocacy, lest by so doing I should expose Washington. Therefore, on the 4th I left City Point to visit Hunter's command, and determine for myself what was best to be done. On arrival there, and after consultation with General Hunter, I issued to him the following instructions: —

MONOCACY BRIDGE, MD.,
August 5, 1864 — 8 P. M.

GENERAL: Concentrate all your available force without delay in the vicinity of Harper's Ferry, leaving only such railroad guards and garrisons for public property as may be necessary. Use, in this concentrating, the railroads, if by so doing time can be saved. From Harper's Ferry, if it is found that the enemy has moved north of the Potomac in large force, push north, following him and attacking him wherever found; follow him if driven south of the Potomac, as long as it is safe to do so. If it is ascertained that the enemy has but a small force north of the Potomac, then push south with the main force, detaching, under a competent commander, a sufficient force to look after the raiders, and drive them to their homes. In detaching such a force, the brigade of cavalry now en route from Washington via Rockville, may be taken into account.

There are now on their way to join you three other brigades of the best cavalry, numbering, at least, five thousand men and horses. These will be instructed, in the absence of further orders, to join you by the south side of the Potomac. One brigade will probably start to-morrow. In pushing up the Shenandoah Valley, where it is expected you will have to go first or last, it is desirable that nothing should be left to invite the enemy to return. Take all provisions, forage, and stock wanted for the use of your command; such as cannot be consumed, destroy. It is not desirable that the buildings should be destroyed — they should rather be protected; but the people should be informed that, so long as an army can subsist among them, recurrences of these raids must be expected, and we are determined to stop them at all hazards.

Bear in mind, the object is to drive the enemy south; and to do this you want to keep him always in sight. Be guided in your course by the course he takes.

Make your own arrangements for supplies of all kinds, giving regular vouchers for such as may be taken from loyal citizens in the country through which you march.

U. S. GRANT, *Lieutenant General.*

MAJOR GENERAL D. HUNTER.

The troops were immediately put in motion, and the advance reached Halltown that night.

General Hunter having, in our conversation, expressed a willingness to be relieved from command, I telegraphed to have General Sheridan, then at Washington, sent to Harper's Ferry by the morning train, with orders to take general command of all the troops in the field, and to call on General Hunter at Monocacy, who would turn over to him my letter of instructions. I remained at Monocacy until General Sheridan arrived, on the morning of the 6th, and, after a conference with him in relation to military affairs in that vicinity, I returned to City Point by way of Washington.

On the 7th of August the Middle Department and the Departments of West Virginia, Washington, and Susquehanna were constituted into the "Middle Military Division," and Major General Sheridan was assigned to temporary command of the same.

Two divisions of cavalry, commanded by Generals Torbert and Wilson, were sent to Sheridan from the army of the Potomac. The first reached him at Harper's Ferry about the 11th of August.

His operations during the month of August and the fore part of September were both of an offensive and defensive character, resulting in many severe skirmishes, principally by the cavalry, in which we were generally successful; but no general engagement took place. The two armies lay in such a position — the enemy on the west bank of the Opequan Creek, covering Winchester, and our forces in front of Berrysville — that either could bring on a battle at any time. Defeat to us would lay open to the enemy the States of Maryland and Pennsylvania for long distances before another army could be interposed to check him. Under these circumstances, I hesitated about allowing the initiative to be taken. Finally, the use of the Baltimore and Ohio Railroad and the Chesapeake and Ohio Canal, which were both obstructed by the enemy, became so indispensably necessary to us, and the importance of relieving Pennsylvania and Maryland from continuously threatened invasion so great, that I determined the risk should be taken. But fearing to telegraph the order for an attack without knowing more than I did of General Sheridan's feelings as to what would be the probable result, I left City Point, on the 15th of September, to visit him at his headquarters, to decide, after conference with him, what should be done. I met him at Charleston, and he pointed out so distinctly how each army lay, what he could do the moment he was authorized, and expressed such confidence of success, that I saw there were but two words of instruction necessary — Go in! For the convenience of forage, the teams for supplying the army were kept at Harper's Ferry. I asked him if he could get out his teams and supplies in time to make an attack on the ensuing Tuesday morning. His reply was, that he could before daylight on Monday. He was off promptly to time, and I may here add that the result was such that I have never since deemed it necessary to visit General Sheridan before giving him orders.

Early on the morning of the 19th General Sheridan attacked General Early at the crossing on the Opequan Creek, and after a most sanguinary and bloody battle, lasting until five o'clock in the evening, defeated him with heavy loss, carrying his entire position from Opequan Creek to Winchester, capturing several thousand prisoners and five pieces of artillery. The enemy rallied and made a stand in a strong position at Fisher's Hill, where he was attacked and again defeated with heavy loss on the 20th. Sheridan pursued him with great energy through Harrisonburg, Staunton, and the gaps of the Blue Ridge. After stripping the upper valley of most of the supplies and provisions for the rebel army, he returned to Strasburg, and took position on the north side of Cedar Creek.

Having received considerable reënforcements, General Early again returned to the Valley, and on the 9th of October his cavalry encountered ours near Strasburg, where the rebels were defeated with the loss of eleven pieces of artillery and three hundred and fifty prisoners. On the night of the 18th the enemy crossed the mountains which separated the branches of the Shenandoah, forded the north fork, and early on the morning of the 19th, under cover of the darkness and the fog, surprised and turned our left flank, and captured the batteries which enfiladed our whole line. Our troops fell back with heavy loss and in much confusion, but were finally rallied between Middletown and Newtown. At this juncture General Sheridan, who was at Winchester when the battle commenced, arrived on the field, arranged his lines just in time to repulse a heavy attack of the enemy, and immediately assuming the offensive, he attacked in turn with great vigor. The enemy was defeated with great slaughter and the loss of most of his artillery and trains and the trophies he had captured in the morning. The wreck of his army escaped during the night, and fled in the direction of Staunton and Lynchburg. Pursuit was made to Mount Jackson. Thus ended this, the enemy's last attempt to invade the north via the Shenandoah Valley. I was now enabled to return the Sixth Corps to the army of the Potomac, and to send one division from Sheridan's army to the army of the James, and another to Savannah, Georgia, to hold

Sherman's new acquisitions on the sea-coast, and thus enable him to move without detaching from his force for that purpose.

Reports from various sources led me to believe that the enemy had detached three divisions from Petersburg to reënforce Early in the Shenandoah Valley. I therefore sent the Second Corps and Gregg's division of cavalry, of the army of the Potomac, and a force of General Butler's army, on the night of the 13th of August, to threaten Richmond from the north side of the James, to prevent him from sending troops away, and, if possible, to draw back those sent. In this move we captured six pieces of artillery and several hundred prisoners, detained troops that were under marching orders, and ascertained that but one division (Kershaw's), of the three reputed detached, had gone.

The enemy having withdrawn heavily from Petersburg to resist this movement, the Fifth Corps, General Warren commanding, was moved out on the 18th, and took possession of the Weldon Railroad. During the day he had considerable fighting. To regain possession of the road, the enemy made repeated and desperate assaults, but was each time repulsed with great loss. On the night of the 20th the troops on the north side of the James were withdrawn, and Hancock and Gregg returned to the front of Petersburg. On the 25th the Second Corps and Gregg's division of cavalry, while at Ream's Station destroying the railroad, were attacked, and after desperate fighting, a part of our line gave way, and five pieces of artillery fell into the hands of the enemy.

By the 12th of September a branch railroad was completed from the City Point and Petersburg Railroad to the Weldon Railroad, enabling us to supply, without difficulty, in all weather, the army in front of Petersburg.

The extension of our lines across the Weldon Railroad compelled the enemy to so extend his that it seemed he could have but few troops north of the James for the defence of Richmond. On the night of the 28th the Tenth Corps, Major General Birney, and the Eighteenth Corps, Major General Ord commanding, of General Butler's army, were crossed to the north side of the James, and advanced on the morning of the 29th, carrying the very strong fortifications and intrenchments below Chapin's farm, known as Fort Harrison, capturing fifteen pieces of artillery and the New Market road and intrenchments. This success was followed up by a gallant assault upon Fort Gillmore, immediately in front of the Chapin farm fortifications, in which we were repulsed with heavy loss. Kautz's cavalry was pushed forward on the road to the right of this, supported by infantry, and reached the enemy's inner line, but was unable to get farther. The position captured from the enemy was so threatening to Richmond that I determined to hold it. The enemy made several desperate attempts to dislodge us, all of which were unsuccessful, and for which he paid dearly. On the morning of the 30th General Meade sent out a reconnoissance, with a view to attacking the enemy's line if it was found sufficiently weakened by withdrawal of troops to the north side. In this reconnoissance we captured and held the enemy's works near Poplar Spring Church. In the afternoon troops moving to get to the left of the point gained were attacked by the enemy in heavy force, and compelled to fall back until supported by the forces holding the captured works. Our cavalry under Gregg was also attacked, but repulsed the enemy with great loss.

On the 7th of October the enemy attacked Kautz's cavalry north of the James, and drove it back with heavy loss in killed, wounded, and prisoners, and the loss of all the artillery — eight or nine pieces. This he followed up by an attack on our intrenched infantry line, but was repulsed with severe slaughter. On the 13th a reconnoissance was sent out by General Butler, with a view to drive the enemy from some new works he was constructing, which resulted in very heavy loss to us.

On the 27th the army of the Potomac, leaving only sufficient men to hold its fortified line, moved by the enemy's right flank. The Second Corps, followed by two divisions of the Fifth Corps, with the cavalry in advance and covering our left flank, forced a passage of Hatcher's Run, and moved up the south side of it towards the Southside Railroad, until the Second Corps and part of the cavalry reached the Boydton plank road, where it crosses Hatcher's Run. At this point we were six miles distant from the Southside Railroad, which I had hoped by this movement to reach and hold. But finding that we had not reached the end of the enemy's fortifications, and no place presenting itself for a successful assault by which he might be doubled up and shortened, I determined to withdraw to within our fortified line. Orders were given accordingly. Immediately upon receiving a report that General Warren had connected with General Hancock, I returned to my headquarters. Soon after I left, the enemy moved out across Hatcher's Run, in the gap between Generals Hancock and Warren (which was not closed, as reported), and made a desperate attack on General Hancock's right and rear. General Hancock immediately faced his corps to meet it, and after a bloody combat drove the enemy within his works, and withdrew that night to his old position.

In support of this movement General Butler made a demonstration on the north side of the James, and attacked the enemy on the Williamsburg road, and also on the York River Railroad. In the former he was unsuccessful; in the latter he succeeded in carrying a work, which was afterwards abandoned, and his forces withdrawn to their former positions.

From this time forward the operations in front of Petersburg and Richmond, until the spring campaign of 1865, were confined to the defence and extension of our lines, and to offensive movements for crippling the enemy's lines of communication, and to prevent his detaching any considerable force to send south. By the 7th of February our lines were extended to Hatcher's Run, and the Weldon Railroad had been destroyed to Hicksford.

General Sherman moved from Chattanooga on the 6th of May, with the armies of the Cumberland, Tennessee, and Ohio, commanded, respectively, by Generals Thomas, McPherson, and Schofield, upon Johnston's army at Dalton; but finding the enemy's position at Buzzard Roost, covering Dalton, too strong to be assaulted, General McPherson was sent through Snake Gap to turn it, whilst Generals Thomas and Schofield threatened it in front and on the north. This movement was successful. Johnston, finding his retreat likely to be cut off, fell back to his fortified position at Resaca, where he was attacked on the afternoon of May 15. A heavy battle ensued. During the night the enemy retreated south. Late on the 17th his rear-guard was overtaken near Adairsville, and heavy skirmishing followed. The next morning, however, he had again disappeared. He was vigorously pursued, and was overtaken at Cassville on the 19th, but, during the ensuing night, retreated across the Etowah. Whilst these operations were going on, General Jefferson C. Davis's division of Thomas's army was sent to Rome, capturing it, with its forts and artillery, and its valuable mills and founderies. General Sherman, having given his army a few days' rest at this point, again put it in motion on the 23d for Dallas, with a view of turning the difficult pass at Allatoona. On the afternoon of the 25th, the advance, under General Hooker, had a severe battle with the enemy, driving him back to New Hope Church, near Dallas. Several sharp encounters occurred at this point. The most important was on the 28th, when the enemy assaulted General McPherson at Dallas, but received a terrible and bloody repulse.

On the 4th of June Johnston abandoned his intrenched position at New Hope Church, and retreated to the strong positions of Kenesaw, Pine, and Lost Mountains. He was forced to yield the two last-named places and concentrate his army on Kenesaw, where, on the 27th, Generals Thomas and McPherson made a determined but unsuccessful assault. On the night of the 2d of July Sherman commenced moving his army by the right flank, and on the morning of the 3d found that the enemy, in consequence of this movement, had abandoned Kenesaw and retreated across the Chattahoochie.

General Sherman remained on the Chattahoochie to give his men rest and get up stores until the 17th of July, when he resumed his operations, crossed the Chattahoochie, destroyed a large portion of the railroad to Augusta, and drove the enemy back to Atlanta. At this place General Hood succeeded General Johnston in command of the rebel army, and assuming the offensive-defensive policy, made several severe attacks upon Sherman in the vicinity of Atlanta, the most desperate and determined of which was on the 22d of July. About one P. M. of this day the brave, accomplished, and noble-hearted McPherson was killed. General Logan succeeded him, and commanded the army of the Tennessee through this desperate battle, and until he was superseded by Major General Howard, on the 26th, with the same success and ability that had characterized him in the command of a corps or division.

In all these attacks the enemy was repulsed with great loss. Finding it impossible to entirely invest the place, General Sherman, after securing his line of communications across the Chattahoochie, moved his main force round by the enemy's left flank upon the Montgomery and Macon roads, to draw the enemy from his fortifications. In this he succeeded, and, after defeating the enemy near Rough and Ready, Jonesboro', and Lovejoy's, forcing him to retreat to the south, on the 2d of September occupied Atlanta, the objective point of his campaign.

About the time of this move the rebel cavalry, under Wheeler, attempted to cut his communications in the rear, but was repulsed at Dalton, and driven into East Tennessee, whence it proceeded west to McMinnville, Murfreesboro,' and Franklin, and was finally driven south of the Tennessee. The damage done by this raid was repaired in a few days.

During the partial investment of Atlanta, General Rousseau joined General Sherman with a force of cavalry from Decatur, having made a successful raid upon the Atlanta and Montgomery Railroad, and its branches near Opelika. Cavalry raids were also made by Generals McCook, Garrard, and Stoneman, to cut the remaining railroad communication with Atlanta. The first two were successful, the latter disastrous.

General Sherman's movement from Chattanooga to Atlanta was prompt, skilful, and brilliant. The history of his flank movements and battles during that memorable campaign will ever be read with an interest unsurpassed by anything in history.

His own report, and those of his subordinate commanders accompanying it, give the details of that most successful campaign.

He was dependent for the supply of his armies upon a single-track railroad from Nashville to the point where he was operating. This passed the entire distance through a hostile country, and every foot of it had to be protected by troops. The cavalry force of the enemy under Forrest, in Northern Mississippi, was evidently waiting for Sherman to advance far enough into the mountains of Georgia to make a retreat disastrous, to get upon his line and destroy it beyond the possibility of further use. To guard against this danger, Sherman left what he supposed to be a sufficient force to operate against Forrest in West Tennessee. He directed General Washburn, who commanded there, to send Brigadier General S. D. Sturgis in command of this force to attack him. On the morning of the 10th of June General Sturgis met the enemy near Guntown, Mississippi, was badly beaten, and driven back in utter rout and confusion to Memphis, a distance of about one hundred miles, hotly pursued by the enemy. By this, however, the enemy was defeated in his designs upon Sherman's line of communications. The persistency with which he followed up this success exhausted him, and made a season for rest and repairs necessary. In the mean time Major General A. J. Smith, with the troops of the army of the Tennessee that had been sent by General Sherman to General Banks, arrived at Memphis on their return from Red River, where they had done most excellent service. He was directed by General Sherman to immediately take the offensive against Forrest. This he did with the promptness and effect which have characterized his whole military career. On the 14th of July he met the enemy at Tupelo, Mississippi, and whipped him badly. The fighting continued through three days. Our loss was small compared with that of the enemy. Having accomplished the object of his expedition, General Smith returned to Memphis.

During the months of March and April this same force under Forrest annoyed us considerably. On the 24th of March it captured Union City, Kentucky, and its garrison, and on the 24th attacked Paducah, commanded by Colonel S. G. Hicks, Fortieth Illinois Volunteers. Colonel Hicks, having but a small force, withdrew to the forts near the river, from where he repulsed the enemy and drove him from the place.

On the 13th of April, part of this force, under the rebel General Buford, summoned the garrison of Columbus, Kentucky, to surrender, but received for reply from Colonel Lawrence, Thirty-fourth New Jersey Volunteers, that, being placed there by his government with adequate force to hold his post and repel all enemies from it, surrender was out of the question.

On the morning of the same day, Forrest attacked Fort Pillow, Tennessee, garrisoned by a detachment of Tennessee cavalry, and the First Regiment Alabama colored troops, commanded by Major Booth. The garrison fought bravely until about three o'clock in the afternoon, when the enemy carried the works by assault; and, after our men threw down their arms, proceeded to an inhuman and merciless massacre of the garrison.

On the 14th, General Buford, having failed at Columbus, appeared before Paducah, but was again driven off.

Guerrillas and raiders, seemingly emboldened by Forrest's operations, were also very active in Kentucky. The most noted of these was Morgan. With a force of from two to three thousand cavalry he entered the state through Pound Gap in the latter part of May. On the 11th of June he attacked and captured Cynthiana, with its entire garrison. On the 12th he was overtaken by General Burbridge, and completely routed, with heavy loss, and was finally driven out of the state. This notorious guerrilla was afterwards surprised and killed near Greenville, Tennessee, and his command captured and dispersed by General Gillem.

In the absence of official reports at the commencement of the Red River expedition, except so far as relates to the movements of the troops sent by General Sherman under A. J. Smith, I am unable to give the date of its starting. The troops under General Smith, comprising two divisions of the Sixteenth and a detachment of the Seventeenth army corps, left Vicksburg on the 10th of March, and reached the designated point on Red River one day earlier than that appointed by General Banks. The rebel forces at Fort De Russey, thinking to defeat him, left the fort on the 14th to give him battle in the open field; but, while occupying the enemy with skirmishing and demonstrations, Smith pushed forward to Fort De Russey, which had been left with a weak garrison, and captured it with its garrison — about three hundred and fifty men, eleven pieces of artillery, and many small arms. Our loss was but slight. On the 15th he pushed forward to Alexandria, which place he reached on the 18th. On the 21st he had an engagement with the enemy at Henderson Hill, in which he defeated him, capturing two hundred and ten prisoners and four pieces of artillery.

On the 28th he again attacked and defeated the enemy under the rebel General Taylor at Cane River. By the 26th General Banks had assembled his whole army at Alexandria, and pushed forward to Grand Ecore. On the morning of April 6, he moved from Grand Ecore. On the afternoon of the 7th his advance engaged the enemy near Pleasant Hill, and drove him from the field. On the same afternoon the enemy made a stand eight miles beyond Pleasant Hill, but was again compelled to retreat. On the 8th, at Sabine Cross-roads and Peach Hill, the enemy attacked and defeated his advance, capturing nineteen pieces of artillery and an immense amount of transportation and stores. During the night General Banks fell back to Pleasant Hill, where another battle was fought on the 9th, and the enemy repulsed with great loss. During the night General Banks continued his retrograde movement to Grand Ecore, and thence to Alexandria, which he reached on the 27th of April. Here a serious difficulty arose in getting Admiral Porter's fleet, which accompanied the expedition, over the rapids, the water having fallen so much since they passed up as to prevent their return. At the suggestion of Colonel (now Brigadier General) Bailey, and under his superintendence, wing-dams were constructed, by which the channel was contracted, so that the fleet passed down the rapids in safety.

The army evacuated Alexandria on the 14th of May, after considerable skirmishing with the enemy's advance, and reached Morganzia and Point Coupée near the end of the month. The disastrous termination of this expedition and the lateness of the season rendered impracticable the carrying out of my plans of a movement in force sufficient to insure the capture of Mobile.

On the 23d of March Major General Steele left Little Rock with the Seventh Army Corps to coöperate with General Banks's expedition on Red River, and reached Arkadelphia on the 28th. On the 16th of April, after driving the enemy before him, he was joined near Elkin's Ferry, in Washita County, by General Thayer, who had marched from Fort Smith. After several severe skirmishes, in which the enemy was defeated, General Steele reached Camden, which he occupied about the middle of April.

On learning the defeat and consequent retreat of General Banks on Red River, and the loss of one of his own trains at Mark's Mill, in Dallas County, General Steele determined to fall back to the Arkansas River. He left Camden on the 26th of April, and reached Little Rock on the 2d of May. On the 30th of April the enemy attacked him while crossing Saline River at Jenkins's Ferry, but was repulsed with considerable loss. Our loss was about six hundred in killed, wounded, and prisoners.

Major General Canby, who had been assigned to the command of the "Military Division of West Mississippi," was therefore directed to send the Nineteenth Army Corps to join the armies operating against Richmond, and to limit the remainder of his command to such operations as might be necessary to hold the positions and lines of communication he then occupied.

Before starting General A. J. Smith's troops back to Sherman, General Canby sent a part of it to disperse a force of the enemy that was collecting near the Mississippi River. General Smith met and defeated this force near Lake Chicot on the 5th of June. Our loss was about forty killed and seventy wounded.

In the latter part of July General Canby sent Major General Gordon Granger, with such forces as he could collect, to coöperate with Admiral Farragut against the defences of Mobile Bay. On the 8th of August Fort Gaines surrendered to the combined naval and land forces. Fort Powell was blown up and abandoned.

On the 9th Fort Morgan was invested, and after a severe bombardment, surrendered on the 23d. The total captures amounted to fourteen hundred and sixty-four prisoners and one hundred and four pieces of artillery.

About the last of August, it being reported that the rebel General Price, with a force of about ten thousand men, had reached Jacksonport, on his way to invade Missouri, General A. J. Smith's command, then en route from Memphis to join Sherman, was ordered to Missouri. A cavalry force was also, at the same time, sent from Memphis, under command of Colonel Winslow. This made General Rosecrans's forces superior to those of Price, and no doubt was entertained he would be able to check Price and drive him back, while the forces under General Steele, in Arkansas, would cut off his retreat. On the 26th day of September Price attacked Pilot Knob, and forced the garrison to retreat, and thence moved north to the Missouri River, and continued up that river towards Kansas. General Curtis, commanding Department of Kansas, immediately collected such forces as he could to repel the invasion of Kansas, while General Rosecrans's cavalry was operating in his rear.

The enemy was brought to battle on the Big Blue and defeated, with the loss of nearly all his artillery and trains and a large number of prisoners. He made a precipitate retreat to Northern Arkansas. The impunity with which Price was enabled to roam over the State of Missouri for a long time, and the incalculable mischief done by him, show to how little purpose a superior force may be used. There is no reason why General Rosecrans should not have concentrated his forces and beaten and driven Price before the latter reached Pilot Knob.

September 20 the enemy's cavalry, under Forrest, crossed the Tennessee near Waterloo, Alabama, and on the 23d attacked the garrison at Athens, consisting of six hundred men, which capitulated on the 24th.. Soon after the surrender, two regiments of reënforcements arrived, and after a severe fight were compelled to surrender. Forrest destroyed the railroad westward, captured the garrison at Sulphur Branch trestle, skirmished with the garrison at Pulaski on the 27th, and on the same day cut the Nashville and Chattanooga Railroad near Tullahoma and Dechard. On the morning of the 30th one column of Forrest's command, under Buford, appeared before Huntsville, and summoned the surrender of the garrison. Receiving an answer in the negative, he remained in the vicinity of the place until next morning, when he again summoned its surrender, and received the same reply as on the night before. He withdrew in the direction of Athens, which place had been regarrisoned, and attacked it on the afternoon of the 1st of October, but without success. On the morning of the 2d he renewed his attack, but was handsomely repulsed.

Another column under Forrest appeared before Columbia on the morning of the 1st, but did not make an attack. On the morning of the 3d he moved towards Mount Pleasant. While these operations were going on every exertion was made by General Thomas to destroy the forces under Forrest before he could recross the Tennessee, but he was unable to prevent his escape to Corinth, Mississippi.

In September an expedition under General Burbridge was sent to destroy the salt-works at Saltville, Virginia. He met the enemy on the 2d of October, about three miles and a half from Saltville, and drove him into his strongly intrenched position around the salt-works, from which he was unable to dislodge him. During the night he withdrew his command and returned to Kentucky.

General Sherman, immediately after the fall of Atlanta, put his armies in camp in and about the place, and made all preparations for refitting and supplying them for future service. The great length of road from Atlanta to the Cumberland River, however, which had to be guarded, allowed the troops but little rest.

During this time Jefferson Davis made a speech in Macon, Georgia, which was reported in the papers of the South, and soon became known to the whole country, disclosing the plans of the enemy, thus enabling General Sherman to fully meet them. He exhibited the weakness of supposing that an army that had been beaten and fearfully decimated in a vain attempt at the defensive could successfully undertake the offensive against the army that had so often defeated it.

In execution of this plan, Hood, with his army, was soon reported to the south-west of Atlanta. Moving far to Sherman's right, he succeeded in reaching the railroad about Big Shanty, and moved north on it.

General Sherman, leaving a force to hold Atlanta, with the remainder of his army fell upon him, and drove him to Gadston, Alabama. Seeing the constant annoyance he would have with the roads to his rear, if we attempted to hold Atlanta, General Sherman proposed the abandonment and destruction of that place, with all the railroads leading to it, and telegraphed me as follows: —

CENTREVILLE, GA., October 10 — Noon.

Despatch about Wilson just received. Hood is now crossing Coosa River, twelve miles below Rome, bound west. If he passes over the Mobile and Ohio road, had I not better execute the plan of my letter sent by Colonel Porter, and leave General Thomas, with the troops now in Tennessee, to defend the state? He will have an ample force when the reënforcements ordered reach Nashville.

W. T. SHERMAN, *Major General.*

LIEUTENANT GENERAL GRANT.

For a full understanding of the plan referred to in this despatch, I quote from the letter sent by Colonel Porter: "I will therefore give my opinion, that your army and Canby's should be reënforced to the maximum; that, after you get Wilmington, you strike for Savannah and the river; that Canby be instructed to hold the Mississippi River, and send a force to get Columbus, Georgia, either by the way of the Alabama or the Apalachicola, and that I keep Hood employed and put my army in final order for a march on Augusta, Columbia, and Charleston, to be ready as soon as Wilmington is sealed as to commerce, and the city of Savannah is in our possession." This was in reply to a letter of mine of date September 12, in answer to a despatch of his containing substantially the same proposition, and in which I informed him of a

34

proposed movement against Wilmington, and of the situation in Virginia, &c.

CITY POINT, VA., October 11, 1864 — 11 A. M.

Your despatch of October 10 received. Does it not look as if Hood was going to attempt the invasion of Middle Tennessee, using the Mobile and Ohio and Memphis and Charleston roads to supply his base on the Tennessee River, about Florence or Decatur? If he does this he ought to be met and prevented from getting north of the Tennessee River. If you were to cut loosé, I do not believe you would meet Hood's army, but would be bushwhacked by all the old men, little boys, and such railroad guards as are still left at home. Hood would probably strike for Nashville, thinking that by going north he could inflict greater damage upon us than we could upon the rebels by going south. If there is any way of getting at Hood's army I would prefer that; but I must trust to your own judgment. I find I shall not be able to send a force from here to act with you on Savannah. Your movements, therefore, will be independent of mine; at least until the fall of Richmond takes place. I am afraid Thomas, with such lines of road as he has to protect, could not prevent Hood from going north. With Wilson turned loose, with all your cavalry, you will find the rebels put much more on the defensive than heretofore.

U. S. GRANT, *Lieutenant General.*

MAJOR GENERAL W. T. SHERMAN.

KINGSTON, GA., October 11 — 11 A. M.

Hood moved his army from Palmetto Station across by Dallas and Cedartown, and is now on the Coosa River, south of Rome. He threw one corps on my road at Acworth, and I was forced to follow. I hold Atlanta with the Twentieth Corps, and have strong detachments along my line. This reduces my active force to a comparatively small army. We cannot remain here on the defensive. With the twenty-five thousand men, and the bold cavalry he has, he can constantly break my roads. I would infinitely prefer to make a wreck of the road and of the country from Chattanooga to Atlanta, including the latter city, send back all my wounded and worthless, and, with my effective army, move through Georgia, smashing things, to the sea. Hood may turn into Tennessee and Kentucky, but I believe he will be forced to follow me. Instead of my being on the defensive, I would be on the offensive; instead of guessing at what he means to do, he would have to guess at my plans. The difference in war is full twenty-five per cent. I can make Savannah, Charleston, or the mouth of the Chattahoochie.

Answer quick, as I know we will not have the telegraph long.

W. T. SHERMAN, *Major General.*

LIEUTENANT GENERAL GRANT.

CITY POINT, VA., October 11, 1864 —11.30 P. M.

Your despatch of to-day received. If you are satisfied the trip to the sea-coast can be made, holding the line of the Tennessee River firmly, you may make it, destroying all the railroad south of Dalton or Chattanooga, as you think best.

U. S. GRANT, *Lieutenant General.*

MAJOR GENERAL W.<sup></sup> T. SHERMAN.

It was the original design to hold Atlanta, and by getting through to the coast, with a garrison left on the southern railroads leading east and west through Georgia, to effectually sever the east from the west — in other words, cut the would-be Confederacy in two again, as it had been cut once by our gaining possession of the Mississippi River. General Sherman's plan virtually effected this object.

General Sherman commenced at once his preparations for his proposed movement, keeping his army in position, in the mean time, to watch Hood. Becoming satisfied that Hood had moved westward from Gadsden across Sand Mountain, General Sherman sent the Fourth Corps, Major General Stanley commanding, and the Twenty-third Corps, Major General Schofield commanding, back to Chattanooga to report to Major General Thomas at Nashville, whom he had placed in command of all the troops of his military division, save the four army corps and cavalry division he designed to move with through Georgia. With the troops thus left at his disposal, there was little doubt that General Thomas could hold the line of the Tennessee, or, in the event Hood should force it, would be able to concentrate and beat him in battle. It was therefore readily consented to that Sherman should start for the sea-coast.

Having concentrated his troops at Atlanta by the 14th of November, he commenced his march, threatening both Augusta and Macon. His coming-out point could not be definitely fixed. Having to gather his subsistence as he marched through the country, it was not impossible that a force inferior to his own might compel him to head for such point as he could reach, instead of such as he might prefer. The blindness of the enemy, however, in ignoring his movement, and sending Hood's army — the only considerable force he had west of Richmond and east of the Mississippi River — northward on an offensive campaign, left the whole country open, and Sherman's route to his own choice.

How that campaign was conducted, how little opposition was

met with, the condition of the country through which the armies passed, the capture of Fort McAllister, on the Savannah River, and the occupation of Savannah on the 21st of December, are all clearly set forth in General Sherman's admirable report.

Soon after General Sherman commenced his march from Atlanta, two expeditions, one from Baton Rouge, Louisiana, and one from Vicksburg, Mississippi, were started by General Canby, to cut the enemy's line of communication with Mobile, and detain troops in that field. General Foster, commanding Department of the South, also sent an expedition, via Broad River, to destroy the railroad between Charleston and Savannah. The expedition from Vicksburg, under command of Brevet Brigadier General E. D. Osband (Colonel Third United States Colored Cavalry), captured, on the 27th of November, and destroyed the Mississippi Central Railroad Bridge and trestle-work over Big Black River, near Canton, thirty miles of the road, and two locomotives, besides large amounts of stores. The expedition from Baton Rouge was without favorable results. The expedition from the Department of the South, under the immediate command of Brigadier General John P. Hatch, consisting of about five thousand men of all arms, including a brigade from the navy, proceeded up Broad River and debarked at Boyd's Neck on the 29th of November, from where it moved to strike the railroad at Grahamsville. At Honey Hill, about three miles from Grahamsville, the enemy was found and attacked in a strongly-fortified position, which resulted, after severe fighting, in our repulse with a loss of seven hundred and forty-six in killed, wounded, and missing. During the night General Hatch withdrew. On the 6th of December General Foster obtained a position covering the Charleston and Savannah Railroad, between the Coosawhatchie and Talifinny Rivers.

Hood, instead of following Sherman, continued his move northward, which seemed to me to be leading to his certain doom. At all events, had I had the power to command both armies, I should not have changed the orders under which he seemed to be acting. On the 26th of October the advance of Hood's army attacked the garrison at Decatur, Alabama, but failing to carry the place, withdrew towards Courtland, and succeeded, in the face of our cavalry, in effecting a lodgment on the north side of the Tennessee River, near Florence. On the 28th Forrest reached the Tennessee, at

Fort Hieman, and captured a gunboat and three transports. On the 2d of November he planted batteries above and below Johnsonville, on the opposite side of the river, isolating three gunboats and eight transports. On the 4th the enemy opened his batteries upon the place, and was replied to from the gunboats and the garrison. The gunboats, becoming disabled, were set on fire, as also were the transports, to prevent their falling into the hands of the enemy. About a million and a half dollars' worth of stores and property on the levee and in storehouses was consumed by fire. On the 5th the enemy disappeared, and crossed to the north side of the Tennessee River, above Johnsonville, moving towards Clifton, and subsequently joined Hood. On the night of the 5th General Schofield, with the advance of the Twenty-third Corps, reached Johnsonville, but, finding the enemy gone, was ordered to Pulaski, and put in command of all the troops there, with instructions to watch the movements of Hood and retard his advance, but not to risk a general engagement until the arrival of General A. J. Smith's command from Missouri, and until General Wilson could get his cavalry remounted.

On the 19th General Hood continued his advance. General Thomas, retarding him as much as possible, fell back towards Nashville for the purpose of concentrating his command and gaining time for the arrival of reënforcements. The enemy, coming up with our main force commanded by General Schofield, at Franklin, on the 30th, assaulted our works repeatedly during the afternoon, until late at night, but were in every instance repulsed. His loss in this battle was seventeen hundred and fifty killed, seven hundred and two prisoners, and thirty-eight hundred wounded. Among his losses were six general officers killed, six wounded, and one captured. Our entire loss was twenty-three hundred. This was the first serious opposition the enemy met with, and I am satisfied was the fatal blow to all his expectations. During the night General Schofield fell back towards Nashville. This left the field to the enemy, — not lost by battle, but voluntarily abandoned, — so that General Thomas's whole force might be brought together. The enemy followed up and commenced the establishment of his line in front of Nashville on the 2d of December.

As soon as it was ascertained that Hood was crossing the Tennessee River, and that Price was going out of Missouri, General Rosecrans was ordered to send to General Thomas the troops of General A. J. Smith's command, and such other troops as he could spare. The advance of this reënforcement reached Nashville on the 30th of November.

On the morning of the 15th of December General Thomas attacked Hood in position, and, in a battle lasting two days, defeated and drove him from the field in the utmost confusion, leaving in our hands most of his artillery and many thousand prisoners, including four general officers.

Before the battle of Nashville I grew very impatient over, as it appeared to me, the unnecessary delay. This impatience was increased upon learning that the enemy had sent a force of cavalry across the Cumberland into Kentucky. I feared Hood would cross his whole army and give us great trouble there. After urging upon General Thomas the necessity of immediately assuming the offensive, I started west to superintend matters there in person. Reaching Washington city, I received General Thomas's despatch announcing his attack upon the enemy, and the result as far as the battle had progressed. I was delighted. All fears and apprehensions were dispelled. I am not yet satisfied but that General Thomas, immediately upon the appearance of Hood before Nashville, and before he had time to fortify, should have moved out with his whole force and given him battle, instead of waiting to remount his cavalry, which delayed him until the inclemency of the weather made it impracticable to attack earlier than he did. But his final defeat of Hood was so complete that it will be accepted as a vindication of that distinguished officer's judgment.

After Hood's defeat at Nashville he retreated, closely pursued by cavalry and infantry, to the Tennessee River, being forced to abandon many pieces of artillery and most of his transportation. On the 28th of December our advance forces ascertained that he had made good his escape to the south side of the river.

About this time, the rains having set in heavily in Tennessee and North Alabama, making it difficult to move army transportation and artillery, General Thomas stopped the pursuit by his main force at the Tennessee River. A small force of cavalry, under Colonel W. J. Palmer, Fifteenth Pennsylvania Volunteers, continued to follow Hood for some distance, capturing considerable transportation and the enemy's pontoon bridge. The details of these operations will be found clearly set forth in General Thomas's report.

A cavalry expedition, under Brevet Major General Grierson, started from Memphis on the 21st of December. On the 25th he surprised and captured Forrest's dismounted camp at Verona, Mississippi, on the Mobile and Ohio Railroad, destroyed the railroad, sixteen cars loaded with wagons and pontoons for Hood's army, four thousand new English carbines, and large amounts of public stores. On the morning of the 28th he attacked and captured a force of the enemy at Egypt, and destroyed a train of fourteen cars; thence, turning to the south-west, he struck the Mississippi Central Railroad at Winona, destroyed the factories and large amounts of stores at Bankston, and the machine shops and public property at Grenada, arriving at Vicksburg January 5.

During these operations in Middle Tennessee, the enemy, with a force under General Breckinridge, entered East Tennessee. On the 13th of November he attacked General Gillem, near Morristown, capturing his artillery and several hundred prisoners. Gillem, with what was left of his command, retreated to Knoxville. Following up his success, Breckinridge moved to near Knoxville, but withdrew on the 18th, followed by General Ammen. Under the directions of General Thomas, General Stoneman concentrated the commands of Generals Burbridge and Gillem, near Bean's Station, to operate against Breckinridge, and destroy or drive him into Virginia — destroy the salt-works at Saltville, and the railroad into Virginia as far as he could go without endangering his command. On the 12th of December he commenced his movement, capturing and dispersing the enemy's forces wherever he met them. On the 16th he struck the enemy, under Vaughn, at Marion, completely routing and pursuing him to Wytheville, capturing all his artillery, trains, and one hundred and ninety-eight prisoners; and destroyed Wytheville, with its stores and supplies, and the extensive lead-works near there. Returning to Marion, he met a force under Breckinridge, consisting, among other troops, of the garrison of Saltville, that had started in pursuit. He at once made arrangements to attack it the next morning; but morning found Breckinridge gone. He then moved directly to Saltville, and destroyed the extensive salt-works at that place, a large amount of stores, and captured eight pieces of artillery. Having thus successfully executed his instructions, he returned General Burbridge to Lexington and General Gillem to Knoxville.

Wilmington, North Carolina, was the most important sea-coast port left to the enemy through which to get supplies from abroad, and send cotton and other products out by blockade-runners, besides being a place of great strategic value. The navy had been making strenuous exertions to seal the harbor of Wilmington, but with only partial effect. The nature of the outlet of Cape Fear River was such that it required watching for so great a distance, that without possession of the land north of New Inlet, or Fort Fisher, it was impossible for the navy to entirely close the harbor against the entrance of blockade-runners.

To secure the possession of this land required the coöperation of a land force, which I agreed to furnish. Immediately commenced the assemblage in Hampton Roads, under Admiral D. D. Porter, of the most formidable armada ever collected for concentration upon one given point. This necessarily attracted the attention of the enemy, as well as that of the loyal north; and through the imprudence of the public press, and very likely of officers of both branches of service, the exact object of the expedition became a subject of common discussion in the newspapers both north and south. The enemy, thus warned, prepared to meet it. This caused a postponement of the expedition until the latter part of November, when, being again called upon by Hon. G. V. Fox, Assistant Secretary of the Navy, I agreed to furnish the men required at once, and went myself, in company with Major General Butler, to Hampton Roads, where we had a conference with Admiral Porter as to the force required and the time of starting. A force of six thousand five hundred men was regarded as sufficient. The time of starting was not definitely arranged, but it was thought all would be ready by the 6th of December, if not before. Learning on the 30th of November that Bragg had gone to Georgia, taking with him most of the forces about Wilmington, I deemed it of the utmost importance that the expedition should reach its destination before the return of Bragg, and directed General Butler to make all arrangements for the departure of Major General Weitzel, who had been designated to command the land forces, so that the navy might not be detained one moment.

On the 6th of December the following instructions were given: —

CITY POINT, VA., December 6, 1864.

GENERAL: The first object of the expedition under General Weitzel is to close to the enemy the port of Wilmington. If successful in this, the second will be to capture Wilmington itself. There are reasonable grounds to hope for success, if advantage can be taken of the absence of the greater part of the enemy's forces now looking after Sherman in Georgia. The directions you have given for the numbers and equipment of the expedition are all right, except in the unimportant matter of where they embark and the amount of intrenching tools to be taken. The object of the expedition will be gained by effecting a landing on the main land between Cape Fear River and the Atlantic, north of the north entrance to the river. Should such landing be effected whilst the enemy still holds Fort Fisher and the batteries guarding the entrance to the river, then the troops should intrench themselves, and, by coöperating with the navy, effect the reduction and capture of those places. These in our hands, the navy could enter the harbor, and the port of Wilmington would be sealed. Should Fort Fisher and the point of land on which it is built fall into the hands of our troops immediately on landing, then it will be worth the attempt to capture Wilmington by a forced march and surprise. If time is consumed in gaining the first object of the expedition, the second will become a matter of after consideration.

The details for execution are intrusted to you and the officer immediately in command of the troops.

Should the troops under General Weitzel fail to effect a landing at or near Fort Fisher, they will be returned to the armies operating against Richmond without delay.

U. S. GRANT, *Lieutenant General.*

MAJOR GENERAL B. F. BUTLER.

General Butler commanding the army from which the troops were taken for this enterprise, and the territory within which they were to operate, military courtesy required that all orders and instructions should go through him. They were so sent; but General Weitzel has since officially informed me that he never received the foregoing instructions, nor was he aware of their existence until he read General Butler's published official report of the Fort Fisher failure, with my indorsement and papers accompanying it. I had no idea of General Butler's accompanying the expedition until the evening before it got off from Bermuda

Hundred, and then did not dream but that General Weitzel had received all the instructions, and would be in command. I rather formed the idea that General Butler was actuated by a desire to witness the effect of the explosion of the powder-boat. The expedition was detained several days at Hampton Roads, awaiting the loading of the powder-boat.

The importance of getting the Wilmington expedition off without any delay, with or without the powder-boat, had been urged upon General Butler, and he advised to so notify Admiral Porter.

The expedition finally got off on the 13th of December, and arrived at the place of rendezvous, off New Inlet, near Fort Fisher, on the evening of the 15th. Admiral Porter arrived on the evening of the 18th, having put in at Beaufort to get ammunition for the monitors. The sea becoming rough, making it difficult to land troops, and the supply of water and coal being about exhausted, the transport fleet put back to Beaufort to replenish; this, with the state of the weather, delayed the return to the place of rendezvous until the 24th. The powder-boat was exploded on the morning of the 24th, before the return of General Butler from Beaufort; but it would seem from the notice taken of it in the southern newspapers that the enemy were never enlightened as to the object of the explosion until they were informed by the northern press.

On the 25th a landing was effected without opposition, and a reconnoissance, under Brevet Brigadier General Curtis, pushed up towards the fort. But before receiving a full report of the result of this reconnoissance, General Butler, in direct violation of the instructions given, ordered the reëmbarkation of the troops and the return of the expedition.

The reëmbarkation was accomplished by the morning of the 27th.

On the return of the expedition, officers and men — among them Brevet Major General (then Brevet Brigadier General) M. R. Curtis, First Lieutenant G. W. Ross, —— regiment Vermont volunteers, First Lieutenant George W. Walling and Second Lieutenant George Simpson, one hundred and forty-second New York volunteers — voluntarily reported to me that when recalled they were nearly into the fort, and, in their opinion, it could have been taken without much loss.

Soon after the return of the expedition, I received a despatch from the Secretary of the Navy, and a letter from Admiral Porter, informing me that the fleet was still off Fort Fisher, and expressing the conviction that, under a proper leader, the place could be taken. The natural supposition with me was, that when the troops abandoned the expedition, the navy would do so also. Finding it had not, however, I answered on the 30th of December, advising Admiral Porter to hold on, and that I would send a force and make another attempt to take the place. This time I selected Brevet Major General (now Major General) A. H. Terry to command the expedition. The troops composing it consisted of the same that composed the former, with the addition of a small brigade, numbering about one thousand five hundred, and a small siege train. The latter it was never found necessary to land. I communicated direct to the commander of the expedition the following instructions: —

CITY POINT, VA., January 3, 1865.

GENERAL: The expedition intrusted to your command has been fitted out to renew the attempt to capture Fort Fisher, N. C., and Wilmington ultimately, if the fort falls. You will, then, proceed with as little delay as possible to the naval fleet lying off Cape Fear River, and report the arrival of yourself and command to Admiral D. D. Porter, commanding North Atlantic blockading squadron.

It is exceedingly desirable that the most complete understanding should exist between yourself and the naval commander. I suggest, therefore, that you consult with Admiral Porter freely, and get from him the part to be performed by each branch of the public service, so that there may be unity of action. It would be well to have the whole programme laid down in writing. I have served with Admiral Porter, and know that you can rely on his judgment and his nerve to undertake what he proposes. I would, therefore, defer to him as much as is consistent with your own responsibilities. The first object to be attained is to get a firm position on the spit of land on which Fort Fisher is built, from which you can operate against that fort. You want to look to the practicability of receiving your supplies, and to defending yourself against superior forces sent against you by any of the avenues left open to the enemy. If such a position can be obtained, the siege of Fort Fisher will not be abandoned until its reduction is accomplished or another plan of campaign is ordered from these headquarters.

My own views are, that if you effect a landing, the navy ought to run a portion of their fleet into Cape Fear River, while the balance of it operates on the outside. Land forces cannot invest Fort Fisher, or cut it off from supplies or reënforcements, while the river is in possession of the enemy.

A siege train will be loaded on vessels and sent to Fort Monroe, in readiness to be sent to you if required. All other supplies can be drawn from Beaufort as you need them.

Keep the fleet of vessels with you until your position is assured. When you find they can be spared, order them back, or such of them as you can spare, to Fort Monroe, to report for orders.

In case of failure to effect a landing, bring your command back to Beaufort, and report to these headquarters for further instructions. You will not debark at Beaufort until so directed.

General Sheridan has been ordered to send a division of troops to Baltimore, and place them on sea-going vessels. These troops will be brought to Fort Monroe, and kept there on the vessels until you are heard from. Should you require them they will be sent to you.

U. S. GRANT, *Lieutenant General.*

BREVET MAJOR GENERAL A. H. TERRY.

Lieutenant Colonel C. B. Comstock, aide-de-camp (now Brevet Brigadier General), who accompanied the former expedition, was assigned in orders as chief engineer to this.

It will be seen that these instructions did not differ materially from those given for the first expedition; and that in neither instance was there an order to assault Fort Fisher. This was a matter left entirely to the discretion of the commanding officer.

The expedition sailed from Fort Monroe on the morning of the 6th, arriving on the rendezvous, off Beaufort, on the 8th, where, owing to the difficulties of the weather, it lay until the morning of the 12th, when it got under way and reached its destination that evening. Under cover of the fleet, the disembarkation of the troops commenced on the morning of the 13th, and by three o'clock P. M. was completed without loss. On the 14th a reconnoissance was pushed to within five hundred yards of Fort Fisher, and a small advance work taken possession of and turned into a defensive line against any attempt that might be made from the fort. This reconnoissance disclosed the fact that the front of the work had been seriously injured by the navy fire. In the afternoon of the 15th the fort was assaulted, and after most desperate fighting was captured with its entire garrison and armament. Thus was secured, by the combined efforts of the navy and army, one of the most important successes of the war. Our loss was — killed, one hundred and ten; wounded, five hundred and thirty-six. On the 16th and 17th the enemy abandoned and blew up

Fort Caswell and the works on Smith's Island, which were immediately occupied by us. This gave us entire control of the mouth of the Cape Fear River.

At my request Major General B. F. Butler was relieved, and Major General E. O. C. Ord assigned to the command of the Department of Virginia and North Carolina.

The defence of the line of the Tennessee no longer requiring the force which had beaten and nearly destroyed the only army threatening it, I determined to find other fields of operation for General Thomas's surplus troops — fields from which they would coöperate with other movements. General Thomas was therefore directed to collect all troops, not essential to hold his communications, at Eastport, in readiness for orders. On the 7th of January General Thomas was directed, if he was assured of the departure of Hood south from Corinth, to send General Schofield with his corps east with as little delay as possible. This direction was promptly complied with, and the advance of the corps reached Washington on the 23d of the same month, whence it was sent to Fort Fisher and Newbern. On the 26th he was directed to send General A. J. Smith's command and a division of cavalry to report to General Canby. By the 7th of February the whole force was en route for its destination.

The State of North Carolina was constituted into a military department, and General Schofield assigned to command, and placed under the orders of Major General Sherman. The following instructions were given him: —

CITY POINT, VA., January 31, 1865.

GENERAL: . . . Your movements are intended as coöperative with Sherman's through the States of South and North Carolina. The first point to be attained is to secure Wilmington. Goldsboro' will then be your objective point, moving either from Wilmington or Newbern, or both, as you deem best. Should you not be able to reach Goldsboro', you will advance on the line or lines of railway connecting that place with the sea-coast — as near to it as you can, building the road behind you. The enterprise under you has two objects: the first is to give General Sherman material aid, if needed, in his march north; the second, to open a base of supplies for him on his line of march. As soon, therefore, as you can determine which of the two points, Wilmington or Newbern, you can best use for throwing supplies from to the interior, you will commence the accumulation of twenty days' rations and forage for sixty thousand men and twenty thousand animals. You will get of these as many as you can house and protect to such point in the interior as you may be able to occupy. I believe General Palmer has received some instructions direct from General Sherman on the subject of securing supplies for his army. You can learn what steps he has taken, and be governed in your requisitions accordingly. A supply of ordnance stores will also be necessary.

Make all requisitions upon the chiefs of their respective departments in the field with me at City Point. Communicate with me by every opportunity, and should you deem it necessary at any time, send a special boat to Fortress Monroe, from which point you can communicate by telegraph.

The supplies referred to in these instructions are exclusive of those required for your own command.

The movements of the enemy may justify, or even make it your imperative duty, to cut loose from your base and strike for the interior to aid Sherman. In such case you will act on your own judgment, without waiting for instructions. You will report, however, what you purpose doing. The details for carrying out these instructions are necessarily left to you. I would urge, however, if I did not know that you are already fully alive to the importance of it, prompt action. Sherman may be looked for in the neighborhood of Goldsboro' any time from the 22d to the 28th of February: this limits your time very materially.

If rolling stock is not secured in the capture of Wilmington, it can be supplied from Washington. A large force of railroad men have already been sent to Beaufort, and other mechanics will go to Fort Fisher in a day or two. On this point I have informed you by telegraph.

U. S. GRANT, *Lieutenant General.*

MAJOR GENERAL J. M. SCHOFIELD.

Previous to giving these instructions I had visited Fort Fisher, accompanied by General Schofield, for the purpose of seeing for myself the condition of things, and personally conferring with General Terry and Admiral Porter as to what was best to be done.

Anticipating the arrival of General Sherman at Savannah,—his army entirely foot-loose, Hood being then before Nashville, Tennessee, the southern railroads destroyed, so that it would take several months to reëstablish a through line from west to east, and regarding the capture of Lee's army as the most important operation towards closing the rebellion,—I sent orders to General Sherman, on the 6th of December, that after establishing a base on the sea-coast, with necessary garrison to include all his artillery and cavalry, to come by water to City Point with the balance of his command.

On the 18th of December, having received information of the defeat and utter rout of Hood's army by General Thomas, and that, owing to the great difficulty of procuring ocean transportation, it would take over two months to transport Sherman's army, and doubting whether he might not contribute as much towards the desired result by operating from where he was, I wrote to him to that effect, and asked him for his views as to what would be best to do. A few days after this I received a communication from General Sherman, of date 16th December, acknowledging the receipt of my order of the 6th, and informing me of his preparations to carry it into effect as soon as he could get transportation. Also that he had expected, upon reducing Savannah, instantly to march to Columbia, South Carolina, thence to Raleigh, and thence to report to me; but that this would consume about six weeks' time after the fall of Savannah, whereas by sea he could probably reach me by the middle of January. The confidence he manifested in this letter of being able to march up and join me pleased me, and, without waiting for a reply to my letter of the 18th, I directed him, on the 28th of December, to make preparations to start, as he proposed, without delay, to break up the railroads in North and South Carolina, and join the armies operating against Richmond as soon as he could.

On the 21st of January I informed General Sherman that I had ordered the Twenty-third Corps, Major General Schofield commanding, east; that it numbered about twenty-one thousand men; that we had at Fort Fisher about eight thousand men; at Newbern about four thousand; that if Wilmington was captured, General Schofield would go there; if not, he would be sent to Newbern; that, in either event, all the surplus force at both points would move to the interior towards Goldsboro', in coöperation with his movement; that from either point railroad communication could be run out; and that all these troops would be subject to his orders as he came into communication with them.

In obedience to his instructions, General Schofield proceeded to reduce Wilmington, North Carolina, in coöperation with the navy under Admiral Porter, moving his forces up both sides of the Cape Fear River. Fort Anderson, the enemy's main defence on the west bank of the river, was occupied on the morning of the 19th, the enemy having evacuated it after our appearance before it.

After fighting on the 20th and 21st, our troops entered Wilmington on the morning of the 22d, the enemy having retreated towards Goldsboro' during the night. Preparations were at once made for a movement on Goldsboro' in two columns, — one from Wilmington, and the other from Newbern, — and to repair the railroads leading there from each place, as well as to supply General Sherman by Cape Fear River, towards Fayetteville, if it became necessary. The column from Newbern was attacked on the 8th of March at Wise's Forks, and driven back with the loss of several hundred prisoners. On the 11th the enemy renewed his attack upon our intrenched position, but was repulsed with severe loss, and fell back during the night. On the 14th the Neuse River was crossed and Kinston occupied, and on the 21st Goldsboro' was entered. The column from Wilmington reached Cox's Bridge, on the Neuse River, ten miles above Goldsboro', on the 22d.

By the 1st of February General Sherman's whole army was in motion from Savannah. He captured Columbia, South Carolina, on the 17th; thence moved on Goldsboro', North Carolina, via Fayetteville, reaching the latter place on the 12th of March, opening up communication with General Schofield by way of Cape Fear River. On the 15th he resumed his march on Goldsboro'. He met a force of the enemy at Averysboro', and after a severe fight defeated and compelled it to retreat. Our loss in the engagement was about six hundred. The enemy's loss was much greater. On the 18th the combined forces of the enemy, under Joe Johnston, attacked his advance at Bentonville, capturing three guns and driving it back upon the main body. General Slocum, who was in the advance, ascertaining that the whole of Johnston's army was in the front, arranged his troops on the defensive, intrenched himself, and awaited reënforcements, which were pushed forward. On the night of the 21st the enemy retreated to Smithfield, leaving his dead and wounded in our hands. From there Sherman continued to Goldsboro', which place had been occupied by General Schofield on the 21st (crossing the Neuse River ten miles above there, at Cox's Bridge, where General Terry had got possession and thrown a pontoon bridge, on the 22d), thus forming a junction with the columns from Newbern and Wilmington.

Among the important fruits of this campaign was the fall of Charleston, South Carolina. It was evacuated by the enemy on the night of the 17th of February, and occupied by our forces on the 18th.

On the morning of the 31st of January General Thomas was directed to send a cavalry expedition under General Stoneman from East Tennessee, to penetrate South Carolina well down towards Columbia, to destroy the railroads and military resources of the country, and return, if he was able, to East Tennessee, by way of Salisbury, North Carolina, releasing our prisoners there, if possible. Of the feasibility of this latter, however, General Stoneman was to judge. Sherman's movements, I had no doubt, would attract the attention of all the force the enemy could collect, and facilitate the execution of this. General Stoneman was so late in making his start on this expedition (and Sherman having passed out of the State of South Carolina), on the 27th of February I directed General Thomas to change his course, and ordered him to repeat his raid of last fall, destroying the railroad towards Lynchburg as far as he could. This would keep him between our garrisons in East Tennessee and the enemy. I regarded it not impossible that in the event of the enemy being driven from Richmond he might fall back to Lynchburg and attempt a raid north through East Tennessee. On the 14th of February the following communication was sent to General Thomas: —

CITY POINT, VA., February 14, 1865.

General Canby is preparing a movement from Mobile Bay against Mobile and the interior of Alabama. His force will consist of about twenty thousand men, besides A. J. Smith's command. The cavalry you have sent to Canby will be debarked at Vicksburg. It, with the available cavalry already in that section, will move from there eastward, in coöperation. Hood's army has been terribly reduced by the severe punishment you gave it in Tennessee, by desertion consequent upon their defeat, and now by the withdrawal of many of them to oppose Sherman. (I take it a large portion of the infantry has been so withdrawn. It is so asserted in the Richmond papers, and a member of the rebel Congress said a few days since in a speech, that one half of it had been brought to South Carolina to oppose Sherman.) This being true, or even if it is not true, Canby's movement will attract all the attention of the enemy, and leave the advance from your stand-point easy. I think it advisable, therefore, that you prepare as much of a cavalry force as you can spare, and hold it in readiness to go south. The object would be three-fold: first, to attract as much of the enemy's force as possible to insure success to Canby; second, to destroy the enemy's line of communications and military resources; third, to destroy or capture their forces brought into the field. Tuscaloosa and Selma would probably be the points to direct the expedition against. This, however, would not be so important as the mere fact of penetrating deep into Alabama. Discretion should be left to the officer commanding the expedition to go where, according to information he may receive, he will best secure the objects named above.

Now that your force has been so much depleted, I do not know what number of men you can put into the field. If not more than five thousand men, however, all cavalry, I think it will be sufficient. It is not desirable that you should start this expedition until the one leaving Vicksburg has been three or four days out, or even a week. I do not know when it will start, but will inform you by telegraph as soon as I learn. If you should hear through other sources before hearing from me, you can act on the information received.

To insure success, your cavalry should go with as little wagon train as possible, relying upon the country for supplies. I would also reduce the number of guns to a battery, or the number of batteries, and put the extra teams to the guns taken. No guns or caissons should be taken with less than eight horses.

Please inform me by telegraph, on receipt of this, what force you think you will be able to send under these directions.

U. S. GRANT, *Lieutenant General.*

MAJOR GENERAL G. H. THOMAS.

On the 15th he was directed to start the expedition as soon after the 20th as he could get it off.

I deemed it of the utmost importance, before a general movement of the armies operating against Richmond, that all communications with the city, north of James River, should be cut off. The enemy having withdrawn the bulk of his force from the Shenandoah Valley and sent it south, or replaced troops sent from Richmond, and desiring to reënforce Sherman, if practicable, whose cavalry was greatly inferior in numbers to that of the enemy, I determined to make a move from the Shenandoah, which, if successful, would accomplish the first at least, and possibly the latter of these objects. I therefore telegraphed General Sheridan as follows: —

CITY POINT, VA., February 20, 1865 — 1 P. M.

GENERAL: As soon as it is possible to travel, I think you will have no difficulty about reaching Lynchburg with a cavalry force alone. From there you could destroy the railroad and canal in every direction, so as to be of no further use to the rebellion. Sufficient cavalry should be left behind to look after Mosby's gang. From Lynchburg, if information you might get there would justify it, you could strike south, heading the streams in Virginia to the westward of Danville, and push on and join General Sherman. This additional raid, with one now about starting from East Tennessee under Stoneman, numbering four or five thousand cavalry, one from Vicksburg, numbering seven or eight thousand cavalry, one from Eastport, Mississippi, ten thousand cavalry, Canby from Mobile Bay with about thirty-eight thousand mixed troops, these three latter pushing for Tuscaloosa, Selma, and Montgomery, and Sherman with a large army eating out the vitals of South Carolina, is all that will be wanted to leave nothing for the rebellion to stand upon. I would advise you to overcome great obstacles to accomplish this. Charleston was evacuated on Tuesday last.

U. S. GRANT, *Lieutenant General.*

MAJOR GENERAL P. H. SHERIDAN.

On the 25th I received a despatch from General Sheridan, inquiring where Sherman was aiming for, and if I could give him definite information as to the points he might be expected to move on this side of Charlotte, North Carolina. In answer, the following telegram was sent him: —

CITY POINT, VA., February 25, 1865.

GENERAL: Sherman's movements will depend on the amount of opposition he meets with from the enemy. If strongly opposed, he may possibly have to fall back to Georgetown, S. C., and fit out for a new start. I think, however, all danger for the necessity of going to that point has passed. I believe he has passed Charlotte. He may take Fayetteville on his way to Goldsboro'. If you reach Lynchburg, you will have to be guided in your after movements by the information you obtain. Before you could possibly reach Sherman, I think you would find him moving from Goldsboro' towards Raleigh, or engaging the enemy strongly posted at one or the other of these places, with railroad communications opened from his army to Wilmington or Newbern.

U. S. GRANT, *Lieutenant General.*

MAJOR GENERAL P. H. SHERIDAN.

General Sheridan moved from Winchester on the 27th of February, with two divisions of cavalry, numbering about five thousand each. On the 1st of March he secured the bridge, which the enemy attempted to destroy, across the middle fork of the Shenandoah, at Mount Crawford, and entered Staunton on the 2d, the enemy having retreated on Waynesboro'. Thence he pushed on to Waynesboro', where he found the enemy in force in an intrenched position, under General Early. Without stopping to make a reconnoissance, an immediate attack was made, the position was carried, and sixteen hundred prisoners, eleven pieces of artillery, with horses and caissons complete, two hundred wagons and teams loaded with subsistence, and seventeen battle-flags, were captured. The prisoners, under an escort of fifteen hundred men, were sent back to Winchester. Thence he marched on Charlottesville, destroying effectually the railroad and bridges as he went, which place he reached on the 3d. Here he remained two days, destroying the railroad towards Richmond and Lynchburg, including the large iron bridges over the north and south forks of the Rivanna River, and awaiting the arrival of his trains. This necessary delay caused him to abandon the idea of capturing Lynchburg. On the morning of the 6th, dividing his force into two columns, he sent one to Scottsville, whence it marched up the James River Canal to New Market, destroying every lock, and in many places the bank of the canal. From here a force was pushed out from this column to Duiguidsville, to obtain possession of the bridge across the James River at that place, but failed. The enemy burned it on our approach. The enemy also burned the bridge across the river at Hardwicksville. The other column moved down the railroad towards Lynchburg, destroying it as far as Amherst Court-house, sixteen miles from Lynchburg; thence across the country, uniting with the column at New Market. The river being very high, his pontoons would not reach across it; and the enemy having destroyed the bridges by which he had hoped to cross the river and get on the Southside Railroad about Farmville, and destroy it to Appomattox Court-house, the only thing left for him was to return to Winchester or strike a base at the White House. Fortunately he chose the latter. From New Market he took up his line of march, following the canal towards Richmond, destroying every lock upon it, and cutting the banks wherever practicable, to a point eight miles east of Goochland, concentrating the whole force at Columbia on the 10th. Here he rested one day, and sent through by scouts information of his whereabouts and purposes, and a request for supplies to meet him at White House, which reached me on the night of the 12th. An infantry force was immediately sent to get possession of White House, and supplies were forwarded. Moving from Columbia in a direction to threaten

Richmond, to near Ashland Station, he crossed the Annas, and after having destroyed all the bridges and many miles of the railroad, proceeded down the north bank of the Pamunkey to White House, which place he reached on the 19th.

Previous to this the following communication was sent to General Thomas: —

CITY POINT, VA., March 7, 1865 — 9.30 A. M.

GENERAL: I think it will be advisable now for you to repair the railroad in East Tennessee, and throw a good force up to Bull's Gap and fortify there. Supplies at Knoxville could always be got forward as required. With Bull's Gap fortified, you can occupy as outposts about all of East Tennessee, and be prepared, if it should be required of you in the spring, to make a campaign towards Lynchburg, or into North Carolina. I do not think Stoneman should break the road until he gets into Virginia, unless it should be to cut off rolling stock that may be caught west of that.

U. S. GRANT, *Lieutenant General.*

MAJOR GENERAL G. H. THOMAS.

Thus it will be seen that in March, 1865, General Canby was moving an adequate force against Mobile and the army defending it under General Dick Taylor; Thomas was pushing out two large and well-appointed cavalry expeditions, — one from Middle Tennessee under Brevet Major General Wilson against the enemy's vital points in Alabama, the other from East Tennessee under Major General Stoneman towards Lynchburg, — and assembling the remainder of his available forces, preparatory to offensive operations from East Tennessee; General Sheridan's cavalry was at White House; the armies of the Potomac and James were confronting the enemy under Lee in his defences of Richmond and Petersburg; General Sherman with his armies, reënforced by that of General Schofield, was at Goldsboro'; General Pope was making preparations for a spring campaign against the enemy under Kirby Smith and Price, west of the Mississippi; and General Hancock was concentrating a force in the vicinity of Winchester, Virginia, to guard against invasion or to operate offensively, as might prove necessary.

After the long march by General Sheridan's cavalry over winter roads, it was necessary to rest and refit at White House. At this time the greatest source of uneasiness to me was the fear that the enemy would leave his strong lines about Petersburg and Richmond for the purpose of uniting with Johnston, before he was driven from them by battle, or I was prepared to make an effectual pursuit. On the 24th of March General Sheridan moved from White House, crossed the James River at Jones's Landing, and formed a junction with the army of the Potomac in front of Petersburg on the 27th. During this move General Ord sent forces to cover the crossings of the Chickahominy.

On the 24th of March the following instructions for a general movement of the armies operating against Richmond were issued: —

CITY POINT, VA., March 24, 1865.

GENERAL: On the 29th instant the armies operating against Richmond will be moved by our left for the double purpose of turning the enemy out of his present position around Petersburg, and to insure the success of the cavalry under General Sheridan, which will start at the same time, in its efforts to reach and destroy the Southside and Danville Railroads. Two corps of the army of the Potomac will be moved at first in two columns, taking the two roads crossing Hatcher's Run nearest where the present line held by us strikes that stream, both moving towards Dinwiddie Court-house.

The cavalry under General Sheridan, joined by the division now under General Davies, will move at the same time by the Weldon road and the Jerusalem plank road, turning west from the latter before crossing the Nottoway, and west with the whole column before reaching Stony Creek. General Sheridan will then move independently, under other instructions which will be given him. All dismounted cavalry belonging to the army of the Potomac, and the dismounted cavalry from the middle military division not required for guarding property belonging to their arm of service, will report to Brigadier General Benham, to be added to the defences of City Point. Major General Parke will be left in command of all the army left for holding the lines about Petersburg and City Point, subject, of course, to orders from the commander of the army of the Potomac. The Ninth Army Corps will be left intact to hold the present line of works so long as the whole line now occupied by us is held. If, however, the troops to the left of the Ninth Corps are withdrawn, then the left of the corps may be thrown back so as to occupy the position held by the army prior to the capture of the Weldon road. All troops to the left of the Ninth Corps will be held in readiness to move at the shortest notice by such route as may be designated when the order is given.

General Ord will detach three divisions, two white and one colored, or so much of them as he can, and hold his present lines, and march for the present left of the army of the Potomac. In the absence of further orders, or until further orders are given, the white divisions will follow the left column of the army of the Potomac, and the colored division the right column. During the movement Major General Weitzel will be left in command of all the forces remaining behind from the army of the James.

The movement of troops from the army of the James will commence on the night of the 27th instant. General Ord will leave behind the minimum number of cavalry necessary for picket duty, in the absence of the main army. A cavalry expedition from General Ord's command will also be started from Suffolk, to leave there on Saturday the 1st of April, under Colonel Sumner, for the purpose of cutting the railroad about Hicksford. This, if accomplished, will have to be a surprise, and therefore from three to five hundred men will be sufficient. They should, however, be supported by all the infantry that can be spared from Norfolk and Portsmouth, as far out as to where the cavalry crosses the Blackwater. The crossing should probably be at Uniten. Should Colonel Sumner succeed in reaching the Weldon road, he will be instructed to do all the damage possible to the triangle of roads between Hicksford, Weldon, and Gaston. The railroad bridge at Weldon being fitted up for the passage of carriages, it might be practicable to destroy any accumulation of supplies the enemy may have collected south of the Roanoke. All the troops will move with four days' rations in haversacks, and eight days' in wagons. To avoid as much hauling as possible, and to give the army of the James the same number of days' supply with the army of the Potomac, General Ord will direct his commissary and quartermaster to have sufficient supplies delivered at the terminus of the road to fill up in passing. Sixty rounds of ammunition per man will be taken in wagons, and as much grain as the transportation on hand will carry, after taking the specified amount of other supplies. The densely wooded country in which the army has to operate making the use of much artillery impracticable, the amount taken with the army will be reduced to six or eight guns to each division, at the option of the army commanders.

All necessary preparations for carrying these directions into operation may be commenced at once. The reserves of the Ninth Corps should be massed as much as possible. Whilst I would not now order an unconditional attack on the enemy's line by them, they should be ready, and should make the attack if the enemy weakens his line in their front, without waiting for orders. In case they carry the line, then the whole of the Ninth Corps could follow up, so as to join or coöperate with the balance of the army. To prepare for this, the Ninth Corps will have rations issued to them, same as the balance of the army. General Weitzel will keep vigilant watch upon his front, and if found at all practicable to break through at any point, he will do so. A success north of the James should be followed up with great promptness. An attack will not be feasible unless it is found that the enemy has detached largely. In that case it may be regarded as evident that the enemy are relying upon their local reserves, principally, for the defence of Richmond. Preparations may be made for abandoning all the lines north of the James, except enclosed works — only to be abandoned, however, after a break is made in the lines of the enemy.

By these instructions a large part of the armies operating against Richmond is left behind. The enemy, knowing this, may, as an only chance, strip their lines to the merest skeleton, in the hope of advantage not being taken of it, whilst they hurl everything against the moving column, and return. It cannot be impressed too strongly upon commanders of troops left in the trenches not to allow this to occur without taking advantage of it. The very fact of the enemy coming out to attack, if he does so, might be regarded as almost conclusive evidence of such a weakening of his lines. I would have it particularly enjoined upon corps commanders that, in case of an attack from the enemy, those not attacked are not to wait for orders from the commanding officer of the army to which they belong, but that they will move promptly, and notify the commander of their action. I would also enjoin the same action on the part of division commanders when other parts of their corps are engaged. In like manner, I would urge the importance of following up a repulse of the enemy.

U. S. GRANT, *Lieutenant General.*

MAJOR GENERALS MEADE, ORD, AND SHERIDAN.

Early on the morning of the 25th the enemy assaulted our lines in front of the Ninth Corps (which held from the Appomattox River towards our left) and carried Fort Steadman and a part of the line to the right and left of it, established themselves, and turned the guns of the fort against us; but our troops on either flank held their ground until the reserves were brought up, when the enemy was driven back with a heavy loss in killed and wounded, and one thousand nine hundred prisoners. Our loss was sixty-eight killed, three hundred and thirty-seven wounded, and five hundred and six missing. General Meade at once ordered the other corps to advance and feel the enemy in their respective fronts. Pushing forward, they captured and held the enemy's strongly intrenched picket line in front of the Second and Sixth Corps, and eight hundred and thirty-four prisoners. The enemy made desperate attempts to retake this line, but without success. Our loss in front of these was fifty-two killed, eight hundred and sixty-four wounded, and two hundred and seven missing. The enemy's loss in killed and wounded was far greater.

General Sherman, having got his troops all quietly in camp about Goldsboro', and his preparations for furnishing supplies to them perfected, visited me at City Point on the 27th of March, and stated that he would be ready to move, as he had previously written me, by the 10th of April, fully equipped and rationed for twenty days, if it should become necessary to bring his command to bear against Lee's army, in coöperation with our forces in front of Richmond and Petersburg. General Sherman proposed in this movement to threaten Raleigh, and then, by turning suddenly to the right, reach the Roanoke at Gaston or thereabouts, whence he could move on to the Richmond and Danville Railroad, striking it in the vicinity of Burkesville, or join the armies operating against Richmond, as might be deemed best. This plan he was directed to carry into execution, if he received no further directions in the mean time. I explained to him the movement I had ordered to commence on the 29th of March. That if it should not prove as entirely successful as I hoped, I would cut the cavalry loose to destroy the Danville and Southside Railroads, and thus deprive the enemy of furthur supplies, and also prevent the rapid concentration of Lee and Johnston's armies.

I had spent days of anxiety lest each morning should bring the report that the enemy had retreated the night before. I was firmly convinced that Sherman's crossing the Roanoke would be the signal for Lee to leave. With Johnston and him combined, a long, tedious, and expensive campaign, consuming most of the summer, might become necessary. By moving out I would put the army in better condition for pursuit, and would, at least, by the destruction of the Danville road, retard the concentration of the two armies of Lee and Johnston, and cause the enemy to abandon much material that he might otherwise save. I therefore determined not to delay the movement ordered.

On the night of the 27th, Major General Ord, with two divisions of the Twenty-fourth Corps, Major General Gibbon commanding, and one division of the Twenty-fifth Corps, Brigadier General Birney commanding, and McKenzie's cavalry, took up his line of march in pursuance of the foregoing instructions, and reached the position assigned him near Hatcher's Run on the morning of the 29th. On the 28th the following instructions were given to General Sheridan:—

CITY POINT, Va., March 28, 1865.

GENERAL: The Fifth Army Corps will move by the Vaughn Road at three A. M., to-morrow morning. The Second moves at about nine A. M., having but about three miles to march to reach the point designated for it to take on the right of the Fifth Corps, after the latter reaching Dinwiddie Court-house. Move your cavalry at as early an hour as you can, and without being confined to any particular road or roads. You may go out by the nearest roads in rear of the Fifth Corps, pass by its left, and, passing near to or through Dinwiddie, reach the right and rear of the enemy as soon as you can. It is not the intention to attack the enemy in his intrenched position, but to force him out, if possible. Should he come out and attack us, or get himself where he can be attacked, move in with your entire force in your own way, and with the full reliance that the army will engage or follow, as circumstances will dictate. I shall be on the field, and will probably be able to communicate with you. Should I not do so, and you find that the enemy keeps within his main intrenched line, you may cut loose and push for the Danville road. If you find it practicable, I would like you to cross the Southside road, between Petersburg and Burkesville, and destroy it to some extent. I would not advise much detention, however, until you reach the Danville road, which I would like you to strike as near to the Appomattox as possible. Make your destruction on that road as complete as possible. You can then pass on to the Southside road, west of Burkesville, and destroy that in like manner.

After having accomplished the destruction of the two railroads, which are now the only avenues of supply to Lee's army, you may return to this army, selecting your road further south, or you may go on into North Carolina and join General Sherman. Should you select the latter course, get the information to me as early as possible, so that I may send orders to meet you at Goldsboro'.

U. S. GRANT, *Lieutenant General.*

MAJOR GENERAL P. H. SHERIDAN.

On the morning of the 29th the movement commenced. At night the cavalry was at Dinwiddie Court-house, and the left of our infantry line extended to the Quaker road, near its intersection with the Boydton plank road. The position of the troops, from left to right, was as follows: Sheridan, Warren, Humphreys, Ord, Wright, Parke.

Everything looked favorable to the defeat of the enemy, and the capture of Petersburg and Richmond, if the proper effort was made. I therefore addressed the following communication to General Sheridan, having previously informed him verbally not to cut loose for the raid contemplated in his orders until he received notice from me to do so:—

GRAVELLY CREEK, March 29, 1865.

GENERAL: Our line is now unbroken from the Appomattox to Dinwiddie. We are all ready, however, to give up all, from the Jerusalem plank road to Hatcher's Run, whenever the forces can be used advantageously. After getting into line south of Hatcher's, we pushed forward to find the enemy's position. General Griffin was attacked near where the Quaker road intersects the Boydton road, but repulsed it easily, capturing about one hundred men. Humphrey's reached Dabney's mill, and was pushing on when last heard from.

I now feel like ending the matter, if it is possible to do so, before going back. I do not want you, therefore, to cut loose and go after the enemy's roads at present. In the morning push around the enemy, if you can, and get on to his right rear. The movements of the enemy's cavalry may, of course, modify your action. We will act all together as one army here until it is seen what can be done with the enemy. The signal officer at Cobb's Hill reported, at 11.30 A. M., that a cavalry column had passed that point from Richmond towards Petersburg, taking forty minutes to pass.

U. S. GRANT, *Lieutenant General.*

MAJOR GENERAL P. H. SHERIDAN.

From the night of the 29th to the morning of the 31st, the rain fell in such torrents as to make it impossible to move a wheeled vehicle, except as corduroy roads were laid in front of them. During the 30th, Sheridan advanced from Dinwiddie Court-house towards Five Forks, where he found the enemy in force. General Warren advanced and extended his line across the Boydton plank road to near the White Oak road, with a view of getting across the latter; but finding the enemy strong in his front and extending beyond his left, was directed to hold on where he was, and fortify. General Humphreys drove the enemy from his front into his main line on the Hatcher, near Burgess's mills. Generals Ord, Wright, and Parke made examinations in their fronts to determine the feasibility of an assault on the enemy's lines. The two latter reported favorably. The enemy confronting us, as he did, at every point from Richmond to our extreme left, I conceived his lines must be weakly held, and could be penetrated if my estimate of his forces was correct. I determined, therefore, to extend my line no further, but to reënforce General Sheridan with a corps of infantry, and thus enable him to cut loose and turn the enemy's right flank, and with the other corps assault the enemy's lines. The result of the offensive effort of the enemy the week before, when he assaulted Fort Steadman, particularly favored this. The enemy's intrenched picket line captured by us at that time threw the lines occupied by the belligerents so close together at some points that it was but a moment's run from one to the other. Preparations were at once made to relieve General Humphreys' corps, to report to General Sheridan; but the condition of the roads prevented immediate movement. On the morning of the 31st, General Warren reported favorably to getting possession of the White Oak road, and was directed to do so. To accomplish this, he moved with one division, instead of his whole corps, which was attacked by the enemy in superior force, and driven back on the second division before it had time to form, and it, in turn, forced back upon the third division, when the enemy was checked. A division of the Second Corps was immediately sent to his support, the enemy driven back with heavy loss, and possession of the White Oak road gained. Sheridan advanced, and with a portion of his cavalry got possession of the Five Forks, but the enemy, after the affair with the Fifth Corps, reënforced the rebel cavalry, defending that point with infantry, and forced him back towards Dinwiddie Court-house. Here General Sheridan displayed great generalship. Instead of retreating with his whole command on the main army, to tell the story of superior forces encountered, he deployed his cavalry on foot, leaving only mounted men enough to take charge of the horses. This compelled the enemy to deploy over a vast extent of woods and broken country, and made his progress slow. At this juncture he despatched to me what had taken place, and that he was dropping back slowly on Dinwiddie Court-house. General McKenzie's cavalry and one division of the Fifth Corps were immediately ordered to his assistance. Soon after, receiving a report from General Meade that Humphreys could hold our position on the Boydton road, and that the other two divisions of the Fifth Corps could go to Sheridan, they were so ordered at once. Thus the operations of the day necessitated the sending of Warren because of his accessibility, instead of Humphreys, as was intended, and precipitated intended movements.

On the morning of the 1st of April, General Sheridan, reënforced by General Warren, drove the enemy back on Five Forks, where, late in the evening, he assaulted and carried his strongly-fortified position, capturing all his artillery and between five and six thousand prisoners. About the close of this battle, Brevet Major General Charles Griffin relieved Major General Warren in command of the Fifth Corps. The report of this reached me after nightfall. Some apprehensions filled my mind lest the enemy might desert his lines during the night, and by falling upon General Sheridan before assistance could reach him, drive him from his position and open the way for retreat. To guard against this, General Miles's division of Humphreys's corps was sent to reënforce him, and a bombardment was commenced and kept up until four o'clock in the morning (April 2), when an assault was ordered on the enemy's lines. General Wright penetrated the lines with his whole corps, sweeping everything before him and to his left towards Hatcher's Run, capturing many guns and several thousand prisoners. He was closely followed by two divisions of General Ord's command, until he met the other division of General Ord's that had succeeded in forcing the enemy's lines near Hatcher's Run. Generals Wright and Ord immediately swung to the right, and closed all of the enemy on that side of them in Petersburg, while General Humphreys pushed forward with two divisions and joined General Wright on the left. General Parke succeeded in carrying the enemy's main line, capturing guns and prisoners, but was unable to carry his inner line. General Sheridan being advised of the condition of affairs, returned General Miles to his proper command. On reaching the enemy's lines immediately surrounding Petersburg, a portion of General Gibbon's corps, by a most gallant charge, captured two strong enclosed works, — the most salient and commanding south of Petersburg, — thus materially shortening the line of investment necessary for taking in the city. The enemy south of Hatcher's Run retreated westward to Sutherland's Station, where they were overtaken by Miles's division. A severe engagement ensued, and lasted until both his right and left flanks were threatened by the approach of General Sheridan, who was moving from Ford's Station towards Petersburg, and a division sent by General Meade from the front of Petersburg, when he broke in the utmost confusion, leaving in our hands his guns and many prisoners. This force retreated by the main road along the Appomattox River. During the night of the 2d, the enemy evacuated Petersburg and Richmond, and retreated towards Danville. On the morning of the 3d, pursuit was commenced. General Sheridan pushed for the Danville road, keeping near the Appomattox, followed by General Meade with the Second and Sixth Corps, while General Ord moved for Burkesville along the Southside road; the Ninth Corps stretched along that road behind him. On the 4th, General Sheridan struck the Danville road near Jettersville, where he learned that Lee was at Amelia Court-house. He immediately intrenched himself, and awaited the arrival of General

Meade, who reached there the next day. General Ord reached Burkesville on the evening of the 5th.

On the morning of the 5th I addressed Major General Sherman the following communication: —

WILSON'S STATION, April 5, 1865.

GENERAL: All indications now are that Lee will attempt to reach Danville with the remnant of his force. Sheridan, who was up with him last night, reports all that is left, horse, foot, and dragoons, at twenty thousand, much demoralized. We hope to reduce this number one half. I shall push on to Burkesville, and if a stand is made at Danville, will in a very few days go there. If you can possibly do so, push on from where you are, and let us see if we cannot finish the job with Lee's and Johnston's armies. Whether it will be better for you to strike for Greensboro', or nearer to Danville, you will be better able to judge when you receive this. Rebel armies now are the only strategic points to strike at.

U. S. GRANT, *Lieutenant General.*

MAJOR GENERAL W. T. SHERMAN.

On the morning of the 6th, it was found that General Lee was moving west of Jettersville, towards Danville. General Sheridan moved with his cavalry (the Fifth Corps having been returned to General Meade on his reaching Jettersville) to strike his flank, followed by the Sixth Corps, while the Second and Fifth Corps pressed hard after, forcing him to abandon several hundred wagons and several pieces of artillery. General Ord advanced from Burkesville towards Farmville, sending two regiments of infantry and a squadron of cavalry, under Brevet Brigadier General Theodore Read, to reach and destroy the bridges. This advance met the head of Lee's column near Farmville, which it heroically attacked and detained until General Read was killed and his small force overpowered. This caused a delay in the enemy's movements, and enabled General Ord to get well up with the remainder of his force, on meeting which the enemy immediately intrenched himself. In the afternoon General Sheridan struck the enemy south of Sailor's Creek, captured sixteen pieces of artillery, and about four hundred wagons, and detained him until the Sixth Corps got up, when a general attack of infantry and cavalry was made, which resulted in the capture of six or seven thousand prisoners, among whom were many general officers. The movements of the Second Corps and General Ord's command contributed greatly to the day's success.

On the morning of the 7th the pursuit was renewed, the cavalry, except one division, and the Fifth Corps moving by Prince Edward's Court-house; the Sixth Corps, General Ord's command, and one division of cavalry, on Farmville, and the Second Corps by the High Bridge road. It was soon found that the enemy had crossed to the north side of the Appomattox; but so close was the pursuit that the Second Corps got possession of the common bridge at High Bridge before the enemy could destroy it, and immediately crossed over. The Sixth Corps and a division of cavalry crossed at Farmville to its support.

Feeling now that General Lee's chance of escape was utterly hopeless, I addressed him the following communication from Farmville:—

April 7, 1865.

GENERAL: The result of the last week must convince you of the hopelessness of further resistance on the part of the army of Northern Virginia in this struggle. I feel that it is so, and regard it as my duty to shift from myself the responsibility of any further effusion of blood by asking of you the surrender of that portion of the Confederate States army known as the army of Northern Virginia.

U. S. GRANT, *Lieutenant General.*

GENERAL R. E. LEE.

Early on the morning of the 8th, before leaving, I received, at Farmville, the following:—

April 7, 1865.

GENERAL: I have received your note of this date. Though not entertaining the opinion you express on the hopelessness of further resistance on the part of the army of Northern Virginia, I reciprocate your desire to avoid useless effusion of blood, and therefore, before considering your proposition, ask the terms you will offer on condition of its surrender.

R. E. LEE, *General.*

LIEUTENANT GENERAL U. S. GRANT.

To this I immediately replied,—

April 8, 1865.

GENERAL: Your note of last evening, in reply to mine of same date, asking the condition on which I will accept the surrender of the army of Northern Virginia, is just received. In reply, I would say that *peace* being my great desire, there is but one condition I would insist upon, namely: that the men and officers surrendered shall be disqualified for taking up arms again against the government of the United States until properly exchanged. I will meet you, or will designate officers to meet any officers you may name for the same purpose, at any point agreeable to you, for the purpose of arranging definitely the terms upon which the surrender of the army of Northern Virginia will be received.

U. S. GRANT, *Lieutenant General.*

GENERAL R. E. LEE.

Early on the morning of the 8th tne pursuit was resumed. General Meade followed north of the Appomattox, and General Sheridan, with all the cavalry, pushed straight for Appomattox Station, followed by General Ord's command and the Fifth Corps. During the day General Meade's advance had considerable fighting with the enemy's rear guard, but was unable to bring on a general engagement. Late in the evening General Sheridan struck the railroad at Appomattox Station, drove the enemy from there, and captured twenty-five pieces of artillery, a hospital train, and four trains of cars loaded with supplies for Lee's army. During this day I accompanied General Meade's column, and about midnight received the following communication from General Lee: —

April 8, 1865.

GENERAL: I received at a late hour your note of to-day. In mine of yesterday I did not intend to propose the surrender of the army of Northern Virginia, but to ask the terms of your proposition. To be frank, I do not think the emergency has arisen to call for the surrender of this army, but as the restoration of peace should be the sole object of all, I desired to know whether your proposals would lead to that end. I cannot, therefore, meet you with a view to surrender the army of Northern Virginia, but as far as your proposal may affect the Confederate States forces under my command, and tend to the restoration of peace, I should be pleased to meet you at ten A. M., to-morrow, on the old stage road to Richmond, between the picket lines of the two armies.

R. E. LEE, *General.*

LIEUTENANT GENERAL U. S. GRANT.

Early on the morning of the 9th I returned him an answer as follows, and immediately started to join the column south of the Appomattox: —

April 9, 1865.

GENERAL: Your note of yesterday is received. I have no authority to treat on the subject of peace; the meeting proposed for ten A. M. to-day could lead to no good. I will state, however, General, that I am equally anxious for peace with yourself, and the whole North entertains the same feeling. The terms upon which peace can be had are well understood. By the South laying down their arms they will hasten that most desirable event, save thousands of human lives, and hundreds of millions of property not yet destroyed. Seriously hoping that all our difficulties may be settled without the loss of another life, I subscribe myself, &c.,

U. S. GRANT, *Lieutenant General.*

GENERAL R. E. LEE.

On the morning of the 9th, General Ord's command and the Fifth Corps reached Appomattox Station just as the enemy was making a desperate effort to break through our cavalry. The infantry was at once thrown in. Soon after a white flag was received, requesting a suspension of hostilities pending negotiations for a surrender.

Before reaching General Sheridan's headquarters, I received the following from General Lee:—

April 9, 1865.

GENERAL: I received your note of this morning on the picket line, whither I had come to meet you, and ascertain definitely what terms were embraced in your proposal of yesterday with reference to the surrender of this army. I now ask an interview in accordance with the offer contained in your letter of yesterday for that purpose.

R. E. LEE, *General.*

LIEUTENANT GENERAL U. S. GRANT.

The interview was held at Appomattox Court-house, the result of which is set forth in the following correspondence:—

APPOMATTOX COURT-HOUSE, VA., April 9, 1865.

GENERAL: In accordance with the substance of my letter to you of the 8th instant, I propose to receive the surrender of the army of Northern Virginia on the following terms, to wit: Rolls of all the officers and men to be made in duplicate, one copy to be given to an officer to be designated by me, the other to be retained by such officer or officers as you may designate. The officers to give their individual paroles not to take up arms against the government of the United States until properly exchanged; and each company or regimental commander sign a like parole for the men of their commands. The arms, artillery, and public property to be parked and stacked, and turned over to the officers appointed by me to receive them. This will not embrace the side-arms of the officers nor their private horses or baggage. This done, each officer and man will be allowed to return to his home, not to be disturbed by United States authority so long as they observe their paroles and the laws in force where they may reside.

U. S. GRANT, *Lieutenant General.*

GENERAL R. E. LEE.

HEADQUARTERS ARMY OF NORTHERN VIRGINIA, April 9, 1865.

GENERAL: I received your letter of this date, containing the terms of the surrender of the army of Northern Virginia as proposed by you. As they are substantially the same as those expressed in your letter of the 8th instant, they are accepted. I will proceed to designate the proper officers to carry the stipulations into effect.

R. E. LEE, *General.*

LIEUTENANT GENERAL U. S. GRANT.

The command of Major General Gibbon, the Fifth Army Corps under Griffin, and McKenzie's cavalry, were designated to remain at Appomattox Court-house until the paroling of the surrendered army was completed, and to take charge of the public property. The remainder of the army immediately returned to the vicinity of Burkesville.

General Lee's great influence throughout the whole South caused his example to be followed; and to-day the result is, that the armies lately under his leadership are at their homes, desiring peace and quiet, and their arms are in the hands of our ordnance officers.

On the receipt of my letter of the 5th, General Sherman moved directly against Joe Johnston, who retreated rapidly on and through Raleigh, which place General Sherman occupied on the morning of the 13th. The day preceding, news of the surrender of General Lee reached him at Smithfield.

On the 14th a correspondence was opened between General Sherman and General Johnston, which resulted, on the 18th, in an agreement for a suspension of hostilities, and a memorandum or basis for peace, subject to the approval of the President. This agreement was disapproved by the President on the 21st, which disapproval, together with your instructions, was communicated to General Sherman by me in person on the morning of the 24th, at Raleigh, North Carolina, in obedience to your orders. Notice was at once given by him to General Johnston for the termination of the truce that had been entered into. On the 25th another meeting between them was agreed upon, to take place on the 26th, which terminated in the surrender and disbandment of Johnston's army upon substantially the same terms as were given to General Lee.

The expedition under General Stoneman, from East Tennessee, got off on the 20th of March, moving by way of Boone, North Carolina, and struck the railroad at Wytheville, Chambersburg, and Big Lick. The force striking it at Big Lick pushed on to within a few miles of Lynchburg, destroying the important bridges, while with the main force he effectually destroyed it between New River and Big Lick, and then turned for Greensboro', on the North Carolina Railroad; struck that road, and destroyed the bridges between Danville and Greensboro', and between Greensboro' and the Yadkin, together with the depots of supplies along it, and captured four hundred prisoners. At Salisbury he attacked and defeated a force of the enemy under General Gardiner, capturing fourteen pieces of artillery and thirteen hundred and sixty-four prisoners, and destroyed large amounts of army stores. At this place he destroyed fifteen miles of railroad and the bridges towards Charlotte. Thence he moved to Slatersville.

General Canby, who had been directed in January to make preparations for a movement from Mobile Bay against Mobile and the interior of Alabama, commenced his movement on the 20th of March. The Sixteenth Corps, Major General A. J. Smith commanding, moved from Fort Gaines by water to Fish River; the Thirteenth Corps, under Major General Gordon Granger, moved from Fort Morgan and joined the Sixteenth Corps on Fish River, both moving thence on Spanish Fort, and investing it on the 27th; while Major General Steele's command moved from Pensacola, cut the railroad leading from Tensas to Montgomery, effected a junction with them, and partially invested Fort Blakely. After a severe bombardment of Spanish Fort, a part of its line was carried on the 8th of April. During the night the enemy evacuated the fort. Fort Blakely was carried by assault on the 9th, and many prisoners captured; our loss was considerable. These successes practically opened to us the Alabama River, and enabled us to approach Mobile from the north. On the night of the 11th the city was evacuated, and was taken possession of by our forces on the morning of the 12th.

The expedition under command of Brevet Major General Wilson, consisting of twelve thousand five hundred mounted men, was delayed by rains until March 22, when it moved from Chickasaw, Alabama. On the 1st of April General Wilson encountered the enemy in force, under Forrest, near Ebenezer Church, drove him in confusion, captured three hundred prisoners and three guns, and destroyed the Central Bridge over the Cahawba River. On the 2d he attacked and captured the fortified city of Selma, defended by Forrest with seven thousand men and thirty-two guns, destroyed the arsenal, armory, naval foundery, machine shops, vast quantities of stores, and captured three thousand prisoners. On the 4th he captured and destroyed Tuscaloosa. On the 10th he crossed the Alabama River, and after sending information of his operations to General Canby, marched on Montgomery, which place he occupied on the 14th, the enemy having abandoned it. At this place many stores and five steamboats fell into our hands. Thence a force marched direct on Columbus, and another on West Point, both of which places were assaulted and captured on the 16th. At the former place we got fifteen hundred prisoners and fifty-two field-guns, destroyed two gunboats, the navy yard, founderies, arsenal, many factories, and much other public property. At the latter place we got three hundred prisoners, four guns, and destroyed nineteen locomotives and three hundred cars. On the 20th he took possession of Macon, Georgia, with sixty field-guns, twelve hundred militia, and five generals, surrendered by General Howell Cobb. General Wilson hearing that Jeff. Davis was trying to make his escape, sent forces in pursuit, and succeeded in capturing him on the morning of May 11.

On the 4th day of May, General Dick Taylor surrendered to General Canby all the remaining rebel forces east of the Mississippi.

A force sufficient to insure an easy triumph over the enemy under Kirby Smith, west of the Mississippi, was immediately put in motion for Texas, and Major General Sheridan designated for its immediate command; but on the 26th day of May, and before they reached their destination, General Kirby Smith surrendered his entire command to Major General Canby. This surrender did not take place, however, until after the capture of the rebel president and vice-president; and the bad faith was exhibited of first disbanding most of his army and permitting an indiscriminate plunder of public property.

Owing to the report that many of those lately in arms against the government had taken refuge upon the soil of Mexico, carrying with them arms rightfully belonging to the United States, which had been surrendered to us by agreement,—among them some of the leaders who had surrendered in person,—and the disturbed condition of affairs on the Rio Grande, the orders for troops to proceed to Texas were not changed.

There have been severe combats, raids, expeditions and movements to defeat the designs and purposes of the enemy, most of them reflecting great credit on our arms, and which contributed greatly to our final triumph, that I have not mentioned. Many of these will be found clearly set forth in the reports herewith submitted; some in the telegrams and brief despatches announcing them, and others, I regret to say, have not as yet been officially reported.

For information touching our Indian difficulties, I would respectfully refer to the reports of the commanders of departments in which they have occurred.

It has been my fortune to see the armies of both the west and the east fight battles, and from what I have seen I know there is no difference in their fighting qualities. All that it was possible for men to do in battle they have done. The western armies commenced their battles in the Mississippi valley, and received the final surrender of the remnant of the principal army opposed to them in North Carolina. The armies of the east commenced their battles on the river from which the army of the Potomac derived its name, and received the final surrender of their old antagonist at Appomattox Court-house, Virginia. The splendid achievements of each have nationalized our victories, removed all sectional jealousies (of which we have unfortunately experienced too much), and the cause of crimination and recrimination that might have followed had either section failed in its duty. All have a proud record, and all sections can well congratulate themselves and each other for having done their full share in restoring the supremacy of law over every foot of territory belonging to the United States. Let them hope for perpetual peace and harmony with that enemy, whose manhood, however mistaken the cause, drew forth such herculean deeds of valor.

I have the honor to be, very respectfully,

Your obedient servant,

U. S. GRANT, *Lieutenant General.*

HON. E. M. STANTON, *Secretary of War.*

ADJUTANT GENERAL'S OFFICE,
November 18, 1865.

Official copy.

E. D. TOWNSEND, *Assistant Adjutant General.*

# VI.

## GRANT'S REPORT AS SECRETARY OF WAR *AD INTERIM* AND GENERAL UNITED STATES ARMY FOR 1867.

WAR DEPARTMENT,
WASHINGTON CITY, November, 1867.

MR. PRESIDENT: I have the honor to submit my report as Secretary of War *ad interim*, and the accompanying reports of the army and bureaus under the War Department, since the last annual report of the Secretary of War.

I assumed the duties of Secretary of War *ad interim* August 12, 1867, in pursuance to the following instructions from the President, to wit:—

"EXECUTIVE MANSION,
"WASHINGTON, D. C., August 12, 1867.

"SIR: The Honorable Edwin M. Stanton having been this day suspended as Secretary of War, you are hereby authorized and empowered to act as Secretary of War *ad interim*, and will at once enter upon the discharge of the duties of that office.

"The Secretary of War has been instructed to transfer to you all records, books, papers, and other public property now in his custody and charge.

"Very respectfully yours,

"ANDREW JOHNSON.

"GENERAL ULYSSES S. GRANT, *Washington, D. C.*"

On receipt of the above I notified the Secretary of War of it, first verbally, and then, at his suggestion, by letter, of which the following is a copy:—

"HEADQUARTERS ARMIES OF THE UNITED STATES,
"WASHINGTON, D. C., August 12, 1867.

"SIR: Enclosed herewith I have the honor to transmit to you a copy of a letter just received from the President of the United States, notifying me of my assignment as Acting Secretary of War, and directing me to assume those duties at once.

"In notifying you of my acceptance, I cannot let the opportunity pass without expressing to you my appreciation of the zeal, patriotism, firmness, and ability with which you have ever discharged the duties of Secretary of War.

"With great respect, your obedient servant,

"U. S. GRANT, *General.*

"HON. E. M. STANTON, *Secretary of War.*"

To this the Secretary of War made this reply: —

"WAR DEPARTMENT,
"WASHINGTON CITY, August 12, 1867.

"GENERAL: Your note of this date, accompanied by a copy of a letter addressed to you, August 12, by the President, appointing you Secretary of War *ad interim*, and informing me of your acceptance of the appointment, has been received.

"Under a sense of public duty I am compelled to deny the President's right, under the constitution and laws of the United States, to suspend me from office as Secretary of War, or to authorize any other person to enter upon the discharge of the duties of that office, or to require me to transfer to you or any other person the records, books, papers, and other property in my official custody and charge as Secretary of War.

"But inasmuch as the President has assumed to suspend me from office as Secretary of War, and you have notified me of your acceptance of the appointment of Secretary of War *ad interim*, I have no alternative but to submit, under protest, to the superior force of the President.

"You will please accept my acknowledgment of the kind terms in which you have notified me of your acceptance of the President's appointment, and my cordial reciprocation of the sentiments expressed.

"I am, with sincere regard, truly yours,

"EDWIN M. STANTON, *Secretary of War*.

"GENERAL ULYSSES S. GRANT."

Immediately after this exchange of notes I assumed the duties of the office assigned to me, in addition to the duties of General of the Army.

A long war had entailed upon the army practices of extravagance totally unjustifiable in times of peace; and as the increase of the regular army since 1860 (now almost the entire army) is officered by men whose army experience does not go back to that period (and therefore they may not know but their indulgences at the expense of the general government are all legitimate), retrenchment was the first subject to attract my attention. During the rebellion, ambulances and mounted orderlies at every headquarters had come into use; and since the rebellion they have been continued, if not at every post of a single company, at least generally throughout the army. A discontinuance of this evil was necessary both to the discipline and efficiency of the army and to the relief of the treasury. Orders were therefore given both for breaking it up and seeing to its execution.

The Bureau of Rebel Archives was transferred to the Adjutant General's Department, as was also the Bureau for the Exchange of Prisoners, &c., thus relieving from government employment a large number of clerks and several officers who had, to that date, been continued in service.

Supplying large armies for a period of four years of hostilities necessarily led to an accumulation of stores of all sorts far beyond the wants of our present establishment for many years to come. Many of these articles were of a perishable nature; besides being borne on the returns of officers accountable for them, they had to be stored and guarded, although the cost of care per annum might be greater than their value. Under my direction all these surplus and useless stores in the Quartermaster's Department are being sold, and the balance distributed for issue to troops as they may be wanted. This releases a large number of storehouses for which rent is being paid, and also discharges a large number of civil employees of government.

During the last summer and summer before I caused inspections to be made of the various routes of travel and supply through the territory between the Missouri River and the Pacific coast. The cost of maintaining troops in that section was so enormous that I desired, if possible, to reduce it. This I have been enabled to do, to some extent, from the information obtained by these inspections; but for the present the military establishment between the lines designated must be maintained at a great cost per man. The completion of the railroads to the Pacific will materially reduce this cost, as well as the number of men to be kept there. The completion of these roads will also go far towards a permanent settlement of our Indian difficulties. There is good reason to hope that negotiations now going on with the hostile tribes of Indians will result, if not in a permanent peace, at least in a suspension of hostilities until the railroads are pushed through that portion of the Indian territory where they are giving the most trouble.

### *Freedmen's Bureau.*

From the report of the Commissioner of the Bureau of Refugees, Freedmen, and Abandoned Lands, I make the following synopsis: —

No changes have been made in the organization and practical working of the Bureau of Refugees, Freedmen, and Abandoned Lands, except such as have been caused by the appointment of district commanders under the Reconstruction Act.

The detail of officers serving with troops has enabled the Commissioner to reduce the number of bureau agents. Twenty-eight (28) civil agents have been discharged, and forty-eight (48) mustered out.

The freedmen, as a people, are making rapid progress in education, in mechanic arts, and in all branches of industry.

The amount of "abandoned land" now in possession of the bureau is 215,024 acres, much of which is swamp land, and scarcely any affording revenue. The number of pieces of town property is 950.

The business of adjusting the claims of colored soldiers has greatly increased in good results. The total number of claims presented during the year is 5,535, of which 755 have been finally adjusted, and 4,266 are now awaiting action in the Treasury Department. The amount collected and paid to claimants has been $64,494.29; certificates received by the commissioner and ordered paid, under act of Congress approved March 29, 1867, amounting to $890,712.99.

*Transportation* has been furnished to 778 refugees, and to 16,931 freedmen, to enable them to reach places where they can provide for themselves. Teachers and agents have also received transportation. Railroad accounts for transportation have been audited, amounting to $102,093.99, and the amount paid by the disbursing officer has been $227,754.63.

*Hospitals* are being rapidly closed and dispensaries substituted, as a more economical mode of giving relief to the sick. The number of refugees treated during the year ending August 31, 1867, is 8,853, of whom 196 died, or 2 2-10 per cent. The number of freedmen treated is 135,296; died, 4,640, or 3 4-10 per cent. The number of commissioned medical officers and private physicians employed by the bureau has been 178, of whom 105 were on duty at the end of the year. No adequate provision has been made for the insane, either by state or municipal authorities; but they are cared for in separate wards of bureau hospitals. The average cost of furnishing medical attendance and medicines during the year has been two dollars and seventy-three cents ($2.73) for each patient.

The total expenditures for the medical department have been $301,800.

*Commissary supplies* have been issued to a limited extent. It has been found impracticable to discontinue such issues altogether. The average number of rations for the year ending September 1, 1867, was 11,658 per day. In the latter part of winter the destitution became so great that urgent appeals were made for a more general distribution of supplies. The total amount of supplies furnished by means of the "relief fund" has been 850,388 pounds of pork and bacon, and 6,809,296 pounds of corn. The number of persons receiving relief is reported to have been 233,372. The average number has been 58,000, the largest number being in July, 82,000. The whole expense has been $445,993.36, i. e., nearly $8 to each person for the period of four months, or $2 per month. This special relief was discontinued in August, the funds and supplies remaining on hand being reserved for those who may require help during the coming winter.

*The schools* have increased in number and usefulness. Normal and training schools are well attended. The total of day and night schools reported, including industrial, but not the Sunday schools, is 2,207, with 2,442 teachers and 130,735 scholars; an increase of 40,000 since the last annual report. Of these, 1,056 schools are sustained wholly or in part by freedmen, and 391 buildings are owned by them. Of the teachers, 699 are colored and 1,388 white.

The average amount of tuition paid per month by the freedmen has been $14,555.

*Finances.*—Appropriation for the year ending July 1, 1868, $3,836,300.

Total expenditures from October 1, 1866, to August 31, 1867, eleven months, $3,597,397.65.

The principal items of expenditures are: for schools and school buildings, $553,915.79; subsistence stores, $1,460,326.28; transportation, $227,754.63; salaries of agents, clerks, &c., $521,421.44; medical department, $331,001.21; quarters and fuel, $135,098.64; clothing, $116,688.80.

The balance of the expenditure, $251,190.86, has been for printing, postage, and other contingencies.

The surplus from the unexpended appropriations of 1866, with the balance of the appropriations of this year, will be sufficient for the purposes of the bureau during the present fiscal year ending June 30, 1868. In addition to the above proper expenditures, the disbursing officer has paid back to colored soldiers, or their heirs, retained state bounties to the amount of $51,720.83, and has paid claims of colored soldiers, under joint resolution of Congress approved March 29, 1867, to the amount of $350,870.96.

*Apprenticeship* in Maryland still holds large numbers of colored children in virtual slavery. The evils and cruelties resulting from this system, sanctioned by the state laws, are matters of constant complaint. As many as two thousand cases have been presented in a single county.

*Education.* — In all the schools in the District of Columbia and West Virginia there have been 7,998 scholars and 229 teachers. In West Virginia the schools have been sustained in part from the public school fund, where an impartial system of free schools exists. In the District of Columbia the colored schools are also entitled to a proportionate share of the public school fund, but the city authorities have not yet paid the entire sum claimed. It is probable, however, that the trustees of the colored schools will recover all that is due, and in future receive an equitable share of the public funds, in which case the colored schools will be independent of the bureau. Several institutions of higher grade than common schools have been established, and have made a good beginning. Among these are the National Theological Institute, in Washington, under the auspices of the Baptist denomination; the normal school and college at Harper's Ferry, conducted by the Free-will Baptists, and the Howard University, in the District of Columbia, which is designed to be national and free to all. The normal and preparatory department has been opened with about sixty scholars, and buildings are now being erected for other departments.

To provide cheap homes for industrious colored men, a farm has been purchased, surveyed into acre lots, and sold at cost. The lots have been taken up rapidly, and payments upon them promptly made.

Expenditures have fallen below the original estimates. No further appropriation of funds is asked for. As the bureau will expire next July, unless extended by Congress, no funds are estimated for the next fiscal year. In case the bureau is not extended, it is recommended by the Commissioner that proper arrangements be made with the state authorities for the care of indigent classes; that the educational work be continued under the direction of the Bureau of Education or other United States agency, with full power and means to maintain and extend the present system; and that the Claim Division be continued in connection with the War Department as long as it may be deemed necessary by the Secretary of War.

This is but a brief abstract of the report of the Commissioner of Refugees, Freedmen, and Abandoned Lands. Special attention to the report itself is respectfully invited. No recommendation is made at the present time respecting the continuance or discontinuance of this bureau. During the session of Congress, facts may develop themselves requiring special legislation in the premises, when the necessary recommendations can be made.

### *Adjutant General.*

The report of the Adjutant General of the army shows the organization and present strength of the army, the force stationed in each military department and district, the number of recruits enlisted, and desertions from October 1, 1866, to September 20, 1867, and the organization of the colored troops.

On the 30th of September, 1867, the aggregate strength of the army (officers and men) was 56,815; the number of recruits, 34,191; and desertions, 13,608.

The recruiting service has been very successful, and men have been supplied as fast as needed.

The greatly enlarged numbers of the army, and of the military posts occupied by it, render it necessary that some change should be made in the present system of courts-martial and of punishments. The organization of "companies of discipline" is recommended. It is also recommended that, for the good of the service, the term of enlistment be changed from three to five years. In the cavalry it is five years, but the other arms of the service only enlist for three.

At the date of the last report, 11,043 volunteers still remained in service. That number has been reduced, and now only 203 commissioned officers remain, and no enlisted men. These officers are kept by special acts authorizing retention of volunteers in Freedmen's Bureau.

The mustering and disbursing officers have all been discontinued, except at Albany, New York; Philadelphia, Pennsylvania; Columbus, Ohio; Louisville, Kentucky; St. Louis, Missouri; Santa Fé, New Mexico; and San Francisco, California. No appropriation is required for the volunteer disbursing branch for the next year.

Attention is called to the great number of desertions, and the necessity for a change in the present system of courts-martial and of punishment to abate the evil.

I would recommend an increase of three assistant adjutants general. This would enable the assignment of one to each of the major generals and brigadier generals of the army, and avoid the necessity of detaching officers from their legitimate duties to act as assistant adjutants general.

### *Inspector General.*

During the year there has been no change in the Inspector General's Department, except that two of the assistant inspectors general have been promoted from majors to lieutenant colonels, under the provisions of the act of Congress approved July 28, 1866. The number of officers in this branch of the service is too small to properly make the required special and stated inspections, whereby many abuses and irregularities have crept into the service. The immediate organization of an inspection department, composed of competent, active officers, is respectfully recommended to the attention of the authorities.

### *The Chief of the Bureau of Military Justice*

Reports, that in the Bureau of Military Justice, during the past year, 11,432 records of military courts were received, reviewed, and registered; 2,135 special reports made as to the regularity of judicial proceedings, the pardon of military offenders, the remission or commutation of sentences, and upon the miscellaneous subjects and questions of law referred for the opinion of the bureau.

The only change made in the conduct of the bureau and the status of its officers during the year has been in the detailing, by the order of the Secretary of War, of the assistant judge advocate general and four judge advocates, for service at the headquarters, respectively, of the five military districts established by the act of Congress of March 2, 1867. From official reports of the district commanders, and other communications, it is believed that the services of these officers have been of an important and valuable character. The satisfactory manner in which they are represented as having performed their duties, which have been both of an advisory and judicial character, is deemed especially to vindicate the policy of Congress in retaining in the army a small body of officers instructed in military and common law, by constituting the corps of judge advocates a part of the permanent regular establishment.

*Quartermaster General.*

The Quartermaster General submits full financial statement and analysis of accounts for fiscal year ending June 30, 1867, showing that during the past year 11,130 accounts have been examined, amounting to $309,738,171.89, and of accounts remaining to be examined 1,544, amounting to $47,451,262.74.

Sixteen thousand and eighty-six horses and mules were purchased during the year for the public service.

The sales of surplus or unserviceable animals during the year amount to $268,572.24. The total sales of this character since the close of active hostilities in 1865 amount to $16,215,716.16.

The supply of clothing and equipage is so large that no purchases of these articles will be necessary for the next year.

The amount of clothing and equipage issued under the act of Congress approved July 14, 1866, to families rendered houseless and destitute by the recent conflagration in Portland, Maine, is fully set forth in report.

The fund of $1,000,000, known as the sheltering fund for the troops on the plains, has been applied to the purposes for which it was intended.

One thousand temporary buildings have been sold during the year for the sum of $112,000.

The erection of the fire-proof warehouse in Philadelphia is in process of construction. The contract price for building is

$138,800. It will probably be ready for occupancy in December next.

The United States not owning any land at or near the city of Jeffersonville, Indiana, and no appropriation having been made to purchase land as a site for the buildings, no steps have been taken to execute the provisions of the fourth section of the act of Congress approved February 2, 1867, authorizing the erection of fireproof buildings at that place.

There are 308 cemeteries in the United States, in which are interred the bodies of United States soldiers. Eighty-one of these are known as "national cemeteries." The total number of United States soldiers interred in cemeteries is 251,827, of which 238,666 are interred in the national cemeteries. Seventy-six thousand two hundred and sixty-three bodies are yet to be interred in these cemeteries, which, when completed, will make the total number 328,090. Twenty thousand eight hundred and sixty-one rebel prisoners of war have been interred. The estimated cost for fencing the cemeteries is $709,000. The amount already expended on cemeteries is estimated at $1,737,000. The total cost of the cemeteries, when completed, is estimated at $3,500,000.

On July 1, 1866, the southern railroads were indebted to the government to the amount of $6,570,074.05. June 30. 1867, this amount was reduced to $5,921,372.10.

The number of troops and the quantity of supplies transported up to the 20th September were as follows: Passengers, 73,196; animals, 7,194; public freight, 306,576 tons, at a cost of $4,048,000.

During the fiscal year there were presented 24,417 claims, amounting to $13,924,764.10, of which —

| | |
|---|---|
| 5,408 claims were approved, amounting to . . . . | $5,440,041 48 |
| 6,513 claims were not allowed, amounting to . . . . | 3,613,866 99 |
| 12,496 claims are awaiting action, amounting to . . | 4,870,855 63 |
| | 13,924,764 10 |

On the 1st of July, 1866, the organization of the department consisted of 67 officers and 12 military storekeepers, — total 79. By the act approved July 28, 1866, the department was reorganized, and now consists of 76 officers and 16 military storekeepers with the rank of captain, making a total of 92. Five assistant quartermasters general have been retired. The number of volunteer officers in the department has been reduced from 107 to 31. Those remaining at the close of the year were fully employed upon important duties.

It is found that the number of officers of the quartermasters' department, as authorized by the act of July 28, 1866, is insufficient to the prompt performance of the duties devolving upon them. It is therefore respectfully recommended that a portion of section 13 of the act approved July 28, 1866, be repealed, and that there be added to the quartermasters' department so many assistant quartermasters, with the rank, pay, and emoluments of captains of cavalry, as will raise the number of officers of that grade to fifty; and that the vacancies thereby created in the grade of assistant quartermaster shall be filled by selection from those persons who have rendered meritorious services in the military service of the United States as assistant quartermasters of volunteers in the late war.

All of the officers of the department are highly commended for the able, conscientious, and faithful manner in which they have discharged the highly important duties devolving upon them in the various details of business pertaining to the department.

*Commissary General.*

The Commissary General of Subsistence reports that during the past year subsistence stores for the army have been procured in the usual manner, by advertising for proposals in the larger markets of the country. Efforts have been made with considerable success to obtain supplies from the producers and dealers established near the point of consumption. The completion and extension of the Union Pacific Railroad already afford great facilities for reaching and supplying distant occupied posts, heretofore supplied by trains of wagons at special seasons of the year. Recent reports from the military division of the Pacific give assurances of success in the efforts to supply the troops of that division with pork made on the coast. This article has heretofore been shipped from New York. Tobacco has been supplied to the enlisted men of the army under the sixth section of the act of March 3, 1865, to the amount of $104,895.84. Subsistence to the amount of $882,684.66 has been furnished by this department, for the fiscal year ending June 30, 1867, to freedmen and others, under the proper and authorized demands of the officers and agents of the Bureau of Refugees, Freedmen, and Abandoned Lands. The total cost of subsistence stores issued or transferred for the subsistence of Indians for the fiscal year ending June 30, 1867, is $644,439.22. The number of claims presented and paid under public resolution No. 56, approved July 25, 1866, up to September 12, 1867, was 2,069, and amounted to $116,187.75. The number presented and passed for payment under section three of the act of March 2, 1867, was five, and amounted to $259.50.

The total number of claims received under the third section of the act approved July 4, 1864, is 4,926, amounting to $2,493,257.45; of which number there have been examined and approved 482, amounting to $146,149.51; examined and rejected, 1,881, amounting to $1,071,194.42; leaving for final action and decision 2,563, amounting to $1,275,913.32.

The number of claims examined and decided since the last annual report is 1,190, amounting to $480,436.60; of which number there have been approved 248, amounting to $60,806.41; rejected, 942, amounting to $419,630.19.

The officers of the department have all performed their duties with zeal and ability.

All of the commissaries of subsistence of volunteers have now been mustered out except two, who are by authority of law on duty in the Bureau of Refugees, Freedmen, and Abandoned Lands.

No appropriation having been made to meet the large expenditures necessary to carry out the provisions of section 25 of the act approved July 28, 1866, an order was issued permitting sutlers to continue to trade with troops until further orders.

The law authorizing the appointment of commissaries of subsistence having expired, it is suggested that it be recommended to Congress to authorize the General commanding the army to appoint from the lieutenants of the line, on the recommendation of the Commissary General of Subsistence, as many assistant commissaries of subsistence as the service may require, not to exceed thirty-two, such officers to be paid $20 a month in addition to their proper pay and emoluments, but without loss of the fourth ration, and to hold their appointment until cancelled by their promotion to the grade of captain or by order of the General.

It is also suggested that it would be highly beneficial to the service could there be authorized a grade of non-commissioned officers, to be called post commissary sergeants, to be selected and appointed as are ordnance sergeants, and to have the same rank, pay, and emoluments — the number not to exceed one to each military post.

The recommendation of the Commissary General for the appointment of thirty-two assistant commissaries is approved. It is absolutely necessary that there should be, and there is, an officer acting as commissary at every post garrisoned by troops. The only bonded officers to act in such capacity are the officers of the subsistence department and the regimental quartermasters. The same bond should be required from assistant commissaries as is required to be given by the latter. The additional pay would only be allowed when the duty of assistant commissary was performed, and they would never perform that duty at a post of less than a full regiment when there was present either a commissary or a regimental quartermaster.

I would recommend that no appropriation be made to execute the requirements of section 25 of the act of Congress entitled "An act to increase and fix the military peace establishment of the United States," and that public resolution of Congress No. 33, approved March 30, 1867, as promulgated in the following orders, be continued in force: —

[*General Orders, No.* 54.]

WAR DEPARTMENT, ADJUTANT GENERAL'S OFFICE,
WASHINGTON, April 15, 1867.

The following resolution of Congress is published for the information and government of all concerned: —

[PUBLIC RESOLUTION — No. 33.]

A RESOLUTION to authorize the commanding general of the army to permit traders to remain at certain military posts.

*Resolved by the Senate and House of Representatives of the United States of America in Congress assembled,* That the commanding general of the army shall be authorized to permit a trading establishment to be maintained, after the first day of July, eighteen hundred and sixty-seven, at any military post on the frontier not in the vicinity of any city or town, and situated at any point between the one hundredth meridian of longitude west from Greenwich and the eastern boundary of the State of California, when, in his judgment, such establishment is needed for the accommodation of emigrants, freighters, and other citizens: *Provided*, That after the commissary department shall be prepared to supply stores to soldiers as required by law, no trader permitted to remain at such post shall sell any goods kept by the commissary department to any enlisted men: *And provided further*, That such traders shall be under protection and military control as camp followers.

Approved March 30, 1867.

By order of the Secretary of War.

E. D. TOWNSEND, *Assistant Adjutant General.*

[*General Orders, No.* 58.]

HEADQUARTERS OF THE ARMY,
ADJUTANT GENERAL'S OFFICE,
WASHINGTON, May 24, 1867.

So much of paragraph II, General Orders No. 6, dated War Department, January 26, 1867, as is inconsistent with the following, is by direction of the Secretary of War revoked:

The Commissary General of Subsistence having reported that no special appropriation has been made by Congress to enable the subsistence department to carry into effect section twenty-five of the act of Congress approved July 28, 1866, which abolishes the office of sutler, and requires said department to furnish for sale to officers and soldiers such articles (heretofore supplied by sutlers) as may be designated by the inspectors general of the army; and in view of the large expenditure of funds necessary to furnish such supplies, and the delay which must ensue before an appropriation can be made for this purpose, it is ordered, that the sutlers at military posts on the frontier, not in the vicinity of any city or town, and situated between the one hundredth meridian of longitude west from Greenwich and the eastern boundary of the State of California, shall, after the 1st of July, 1867, be retained, until further orders, as traders at such military posts, under the resolution of Congress approved March 30, 1867, authorizing the commanding general of the army to permit traders to remain at certain military posts.

Should the commanding officer of any post included in this order consider the present sutler of his post an unfit person to hold the office of trader, he will forward a report to that effect through intermediate commanders to these headquarters.

By command of General Grant.

E. D. TOWNSEND, *Assistant Adjutant General.*

[*General Orders, No.* 68.]

HEADQUARTERS OF THE ARMY,
ADJUTANT GENERAL'S OFFICE,
WASHINGTON, July 19, 1867.

*Traders at military posts.*

General Order No. 58, of May 24, 1867, is modified so as to permit any persons, without limit as to number, to trade at the military posts situated between the one nundredth meridian of longitude west from Greenwich and the eastern boundary of the State of California, subject only to such regulations and restrictions as may be imposed by department commanders.

By command of General Grant.

E. D. TOWNSEND, *Assistant Adjutant General.*

### *Surgeon General.*

From the report of the Surgeon General it will be found that, since October 20, 1866, three surgeons, six assistant surgeons, and seven acting assistant surgeons have died. Of these five died of yellow fever and three of Asiatic cholera.

In the month of June of the present year Asiatic cholera appeared among the troops at various points in the west and northwest; and for a time fears of a wide-spread epidemic were entertained. Recent reports from the infected command show that the disease has subsided, or has been eradicated by vigorous hygienic measures.

The valuable medical and mortuary records of this department were transferred to the fire-proof building on Tenth Street, in December, 1866. During the year official evidence has been furnished from these records of the death or discharge for disability in 55,500 cases.

Four thousand and eight monthly reports of sick and wounded, 315 special reports, 598 folio records of hospital records, 2,365 burial records, and 1,262 hospital muster and pay-rolls have been received during the year. The alphabetical registers of the dead, as far as completed, contain the names of 244,747 white soldiers, 29,796 colored soldiers, and 30,204 rebel soldiers.

In the division of surgical records the histories of 45,551 wounded men have been traced out and entered upon the permanent registers. The number thus entered now amounts to 207,941. The histories of the graver injuries, and of those cases in which important operations were performed, are very fully recorded.

Fifty-nine thousand five hundred and nineteen cases of wounds and operations occurring previous to the present system of registration and return of injuries have been compiled, and will be entered upon the permanent registers.

The average annual strength of white troops is represented by the reports at 41,104. The number taken on sick report for diseases, wounds, and injuries, 122,181, an average of nearly three entries on sick report for each man. The mortality during the year was 1,527. The average annual strength of the colored troops, as shown by the reports, is 6,561. The number taken on sick report for disease, wounds, and injuries was 19,694, an average of three entries on sick report for each man. The total number of white and colored soldiers discharged during the year on surgeons' certificate of disability is 618.

The Army Medical Museum was removed to the building on Tenth Street in April last. Eight thousand five hundred and forty-two specimens have been catalogued, and a small appropriation will be required to continue and preserve this invaluable collection.

In September, 1867, a medical board was convened in New York city for the examination of candidates for the position of assistant surgeons in the army and the promotion of assistant surgeons, which resulted in the appointment of forty-seven as assistant surgeons in the army, and the promotion of fourteen assistant surgeons.

Of artificial legs, arms, &c., there were issued during the past year, to wounded soldiers, 573 pieces.

| | |
|---|---|
| The funds of the medical and hospital department for the fiscal year ending June 30, 1867, consisted of a balance remaining in the treasury June 30, 1866 . . . . | $2,546,457 14 |
| Amount issued by the treasury in June, 1866, to disbursing officers, but which had not come to hand July 1, 1866 . | 37,000 00 |
| Balance of appropriation for artificial limbs under act of July 16, 1862 . . . . . . . . . . | 540 00 |
| Appropriation for the year ending June 30, 1867, by act of July 13, 1866 . . . . . . . . . . | 500,000 00 |
| Amount derived from the sale of old and surplus hospital property . . . . . . . . . . . | 293,002 82 |
| From boards of officers in hospitals . . . . . . | 327 85 |
| For care of citizen patients in United States hospital at Louisville, Kentucky . . . . . . . . . | 1,270 88 |
| Refunded from appropriation for prisoners of war . . | 1,420 87 |
| Amounts in the hands of disbursing officers, including suspended vouchers . . . . . . . . . | 446,139 47 |
| | 3,826,159 03 |
| Deduct balances in favor of various disbursing officers . . | 751,555 81 |
| | 3,074,603 22 |

| | |
|---|---|
| There was disbursed for purchase of medical and hospital supplies . . . . . . . . . . . . . . | $176,556 40 |
| For pay of private physicians . . . . . . . . | 225,531 40 |
| For pay of hospital employees . . . . . . . . | 40,894 44 |
| For expense of purveying depots . . . . . . . . | 102,253 06 |
| For artificial limbs for soldiers and seamen . . . | 35,206 50 |
| For care of sick soldiers in private hospitals . . . | 3,229 04 |
| For miscellaneous expenses of the medical department . | 48,835 19 |
| For internal revenue tax . . . . . . . . . . | 2,133 12 |
| Refundment of amounts erroneously deposited in the previous year . . . . . . . . . . . . . . | 125 60 |
| Transferred to the pay department for the payment of contract surgeons . . . . . . . . . . . . | 200,000 00 |
| Balance of appropriation for artificial limbs turned into the surplus fund . . . . . . . . . . . . | 190 00 |
| Balance in the treasury June 30, 1867 . . . . . . | 2,909,614 08 |
| Amount of previous disallowances now admitted, proper vouchers being furnished . . . . . . . . | 33,789 33 |
| In the hands of disbursing officers . . . . . . . | 72,526 25 |
| Amounts chargeable to disbursing officers on suspended vouchers awaiting explanation and correction . . . . | 65,769 52 |
| | 3,916,653 94 |
| Deduct balances due disbursing officers . . . . . . | 842,050 72 |
| | 3,074,603 22 |

*Paymaster General.*

The Paymaster General reports that at the date of the last annual report there were 25 paymasters of the old establishment, and 58 additional paymasters, making a total of 83. There have since been 35 appointed in the permanent establishment, the complement authorized by the "Act to increase and fix the military peace establishment," approved July 28, 1866, making of regular paymasters created and now in service 60; reduction of additional paymasters during the fiscal year, 37, leaving still in service 21. Total of both classes now in service, 81.

The explanation given in the last annual report of the necessity of continuing in service some of the additional paymasters still exists in all its force, though it is expected that a further reduction may be practicable before the end of the current year.

| | |
|---|---|
| The financial summary exhibits a balance on hand at the beginning of the fiscal year of | $23,941,899 82 |
| Received from treasury and other sources during the year | 34,933,958 27 |
| Total | 58,875,558 09 |

Accounted for as follows:

| | |
|---|---|
| Disbursements to the regular army and the Military Academy | $14,369,243 62 |
| Disbursements to volunteers | 28,389,213 43 |
| Requisitions cancelled | 8,100,000 00 |
| Amount refunded to treasury | 38,000 00 |
| Amount of paymasters' balances on deposit in Merchants' National Bank at date of closing, not heretofore accounted for | 107,614 65 |
| Unissued requisitions in treasury | 3,550,000 00 |
| In hands of paymasters | 4,321,786 39 |
| Total | 58,875,558 09 |

The total disbursements of each class during the fiscal year are as follows: —

| | |
|---|---|
| To troops in service | $20,078,855 09 |
| To troops on muster-out | 3,300,000 00 |
| To treasury certificates | 10,614,000 00 |
| To referred claims | 8,765,602 00 |
| Total | 42,758,457 09 |

There have been received and recorded to October 20, 1867, 407,857 bounty claims under the act of Congress approved July 28, 1866. Of this number, 105,378 have been fully settled and disposed of at an expenditure of $9,352,797; 302,479 claims remain on hand to be settled.

Thirty-one thousand claims for ordering bounty and arrears of pay have also been settled and disposed of within the year, at an expenditure of $3,353,203.

Under the joint resolutions of Congress, the one approved March 30, 1867, and the other July 19, 1867, $1,500,000 was appropriated for expenditure in the five military districts of the South. Of this amount there has been drawn from the treasury $1,454,728.93, leaving a balance in the treasury of $45,271.07, which balance is to the credit of the second military district.

### *Chief Engineer.*

The corps of engineers consists of one hundred and seven officers and the battalion of engineer troops. Seventeen officers are on detached duty, serving on the staff of the General of the army, on the staffs of the general officers commanding military divisions and departments, at the Military Academy, on the Light-house Board, and in the Interior Department. The remainder are engaged, under the orders of the Chief of Engineers, upon the permanent defences of the country, the survey of the lakes, the improvement of rivers and harbors and the surveys relating thereto, upon explorations, in the command and instruction of the engineer troops, and in the charge of public buildings, grounds, and works in Washington.

The work of strengthening the permanent defences of the country, and of adapting them to receive more powerful armaments, has been continued during the past fiscal year.

Experimental targets and other structures have been in the course of construction for the purpose of determining the further modifications which sea-coast defence must undergo in view of the great power of modern ordnance, and the best and most economical manner of using iron as shields or scarps, or in other modes for defence.

The estimates for the sea-coast defences during the next fiscal year are for the construction of such interior and other portions of the works now in progress as are not affected by the improved means of naval warfare and of siege operations, or where the increased strength required can be secured by simple means, such as greater thickness of earth-covering, &c.

The headquarters of the engineer battalion, with three companies, have been established at Willett's Point, the chief depot of engineer supplies; a second depot has been fixed at Jefferson Barracks, with one company; and a third, near San Francisco, with one company. A detachment from the engineer battalion is at the Military Academy, to aid in giving instruction in practical engineering.

Some legislation for improving the discipline and instruction of the engineer troops is recommended by the Chief of Engineers, and appears to be required.

The operations of the corps relating to reconnoissances and surveys for military and commercial purposes, and to the improvement of rivers and harbors, have progressed during the fiscal year in a satisfactory manner.

The maps of the country from the Mississippi to the Pacific, prepared chiefly from the first-named surveys, are indispensable to the troops now occupying that region. The explorations and surveys in progress, and those in contemplation, will continue to supply such wants, and to furnish, besides, information of great value to the country.

The surveys for river and harbor improvements supply the information essential for legislation, as well as for the proper location and construction of the works. They should be continued, especially upon the western rivers, where changes in the channels and bars, and other obstacles to navigation, are constantly going on.

The survey of the lakes has made satisfactory progress in the waters of Lakes Superior and Michigan, to which attention has been confined for the most part, to meet the demands of commerce now being developed upon the borders of those waters.

The report of the Chief of Engineers and accompanying papers contain all the information required to be presented by the acts of 1866 and 1867, making appropriations for certain river and harbor improvements and surveys. These works have been carried on in a highly satisfactory manner.

Embarrassments have been experienced in the execution of the acts, modifications of which are suggested by the Chief of Engineers.

A large number of detailed maps, intended to illustrate some of the principal campaigns and battle-fields, have been prepared, and others are in course of preparation. They contain information not only useful for the purposes intended, but highly valuable in connection with other objects, military and civil. The Chief of Engineers recommends an appropriation of fifty thousand dollars for the engraving and printing of the most important, a recommendation which is concurred in.

*Ordnance Bureau.*

The expenditures of the Ordnance Bureau during the past fiscal year were less than one third of those of the preceding year. They were applied chiefly to work previously begun and partially executed, and to the settlement of war claims. The estimates for the next year are for defraying expenses of ordinary peace operations, and executing such work as have been authorized and directed by law.

The operations at the arsenals have been confined to the manufacture of iron gun-carriages and implements for sea-coast cannon, and of articles required for issue to troops, the reception, care, and preservation of ordnance and ordnance stores, the breaking up of unserviceable ammunition, and the construction of authorized buildings, and other permanent improvements. The hired men employed at the arsenals have been reduced from last year by about seventeen per cent., and the reduction is in further progress. There were, at the end of the year, 987 enlisted ordnance men employed at the arsenals in guard, police, and other military duties, and as mechanics and laborers in the workshops, magazines, and laboratories.

A title to the property on Rock Island, Illinois, having been acquired, the construction of the arsenal and armory at that place, in accordance with the act of April 19, 1864, has been carried forward rapidly. The estimate for continuing that work during the next fiscal year is in accordance with its character and design as authorized and directed by law. The conditions connected with the appropriation in March last for the erection of a bridge at Rock Island having not yet been fulfilled by the railroad company, no part of that appropriation has been expended. From correspondence and negotiations with the railroad company in reference to the guarantee required from them by the appropriation act, it is understood that the company will agree to pay, and will satisfactorily guarantee the payment of, half the cost of building the bridges across the main channel of the Mississippi River and across the slough on the Illinois side, and is anxious to have the bridges built as soon as practicable upon those conditions. As there is some doubt whether the guarantee which the company is willing to give would fulfil the exact requirements of the law, this subject is recommended to be brought to the notice of Congress for such further legislation as may be deemed necessary and proper. It is very desirable that the bridges should be built as soon as practicable, and that a sufficient appropriation for the purpose be made. When the work is done, one half of its expense will be returned to the government by the railroad company.

The arms and other ordnance stores which had accumulated at the Southern arsenals, excepting one in Florida turned over for use by the Freedmen's Bureau, and one at Little Rock, Arkansas, occupied as a military station, have been repossessed, and are now in charge of the ordnance department. The buildings and other public property at these arsenals should be kept from decay and in proper preservation, and the ordnance estimates include the amount necessary for that purpose. The arsenal at Augusta, Georgia, from its position and healthfulness, is peculiarly suitable for a large arsenal of deposit, and its advantages in this respect should be made available as soon as it may be considered necessary and proper to store arms in the South. The establishment of an arsenal at a suitable point between the Missouri and the Rocky Mountains, for supplying troops serving in that region, is considered necessary, and an appropriation for that purpose is recommended. The sale of the small arsenals at Rome, New York, Vergennes, Vermont, and Liberty, Missouri, which may be soon abandoned without disadvantage to the public service, is also recommended, as well as the sale of the North Carolina arsenal, the Macon armory, and the powder works at Augusta, Georgia, which were captured from the rebel government. The land and other property at Harper's Ferry, formerly used for an armory, are not now required by the department, and their sale is recommended, if it be decided that it can be done under the government title. If not sold, it is suggested that it be leased for a term of years.

There were 23,083 Springfield rifle muskets converted into breech-loaders during the past fiscal year at the national armory, and about 100,000 muskets, carbines, and sabres were cleaned and repaired there. All of the converted arms have been issued to troops, and nearly all the infantry serving in the departments of the Missouri and the Platte have been armed with them. Monthly reports received from the commanders of the companies so armed have been highly favorable to the arm, and furnish abundant evidence of its excellence and fitness for the military service. The almost unanimous opinion expressed by the officers is, that the musket is simple, strong, not liable to get out of order, and extremely accurate in firing. Not a single officer has expressed the opinion that the calibre (reduced from that of the muzzle-loader) is too small, while a few have recommended a further reduction. These arms have done excellent service in an Indian campaign during the past summer; very few of them have been reported as rendered unserviceable, and of these, more were made unserviceable through carelessness than from all other causes. In July, 1866, the Secretary of War directed the conversion of 25,000 Springfield rifle muskets into breech-loaders, and the preparation of an adequate supply of proper ammunition. He afterwards ordered the conversion of these arms to be continued, without fixing a limit as to number; and the work was carried on rapidly until August, 1867, when it was directed to be suspended, after 50,000 arms had been altered. That number is nearly completed, and there have been prepared the requisite tools for converting about 400 muskets per day, at which rate their conversion can be resumed at short notice. It is confidently believed that no converted breech-loader, in this country or in Europe, has been produced which is superior to the converted Springfield musket, as altered at the armory, and that none equal to it in serviceable qualities can be produced at less cost. In view of the fact that the 50,000 converted muskets will very soon be issued to troops, leaving no breech-loading muskets on hand in store, it is recommended that the conversion of the Springfield musket be resumed. The chief difficulties which have been interposed against the production of a good breech-loading musket, by the ordnance department, have been the immediate claim of almost every improvement under some of the many patents which have been granted for improvements in fire-arms, and the extreme eagerness and strong efforts of some inventors, and others interested in patents, to have their particular inventions used in the government military service. There are many claims of patent rights in the methods used to convert the Springfield muskets. Several parties, in some instances, claim to hold patents for the same thing;

and every improvement, it is believed, is claimed by more than one inventor. The validity of such patent claims for the improvements used at the national armory in converting the muskets have not been acknowledged by the ordnance bureau, which believes that the proper course for the various claimants to take is to establish their respective rights, and then apply to Congress for remuneration for their use by the government.

The cartridges used for breech-loading arms are known as "central fire," about 7,000,000 of which have been fabricated. Extensive trials of them, made by troops and in proofs, resulted in an average failure of only one third of one per cent.

Smooth-bore cannon of less than eight inches calibre being ineffective against iron-clad war vessels, it has been determined to supersede all such now in the sea-coast forts by those of heavier calibre, and by rifled cannon. A board of engineer, ordnance, and artillery officers, especially appointed to consider the subject of arming the permanent forts, reported that 1,915 pieces of the calibre of 13, 15 and 20 inches for smooth-bores, and of 10 and 12 inches for rifles, were required for the permanent fortifications, and should be provided; and their report was approved by the Secretary of War. None of these guns have yet been provided, and there are no existing orders or contracts for heavy cannon. This stoppage of the procurement of heavy cannon has been mainly occasioned by "persistent efforts for some time past by ignorant or designing persons to destroy public confidence in the heavy guns which have been provided by the ordnance department of the army and navy." This subject, as also the experiments which have been made to test the durability and efficiency of these cannon, are stated more fully and in detail in the report of the Chief of Ordnance. The experiments have resulted in establishing the fact that our heavy cast-iron cannon are the cheapest and most effective guns that are possessed by any nation. While this is fully proved so far as regards the smooth-bore heavy guns, and the same results have followed in respect to the rifles, so far as the tests have yet been applied to them, it is not deemed prudent to enter upon the manufacture of these latter to a large extent without the previous trial of a greater number of these guns.

Since the delivery of the report of the Chief of Ordnance, that officer has received such information as to materially change his views in regard to additional legislation, which he thinks necessary to secure the interests of the United States, before expending any money on the railroad bridge at Rock Island.

His views will be submitted in special report hereafter.

### *Signal Corps.*

The chief signal officer of the army reports that the course of tuition in military signalling and telegraphing has been definitely established and commenced at West Point; that the preliminary steps have been taken to secure the arrangement, upon similar plans, in so far as is practicable, of the studies of these duties, at the Military and Naval Academies; that a project for the general communication of the army and navy, by signals common to both services, has been brought under consideration; that a general order, publishing regulations for the equipment and instruction of the army, has been authorized. When these plans shall have been carried into effect, the active forces of the United States will be prepared to use, in the contingencies of the service, either aerial or electric telegraphy.

### *Military Academy.*

The corps of cadets at the examination in June last numbered two hundred and fifty-five. Of these sixty-three graduated, and were commissioned in the army.

The report of the Board of Visitors exhibits fully the excellent condition of the institution, and bears ample testimony of its usefulness. They renew the recommendation made by the board of the previous year to increase the number of cadets, giving substantially, but perhaps more elaborately, the same arguments for the increase. They also recommend that the pay and emoluments of the superintendent should be not less than those of a brigadier general, and give various strong reasons therefor. They rightly say that "the continuous and increasing visits of official persons from abroad and from our own country exact expenditures which ought not to be permitted by a generous people any longer to diminish his income." The erection of a fire-proof building, for the preservation and safety of the records and archives of the academy, is also recommended. Congress appropriated fifteen thousand dollars to accomplish this object, but it is found inadequate, and an additional appropriation of fifteen thousand dollars is asked for this year. Other recommendations are made by the board, but for which no estimates are submitted by the inspector. The inspector bears liberal testimony to the unusual degree of interest and patience manifested by the board to examine and investigate all the affairs, faults, and errors of administration of the institution; and he says that it will be the pleasure and endeavor of the academic authorities to profit by and carry out the views and suggestions of the board where no legal obstacle intervenes.

| | |
|---|---|
| The total estimate of military appropriations for the fiscal year ending June 30, 1869, is | $77,124,707 08 |
| For office of the General of the army | 5,000 00 |
| For Adjutant General's office, recruiting service | 300,000 00 |
| For Inspector General's office — no appropriation. | |
| For Military Academy | $146,305 00 |
| For pay of cadets, &c. | 188,707 00 |
| | 335,012 00 |
| For Bureau of Military Justice — no appropriation. | |
| For Quartermaster General's department | $28,180,066 ,20 |
| For ditto — deficiency estimate | 13,500,000 00 |
| For ditto — for contingencies | 100,000 00 |
| | 41,780,066 20 |
| For subsistence department — no appropriation. | |
| For medical department | $15,000 00 |
| For pay department | 22,412,068 00 |
| For engineer bureau | 10,528,769 88 |
| For ordnance bureau | 1,533,084 00 |
| For Bureau Refugees, Freedmen, and Abandoned Lands — no appropriation. | |
| For signal service | 27,000 00 |

The foregoing estimates for the approaching fiscal year are taken from the estimate of the different bureau chiefs, without change of the items. They are based upon the expenditures of the current year, and will probably exceed the amount which will be required. A season of peace with the Indians on the plains will of itself materially diminish the expenditures of the army, and justify a reduction in the number of enlisted men in a company.

Attention may be attracted to the great increase of appropriation for the bureaus of the War Department asked for this year over the estimates of last year, and requires explanation. The expenses for the next fiscal year will necessarily be much below those for the present year. It will be observed that $13,600,000 of the present estimate is to cover deficiency in appropriation of last year. The last Congress made large appropriations for river and harbor improvements, for which no estimates were then made. The work having been commenced under such authority, it is now necessary to make large estimates for its continuance. The appropriations for the fiscal year ending June 30, 1867, having been made during the existence of war, were very large; far in excess of requirements after cessation of hostilities. This left a large balance, already appropriated, to commence the present fiscal year with, and reduced the estimate. No such balance will exist to commence the year 1868–'69 with.

The small regular army sustained by the United States prior to 1861 was kept well supplied with officers educated at the National Military Academy. After the rebellion, however, it was found necessary to increase this standing force about four-fold. The war educated soldiers to fill well, by judicious selections, this increase to the army, but not to keep up the supply. The original vacancies created by this increase of the army are now filled, and appointments hereafter to fill vacancies must go in at the foot of the army register. For this reason, the time has passed, or soon will, when efficient volunteer soldiers, educated in the rebellion, will be willing to accept such positions; or, if willing, will be of an age making it unadvisable to accept them. While the army has been so much increased, no addition has been made to the number of cadets admitted at West Point. I would now respectfully recommend an increase to the full number that can be accommodated without additional buildings. The present number of cadets is limited by the number of representatives and delegates in the lower house of Congress, and ten *at large* each year appointed by the President. Four hundred cadets can be accommodated without increase of expense to the government further than the pay to the additional number. The manner of making these appointments, I would suggest, should be by adding three *at large* additional, to be appointed by the President, and by regarding a vacancy as existing in each congressional district when the cadet representing it enters the second class.

I would recommend the continuance for another year of the additional pay allowed to officers of the army by the last Congress.

The 37th section of the act of July 28, 1866, appropriates $20,000 for the procurement of an equestrian statue of Lieutenant General Winfield Scott. It has been found that the work cannot be contracted for for less than from three to four times the appropriation; hence no contract has been entered into.

Special report will be submitted hereafter of plans and estimates that have been prepared for the erection of new War Department buildings.

By act of Congress the ten Southern States which have no representation in the national councils are divided into five military districts, each commanded by an officer of the army of not less rank than brigadier general. The powers of these commanders are both civil and military. So far as their military duties are concerned they are under the same subordination to the General of the army and Secretary of War that department commanders are. In their civil capacity they are entirely independent of both the General and Secretary, except in the matters of removals, appointment, and detail, where the General of the army has the same powers as have district commanders. It is but fair to the district commanders, however, to state that, while they have been thus independent in their civil duties, there has not been one of them who would not yield to a positively expressed wish, in regard to any matter of civil administration, from either of the officers placed over them by the Constitution or acts of Congress, so long as that wish was in the direction of a proper execution of the law for the execution of which they alone are responsible. I am pleased to say that the commanders of the five military districts have executed their difficult trust faithfully and without bias from any judgment of their own as to the merit or demerit of the law they were executing.

*First Military District*

Comprises the State of Virginia, Brevet Major General J. M. Schofield commanding. In assuming command, the principle was announced by General Schofield that the military power conferred by act of Congress on the district commander would be used only so far as was necessary to accomplish the purposes for which the power was conferred. The civil government was interfered with only when necessary, and the wisdom of the policy has been demonstrated by the result. The instances of complaint of the action of the civil courts became exceedingly rare. Still the evil which existed prior to the act of Congress of March 2, 1867, though mitigated by the increased efficiency of civil officers, was not removed. It was an evil in the jury system, apparent at all times, and fully developed by the natural antagonism between loyalist and rebel, or the prejudice between white and black, existing throughout the South since the rebellion. The first idea was to admit blacks on juries, and prescribe a test of loyalty. But as the requirement of a unanimous verdict must give very inadequate protection where strong prejudice of class or caste exists, and as a military change of jury system would be but temporary, it was determined to leave its change to the convention soon to meet, and be content with a system of military commissions. Such commissioners were appointed from officers of the army and Freedmen's Bureau for the different cities and counties of the State, with powers of justices of the peace, while the State was divided into sub-districts under commanders whose powers were ultimately increased to those of circuit judges, taking jurisdiction only in cases where civil authorities failed to do justice. The system has given a large measure of protection to all classes of citizens, with slight interference with the civil courts.

Since the publication of the act of March 23, 1867, all elections have been suspended. Existing State, county, and municipal officers were continued in office. Vacancies have been filled by the district commander. The number of removals has been five, and of appointments to fill vacancies one hundred and five.

In executing the registration, a board of officers was first appointed to select registering officers. The selections were made with great care, and the officers so selected have, with few exceptions, done their duty in a most satisfactory manner. Carefully prepared regulations for the boards of registration were issued, being made as specific as possible, so as to secure a uniform rule of disfranchisement throughout the State. In prescribing them, the district commander was controlled by the belief that the law made him responsible for its correct interpretation, as well as its faithful execution.

The results of the first session of the registering boards were all received on September 15. One hundred and fifteen thousand and sixty-eight whites, and one hundred and one thousand three hundred and eighty-two colored, registered; one thousand six hundred and twenty whites, and two hundred and thirty-two colored, being rejected. The tax list of 1866–'67 (not quite complete) returns about one hundred and thirty-six thousand white male adults, and eighty-seven thousand colored male adults. This indicates that the number of whites disfranchised, or who have failed to register, is about nineteen thousand, and that about fifteen thousand more colored men have registered than were on the tax lists. Hence it may be inferred that nearly all male adults, white or colored, not disfranchised, have registered.

The principle upon which the apportionment was made was to give separate representations to the smallest practicable subdivisions of the State, and where fractions remained over, to so combine counties in election districts as to justly represent those portions. This is believed to be the fairest mode of apportionment practicable under the law.

### *Second Military District*

Comprises the States of North Carolina and South Carolina, Brevet Major General E. R. S. Canby commanding. Major General Daniel E. Sickles, who was originally assigned to the command of this district, was relieved, and General Canby assigned by the following order of the President: —

[*General Orders, No.* 80.]

HEADQUARTERS OF THE ARMY, ADJUTANT GENERAL'S OFFICE,
WASHINGTON, August 27, 1867.

I. The following orders have been received from the President: —

"EXECUTIVE MANSION,
"WASHINGTON, D. C., August 26, 1867.

"Brevet Major General Edward R. S. Canby is hereby assigned to the command of the second military district, created by the act of Congress of March 2, 1867, and of the military department of the South, embracing the States of North Carolina and South Carolina. He will, as soon as practicable, relieve Major General Daniel E. Sickles, and, on assuming the command to which he is hereby assigned, will, when necessary to a faithful execution of the laws, exercise any and all powers conferred by acts of Congress upon district commanders, and any and all authority pertaining to officers in command of military departments.

"Major General Daniel E. Sickles is hereby relieved from the command of the second military district.

"The Secretary of War *ad interim* will give the necessary instructions to carry this order into effect.

"ANDREW JOHNSON."

II. In pursuance of the foregoing order of the President of the United States, Brevet Major General Canby will, on receipt of the order, turn over his present command to the officer next in rank to himself, and proceed to Charleston, South Carolina, to relieve Major General Sickles of the command of the second military district.

III. Major General Sickles, on being relieved, will repair to New York city, and report by letter to the Adjutant General.

By command of General Grant.

E. D. TOWNSEND, *Assistant Adjutant General.*

"In order to secure a more efficient administration of justice it was deemed necessary to place all sheriffs and other municipal officers under the immediate control of a military officer. Accordingly all such officers were directed to report to the provost marshal general, and to make monthly reports of 'crimes committed' and 'prisoners confined.' The reports of prisoners confined has aided materially in detecting illegal imprisonments or punishments, and has enabled the district commander to secure the release of many Union men and freedmen, against whom much gross injustice had been committed.

"A bureau of civil affairs was established to take charge of all matters pertaining to registration; and its duties were afterwards extended to include all questions of protection to person or property arising under the laws of Congress. One hundred and seventy registration precincts were established in North Carolina, and one hundred and nine in South Carolina.

"In North Carolina there were registered 103,060 whites, and 71,657 blacks; and in South Carolina, 45,751 whites, and 79,585 blacks. Registration proceeded very slowly on account of slowness of communication with distant parts of the district.

"Of the appropriation made by Congress, $54,802.87 have been expended, and outstanding liabilities will exceed the balance on hand $194,802.87.

"The present condition of the district is so satisfactory as to warrant the belief that after elections the number of military posts in both States can be diminished."

*Third Military District*

Comprises the States of Georgia, Florida, and Alabama, Brevet Major General John Pope commanding.

"On assuming command, an order was issued" by General Pope "continuing in office State officials, but forbidding their opposing the reconstruction acts; prohibiting elections except under those acts, and giving notice that all vacancies in civil offices would be filled by the district commander. Becoming satisfied subsequently that State officials, while obeying the order personally, yet officially, by their patronage, encouraged papers opposing the reconstruction act, an order was issued forbidding official patronage to such papers.

"In consequence of the riot at Mobile, an order was issued holding city and county officers responsible for the preservation of peace at all public meetings, and requiring the United States troops to assist them when called on. No disturbances have since occurred.

"Under the laws of the State, no colored person could be admitted to the jury box, and there was no surety of justice to Union men, to people from the North (and especially ex-Union soldiers), or to colored persons, from juries inflamed with hostility towards such classes.

"There is a very large number of cases of wrong perpetrated by such juries in the district on file.

"Accordingly an order was issued directing all juries to be drawn indiscriminately from the list of voters registered by the boards of registration.

"Very few civil officers have been removed, and those, in almost every case, were removed for refusing to comply with orders. Appointments to fill vacancies have only been made where the daily business of the people demanded it.

"The State treasurers of Georgia, Alabama, and Florida have been ordered to make no payments after the appropriations of the present fiscal year have expired, save on warrants approved by the district commander, as it is believed that a new legislature will not continue or approve many of the appropriations made.

"In executing the registration, it was deemed advisable that no officer nor soldier of the United States should be employed, and accordingly each board of registration was appointed from among the citizens living in the district, and to consist of two white men and one colored. A fixed sum was paid for registering each name, the average for the district being twenty-six cents per name.

"There were registered in Georgia, 95,214 whites, and 93,457 colored; in Alabama, 74,450 whites, and 90,350 colored; and in Florida, 11,180 whites, and 15,357 colored. The amount expended in registration, &c., has been $162,325.

"The appointment of delegates was made in Georgia for State senatorial districts, and in Alabama for representative districts, fixed by an order. Polls were ordered to be opened at each county seat."

*Fourth Military District*

Comprises the States of Mississippi and Arkansas, Brevet Major General E. O. C. Ord commanding.

"The reconstruction measures of Congress are unpopular with a majority of the white people, but their execution has met with slight opposition, the ignorant and lawless, from whom alone trouble was to be apprehended, having been kept in order by the troops distributed through the States.

"The civil laws have not been interfered with when equally administered, except to remove from the civil courts cases of crime charged against persons who, being opposed to the rebellion, had reason to fear prejudice. Also freedmen's cases, where the courts were practically closed against them; and cases of horse stealing, and violations of acts of Congress, for all of which military commissions have been organized.

"The officers of the provisional State government have continued in office, except where they have failed to perform their duties. It is difficult to find competent men who can qualify to fill vacancies in civil offices, some of which are consequently vacant.

"In consequence of the indisposition (as manifested of late) of the civil authorities in Arkansas to take action in offences of an aggravated nature against freedmen, orders have been issued for the trial of all such cases by military commission, and for prompt action to be taken for the punishment of civil officers who fail to issue writs against offenders committing assaults, &c., against freedmen, and prohibiting bail for the appearance of such criminals."

The extension of suffrage to freedmen has evidently aroused a sentiment of hostility to the colored race, and to northern men in many parts of the district, which did not exist before; and General Ord is convinced that a larger force than is now stationed in those States to preserve order and organize conventions will be required hereafter to protect them and secure the freedmen the use of the suffrage.

"In a majority of the counties of this district there are very few men who can take the test oath, and these are not disposed to defy public opinion by accepting office, unless supported by a military force afterwards.

"The will of the colored people may be in favor of supporting loyal office-holders, but their intelligence is not now sufficient to enable them to combine for the execution of their will. All their combinations are now conducted by white men, under the protection of the military; if the protection is withdrawn, the white men now controlling would withdraw with it; and some of the southern people, now exasperated at what they deem the freedmen's presumption, would not be very gentle towards them, so that the presence of a larger military force will be required for some time to maintain the freedmen in the right of suffrage."

### *Fifth Military District*

Comprises the States of Louisiana and Texas, Brevet Major General J. A. Mower commanding.

No report has yet been received from General Mower, but it is expected in time for the meeting of Congress.

Major General P. H. Sheridan, who was originally assigned to the command of this district, was relieved, and General Hancock assigned, by the following orders of the President. On the decease of Brevet Major General Charles Griffin, designated as the officer next in rank to whom General Sheridan should turn over the command until General Hancock assumed it, General Mower succeeded to the command: —

[*General Orders, No.* 77.]

HEADQUARTERS OF THE ARMY,
ADJUTANT GENERAL'S OFFICE,
WASHINGTON, August 19, 1867.

I. The following orders have been received from the President: —

"EXECUTIVE MANSION,
"WASHINGTON, D. C., August 17, 1867.

"Major General George H. Thomas is hereby assigned to the command of the fifth military district, created by the act of Congress passed on the 2d day of March, 1867.

"Major General P. H. Sheridan is hereby assigned to the command of the department of the Missouri.

"Major General Winfield S. Hancock is hereby assigned to the command of the department of the Cumberland.

"The Secretary of War *ad interim* will give the necessary instructions to carry this order into effect.

"ANDREW JOHNSON."

II. In pursuance of the foregoing order of the President of the United States, Major General G. H. Thomas will, on receipt of the order, turn over his present command to the officer next in rank to himself, and proceed to New Orleans, Louisiana, to relieve Major General P. H. Sheridan of the command of the fifth military district.

III. Major General P. H. Sheridan, on being relieved from the command of the fifth military district by Major General G. H. Thomas, will proceed to Fort Leavenworth, Kansas, and will relieve Major General W. S. Hancock in the command of the department of the Missouri.

IV. Major General W. S. Hancock, on being relieved from the command of the department of the Missouri by Major General Sheridan, will proceed to Louisville, Kentucky, and will assume command of the department of the Cumberland.

V. Major General G. H. Thomas will continue to execute all orders he may find in force in the fifth military district at the time of his assuming command of it, unless authorized by the General of the army to annul, alter, or modify them.

VI. Major General Sheridan, before relieving Major General Hancock, will report in person at these headquarters.

By command of General Grant.

E. D. TOWNSEND, *Assistant Adjutant General.*

[*General Orders, No.* 81.]

HEADQUARTERS OF THE ARMY,
ADJUTANT GENERAL'S OFFICE,
WASHINGTON, August 27, 1867.

I. The following orders have been received from the President: —

"EXECUTIVE MANSION,
"WASHINGTON, D. C., August 26, 1867.

"SIR: In consequence of the unfavorable condition of the health of Major General George H. Thomas, as reported to you in Surgeon Hasson's despatch of the 21st instant, my order dated August 17, 1867, is hereby modified so as to assign Major General Winfield S. Hancock to the command of the fifth military district, created by the act of Congress, passed March 2, 1867, and of the military department comprising the States of Louisiana and Texas. On being relieved from the command of the department of the Missouri by Major General P. H. Sheridan, Major General Hancock will proceed directly to New Orleans, Louisiana, and, assuming the command to which he is hereby assigned, will, when necessary to a faithful execution of the laws, exercise any and all powers conferred by acts of Congress upon district commanders, and any and all authority pertaining to officers in command of military departments.

"Major General P. H. Sheridan will at once turn over his present command to the officer next in rank to himself, and proceeding, without delay, to Fort Leavenworth, Kansas, will relieve Major General Hancock of the command of the department of the Missouri.

"Major General George H. Thomas will, until further orders, remain in command of the department of the Cumberland.

"Very respectfully, yours,
"ANDREW JOHNSON.

"GENERAL U. S. GRANT,
"*Secretary of War ad interim.*"

II. In compliance with the foregoing instructions of the President of the United States, Major General P. H. Sheridan will, on receipt of this order, turn over his present command to Brevet Major General Charles Griffin, the officer next in rank to himself, and proceed, without delay, to Fort Leavenworth, Kansas, and will relieve Major General Hancock in command of the department of the Missouri.

III. On being relieved by Major General Sheridan, Major General Hancock will proceed, without delay, to New Orleans, Louisiana, and assume command of the fifth military district, and of the department composed of the States of Louisiana and Texas.

IV. Major General George H. Thomas will continue in command of the department of the Cumberland.

By command of General Grant.

E. D. TOWNSEND, *Assistant Adjutant General.*

Generals Sheridan and Sickles having been relieved before the period for submitting their annual reports, none have been received from them. They have, however, been called on recently to submit reports, which may be expected before the meeting of Congress.

The territory of the United States not embraced in the five military districts is divided into military divisions (they subdivided into departments) and departments.

## ABSTRACT OF REPORTS FROM MILITARY DIVISION AND DEPARTMENT COMMANDERS.

### *Military Division of the Missouri,*

Commanded by Lieutenant General W. T. Sherman, embraces the departments of Dakota, the Platte, and the Missouri; commanded respectively by Brevet Major General A. H. Terry, Brevet Major General C. C. Augur, and Major General P. H. Sheridan.

During the latter part of the year 1866, the operations of this command were embarrassed by the necessity of mustering out the volunteer troops that had been organized for the war of the rebellion, before a sufficient number of regular troops could be raised and forwarded to remote parts of the frontier, to replace them. The winter of 1866–'67 proved to be unprecedentedly severe, so that it was a physical impossibility to keep open communication with some of the most remote posts. The garrison of Fort Phil Kearney, on Powder River, 223 miles distant from old Fort Laramie, suffered severely from an attack made by Indians, December 21, 1866, upon a wagon-train and its escorts, that had been sent a short distance from the fort to procure lumber, in which Brevet Lieutenant Colonel W. J. Fetterman and a detachment of forty-nine men were killed. In December other bands of hostile Indians made their appearance at Fort Buford, and rumors were received of the massacre of the entire garrison. All communication being cut off by the severity of the weather, great anxiety was felt for the safety of the garrison for two months, when reports were received contradicting the capture of the post.

In the spring of 1867 rumors were received from all quarters of a renewal of Indian hostilities. Though many proved to be greatly exaggerated, yet depredations and attacks on the principal emigrant routes increased to such an extent that it required the utmost activity on the part of the troops to keep open communication with our Territories, and protect working parties on the important railroads now in process of construction.

A village of the Cheyennes and Sioux, on Pawnee Fork, was burned April 19, as a punishment for depredations previously committed.

Department commanders visited the scenes of hostilities in person, and made every effort with the means at hand to afford protection. They have at times been greatly embarrassed by a disposition on the part of irresponsible persons to precipitate hostilities by false rumors and sensation reports.

Since the Indian commission, provided by act of July 20, 1867, commenced its labors, the operations of the troops have been confined to the defensive, and they are now principally engaged in garrisoning the most important posts.

Indians have been employed as soldiers under the provisions of the act of July 28, 1866, with some success. The attention of Congress is respectfully invited to the remarks of Lieutenant General Sherman on this subject, and also in regard to providing for a more efficient civil government in the Indian country.

The following number of trains have passed Fort Sedgwick, Colorado Territory, from February 1 to September 28: —

Trains, 124; wagons, 3,074; men, 4,587; women, 556; children, 587; mules, 5,738; oxen, 11,096; horses, 1,062; led animals, 948.

*Department of the Cumberland,*

Major General G. H. Thomas commanding, embraces the States of Kentucky, Tennessee, and West Virginia.

General Thomas reports that with his present force he is able partially to hold in check the disloyal tendencies of the people, and to punish, if not prevent, unlawful proceedings; that, although there still remains much to be desired in the way of protection to life and property throughout his command, outrages are not so prevalent as formerly; but the feeling of the people is still hostile to the government.

A small force is retained in West Virginia, as it is believed that without it the laws would not be impartially executed.

In anticipation of trouble in Tennessee at the period of the

August elections, the troops were so disposed as to be able to render proper assistance to the civil authorities in suppressing riots or violence of any kind. The department commander was directed to proceed in person to Memphis, and to make the best disposition to guard against an outbreak. The election, however, passed off quietly, and the services of the troops were not required. Trouble was again apprehended at Nashville at the charter election in September, and General Thomas was directed to go in person to that city, and take every precaution against a disturbance, with the usual instructions to employ the troops only to preserve peace, not permit them to take sides in political differences, and to prevent mobs from aiding any party. General Thomas, by his presence and advice, again rendered the interposition of troops unnecessary.

*The Department of the Lakes,*

Brevet Major General J. C. Robinson commanding, embraces the States of Ohio, Indiana, Illinois, Michigan, and Wisconsin.

The few troops stationed in this department have been employed in garrisoning the forts on our northern frontier.

*The Department of Washington,*

Brevet Major General W. H. Emory commanding. A disturbance being apprehended in Baltimore upon the occasion of the threatened removal of the police commissioners by the governor of Maryland, the headquarters of this department were temporarily transferred to that city November 6, 1866, and the troops were held in readiness to preserve the peace in case it should become necessary to employ them. Their services, however, were not required.

*The Military Division of the Pacific,*

Major General H. W. Halleck commanding, embraces the department of the Columbia and the department of California, commanded respectively by Brevet Major General F. Steele and Brevet Major General Irwin McDowell. The territory, including the district of Alaska, or Russian America, contains 1,235,000 square miles, or more than one third of our entire territory, estimating it at 3,579,002 square miles. Coast line is estimated at 12,750 statute miles — more than three times the length of our Atlantic coast.

Number of tribal Indians is about 130,000, or more than one third the whole number in the United States, estimating this number at 330,000.

White population is about one sixtieth part of the entire civilized population of the United States.

Though some depredations have been committed upon white settlers in nearly every part of the military division, active military operations have been limited to Arizona, southern Idaho, south-eastern Oregon, and the northern portions of Nevada and California. Most of the troops engaged in hostile operations in the latter district have been under command of Brevet Major General Crook, who has exhibited skill, bravery, and untiring energy.

Indians have no principal chiefs, but roam in small bands, and fight independently; hence the impossibility to make treaties with them. As their hunting-grounds are gradually taken from them by the settlers, they are obliged either to rob or starve. The Apaches are the most hostile Indians. They will observe no treaties, agreements, or truces. With them there is no alternative but active and vigorous war till they are completely destroyed, or forced to surrender as prisoners of war.

Though, from various causes, operations against hostile tribes during the past year have not been as active and successful as was expected, considerable progress has been made in breaking up their haunts and punishing their depredations.

Services of Indian scouts employed under act of Congress have been of the greatest value in this military division. Officers are unanimously in favor of increasing the number. As guides and scouts they have been almost indispensable. At least a thousand could be employed on the Pacific coast.

Commanders have been embarrassed by the number of Indians in their hands taken as prisoners of war. They require troops to guard them, and have to be fed by the commissary. They cannot be set to work unless reservations of land and farming implements are provided. General Halleck recommends the transfer of the Indian Bureau to the War Department, and the removal of the Indians to large reservations placed entirely under military authority, and from which all white settlers should be excluded. He condemns the present Indian system, but does not cast reflections on the officers of the Indian Bureau in his military division. They have endeavored to do as much good as possible with their limited means.

*The Department of the East,*

Major General G. G. Meade commanding. This department embraces the New England States, New York, New Jersey, Pennsylvania, and Delaware. The troops have been employed in garrisoning the forts on our northern frontier and North Atlantic coast, and the operations have been confined to improving the posts and collecting and forwarding recruits to the army.

Acting in the double capacity of Secretary of War and General of the army, this report is made to embrace both.

U. S. GRANT,
*Secretary of War ad interim and General U. S. A.*

---

## VII.

### CORRESPONDENCE BETWEEN GENERAL GRANT AND THE PRESIDENT CONCERNING MR. STANTON'S REINSTATEMENT AS SECRETARY OF WAR.

THE following is the correspondence between General Grant and the President relative to the reinstatement of Hon. Edwin M. Stanton as Secretary of War, which was presented to Congress by Mr. Stanton: —

### MR. STANTON'S COMMUNICATION TO THE HOUSE.

WAR DEPARTMENT, Feb. 4, 1868.

SIR: In answer to the resolution of the House of Representatives of the 8th, I transmit herewith copies furnished me by General Grant of the correspondence between him and the President relating to the Secretary of War, and which he reports to be all the correspondence he had with the President on the subject. I have had no correspondence with the President since the 17th of August last.

After the action of the Senate on his alleged reason for my suspension from the office of Secretary of War, I resumed the duties of that office as required by the act of Congress, and have continued to discharge them without any personal or written communication with the President. No orders have been issued from the Department in the name of the President with my knowledge, and I have received no orders from him.

The correspondence sent herewith embraces all the correspondence known to me on the subject referred to in the resolution of the House of Representatives.

I have the honor to be, sir, with great respect,

Your obedient servant,

EDWIN M. STANTON,

*Secretary of War.*

HON. SCHUYLER COLFAX,

*Speaker of the House of Representatives.*

## GENERAL GRANT TO THE PRESIDENT.

HEADQUARTERS ARMY OF THE UNITED STATES,
WASHINGTON, D. C., January 25, 1868.

HIS EXCELLENCY ANDREW JOHNSON,

*President of the United States.*

SIR: On the 24th instant, I requested you to give me in writing the instructions which you had previously given me verbally, not to obey any order from the Hon. E. M. Stanton, Secretary of War, unless I knew that it came from yourself. To this written request I received a message that has left doubt in my mind of your intentions. To prevent any possible misunderstanding, therefore, I renew the request that you will give me written instructions, and I, until they are received, will suspend action on your verbal ones. I am compelled to ask these instructions in writing in consequence of the many gross misrepresentations affecting my personal honor, circulated through the press for the last fortnight, purporting to come from the President, of conversations which occurred either with the President privately in his office, or in Cabinet meeting. What is written admits of no misunderstanding. In view of the misrepresentations referred to, it will be well to state the facts in the case.

Some time after I assumed the duties of Secretary of War *ad interim*, the President asked my views as to the course Mr. Stanton would have to pursue, in case the Senate should not concur in his suspension, to obtain possession of his office. My reply was, in substance, that Mr. Stanton would have to appeal to the courts to reinstate him, illustrating my position by citing the grounds I had taken in the case of the Baltimore Police Commissioners. In that case I did not doubt the technical right of Governor Swann to remove the old Commissioners and to appoint their successors, as the old Commissioners refused to give up. However, I contended that no recourse was left but to appeal to the courts. Finding that the President was desirous of keeping Mr. Stanton out of office, whether sustained in the suspension or not, I stated that I had not looked particularly into the Tenure of Office bill, but that what I had stated was a general principle, and if I should change my mind in this particular case, I would inform him of the fact. Subsequently, on reading the Tenure of Office bill closely, I found that I could not, without violation of the law, refuse to vacate the office of Secretary of War the moment Mr. Stanton was reinstated by the Senate, even though the President ordered me to retain it, which he never did. Taking this view of the subject, and learning on Saturday, the 11th instant, that the Senate had taken up the subject of Mr. Stanton's suspension, after some conversation with Lieutenant General Sherman and some members of my staff, in which I stated that the law left me no discretion as to my action should Mr. Stanton be reinstated, and that I intended to inform the President, I went to the President for the sole purpose of making this decision known, and did so make it known. In doing this I fulfilled the promise made in our last preceding conversation on the subject. The President, however, instead of accepting my view of the requirements of the Tenure of Office bill, contended that he had suspended Mr. Stanton under the authority given by the Constitution, and that the same authority did not preclude him from reporting, as an act of courtesy, his reasons for the suspension to the Senate; that having been appointed under the authority given by the Constitution, and not under any act of Congress, I could not be governed by the act. I stated that the law was binding on me, constitutional or not, until set aside by the proper tribunal. An hour or more was consumed, each reiterating his views on this subject, until, getting late, the President said he would see me again. I did not agree to call again on Monday, nor at any other definite time, nor was I sent for by the President until the following Tuesday. From the 11th till the Cabinet meeting on the 14th instant, a doubt never entered my mind about the President's fully understanding my position, namely: That if the Senate refused to concur in the suspension of Mr. Stanton, my powers as Secretary of War *ad interim* would cease, and Mr. Stanton's right to assume at once the functions of his office would, under the law, be indisputable; and I acted accordingly. With Mr. Stanton I had no communication, direct or indirect, on the subject of his reinstatement during his suspension. I knew it had been recommended to the President to send in the name of Governor Cox, of Ohio, for Secretary of War, and thus save all embarrassment, — a proposition that I sincerely hoped he would entertain favorably, — General Sherman seeing the President, at my particular request, to urge this on the 13th instant. On Tuesday, the day Mr. Stanton reëntered the office of the Secretary of War, General Comstock, who had carried my official letter, announcing that, with Mr. Stanton's reinstatement by the Senate, I had ceased to be Secretary of War *ad interim*, and who saw the President open and read the communication, brought back to me, from the President, a message that he wanted to see me that day at the Cabinet meeting, after I had made known the fact that I was no longer Secretary of War *ad interim*. At this meeting, after opening it as though I were a member of his Cabinet, when reminded of the notification already given him that I was no longer Secretary of War *ad interim*, the President gave a version of the conversation alluded to already. In this statement it was asserted that in both conversations I had agreed to hold on to the office of Secretary of War until displaced by the courts, or resign, so as to place the President where he would have been had I never accepted the office. After hearing the President through, I stated our conversations substantially as given in this letter. I will add that my conversation before the Cabinet embraced other matter not pertinent here, and is therefore left out. I in no wise admitted the correctness of the President's statement of our conversation, though, to soften the evident contradiction my statement gave, I said, alluding to our first conversation on the subject, the President might have understood me the way he said, namely, "That I had promised to resign if I did not resist the reinstatement." I made no such promise.

I have the honor to be, very respectfully,

Your obedient servant,

(Signed) U. S. GRANT, *General.*

ANOTHER LETTER, AND THE PRESIDENT'S INDORSEMENT.

HEADQUARTERS ARMY OF THE UNITED STATES,
WASHINGTON, January 24, 1868.

HIS EXCELLENCY ANDREW JOHNSON,
*President of the United States.*

SIR: I have the honor very respectfully to request to have in writing the order which the President gave me verbally on Sunday, the 19th instant, to disregard the orders of the Hon. E. M. Stanton, as Secretary of War, until I knew from the President himself that they were his orders.

I have the honor to be, very respectfully,

Your obedient servant,

(Signed) U. S. GRANT, *General.*

The following is the indorsement on the above note: —

As requested in this communication, General Grant is instructed, in writing, not to obey any order from the War Department, assumed to be issued by the direction of the President, unless such order is known by the General commanding the armies of the United States to have been authorized by the Executive.

(Signed) ANDREW JOHNSON.

January 29, 1868.

GENERAL GRANT TO THE PRESIDENT.

HEADQUARTERS ARMY OF THE UNITED STATES,
WASHINGTON, January 30, 1868.

HIS EXCELLENCY ANDREW JOHNSON,
*President of the United States.*

SIR: I have the honor to acknowledge the return of my note of the 24th instant, with your indorsement thereon, "That I am not to obey any order from the War Department, assumed to be issued by direction of the President, unless such order is known by me to have been authorized by the Executive;" and in reply thereto to say, that I am informed by the Secretary of War that he has not received from the Executive any order or instructions limiting or impairing his authority to issue orders to the army, as has heretofore been his practice under the law and customs of the Department. While his authority to the War Department is not countermanded, it will be satisfactory evidence to me that any orders issued from the War Department by direction of the President are authorized by the Executive.

I have the honor to be, very respectfully,

Your obedient servant,

(Signed) U. S. GRANT, *General.*

PRESIDENT JOHNSON TO GENERAL GRANT.

EXECUTIVE MANSION, January 31, 1868.

GENERAL: I have received your communication of the 28th instant, renewing your request of the 24th, that I should repeat in a written form my verbal instructions of the 19th instant, viz.: "That you obey no order from the Hon. Edwin M. Stanton, as Secretary of War, unless you have information that it was issued by the President's direction." In submitting this request, with which I complied on the 29th instant, you take occasion to allude to recent publications in reference to the circumstances connected with the vacation by yourself of the office of Secretary of War *ad interim*, and with the view of correcting the statements which you term "gross misrepresentations," and give at length your own recollection of the facts under which, without the sanction of the President, from whom you had received and accepted the appointment, you yielded the Department of War to the present incumbent. As stated in your communication some time after you had assumed the duties of Secretary of War *ad interim*, we interchanged views respecting the course that should be pursued in the event of the non-concurrence by the Senate in the suspension of Mr. Stanton. I sought that interview, calling myself at the War Department. My sole object in then bringing the subject to your attention was to ascertain definitely what would be your own action should such an attempt be made for his restoration to the War Department. That object was accomplished, for the interview terminated with the distinct understanding, that if upon reflection you should prefer not to become a party to the controversy, or should conclude that it would be your duty to surrender the Department to Mr. Stanton, upon action in his favor by the Senate, you were to return the office to me prior to a decision by the Senate, in order that, if I desired to do so, I might designate some one to succeed you. It must have been apparent to you that had not this understanding been reached, it was my purpose to relieve you from the further discharge of the duties as Secretary of War *ad interim*, and to appoint some other person in that capacity. Other conversations upon the subject ensued, all of them having on my part the same object, and leading to the same conclusion as the first. It is not necessary, however, to refer to any of them, excepting that of Saturday, the 11th instant, mentioned in your communication. As it was then known that the Senate had proceeded in the case of Mr. Stanton, I was anxious to learn your determination. After a protracted interview, during which the provisions of the Tenure of Office bill were fully discussed, you said, that as it had been agreed upon in our first conference, you would either return the office to my possession in time to enable me to appoint a successor before final action by the Senate upon Mr. Stanton's suspension, or would remain as its head, awaiting a decision of the question by judicial proceedings. It was then understood that there would be a further conference on Monday, by which time I supposed you would be prepared to inform me of your final decision. You failed, however, to fulfil the engagement, and on Saturday notified me in writing of the receipt of your official notification of the action of the Senate in the case of Mr. Stanton, and at the same time informed me that, according to the act regulating the tenure of certain civil offices, your functions as Secretary of War *ad interim* ceased from the moment of receipt of notice. You thus, in disregard of the understanding between us, vacated the office without having given me notice of your intention to do so. It is but just, however, to say, that in your communication, you claim that you did inform me of your purpose, and thus fulfilled the promise made in our last preceding conversation on the subject. The fact that such a promise existed is evidence of an arrangement of the kind I have mentioned. You had found in our first conference that the President was desirous of keeping Mr. Stanton out of office, whether sustained in the suspension or not. You knew what reasons had induced the President to ask from you a promise. You also knew that in case your views of duty did not accord with his own convictions, it was his purpose to fill your place by another appointment, even ignoring the existence of a positive understanding between us. These conclusions were plainly deducible from our various conversations. It is certain, however, that even under these circumstances you did not offer to return the place to my possession, but, according to your own statement, placed yourself in a position where, could I have anticipated your action, I would have been compelled to ask of you, as I was compelled to ask of your predecessor in the War Department, a letter of resignation, or else to resort to the more disagreeable expedient of suspending you by the appointment of a successor. As stated in your letter, the nomination of Governor Cox, of Ohio, for the office of Secretary of War was suggested to me. This appointment as Mr. Stanton's successor was urged in your name, and it was said that his selection would save further embarrassment. I did not think that in the selection of a Cabinet officer I should be trammelled by such considerations. I was prepared to take the responsibility of deciding the question in accordance with my ideas of constitutional duty, and, having determined upon a course which I deemed right and proper, was anxious to learn the steps you would take should the possession of the War Department be demanded by Mr. Stanton. Had your action been in conformity with the understanding between us, I do not believe that the embarrassment would have attained its present proportions, or that the probability of its repetition would have been so great. I know that, with a view to an early termination of a state of affairs so detrimental to the public interests, you voluntarily offered, both on Monday the 15th instant, and on the succeeding Sunday, to call upon Mr. Stanton and urge upon him that the good of the service required his resignation. I confess that I considered your proposal as a sort of reparation for the failure on your part to act in accordance with an understanding more than once repeated, which I thought had received your full assent, and under which you could have returned to me the office which I had conferred upon you, thus saving yourself from embarrassment, and leaving the responsibility where it properly belonged, with the President, who is accountable for the faithful execution of the law. I have not yet been informed by you whether, as twice proposed by yourself, you had called upon Mr. Stanton and made an effort to induce him voluntarily to resign from the War Department. You conclude your communication with a reference to our conversation at the meeting of the Cabinet held on Tuesday, the 14th instant. In your account of what then occurred, you say that, "after the President had given his version of our previous conversations, you stated them substantially as given in your letter, and that you in no wise admitted the correctness of his statement of them; though, to soften the evident contradiction my statement gave, I said, alluding to our first communication on the subject, the President might have understood in the way he said, viz., that I had promised to resign if I did not resist the reinstatement. I made no such promise." My recollection of what then transpired is diametrically the reverse of your narration. In the presence of the Cabinet I asked you, first, if, in a conversation which took place shortly after your appointment as Secretary of War *ad interim*, you did not agree either to remain at the head of the War Department, and abide any judicial proceedings that might follow the non-concurrence by the Senate in Mr. Stanton's suspension, or, should you wish not to become involved in such a controversy, to put me in the same position with respect to the office as I occupied previous to your appointment, by returning it to me in time to anticipate such action by the Senate? This you admitted. Second: I then asked you if, at the conference on the preceding Saturday, I had not, to avoid misunderstanding, requested you to state what you intended to do; and further, if in reply to that inquiry you had not referred to my former conversations, saying that from them I understood your position, and that your action would be consistent with the understanding which had been reached? To these questions you also replied in the affirmative. Third: I next asked if, at the conclusion of our interview on Saturday it was not understood that we were to have another conference on Monday, before final action by the Senate on the case of Mr. Stanton? You replied that such was the understanding, but that you did not suppose the Senate would act so soon; that on Monday you had been engaged in a conference with General Sherman, and were occupied with "many little matters," and asked if General Sherman had not called on that day. What relevancy General Sherman's visit to me on Monday had with the purpose for which you were to have called, I am at a loss to perceive, as he certainly did not inform me whether you had determined to retain possession of the office, or to afford me an opportunity to appoint a successor in advance of any attempted reinstatement of Mr. Stanton.

This account of what passed between us at the Cabinet meeting on the 14th instant widely differs from that contained in your communication, for it shows that instead of having "stated our conversations as given in the letter," which has made this reply necessary, you admitted that my recital of them was entirely accurate. Sincerely anxious, however, to be correct in my statements, I have to-day read this narration of what occurred on the 14th instant to the members of the Cabinet who were then present. They, without exception, agree in its accuracy. It is only necessary to add that on Wednesday morning, the 15th, you called on me in company with Lieutenant General Sherman. After some preliminary conversation, you remarked that an article in the National Intelligencer of that date did you much injustice. I replied that I had not seen the Intelligencer of that morning. You first told me that it was your intention to urge Mr. Stanton to resign his office. After you had withdrawn, I carefully read the article of which you had spoken, and found that its statement of the understanding between us was substantially correct. On the 17th, I caused it to be read to four of the five members of the Cabinet, who were present at our conference on the 14th, and they concurred in the general accuracy of its statements respecting our conversation upon that occasion. In reply to your communication, I have deemed it proper, in order to prevent further misunderstanding, to make this simple recital of facts.

Very respectfully yours,

ANDREW JOHNSON.

GENERAL U. S. GRANT,
*Commanding United States Armies.*

## GENERAL GRANT TO THE PRESIDENT.

HEADQUARTERS ARMY OF THE UNITED STATES,
WASHINGTON, D. C., February 3, 1868.

TO HIS EXCELLENCY ANDREW JOHNSON,
*President of the United States.*

SIR: I have the honor to acknowledge the receipt of your communication of the 31st ultimo, in answer to mine of the 28th ultimo. After a careful reading and comparison of it with the article in the National Intelligencer of the 15th ultimo, the article over the initials "J. B. S." in the New York World of the 27th ultimo, purporting to be based upon your statement and that of the members of the Cabinet therein named, I find it to be but a reiteration, only somewhat more in detail, of the many and gross misrepresentations contained in these articles, and which my statement of facts, set forth in my letter of the 28th ultimo, was intended to correct; and here I reassert the correctness of my statements in that letter, anything in yours in reply to it to the contrary notwithstanding.

I confess my surprise that the Cabinet officers referred to should so greatly misapprehend the facts in the matter of admissions alleged to have been made by me at the Cabinet meeting on the 14th ultimo, as to suffer their names to be made the basis of the charges in the newspaper article referred to, or agree to the accuracy, as you affirm they do, of your account of what occurred at that meeting. You know that we parted on Saturday, the 11th ultimo, without any promise on my part, either expressed or implied, to the effect that I would hold on to the office of Secretary of War *ad interim*, against the action of the Senate, or, declining to do so myself, would surrender it to you before such action was had, or that I would see you again at any fixed time on the subject. The performance of the promises, alleged to have been made by me, would have involved a resistance of the law, and an inconsistency with the whole history of my connection with the suspension of Mr. Stanton. From our conversation, and my written protest of August 1, 1867, against the removal of Mr. Stanton, you must have known that my greatest objection to his removal was the fear that some one would be appointed in his stead who would, by opposition to the laws relating to the restoration of the

Southern States to their proper relation to the government, embarrass the army in the performance of the duties especially imposed upon it by the laws, and that it was to prevent such an appointment that I accepted the appointment of Secretary of War *ad interim*, and not for the purpose of enabling you to get rid of Mr. Stanton by my withholding it from him in opposition to the law, or, not doing so myself, surrender to one who, as the statement and assumption in your communication plainly indicate, was sought; and it was to avoid this danger, as well as to relieve you from the personal embarrassment in which Mr. Stanton's reinstatement would place you, that I urged the appointment of Governor Cox, believing that it would be agreeable to you, and also to Mr. Stanton, satisfied as I was that it was the good of the country and not the office the latter desired. On the 13th ultimo, in the presence of General Sherman, I stated to you that I thought Mr. Stanton would resign, but did not say I would advise him to do so. On the 18th I did agree with General Sherman to go and advise him to that course; and on the 19th I had an interview alone with Mr. Stanton, which led me to the conclusion that any advice to him of this kind would be useless, and so informed General Sherman. Before I consented to advise Mr. Stanton to resign, I understood from him, in a conversation on the subject immediately after his reinstatement, that it was his opinion that the act of Congress, entitled "An act temporarily to supply vacancies in the Executive Department in certain cases," approved February 20, 1863, was repealed by subsequent legislation, which materially influenced my action. Previous to this time I had no doubt that the law of 1863 was still in force; and notwithstanding my action, a fuller examination of the law leaves a question in my mind whether it is or is not repealed. This being the case, I could not now advise his resignation, lest the same danger I apprehended from his first removal might follow. The course you have understood I agreed to pursue was in violation of law, and that without orders from you; while the course I did pursue, and which I never doubted you fully understood, was in accordance with law, and not in disobedience to any orders of my superior. And now, Mr. President, when my honor as a soldier and integrity as a man have been so violently assailed, pardon me for saying that I can but regard this whole matter, from beginning to end, as an attempt to involve me in the resistance of law, for which you hesitated to assume the responsibility in orders, and thus to destroy my character before the country. I am in a measure confirmed in this conclusion, by your recent orders directing me to disobey orders from the Secretary of War, my superior and your subordinate. Without having countermanded his authority, I am to disobey. With assurance, Mr. President, that nothing less than a vindication of my personal honor and character could have induced this correspondence on my part,

I have the honor to be, very respectfully,

Your obedient servant,

U. S. GRANT, *General.*

### THE PRESIDENT TO GENERAL GRANT.

EXECUTIVE MANSION, February 10, 1868.

GENERAL: The extraordinary character of your letter of the 3d instant would seem to preclude any reply on my part; but the manner in which publicity has been given to the correspondence of which that letter forms a part, and the grave questions which are involved, induce me to take this mode of giving, as a proper sequel to the communications which have passed between us, the statements of the five members of the Cabinet who were present on the occasion of our conversation on the 14th ultimo. Copies of the letters which they have addressed to me upon the subject are accordingly herewith enclosed.

You speak of my letter of the 31st ultimo as a reiteration of the many and gross misrepresentations contained in certain newspaper articles, and reassert the correctness of the statement contained in your communication of the 28th ultimo, adding, — and here I give your own words, — "Anything in yours in reply to it to the contrary notwithstanding." When a controversy upon matters of fact reaches the point to which this has been brought, further assertion or denial between the immediate parties should cease, especially when upon either side it loses the character of the respectful discussion which is required by the relations in which the parties stand to each other, and degenerates in tone and temper. In such a case, if there is nothing to rely upon but the opposing statements, conclusions must be drawn from those statements alone, and from whatever intrinsic probabilities they afford in favor of or against either of the parties, I should not shrink from the controversy.

But, fortunately, it is not left to this test alone. There were five Cabinet officers present at the conversation, the details of which, in my letter of the 28th ultimo, you allow yourself to say contain "many and gross misrepresentations." These gentlemen heard that conversation, and have read my statement. They speak for themselves, and I leave the proof without a word of comment.

I deem it proper before concluding this communication to notice some of the statements contained in your letter. You say that a performance of the promise alleged to have been made by you to the President "would have involved a resistance to law, and an inconsistency with the whole history of my connection with the suspension of Mr. Stanton." You then state that you had fears the President would, on the removal of Mr. Stanton, appoint some one in his place who would embarrass the army in carrying out the reconstruction acts, and add: "It was to prevent such an appointment that I accepted the office of Secretary of War *ad interim*, and not for the purpose of enabling you to get rid of Mr. Stanton by my withholding it from him, in opposition to the law, or, not doing so myself, surrendering it to one who would, as the statements and assumptions in your communication plainly indicate was sought, first of all."

You here admit that from the very beginning of what you term the whole history of your connection with Mr. Stanton's suspension, you intended to circumvent the President. It was to carry out that intent that you accepted the appointment: this was in your mind at the time of your acceptance. It was not, then, in obedience to the order of your superior, as has heretofore been supposed, that you assumed the duties of the office. You knew it was the President's purpose to prevent Mr. Stanton from resuming the office of Secretary of War, and you intended to defeat that purpose. You accepted the office, not in the interest of the President but of Mr. Stanton.

If this purpose, so entertained by you, had been confined to yourself, — if, when accepting the office, you had done so with a mental reservation to frustrate the President, — it would have been a tacit deception. In the ethics of some persons such a course is allowable, but you cannot stand even upon that questionable ground. The history of your connection with this transaction, as written by yourself, places you in a different predicament, and shows that you not only concealed your design from the President, but induced him to suppose that you would carry out his purpose to keep Mr. Stanton out of office by retaining it yourself, after an attempted restoration by the Senate, so as to require Mr. Stanton to establish his right by judicial decision.

I now give that part of this history as written by yourself in your letter of the 28th ultimo: "Some time after I assumed the duties of Secretary of War *ad interim*, the President asked me my views as to the course Mr. Stanton would have to pursue in case the Senate should not concur in his suspension, to obtain possession of his office. My reply was, in substance, that Mr. Stanton would have to appeal to the courts to reinstate him, illustrating my position by citing the ground I had taken in the case of the Baltimore Police Commissioners."

Now, at that time, you admit in your letter of the 3d instant, you held the office for the very object of defeating an appeal to the courts; in that letter you say that in accepting the office, one motive was to prevent the President from appointing some other person who would retain possession, and thus make judicial proceedings necessary. You knew the President was unwilling to trust the office with any one who would not, by holding it, compel Mr. Stanton to resort to the courts. You perfectly understood that in this interview. Some time after you accepted the office, the President, not content with your silence, desired an expression of your views, and you answered him that Mr. Stanton "would have to appeal to the court." If the President had reposed confidence "before" he knew your views, and that confidence had been violated, it might have been said he made a mistake; but a violation of confidence reposed "after" that conversation was no mistake of his, nor of yours; it is the fact only that needs be stated, that at the date of this conversation you did not intend to hold the office with the purpose of forcing Mr. Stanton into court, but did hold it then, and had accepted it, to prevent that course from being carried out. In other words, you said to the President, "That is the proper course," and you said to yourself, "I have accepted this office, and now hold it, to defeat that course."

The excuse you make in a subsequent paragraph of that letter of the 28th ultimo, that afterwards you changed your views as to what would be a proper course, has nothing to do with the point now under consideration. The point is, that before you changed your views you had secretly determined to do the very thing which at last you did — surrender the office to Mr. Stanton. You may have changed your views as to the law, but you certainly did not change your views as to the course you had marked out for yourself from the beginning.

I will only notice one more statement in your letter of the 3d instant, that the performance of the promises which it is alleged were made by you would have involved you in the resistance of law. I know of no statute that would have been violated had you, carrying out your promises in good faith, tendered your resignation when you concluded not to be made a party in any legal proceeding.

You add: "I am in a measure confirmed in this conclusion by your recent order directing me to disobey orders from the Secretary of War, my superior and your subordinate, without having countermanded his authority to issue the orders I am to disobey."

On the 24th ult., you addressed a note to the President requesting in writing an order given to you verbally five days before, to disregard orders from Mr. Stanton, as Secretary of War, until you knew from the President himself that they were his orders. On the 29th, in compliance with your request, I did give you instructions in writing not to obey any order from the War Department assumed to be issued by the direction of the President, unless such order is known by the General commanding the armies of the United States to have been authorized by the Executive. There are some orders which a Secretary of War may issue without the authority of the President. There are others which he issues simply as the agent of the President, and which purport to be by direction of the President. For such orders the President is responsible, and he should therefore know and understand what they are before giving such direction. Mr. Stanton states, in his letter of the 4th instant, which accompanies the published correspondence, that he has had no correspondence with the President since the 12th of August last. And he further says, that since he resumed the duties of the office, he has continued to discharge them without any personal or written communication with the President, and he adds: "No orders have been issued from this Department in the name of the President, with my knowledge, and I have received no orders from him."

It thus seems that Mr. Stanton now discharges the duties of the War Department without any reference to the President, and without using his name. My orders to you had only reference to orders assumed to be issued by the President.

It would appear from Mr. Stanton's letter that you have received no such orders from him. In your note to the President of the 13th ultimo, in which you acknowledge the receipt of the written order of the 29th, you say that you have been informed by Mr. Stanton that he has not received any order limiting his authority to issue orders to the army, according to the practice of the Department, and state that, "while this authority to the War Department is not countermanded, it will be satisfactory evidence to me that any orders issued from the War Department, by direction of the President, are authorized by the Executive."

The President issues an order to you to obey no order from the War Department purporting to be made "by the direction of the President" until you have referred it to him for his approval. You reply that you have received the President's order and will not obey it, but will obey an order purporting to be given by his direction if it comes from the War Department. You will obey no direct order of the President, but will obey his indirect order. If, as you say, there has been a practice in the War Department to issue orders in the name of the President, without his direction, does not the precise order you have requested and have received change the practice as to the General of the Army? Could not the President countermand any such order issued to you from the War Department? If you should receive an order from that Department, issued in the name of the President to do a special act, and an order directly from the President himself not to do the act, is there a doubt which you are to obey? You answer the question when you say to the President in your letter of the 3d instant, the "Secretary of War is your superior and my subordinate." And yet you refuse obedience to the superior out of deference to the subordinate! Without further comment upon the insubordinate attitude which you have assumed, I am at a loss to know how you can relieve yourself from the orders of the President, who is made by the Constitution, the Commander-in-Chief of the Army and Navy, and is, therefore, the official superior as well of the General of the Army as of the Secretary of War.

Respectfully yours,

ANDREW JOHNSON.

GENERAL U. S. GRANT,
*Commanding Armies of the United States,*
*Washington, D. C.*

---

## VIII.

### LETTERS FROM CABINET OFFICERS.

THE following is a copy of a letter addressed to each of the members of the Cabinet present at the conversation between the President and General Grant on the 14th of January, 1868: —

EXECUTIVE MANSION,
WASHINGTON, D. C., February 5, 1868.

SIR: The Chronicle of this morning contains a correspondence between the President and General Grant, reported from the War Department in answer to a resolution of the House of Representatives.

I beg to call your attention to that correspondence, and especially to that part of it which refers to the conversation between the President and General Grant at the Cabinet meeting on Tuesday, the 14th of January, and to request you to state what was said in that conversation.

Very respectfully, yours,

ANDREW JOHNSON.

### REPLY OF SECRETARY WELLES.

WASHINGTON, February 5, 1868.

SIR: Your note of this date was handed to me this evening. My recollection of the conversation of the Cabinet meeting on Tuesday, the 14th of January, corresponds with your statement of it in the letter of the 31st ultimo, in the published correspondence. The three points specified in that letter giving your recollection of the conversation are correctly stated.

Very respectfully,

GIDEON WELLES.

### REPLY OF SECRETARY McCULLOCH.

TREASURY DEPARTMENT, February 6, 1868.

SIR: I have received your note of the 5th instant, calling my attention to the correspondence between yourself and General Grant, as published in the Chronicle of yesterday, especially to that part of it which relates to what occurred in the Cabinet meeting on Tuesday, the 14th ultimo, and requesting me to state what was said in the conversation referred to. I cannot undertake to state the precise language used, but I have no hesitation in saying that your account of that conversation, as given in your letter to General Grant, under date of the 31st ultimo, substantially, in all important particulars, accords with my recollection of it.

With great respect, your obedient servant,

HUGH McCULLOCH.

TO THE PRESIDENT.

### REPLY OF POSTMASTER-GENERAL RANDALL.

POST-OFFICE DEPARTMENT,
WASHINGTON, February 6, 1868.

SIR: I am in receipt of your letter of the 5th February, calling my attention to the correspondence published in the Chronicle between the President and General Grant, and especially to that part of it which refers to the conversation between the President and General Grant at the Cabinet meeting on the 14th of January, with a request that I state what was said in that conversation.

In reply, I have the honor to state that I have read carefully the correspondence in question, and particularly the letter of the President to General Grant, dated January 31, 1868.

The following extract from your letter of the 31st of January to General Grant is according to my recollection of the conversation that took place between the President and General Grant at the Cabinet meeting on the 14th of January last: —

In the presence of the Cabinet the President asked General Grant whether, in the conversation which took place after his appointment as Secretary of War *ad interim*, he did not agree either to remain at the head of the War Department and abide any judicial proceedings that might follow the non-concurrence by the Senate in Mr. Stanton's suspension, or, should he not wish to become involved in such a controversy, to put the President in the same position with respect to the office as he occupied previous to General Grant's appointment, by returning it to the President in time to anticipate such action by the Senate.

This General Grant admitted.

The President then asked General Grant if, at the conference on the preceding Saturday, he had not, to avoid misunderstanding, requested General Grant to state what he intended to do. And further, if in reply to that inquiry, he (General Grant) had not referred to their former conversations, saying that from them the President understood his position, and that his (General Grant's) action would be consistent with the understanding which had been reached.

To these questions General Grant replied in the affirmative. The President asked General Grant if, at the conclusion of their interview on Saturday, it was not understood that they were to have another conference on Monday before final action by the Senate in the case of Mr. Stanton? General Grant replied that such was the understanding, but that he did not suppose the Senate would act so soon; that on Monday he had been engaged in a conference with General Sherman, and was occupied with many little matters, and asked if General Sherman had not called on that day.

I take this mode of complying with the request contained in the President's letter to me, because my attention had been called to the subject before, when the conversation between the President and General Grant was under consideration.

Very respectfully, your obedient servant,

ALEXANDER W. RANDALL,
*Postmaster-General.*

TO THE PRESIDENT.

## REPLY OF SECRETARY BROWNING.

DEPARTMENT OF THE INTERIOR,
WASHINGTON, D. C., February 6, 1868.

I am in receipt of yours of yesterday, calling my attention to a correspondence between yourself and General Grant, published in the Chronicle newspaper, and especially to that part of said correspondence which refers to the conversation between the President and General Grant at the Cabinet meeting on Tuesday, the 14th of January, and requesting me to state what was said in that conversation. In reply, I submit the following statement: —

At the Cabinet meeting on Tuesday, the 14th of January, 1868, General Grant appeared and took his accustomed seat at the board. When he had been reached in the order of business, the President asked him as usual if he had anything to present. In reply, the General, after referring to a note which he had that morning addressed to the President, enclosing a copy of the resolution of the Senate refusing to concur in the reasons for the suspension of Mr. Stanton, proceeded to say that he regarded his duties as Secretary of War *ad interim* terminated by that resolution, and that he could not lawfully exercise such duties for a moment after the adoption of the resolution by the Senate. That the resolution reached him last night, and that this morning he had gone to the War Department, entered the Secretary's room, bolted one door on the inside, locked the other on the outside, delivered the key to the Adjutant-General, and proceeded to the headquarters of the army, and addressed the note above mentioned to the President, informing him that he (General Grant) was no longer Secretary of War *ad interim.*

The President expressed great surprise at the course which General Grant had thought proper to pursue, and addressing himself to the General, proceeded to say in substance, that he had anticipated such action by the Senate, and being very desirous to have the constitutionality of the Tenure of Office bill tested, and his right to suspend or remove a member of the Cabinet decided by the judicial tribunal of the country, he had some time ago, and shortly after General Grant's appointment as Secretary of War *ad interim*, asked the General what his action would be in the event that the Senate should refuse to concur in the suspension of Mr. Stanton, and that the General had then agreed either to remain at the head of the War Department till a decision could be obtained from the court, or resign the office into the hands of the President before the case was acted upon by the Senate, so as to place the President in the same situation he occupied at the time of his (Grant's) appointment.

The President further said that the conversation was renewed on the preceding Saturday, at which time he asked the General what he intended to do if the Senate should undertake to reinstate Mr. Stanton; in reply to which the General referred to their former conversation upon the same subject, and said, "You understand my position, and my conduct will be conformable to that understanding;" that he (the General) then expressed a repugnance to being made a party to a judicial proceeding, saying that he would expose himself to fine and imprisonment by doing so, as his continuing to discharge the duties of Secretary of War *ad interim* after the Senate should have refused to concur in the suspension of Mr. Stanton, would be a violation of the Tenure of Office bill; that in reply to this, he (the President) informed General Grant he had not suspended Mr. Stanton under the Tenure of Office bill, but by virtue of the powers conferred on him by the Constitution, and that as to the fine and imprisonment, he (the President) would pay whatever fine was imposed, and submit to whatever imprisonment might be adjudged against him (the General); that they continued the conversation for some time, discussing the law at length, and that they finally separated without having reached a definite conclusion, and with the understanding that the General would see the President again on Monday.

In reply, General Grant admitted that the conversations had occurred, and said that at the first conversation he had given it as his opinion to the President that in the event of non-concurrence by the Senate in the action of the President in respect to the Secretary of War, the question would have to be decided by the court; that Mr. Stanton would have to appeal to the court to reinstate him in office; that the *ins* would remain in till they could be displaced, and the outs put in by legal proceedings, and that he then thought so, and had agreed that if he should change his mind he would notify the President in time to enable him to make another appointment. But at the time of the first conversation he had not looked very closely into the law; that it had recently been discussed by the newspapers, and that this had induced him to examine it more carefully, and that he had come to the conclusion that if the Senate should refuse to concur in the suspension, Mr. Stanton would thereby be reinstated, and that he (Grant) could not continue thereafter to act as Secretary of War *ad interim* without subjecting himself to fine and imprisonment, and that he came over on Saturday to inform the President of the change in his views, and did so inform him; that the President replied that he had not suspended Mr. Stanton under the Tenure of Office bill, but under the Constitution, and had appointed him (Grant) by virtue of the authority derived from the Constitution, &c.; that they continued to discuss the matter some time, and finally he left without any conclusion having been reached, expecting to see the President again on Monday. He then proceeded to explain why he had not called on the President on Monday, saying that he had a long interview with General Sherman; that various little matters had occupied his time till it was late, and that he did not think the Senate would act so soon; and asked, "Did not General Sherman call on you on Monday?"

I do not know what passed between the President and General Grant on Saturday, except as I learned it from the conversation between them at the Cabinet meeting on Tuesday; and the foregoing is substantially what then occurred. The precise words used on the occasion are not, of course, given exactly in the order in which they were spoken, but the ideas expressed and the facts stated are faithfully preserved and presented.

I have the honor to be, sir, with great respect,

Your obedient servant,

(Signed) O. H. BROWNING.

THE PRESIDENT.

REPLY OF SECRETARY SEWARD.

DEPARTMENT OF STATE,
WASHINGTON, February 6.

SIR: The meeting to which you refer in your letter was a regular Cabinet meeting. While the members were assembling, and before the President had entered the council chamber,

General Grant, on coming in, said to me that he was there, not as a member of the Cabinet, but upon invitation, and I replied by the inquiry whether there was a change in the War Department.

After the President had taken his seat, business went on in the usual way of hearing matters submitted by the several Secretaries. When the time came for the Secretary of War, General Grant said that he was now there, not as Secretary of War, but upon the President's invitation; that he had retired from the War Department.

A slight difference then appeared about the supposed invitation, General Grant saying that the officers who had borne his letter to the President that morning, announcing his retirement from the War Department, had told him that the President desired to see him at the Cabinet, to which the President answered: That when General Grant's communication was delivered to him, the President simply replied that he supposed General Grant would be very soon at the Cabinet meeting.

I regarded the conversation thus begun as an incidental one. It went on quite informally, and consisted of a statement on your part of your views in regard to the misunderstanding of the tenure upon which General Grant had assented to hold the War Department *ad interim*, and of his replies by way of answer and explanation.

It was respectful and courteous on both sides, being in this conversational form, as details could only have been presented by a *verbatim* report. So far as I know no such report was made at the time. I can give only the general effect of the conversation.

Certainly you stated that although you had reported the reasons for Mr. Stanton's suspension to the Senate, you nevertheless held that he would not be entitled to resume the office of Secretary of War even if the Senate should disapprove of his suspension, and that you had proposed to have the question tested by judicial process to be applied to the person who should be the incumbent of the Department. Under your designation of Secretary of War *ad interim* in the place of Mr. Stanton you contended that this was well understood between yourself and General Grant. That when he entered the War Department as Secretary *ad interim* he expressed his concurrence in a belief that the question of Mr. Stanton's restoration would be a question for the courts.

That in a subsequent conversation you had with General Grant you had adverted to the understanding thus had, and that General Grant expressed his concurrence in it.

That at some conversation which had been previously held, General Grant said he still adhered to the same construction of the law, but said that if he should change his opinion he would give you reasonable notice of it, so that you should, in any case, be placed in the same position in regard to the War Department that you were while General Grant held it *ad interim.*

I did not understand General Grant as denying, nor as explicitly admitting these statements in the firm and full extent to which you made them. His admission of them was rather indirect and circumstantial, though he did not understand it to be an evasive one. He said that reasoning from what occurred in the case of the police in Maryland, which he regarded as a parallel one, he was of opinion, and so assured you, that it would be his right and duty, under your instructions, to hold the War Office after the Senate should disapprove of Mr. Stanton's suspension until the question should be decided upon by the courts; that he remained until very recently of that opinion, and that on the Saturday before the Cabinet meeting a conversation was held between yourself and him, in which the subject was generally discussed. General Grant's statement was that in that conversation he had stated to you the legal difficulties which might arise, involving fine and imprisonment under the Civil Tenure bill, and that he did not care to subject himself to those penalties; that you replied to this remark that you regarded the Civil Tenure bill as unconstitutional, and did not think its penalties were to be feared, or that you would voluntarily assume them; and you insisted that General Grant should either retain the office until relieved by yourself, according to what you claimed was the original understanding between yourself and him, or, by seasonable notice of change of purpose on his part, put you in the same situation which you would be in if he adhered. You claim that General Grant finally said in that Saturday's conversation that you understood his views, and his proceedings thereafter would be consistent with what had been so understood. General Grant did not controvert, nor can I say that he admitted, his last statement.

Certainly General Grant did not at any time in the Cabinet meeting insist that he had in the Saturday's conversation either distinctly or finally advised you of his determination to retire from the charge of the War Department, otherwise than under your own subsequent direction. He acquiesced in your statement that the Saturday's conversation ended with an expectation that there would be a subsequent conference on the subject, which he as well as yourself supposed could seasonably take place on Monday.

You then alluded to the fact that General Grant did not call upon you on Monday, as you had expected from the conversation. General Grant admitted that it was his expectation or purpose to call upon you on Monday. General Grant assigned reasons for the omission. He said he was in conference with General Sherman, that there were many little matters to be attended to. He had conversed upon the matter of the incumbency of the War Department with General Sherman, and he expected that General Sherman would call on you on Monday. My own mind suggested a further explanation, but I do not remember whether it was mentioned or not, viz.: That it was not supposed by General Grant on Monday that the Senate would decide the question so promptly as to anticipate further explanation between yourself and him, if delayed beyond that day.

General Grant made another explanation, that he was engaged on Sunday with General Sherman, and, I think, also on Monday, in regard to the War Department matter, with a hope, though he did not say in an effort, to procure an amicable settlement of the affair of Mr. Stanton, and he still hoped that it would be brought about.

I have the honor to be, with great respect,

Your obedient servant,

WILLIAM H. SEWARD.

TO THE PRESIDENT.

WASHINGTON, February 11.

The accompanying letter from General Grant, received since the transmission to the House of Representatives of my communication of this date, is submitted to the House, as a part of the correspondence referred to in the resolution of the 10th instant.

ANDREW JOHNSON.

HEADQUARTERS ARMY OF THE UNITED STATES,
WASHINGTON, D. C., February 11, 1868.

HIS EXCELLENCY ANDREW JOHNSON,
*President of the United States.*

SIR: I have the honor to acknowledge the receipt of your communication of the 10th instant, accompanied by the statements of five Cabinet ministers of their recollection of what occurred on the 14th of January.

Without admitting anything contained in these statements, where they differ from anything heretofore stated by me, I propose to notice only that portion of your communication wherein I am charged with insubordination. I think it will be plain to the reader of my letter of the 30th of January, that I did not propose to disobey any legal order of the President distinctly given, but only gave an interpretation of what would be regarded as satisfactory evidence of the President's sanction to orders communicated by the Secretary of War. I will say here, that your letter of the 10th instant contains the first intimation I have had that you did not accept that interpretation. Now for reasons for giving that interpretation: —

It was clear to me, before my letter of January 30 was written, that I, the person having more public business to transact with the Secretary of War than other of the President's subordinates, was the only one who had been instructed to disregard the authority of Mr. Stanton, where his authority was derived as agent from the President.

On the 27th of January I received a letter from the Secretary of War (copy herewith), directing me to furnish an escort to the public treasure from the Rio Grande to New Orleans, &c., at the request of the Secretary of the Treasury to him.

I also send two other enclosures showing the recognition of Mr. Stanton as Secretary of War by the Secretary of the Treasury and the Postmaster-General, in all of which cases the Secretary of War had to call upon me to make the orders requested, or give the information desired, and where his authority is derived, in my view, as agent of the President.

With an order so clearly ambiguous as that of the President's here referred to, it was my duty to inform the President of my interpretation of it, and to abide by that interpretation until I received other orders.

Disclaiming any intention, now or heretofore, of disobeying any legal order of the President, distinctly communicated, I remain,

Very respectfully,

Your obedient servant,

U. S. GRANT, *General.*

www.ingramcontent.com/pod-product-compliance
Lightning Source LLC
LaVergne TN
LVHW021055110826
845150LV00001B/80